P9-DGS-304

JOAN OF ARC

JOAN OF ARC

HER STORY

Régine Pernoud
Marie-Véronique Clin

Translated and Revised by Jeremy duQuesnay Adams

Edited by Bonnie Wheeler

St. Martin's Griffin

JOAN OF ARC: HER STORY

Copyright © for this translation and revision, Jeremy duQuesnay Adams, 1998. All rights reserved. Printed in the United States of America. No part of this book may be used or reproduced in any manner whatsoever without written permission except in the case of brief quotations embodied in critical articles or reviews. For information, address St. Martin's Press, 175 Fifth Avenue, New York, N.Y. 10010.

Originally published as *Jeanne d'Arc*, Régine Pernoud and M.-V. Clin (Paris: Librairie Arthème Fayard, 1986).

ISBN 0-312-22730-2

Library of Congress Cataloging-in-Publication Data

Pernoud, Régine, 1909-
  [Jean d'Arc. English]
  Joan of Arc : her story / by Régine Pernoud and Marie-Véronique Clin ; translated by Jeremy duQuesnay Adams.
      p. cm.
 Includes bibliographical references and index.
 ISBN 0-312-21442-1 (cloth) 0-312-22730-2 (pbk)
 1. Joan, of Arc, Saint, 1412-1431. 2. Christian women saints-
-France—Biography. 3. France—History—Charles VII, 1422-1451.
 I. Clin, Marie-Veronique. II. Title.
 DC103.P378131999
 944'.026'092—dc21
 [B]   98-45059
                                                         CIP

Design by Acme Art Inc.

First published in hardcover in the United States of America in 1999
First St. Martin's Griffin edition: September 1999

10 9 8 7 6 5 4 3 2 1

DC
103
.P37813
1999

116054

NOV 16 1999

This revised translation
is dedicated with abiding respect to
Régine Pernoud
(June 17, 1909–April 22, 1998)
for her generation and more
the grande dame
of French historical writing on the Middle Ages

CONTENTS

PART I:
THE DRAMA

PART II:
THE CAST OF PRINCIPAL CHARACTERS
(In Three Alphabetical Lists)

THE THREE NOBLE PRINCES

THEIR SUBJECTS

HER JUDGES AT ROUEN

PART III:
ISSUES AND IMAGES

APPENDICES

8 pages of illustrations appear between pages 164 and 165.

FOREWORD

Jeanne d'Arc in English! Witticisms in dubious taste were uttered about this possibility only a hundred years ago, when serious books about her in any language numbered only a few dozen.

Yet by then the Joan of Arc Chapel had been dedicated in London's Westminster Cathedral. Joan was soon recognized across the Atlantic in an official capacity: When I made my first visit to the United States, in 1950, I was told of no fewer than twenty-eight Roman Catholic parishes dedicated to her in that country—my hosts assumed that this information would please me because I was French, even though I made a point in those days of declaring (quite truthfully) my indifference to Joan of Arc.

But soon after that moment, I was imprudent enough to open the documents of her nullification trial and I found myself literally incapable of closing them. Since then Joan has led me to new horizons and fresh interests, made possible in part by the publication of several scholarly editions, beginning with those of Père Doncoeur and Yvonne Lanhers, and including the new edition of the trial documents by Pierre Tisset and Pierre Duparc, published by the Société de l'Histoire de France. The new editions of relevant documents now in progress reflect refined editorial practices and techniques, combined with a continuous desire for more exact knowledge of Joan and her contexts.

We hope that this work, on which Marie-Véronique Clin, my sister Madeleine, and I worked so long at the Centre Jeanne d'Arc at Orléans, and which Professor Adams has translated, revised, and amended with expert competence, may allow new audiences to gain better understanding of Joan's short life. She defines the shaping significance of the subject in history: Her élan reversed the course of historical events and gave a downtrodden people rekindled hope for their lost liberty.

This book presents what is known with relative certainty about the inexhaustibly fascinating Joan of Arc. The historian is caught up in hesitations, dilemmas, and questions at every step in the narrative recounting the deeds of this girl who died at age nineteen. Even her name is problematic. The person we call Joan of Arc was known to herself and to her contemporaries as Jeanne la Pucelle (Joan the

Maid). This biography is organized in three sections: first, the narrative of her life; second, biographical information about contemporaries who bore some relation to her life; and third, brief treatments of current historiographic questions and disputes. Readers are therefore provided with precise data about places, dates, identities, difficult questions of interpretation as well as counter-arguments that can be resolved only with recourse to documentary evidence.

Part I presents the story of one of the most surprising lives known to history from the perspective of documentary evidence. Words like "myth," "legend," and "folklore" dominate writings about Joan, though historians do not generally use such terms. If any person from the past is an apt historical subject—that is, one with a verifiable history, founded on documents rigorously sifted by the most demanding historical methods—that person is Joan of Arc. She surprised her contemporaries just as she surprises us; there is scarcely a chronicle or memoir from her time and place that does not mention her. She is amply evident in public and private letters, and on the pages of the register of the Parlement of Paris. Above all, we possess the texts of two of the contemporary trials she underwent, the first during her life, the other (which we call the nullification trial) only decades after her death, represented in each case by three authentic manuscripts bearing the signatures of notaries. No historian legitimately uses the term "legend" in connection with such heavily attested life records, but since her life continued to interest succeeding ages, "legends" developed about Joan, and her fame—a mixture of history and myth—now extends across the globe.

This is not a conventional biography that tells a life story from birth to death. We chose instead to write the documented life of Joan as it unfolded in time. Staying as close as possible to the historical documents (many of which are being reedited, but all of which are available for scholars to consult today on microfiche at the Centre Jeanne d'Arc at Orléans) allowed us to grasp each event according to the best-situated witnesses and to perceive Joan in a sequence of historically attested moments. History does not exist until it is recorded or told. Our narrative thus begins with the first rumor that spread about Joan of Arc in the year 1429; from thence we follow her footsteps into public life. Who was Joan of Arc? To answer that question we pose another: What is the historical record of Joan? Therefore, we chose not to evoke her childhood or her youth until the narrative's end, since history did not record sustained knowledge of that childhood and youth until the investigation that nullified her condemnation—when ecclesiastical delegates went to interrogate the people of Domrémy-Greux among whom Joan had spent her early years. This book follows the movement of recorded history rather than the chronological sequence of a life.

This structure allows our readers to focus on Joan's imprisonment and trial. Her brilliant and brief career is a diptych: one year of combat, one year of prison. Historians have not always made this fact clear: Prototype of the glorious military heroine, Joan is also prototype of the political prisoner, of the hostage, and of the victim of oppression. The panel of her victories faces the equally important panel of her pain, as an isolated human being facing suffocating ideology and murderous fanaticism. We do not add here the names of such victims in our world today—the list would be too long and the sufferings that they endure are every day replaced by others yet more horrific.

Régine Pernoud
Paris, January 1998

PREFACE

JEREMY DUQUESNAY ADAMS

[T]he biographical shape of her book is Gallic in style, as opposed to being the more straightforward kind of profile familiar among American or British writers.

The French approach demands a distinctive point of view, an interpretation rather than a reproduction of the life under scrutiny, in which the biographer must be clearly perceived as mediator between the reader and the figure portrayed. . . . Her book is in essence an exegetical work. . . .

—Jonathan Keates,
in his review of Lydia Flem's
Casanova: The Man Who Really Loved Women
(*The New York Times Book Review*)

All attempts to account rationally for Joan of Arc's life end no better than those which try to shape it to fit some fantastic theory. She is unique, she is a mystery, and as you read about her and think about her life, you are led up to a threshold beyond which she eludes you, you cannot cross it."

—Katherine Anne Porter,
in her Foreword to Régine Pernoud,
The Retrial of Joan of Arc

One need not be a patriotic French nationalist, or a Christian, or a feminist to find Joan of Arc fascinating and her treatment by the several male establishments of her time an outrage. That she took command of an army at age seventeen (which awed Civil War deserter Mark Twain) and was burned alive at nineteen; that she was probably illiterate yet held a massed battery of the male professional intelligentsia at bay for four months, finally frustrating them even though they won; that she was not only young and female, but also a peasant, from the far frontier of the country she set out to save; that thanks to transcripts of her trials we know more details of her short life than we do of any other human being before her time (including Plato, or Alexander of Macedon, or Julius Caesar, or Jesus Christ) and for several centuries thereafter, is extraordinary. This translator is not abashed to confess that he agrees with Régine Pernoud in finding Joan's story "all too beautiful"—and terrible—to ignore.

Thus, it is a particular pleasure to offer the English reader a revision of Régine Pernoud and Marie-Véronique Clin's *Jeanne d'Arc*. Translation is always a modesty-reinforcing experience. I soon gave up any hope of rendering into my English the distinctive and famous style of Régine Pernoud that I have long admired and enjoyed. Her gift for heightening the objective through the emotive, endowing historical precision with dramatic coloration, while adhering with ruthless fidelity to the sense of documentary evidence expected of a distinguished graduate of the École des Chartes has made her prose famous. The Pernoudian sentence—shaped by the latinity of her studious Provençal child-hood, by the deceptively casual sonorities of Dickens (which she absorbed both in the original and in nineteenth-century French translation) and by the conventions of French literary conversation, at once colloquial and classic—is here shortened, decolorized, blunted. Abandoning any sustained effort to convey the repertory of nuances this grande dame of French letters commands (she wields the slim blade of irony with particular deftness), I have been content to transmit with occasional revisions and amplifications the historical argument of this book, along with the extremely useful battery of data its two authors offer the serious student of Joan's historical moment. Part I, "The Drama," is directed to all readers; part II, "The Cast of Principal Characters," part III, "Issues and Images" (focusing on some of the vexing questions that arise concerning her life, and its later interpretations), and the Appendices (Joan's letters and a chronological itinerary) will interest not only the general reader who wishes to go deeper in any given direction but also the committed student of the later European Middle Ages. The revisions of parts II and III have been at times substantive as well as substantial, occasionally drastic. In the appendix of Joan's letters, I have fulfilled Pernoud's strongly expressed desire that the original fifteenth-century French text of all her dictated letters be restored. I am grateful throughout for the authors' generous sense that adaptation to a new audience a dozen years later was a good thing. I have added a short prelude sketching the larger historical context for the convenience of American readers.

Even the seasoned historian will find a fresh approach in part I. The authors structure the narrative according to the sequence of Joan's appearance in the documentary record rather than the sequence of her life as reconstructed from that record. Most previous biographers of Joan, including Régine Pernoud herself in *Jeanne d'Arc par elle-même et ses témoins* (1962; translated as *Joan of Arc: By Herself and Her Witnesses*, 1966), have followed the norms of historical biography, in which the author tracks the subject chronologically from birth to death, rendering seamless the modalities of private and public identity. Here instead it is history itself—as accumulation of written record—that is tracked. This retelling of the tale of Joan of Arc reports her *historia* as contemporary inscription rather than as a reconstituted narrative, a purported chain of events.

This narrative strategy does not, however, register the elements of Joan's story only in the order in which they were recorded in written documents. Although we read Joan's history as it unfolds, our views are inescapably retrospective. We read with the knowledge of her horrible death and in the context of the nullification trial, a parade in which those who knew her provide cross-checked testimony about the ordinary quality of Joan's childhood and about the extraordinary character of her later speech and deeds. Chapter 1 of part I opens, for example, with an account of the way in which the rumor of Joan's mission, swiftly followed by Joan herself, reached the dauphin's court at Chinon. The most extended report of that story is given through the recollections of the duke of Alençon, as recorded in the transcript of Joan's nullification trial in 1456. Such retrospective evidence must of course be regarded with suspicion. Pernoud and Clin are fully aware of that and frequently indicate that historians inevitably weigh their documents. Alençon's account they credit, as recalling with basic veracity what the duke and his immediate entourage had said and done about that rumor of Joan's mission twenty-seven years before. In other words, Pernoud and Clin retell Joan's story as a series of contemporary statements, some of which were written down shortly after utterance, some later. Partly to free this inscribed narrative from visual distraction, the authors followed the French tradition of avoiding footnotes in part I—a tradition dating back to the earliest years of this century, strongly advocated by the magisterial Achille Luchaire for serious works intended for wide readership, such as his *Social France in the Time of Philip Augustus* (to cite the title of its English translation). Sympathetic to that commitment, Marc Bloch kept footnoting to a bare minimum in *The Feudal Society*. The footnotes Pernoud and Clin provided for parts II and III of this book have been included in the running text as parenthetical citations. If the source of quotations in part I is not self-evidently either the condemnation trial of 1431 or the nullification trial of 1456, I have taken the liberty of indicating it, as I have in the case of some other documentary sources.

Régine Pernoud's discursive strategy in this work obviates some of the charges of partisanship leveled against her massive earlier work on Joan by some reviewers who alleged that she invents a national heroine tritely Catholic in piety and Gaullist in politics. I for one find such criticisms superficial. As she has made clear in her autobiographical memoir, *Villa Paradis* (1992), Pernoud evinced little interest in Joan of Arc before the 1950s; if anything, she found the subject distasteful, a sad case of the exploitive deformation of a historical figure by political and religious interests concerned primarily with recruitment propaganda. In an interview at her Paris apartment on August 3, 1995, Pernoud recalled her active dislike even as a child of processions in honor of Joan organized either by the rightist Action Française or by the Communist Party. Pernoud's conversion (it does not seem too strong a word) to Joan of Arc occurred on Christmas Eve, 1952, in the French Archives Nationales. Her friend Marcel Thiébault, editor of the *Revue de Paris*, had been pressing her for some time to write an article on Joan's nullification trial. She had refused, reminding him repeatedly that her specialty was the twelfth century, not the fifteenth; occasionally, she had ventured a bit forward in time, but only in conjunction with her work on urban statutes and the history of the bourgeoisie. Finally, as a courtesy to her good friend Thiébault, Pernoud interrupted her schedule during a busy holiday season and went to the nearly empty Archives Nationales on December 24 just to glance through Jules Quicherat's nineteenth-century edition of the nullification trial. Hours later, still perched high on a ladder in the stacks, she heard the janitor insist politely but firmly that he had to close the library; everyone else had left hours ago. Clutching all five volumes of Quicherat's cornerstone edition, she descended the ladder and called Thiébault.

Pernoud told him that she would do not an article but a whole book on Joan's second trial: "It is all too beautiful; this is an extraordinary person." She began work on January 8, 1953; by the end of the year, Hachette published her *Vie et mort de Jeanne d'Arc (les témoignages du Procès de réhabilitation, 1450–1456)*, which later appeared as a paperback and was last reedited in 1982. When I pressed her on the subject of her own political views and potential bias, she answered that she had never had any political sensibility, never been politically active, not even on the fringe of the Resistance during World War II—she was then in straitened circumstances, nursing a dying mother and a sister in poor health, and moonlighting all the while as a substitute teacher. As for Gaullism, she was grateful to André Malraux (whom she respected as a writer) for founding the Centre Jeanne d'Arc at Orléans, but beyond that . . .

So why her prolific dedication to the memory of Joan over the last four decades? Régine Pernoud sees herself as simply another voice among the many readers of diverse temperament and commitment who have been drawn to that compelling personality who burst upon European consciousness in 1429 and has recruited more partisans in the modern world than in her own time.

Joan of Arc is not for most of us what she was, for instance, in the nineteenth century for Jules Michelet and later for Charles Péguy. For Michelet (1798–1874), the freethinking prophet of socialism, Joan both incarnated and in a sense gave birth to the *Patrie*. He concluded the introduction to his popular *Jeanne d'Arc*, which first appeared in 1833 as part of his multivolume *Histoire de France* and was published separately twenty years later, with this affirmation:

She loved France so much! . . . And France, touched by that love, began to love her.

One can see it from the first day she appeared before Orléans. The whole people forgot the danger facing it; this ravishing image of the Fatherland, seen for the first time, seized its imagination and led it away; it sortied bravely from the walls, it unfurled its flag, it marched beneath the eyes of the English, who did not dare leave their fortifications.

Let us remember always, O Frenchmen, that our Fatherland was born in the heart of a woman, from her tenderness and her tears, from her blood which she shed for us.

This effusion of high Romantic patriotism is set in sharp relief by Michelet's commentary on Joan's judge Cauchon, whom he sees finally as an agent more of the devil than of the English. But most astonishing is Michelet's excursus on the English, a "great people" distinguished by "good and solid qualities," yet vitiated by their persistent vice of pride. "From Shakespeare to Milton, from Milton to Byron, their beautiful and simple literature remains skeptical, Judaic, Satanic."

Péguy (1873–1914), a working-class boy from Orléans who dropped out of the École Normale Supérieure and published an opinionated fortnightly journal in Paris, died with a German bullet in his forehead at the Battle of the Marne. Joan of Arc joined Mother Eve in inspiring the pinnacles of his poetry. A passionate socialist who first rejected and then passionately reconciled with the Roman Catholic church, Péguy saw in Joan everything good about the soul of France.

In later adaptations of these public visions, French fascism tried to enlist Joan in the cause of anti-Semitism, and the Vichy government appealed to her execution as a rallying point for resistance to the English and their allies: "They Always Return to the Scene of Their Crimes," declared a poster showing Joan at the stake surrounded by Rouen in flames, with British bombers flying overhead. Ethnocentric nationalism, like that of Jean-Marie Le Pen's movement, has frequently exploited her image.

For many, Joan the Maid has other and sometimes new meanings. She embodies for some the fierce resistance to oppression of a working class that has so often limited itself to reactive passivity, even when savaged by bloody anarchy serving not even some coherent exploitive interest but simply (as in France during the ghastly Hundred Years War) the opportunism of patriarchal violence. For others, she embodies the political prisoner, who—as Pernoud remarks here in her preface—has always been with us but whose plight is seen with special sharpness in the twentieth century. How could Joan have had the courage to do what she did? Where could she have found it?—and there lies the ultimate question, the final *mystère* of Joan of Arc.

For Régine Pernoud, Joan is not mysterious, though she is exceptional. Thanks to a superbly documented dossier of authentic sources, Joan can be explained as a person formed by her circumstances. Not all readers will agree. This translator is not sure that he does.

Three explanations are in order, regarding changes in this revision, name forms, and monetary units.

Limitations of space and the need to adapt this very French book have required several additions to Pernoud and Clin's original, and some omissions. I have rearranged parts of the text, especially part II, "The Cast of Principal Characters." Several biographical sketches—among them Philip the Good, Arthur de Richemont, Georges de La Trémoïlle, Bertrand Du Guesclin, Christine de Pisan, and many proponents of the English cause—have been added, along with elements of other sketches. Several items in part III have been dropped and several of them substantively revised. If a historical character appearing in part I is discussed further in parts II or III, that later treatment is indicated by a cross reference at the character's first appearance. I have provided a reduced basic bibliography of French and English titles, including several English-language titles published since the Pernoud-Clin original. Readers with research in mind should seek out the original bibliography, which contains an ample analytical sampling of the last two centuries' worth of books, articles, pamphlets, colloquium papers, and occasional newspaper pieces on Joan. It is an indispensable tool for serious research on Joan and her context.

Translating the names of non-English Europeans presents a curious problem. We are quite used to reading that Usamah ibn-Munqidh was the name of a Muslim Syrian nobleman who wrote about contemporary crusaders, although scholars of Islamic studies will argue about the placement of accents and other conventions of transliteration. When we move closer in culture, however, disagreement multiplies. Should the Byzantine emperor who reconquered Constantinople from the Franks be Michael VIII Palaiologos (a purist rendering) or Palaeologus (the more usual English form)? Francophone convention agrees that he should be Paléologue in a French-language text; English, alas, has reached no such consensus. One solution, now obsolete, was to anglicize resolutely every foreign name, so that Louis IX of France became St. Lewis, and his biographer, John of Joinville. In an absolute and opposite reaction, Margaret R. B. Shaw rendered French names and some titles in their standard Modern French forms, with the result that "Jean, Lord of Joinville" shared a galley bound for Damietta with "the worthy Comte Pierre de Bretagne, the Comte Guillaume de Flandre, my lord Imbert de Beaujeu, High Constable of France, the good knight Baudouin d'Ibelin and his brother Guy" (in her 1963 Penguin translation, *Chronicles of the Crusades*, p. 250). Most contemporary British and American publishers prefer to render St. Louis's son as Philip III rather than Philippe III; it would be unusual to read of King Felipe II of Spain, yet we are just as likely to encounter Kaiser Wilhelm as Frederick the Great. One current English publishing convention prefers to anglicize the names of kings, dukes, and other persons of top social rank, while leaving lesser persons' names in the original language: thus, the Garland *Medieval France: An Encyclopedia* (1995) has articles on King John II and Duke John the Fearless of Burgundy, on Jean Gerson and Jean de Joinville. This translation has striven to follow that model, with a few exceptions that seemed inevitable. In these pages the duke of Alençon and the bastard prince of the blood royal who became count of Dunois both appear as John, whereas the steward of Joan of Arc is Jean d'Aulon and that widely read intellectual statesman who wrote in her defense is Jean Gerson. I was tempted to call this book's peasant heroine Jeanne Darc rather than Jeanne d'Arc; but the American public knows her as Joan of Arc, so that using any other name form seems merely eccentric. That led, however, to the complicated incongruity of "Joan's" extended encounter with "the three Jeannes"—Jeanne de Luxembourg, Jeanne de Béthune, and Jeanne de Bar — during her imprisonment at Beaurevoir; the best solution seemed to be calling all four of them Joan.

The same general guidelines have been followed for surnames. Regnault (not Reginald) "of Chartres" is so called because he happened to come from that major city, whereas Xaintrailles was the extremely obscure site of the redoubtable Poton's origin; more important, whether Poton actually was born there or not, "de Xaintrailles" had already become a toponymic designation of his noble lineage. Was Jean "de Nouillonpont" just *from* that minor place, or was it in some sense his family's? In either case, that name form sounded right to this translator's eyes and ears; one envies the polyvalent neutrality of the French *de*.

I also have made compromises in translating medieval French titles and offices. I am well aware that any *bailli* of the Valois administration was vastly more than a modern American or British bailiff, but what modern English title could serve as a translation? 'Governor,' perhaps? I concluded that 'Receiver General' rendered *Receveur Général* better than 'Chief Tax Collector' could. I can only hope that most such titles crossed the inevitable gaps of time, institutional evolution, and language in recognizable shape.

In addition, responding to shifts in contextual nuance, both Clin and Pernoud occasionally differed in their translation of the original Latin and Old French. I have attempted to preserve the spirit of their quotes, and it is for this reason that some slight discrepancies in translation appear throughout the work.

Monetary units other than the pound (French livre) have generally been kept in French. When the text makes a distinction among the varieties of pound/livre circulating in medieval France—as in livres tournois, pounds of Tours (five of which were worth four pounds of Paris), I have retained the original.

Calculations in anything like modern terms of the values of any of these units of monetary exchange are hopelessly misleading, but some of the following descriptions may be of use to the reader. The medieval libra (Latin)/livre/pound was traditionally divided into twenty solidi or scuti/sous or écus/shillings, and each of those into twelve denarii/deniers/pennies. The exchange value of the sou varied widely: Practically every province minted its own sou, in silver, base metal, or some alloy thereof. In the fifteenth century, twenty sous tournois were supposed to be worth one livre tournois, but twenty-four were required to equal one livre parisis.

The *gros tournois,* a gold coin first minted in 1266 as part of Saint Louis's monetary reform, was to equal one standard écu tournois in official accounting transactions. The franc, a gold coin first minted in 1360 to pay the ransom of King John the Good (then a prisoner in England), was supposed to be worth one livre tournois in money of account. The salut, minted first in France under Charles VI and then in England as well as France under Henry VI, was a gold coin of varying exchange value with an image of the Virgin receiving the salutation of the angel Gabriel.

ACKNOWLEDGMENTS

JEREMY DUQUESNAY ADAMS

I am deeply grateful for the astuteness of my editor and dear spouse Bonnie Wheeler, who had the idea for this translated and revised edition, and who has with her usual energy seen it through to completion. She has in fact revised this edition at least as much as I have. I am grateful also for the preternatural editorial gifts of Gary Kuris and Charles T. Wood. Professor Wood's high expertise in all aspects of Joan's history, the constitutional and military histories of the French and English monarchies, of political religion, and indeed of the whole context of the European fifteenth century, has been of incalculable assistance to this project. Whatever infelicities remain are entirely my doing.

Many generous people have made this translation and revision possible. My thanks go first of all to the authors, who, after the initial kindness of agreeing to this translation and then approving its substance, have been unfailingly gracious in revising and adding key sections to the text as well as in providing me with supplementary documentation. Secretarial support for the project was provided by Helen Hunt and the Sisterfund Foundation. Judy Bland worked long hours at great speed (and despite her assurances, at what must have been great inconvenience) to incorporate my revisions in the growing text, ably and gallantly assisted thereafter by Gabriela Boldea, Amy Dahm, Olivia Franklin, and Xiaodi Zhang. Matthew Ervin has immeasurably aided the final polishing of the text and contributed much in the way of basic and sustained research. I am grateful to my colleagues in French at Southern Methodist University, notably William Beauchamp, Martine Prieto, and Zoë Urbanek. Michael Flamini, Alan Bradshaw, and Jennifer Simington of St. Martin's Press, along with their collaborators, have seen this book through to publication with dispatch and finesse. It is finally a pleasure to acknowledge the sound counsel on many points of the Comte de Saulieu, a scientifically rigorous expert on historical genealogy and an unfailingly kind friend.

PRELUDE

JEREMY DUQUESNAY ADAMS

READERS MAY FIND USEFUL a rapid sketch of two great crises that shaped Joan's historical moment, the Hundred Years War and the Great Schism of the Western church.

THE HUNDRED YEARS WAR

A series of destructive wars between France and England occurred between 1337 and 1453. The conflict began with a long-standing dispute about the proper relationship between the crown of France and several rich feudal principalities within that kingdom's territory. The problem was compounded by the fact that the two mightiest feudal princes, the dukes of Aquitaine and Burgundy, were also lords of territories beyond the kingdom's boundaries, which often made them richer in money and military power than their royal suzerain, the French king. The duke of Aquitaine was also king of England, the most efficient monarchy in Western Europe; the duke of Burgundy was also count of Flanders and of a cluster of neighboring states in the Low Countries and the Rhineland, scene of some of the most vigorous and profitable activity of nascent capitalism.

Yet more serious was a succession crisis that embroiled the closely related dynasties of France, England, and Burgundy. In 1328, the steady father-to-son succession that had blessed the French monarchy since 996 came to an end. Charles IV, the last of three royal sons of Philip IV (1285–1314), died without surviving sons; thus, he ended the eldest male line of the Capetian family. Upon his death, two assertive cousins claimed the crown of France: Philip of Valois, eldest nephew of Philip IV, the son of that king's brother Charles of Valois, who thus was able to claim unbroken descent in the male line from former Capetian kings; and Edward III of England, whose mother was Isabella, Philip IV's daughter.

Inheritance law of both countries would have considered Edward the most direct heir to his grandfather Philip IV—that is, had the inheritance in question been anything other than the kingdom of France, then the most populous, largest, and richest realm in Christendom. The equivalent of a French Supreme Court decided in favor of the Valois line and rejected the claims of Edward's Plantagenet dynasty. Nine years later, in 1337, Edward challenged Philip of Valois, by then King Philip VI, to a trial by combat.

Modern historians generally discern four phases in the Hundred Years War. In the first phase, 1337 to 1360, the Plantagenet party was triumphant. Smashing victories at sea (at Sluis, 1340) and on land (at Crécy in 1346 and at Poitiers in 1356) led to the captivity of the Valois king John II (from 1350 to 1364) and the Treaty of Brétigny (1360), which awarded Aquitaine and two counties in northern France to Edward in outright sovereignty and set King John's ransom at a sum designed to bankrupt the French treasury. Not surprisingly, many Frenchmen outside those conquered territories began to establish links with the English king; they evolved into a Plantagenet faction on French soil.

King Charles V (1364–1380), known thereafter as Charles the Wise, began the second phase of the war, from 1360 to 1413, by chipping away at the concessions of the Peace of Brétigny; he recovered much of the territory his father had lost. He also had to reestablish order within France, badly torn by massive peasant uprisings that the nobility bloodily repressed. His right hand in these efforts was the Breton knight Bertrand Du Guesclin, a master of guerrilla tactics as well as the more conventional forms of warfare. Charles the Wise was assisted by the fact that the eldest son of Edward III—the Black Prince—died before his father, and consequently the unfortunate Richard II (1377–1399) acceded to the English throne. Richard was eventually deposed by his cousin Henry of Lancaster, thereafter King Henry IV, as the Plantagenet family generated its own succession crisis.

The Valois recovery of control initiated by Charles V was weakened by the outbreak after the Wise King's death of a fierce rivalry between the faction of Duke John the Fearless of Burgundy and that of his first cousin Duke Louis of Orléans, a younger son of Charles V and thus brother of King Charles VI (1380–1422). In 1407, Louis of Orléans was assassinated by an agent of John the Fearless. The royalist Valois faction that sought revenge for his unchivalrous murder was led by Count Bernard VII of Armagnac; it took the name 'Armagnacs' from him. (The county of Armagnac lay on the border between Plantagenet Aquitaine and loyalist France deep in the southern part of the kingdom.) All this time, Charles VI seemed to vacillate between sanity and madness; eventually he became known as Charles the Mad.

The third phase of the Hundred Years War, 1413 to 1428, lasted from the accession of the second Lancastrian king, Henry V, to the siege of Orléans. Henry V invaded France, won an overwhelming victory at Agincourt (1415), and dictated the terms of the Treaty of Troyes (1420), which awarded him Charles VI's daughter Catherine and declared that their future son (Henry VI, 1422–1471; see II, 2) would be king of the dual monarchy of England and France. That provision disinherited the dauphin Charles, fifth son of Charles the Mad and the only one left alive in 1422 (II, 1). The dauphin fled to Bourges in the geographical center of France. His fumbling efforts to retain some form of control were badly shaken in 1419, when John the Fearless was murdered by an emissary of the dauphin on a bridge at Montereau, where they were supposed to be in a parley under truce. Some Armagnacs saw that as an appropriate act of revenge, but most historians believe that the dauphin later became obsessed by guilt for this violation of the laws of chivalry.

The dynamic Henry V died in 1422, but his brother, the duke of Bedford (II, 9), prosecuted the war in a vigorous manner, greatly assisted by his alliance with Duke Philip the Good of Burgundy (II, 3), with whose cry for vengeance many of the French felt sympathy. In 1428 Bedford laid siege to Orléans to clear the way for an all-out attack on the dauphin's position at Bourges. By the late spring of 1429, English victory seemed close if not inevitable.

At that moment, Joan the Maid appeared on the scene. To universal astonishment, she inspired the deliverance of Orléans and led the dauphin Charles to Reims for his anointing and coronation, which weakened decisively the claims of the boy-king Henry VI. Even though leaders of the Anglo-Burgundian alliance engineered Joan's death at the stake in Rouen on May 30, 1431, they proved incapable of reversing the French military recovery she had started. Four years later the Treaty of Arras (1435) put an end to the Armagnac–Burgundian feud. This fourth phase of the Hundred Years War ended with nearly complete expulsion of the English from French soil in 1453.

How responsible was the Maid for this unlikely victory? An old debate continues on this point, with most professional historians (such as Edouard Perroy, Bernard Guenée, Christopher Allmand, and Philippe Contamine) conceding her a minor role at best. For such historians, the military expertise of commanders like Dunois (II, 16) and the artillery he eventually had at his disposal were more decisive. Most professional historians would agree that Joan catalyzed popular support for the Valois cause, which by then had become an issue of national patriotism. Some students of the period feel that Joan's role was far more decisive than that of a mere catalyst; Americans mindful of the role of popular resistance to the Vietnam War tend to this judgment.

It is important to recognize how badly France had suffered by the time Joan entered the story. As recently as a century before, the kingdom of France had appeared to be the ideal Christian state. Its prosperity and internal peace under an unbroken dynasty of kings who dispensed justice rather than oppression (as those values were generally understood) seemed to many a sign of divine approval for the constitution and mores of the French. Yet almost all the fighting of the Hundred Years War had taken place in France, and the vast majority of the casualties were French civilians. The ferocity of the conflict banished the restraints of chivalric warfare, which for several centuries had sought profitable prisoners rather than mere bloodshed. Between major campaigns, companies of mercenary soldiers made an easy and pleasurable living from pillage, rapine, and the indiscriminate slaughter of a population that had lost the habit of self-defense under the long Capetian peace. "Fair France" had not been so savaged since the time of the Vikings five centuries before, and the devastation spread beyond the kingdom's borders into Spain, Italy, and Germany. Those who have seen Joan of Arc as an improbable saint, given her conviction that God had sent her to lead the armies of one "Christian" nation against another, generally have not taken into account the dimensions of the misery suffered by the common people of France and some neighboring countries because of that endless and pitiless war. For some of a radically populist temper, Joan's mission now seems entirely valid in larger spiritual terms and something of a model for modern movements of popular resistance to colonial imperialism.

THE GREAT SCHISM

The other great crisis of European civilization against which Joan's drama was staged was the Great Schism of the Roman Catholic church. Between 1378 and 1417 church leadership was claimed by two popes, one residing at Rome and the other at Avignon. From 1409 to 1415, there was also a third claimant. But the roots of the problem and its consequences for believers such as Joan the Maid stretched farther backward and forward in time than those dates might suggest.

One of the victories of King Philip IV of France was the humiliation of the papacy in the person of Pope Boniface VIII (1294–1303), who died after escaping from a detachment of French troops come to arrest him in Italy. Boniface's successor, an archbishop of Bordeaux who took the name Clement

V, seconded Philip's major religious policies: He annulled his predecessor's offensive acts, confirmed Philip's destruction of the Knights Templar, and in 1309 moved the permanent residence of the pope from Rome to Avignon, a papal city on the Rhone River directly opposite the kingdom of France. Public opinion in much of the rest of Europe was so consistently distressed, sometimes outraged, by that surrender of the papacy's ancient role and symbolic seat that the papacy returned to Rome in 1376 amid general rejoicing, even in France.

Two years after the return, however, a disputed election split the papacy once more. One line of popes claiming exclusive legitimacy remained in Rome thereafter; another line claiming the same legitimacy returned to Avignon. In 1409, a church council meeting at Pisa succeeded in producing a third claimant. This stubborn scandal was resolved only in 1415 thanks to a major alteration in the constitution of the church, the recognition of a broadly representative General Council as finally superior to the office of pope. The restored Roman papacy, headed by a native Roman of ancient lineage, Martin V (1417–1431), committed itself to undercutting this innovation at every turn.

During the years of the schism, the English king and Parliament had supported the Roman pope, at least partly because the French kings supported the Avignonese pope. Since Scotland was determined to remain independent of English pressure, the Scots supported the Avignonese claimant; parallel situations arose throughout Christendom. The Avignonese and Roman popes excommunicated their rivals and their rivals' supporters, thus denying them the sacraments of the true church. But how could one be sure which pope was the valid dispenser of the sacraments? One apocalyptic preacher even claimed to have been shown in a vision that no one had entered heaven since the Great Schism began.

Some of the best minds and most idealistic spirits of European society committed their hope for the reform of this scandal and of the church as a whole to the institution of the General Council. One such council, attended by thousands of clerics and laymen from every province and interest group in Christendom, met at the city of Constance on the upper Rhine between 1414 and 1417, and a second met at the nearby city of Basel between 1431 and 1437. The intellectual leadership of the University of Paris was overwhelmingly in favor of conciliar reform. Not surprisingly, the majority of that university's faculty also supported the Plantagenet claimant to the crown of France: A dual monarch would be likely to have his hands so full that he would need to rely on the parliamentary institutions of the two kingdoms. Edward III had shown the way by his cultivation of the English Parliament during his long and popular reign (1327–77); his young and insecure great-great-grandson Henry VI clearly would have to go even further in ruling his French kingdom through the Estates-General, an institution that tended (for good reason) to make the Valois kings nervous.

Modern admirers of Joan who also revere the tradition of representative democracy may feel a certain conflict on that score. The merciless fury of the Paris intelligentsia against the Maid is disturbing, especially to liberal intellectuals, but it is easy to see how she must have represented for them a mindless regression to the inept tyranny of monarchic absolutism, whether royal or papal. This ambivalence makes the reactions of Jacques Gélu (II, 19) and especially of Jean Gerson (II, 20), a consummate intellectual who supported both the General Council and the Valois cause, all the more important to understand.

THE DRAMA

HER STORY BEGINS

The city of Orléans, the bridge between northern and southern France, was sorely besieged by a large English force from October 12, 1428, to the following May. Its ruler, Duke Charles of Orléans (see Part II, Section 31), had been a prisoner in England since the Battle of Agincourt in 1415. The city's defense was commanded by his half-brother John, the Bastard of Orléans (later to be count of Dunois; II, 16). Over those seven months, reinforcements came sporadically to the aid of both the besieged French and the besieging English. Inconclusive skirmishing failed to mask the steady tipping of the balance in favor of the English. By March 1429, Orléans seemed ready to fall at the next serious push.

Then, in early March, came the rumor that a maid from the kingdom's eastern frontier had ridden to meet the Dauphin Charles (II, 1), promising to restore his kingdom to him by saving Orléans and by working other wonders. Joan of Arc enters the historical record; her story begins.

"THEY SAY THAT A MAID PASSED BY THE CITY OF GIEN, a maid who presented herself to the noble dauphin to raise the siege of Orléans and to lead the dauphin to Reims so that he might be anointed." This "they say" in February 1429 is the first appearance in the historical record of the woman we now call Joan of Arc.

These lines were written by one of the principal characters in the opening scenes of Joan's drama, the man best situated to be informed about it: John the Bastard, better known by his later title, the count of Dunois. His testimony from Joan's nullification trial continues: "Since I was the guardian of the city of Orléans, being lieutenant-general once the war began, I sent to the king's court the sire de Villars, who was seneschal of Beaucaire, and Jamet du Tillet, who later was bailiff of the Vermandois, for fuller information concerning this maiden."

On the fate of Orléans hung that of the entire kingdom. Orléans was the key to the south of France. It was the key to Bourges, the stronghold of the dauphin Charles, known contemptuously to his opponents as "the king of Bourges." It was the key to Auxerre, where Burgundian troops were stationed, ready to take up arms in what might well be the final move to checkmate the dauphin. Past Bourges ran the road to Guyenne, where the English were at home, where they did not need to behave like conquerors, since Guyenne was the core of the fief of Aquitaine, the legacy of Eleanor of Aquitaine, and so had belonged to the kings of England, her descendants, for more than 300 years.

The Bastard of Orléans was defending the city of his half brother, Charles, duke of Orléans (II, 31), who was at that time being held as a prisoner somewhere beyond the English Channel. The Bastard was recovering with difficulty from the wound he had received in the ill-fated attack against an English convoy bringing reinforcements to the besiegers—the shaft of an arbalest hit him in the foot almost at the beginning of the attack; two archers were barely able to free him and put him back on his horse, after which the engagement proved disastrous for the French. Several of his most effective companions remained on the battlefield—Louis de Rochechouart, Guillame d'Albret, and the valiant Scotsman John Stuart of Darnley, who was responsible for the rout, because he began the attack without waiting for the arrival of French rearguard cavalry reinforcements. This move against the handful of men escorting the English relief convoy collapsed in total confusion. The English enemy taunted the French for this "Day of the Herrings" (see III, 7)—the convoy consisted mostly of herring pickled in brine destined for the English army in that Lenten season. In Orléans, the defenders' morale sank further. The count of Clermont's reputation had already been compromised by his delay in arriving on the field of the Battle of the Herrings on the pivotal twelfth of February 1429; he left Orléans leading his troops in serious disorder. Several captains imitated him, including, despite his constant readiness for battle, Étienne de Vignolles, better known as "La Hire" (II, 22).

The fate of Orléans now seemed sealed. The Bastard, powerless to reverse it, recalled the fine days of the siege of Montargis two years earlier. With the same La Hire, he had swiftly dislodged the English, who, under the command of their captain, Salisbury (II, 38), had begun to surround the city. On September 5, 1427, Salisbury and his men were forced to abandon the field. Desiring vengeance, the same captain had come one year later to besiege Orléans, where he installed in orderly sequence, before each of the city's gates, like so many bolts, his fortified bastides—temporary fortifications, usually of wooden construction, connected with earthworks, set up to block a defensive structure, such as a tower or gateway. They could be as small as blockhouses or grow to have turrets and gates of their own. Some of the larger bastides could house sizable garrisons of troops.

Distrust of the defender of Orléans increased. The inhabitants had gone so far as to send an embassy to the duke of Burgundy (II, 3), asking him to spare the city since its lord was a prisoner. This appeal to what survived of chivalric sentiments was their last hope; in the age of chivalry, one would never have besieged a castle or a city whose "natural lord" was a prisoner. This popular appeal to the enemy was yet one further humiliation for John the Bastard, who substituted for his brother as defender.

At this critical juncture in February 1429, John the Bastard had leisure to reflect upon his situation. Immobilized by his wound, he found himself in an encircled city, with all but one of its exits closed up. The inhabitants' immediate concern was food. Relating the events of those days, the Journal of the Siege of Orléans records hardly anything other than the arrival of fresh provisions: One day, that was "seven horses loaded with herring and other foodstuffs"; two days later, nine horses came, also loaded with foodstuffs, entering by the Burgundy Gate at the east end of the city—the only gate that the English besiegers had not cut off. Everyone remembered stories of the siege of Rouen ten years before, during which inhabitants had been reduced to eating horses, dogs, cats, and rats before finally opening the city's gates to the victors.

The siege strategy at Orléans was the same as it had been for Rouen. The English applied it slowly and methodically since they knew that their most powerful allies—famine and discouragement—were to be found inside the city.

Shortly after his arrival at the head of the English forces, Salisbury, an experienced man of war, attacked the "Tourelles," those fortifications that defended the approach to the bridge on the left bank of the Loire River. Those two towers allowed whoever held them to close off the southern end of the imposing, nineteen-arch stone bridge that rested on one of the midpoint islands of the river. The city of Orléans was itself a bridge across which the two Frances, the north and the south, communicated.

The people of Orléans were subject to offensive action from July 1428, when the English occupied the small villages of the Beauce one after the other, including Angerville, Toury, Janville, Artenay, and Patay. Once Olivet was taken by one of Salisbury's companions, John de la Pole (II, 41)—known to the French army as La Poule (III, 4)—on October 7, the people of Orléans acted on their acceptance of the inevitable. They began to destroy their own buildings on the left bank of the Loire: the Portereau, along with the church and convent of the Augustinians. Such self-destruction had become practically routine. Since the disaster of Agincourt in 1415 the population of Orléans had been living in a state of alert. The financial registers of the city and its fortress testify to the way that this condition had become a part of daily life: the dispatching of messengers (that is, spies—often women); the coming and going of horsemen who surveyed the movements of mercenary troops, especially toward Étampes and Sully-sur-Loire; the strengthening of the watch on the city's walls; the purchasing of arbalest shafts and defensive artillery (paid for by a rise in taxes). Worse was yet to come. The old remembered that it had been necessary in 1359 to destroy the venerable church of Saint-Aignan, site of an early skirmish between French and English troops. This ancient collegial church had its roots in the region's Christianity. All newly installed bishops of Orléans visited it to venerate the relics of their great predecessor, St. Aignan, who in earlier times had defended the city against the attacks of Attila the Hun. The basilica was rebuilt in 1376 only on the orders of the wise King Charles V, well after the Peace of Brétigny, which ended the first phase of the Hundred Years War.

Public memory remained equally sensitive to attacks and alerts, sometimes caused by bands of mercenary troops, sometimes by the raids of English captains. Based in the surrounding territory, they fell like eagles on their prey: on Olivet, on the abbey of Saint-Bénoît-sur-Loire, or on Orléans itself, as on the day of the "Great Fear" in 1418, when all were certain that the siege would soon commence, for the English were then attacking both Rouen and Paris.

The English defeat at Montargis in 1427—"the first moment of happiness that came my way," the dauphin Charles had cried from his refuge at Bourges—gave Orléans some fleeting hope. Yet it soon became necessary to destroy the suburbs once again, to accommodate refugees within the city, and to make other preparations for siege. At the very moment that the English attacked the Tourelles, they destroyed the twelve water mills that the city used to make its flour. Very quickly, inside Orléans itself, people organized the eleven horse-powered mills that replenished the city's food supply.

Hostilities recommenced on October 17, 1428. One of the three bombards that the English had just installed at Saint-Jean-le-Blanc, near the Augustinian convent that had earlier been abandoned, caused some damage in the city and killed "a woman named Belle near the postern gate of Chesneau." Five days later, the watchtower bell sounded the alarm once more. The citizens of Orléans destroyed one of the arches of the bridge and fortified the islet of Belle-Croix, on which the bridge rested. They would no longer defend the fort of the Tourelles, to which they set fire. The siege progressed with English bastides methodically set up on the principal highways: the bastide named Saint-Laurent near the route to Blois; those that the English called "London" and "Paris" on the routes to Châteaudun and Paris. Another bastide, "Rouen," served as a connection between those two. The bastide of Saint-Loup blocked the way to Gien at its crossroads with the route to

Pithiviers—but on that side, to the east, the blockade would never become complete, despite the invaders' best efforts.

Such was the situation that the Bastard of Orléans discovered on October 25, 1428, when he arrived at his half brother's city. He quickly undertook new strategic arrangements. He had some of the churches and buildings outside of the ramparts destroyed—Saint-Loup, Saint-Euverte, Saint-Gervais, Saint-Marc—and had artillery installed at key points. Some reinforcements came his way with the arrival of Louis de Culant, at the head of 200 fighting men, and Charles de Bourbon, count of Clermont (II, 11), on January 30. The Scotsman John Stuart came on February 8, but the disastrous "Day of the Herrings," on February 12, put an end to his hopes. The citizens of Orléans sent a delegation to the duke of Burgundy. Poton de Xaintrailles (II, 44) and Pierre d'Orgui proposed to Duke Philip the Good (II, 3) that he take the city under his command on the condition of guaranteeing its neutrality—a humiliating development for the Bastard but understandable on the part of the inhabitants, who felt themselves abandoned; they were, after all, making an appeal to a representative of the royal house of France, the cousin of their natural protector, the duke of Orléans.

The negotiations failed. The duke of Burgundy would have been delighted to acquire Orléans without striking a blow, but his ally Bedford, the English regent (II, 9), opposed such an acquisition vehemently: "I would be mighty angry to cut down the bushes so that someone else could get the little birds from the branches!" At least, the duke reestablished contact with some of his men fighting alongside the English besiegers. How much difference did this Burgundian garrison make, or what relief might its departure produce? It may have amounted to little more than a few men-at-arms enlisted among the troops paid by English captains.

The fate of Orléans would surely be settled in a few days, perhaps a few hours, since a decisive offensive could be launched at any minute.

Under these circumstances, increasingly urgent reports of an unexpected rescue sent from heaven and conveyed by an unknown girl said to be called "Joan the Maid" were particularly attractive: Only divine intervention, people said, could save the city. The people of Orléans would later come to explain the feeling that seized them once the rumor about the Maid began to circulate. As the Journal of the Siege of Orléans remarks: "It was said . . . that she had been sent by God to raise the siege of the city. The inhabitants found themselves so hard-pressed by necessity due to the enemies who besieged them that they did not know whom to beg for remedy, if not God Himself."

This report did not comfort the Bastard, an experienced warrior. Even the arrival of two contingents of reinforcement, one French and the other Scottish, had not brought him relief. He testified later that he remained skeptical of this purportedly heaven-sent relief until months later, when he actually met Joan the Maid. But, because he was a pious man, he sent two trustworthy companions to check on this unusual rumor. Since the king was at Chinon, the Bastard sent Archambaut de Villars and Jamet du Tillet there, where they were also likely to find Raoul de Gaucourt (II, 18), governor of Orléans, who had gone to Chinon to inform the dauphin of the city's desperate condition. The Bastard's two envoys soon returned to Orléans to report. The Bastard testified about that conversation in Joan's nullification trial:

> They returned from the king's presence, reporting publicly to me, in the presence of all the people in Orléans who yearned to learn the truth concerning this maiden's arrival, that they had seen the aforesaid maid arrive at the king's court in the city of Chinon themselves. They said that the king himself had not wished to receive her; it was deemed appropriate that this maid wait two days before she should be permitted to come into the king's presence, even though she had said again and again that she came to raise the siege of Orléans and to lead the noble dauphin to Reims, so that he could be anointed king, demanding constantly that she be given men, horses, and arms.

Jeanne la Pucelle, whom we call Joan of Arc (for a discussion of her name, see III, 1), here makes her entry into history.

CHAPTER TWO

JOAN MEETS HER DAUPHIN

This chapter tracks Joan's improbable quest from its visible beginnings in her native Domrémy in the spring of 1428 to her enlisting the reluctant support of Robert of Baudricourt, the captain of neighboring Vaucouleurs (see Part II, Section 7), who gave her a small escort of armed men and sent her to the dauphin's court on February 22, 1429 (II, 1). For six days, that troupe of seven gingerly crossed hostile territory; five days later, they reached the dauphin's court at Chinon in the Loire valley. Two days later, the dauphin received Joan. Moved by the conviction she evinced for her mission to save him, his crown, and France, the dauphin sent Joan farther west, to Poitiers, to undergo an examination by a panel of learned clergymen. Within the fortnight, she had won their approval and returned to join the dauphin's court. However great the doubts about her, Joan had already restored an amazing degree of hope to the French cause.

When I arrived at the town of Sainte-Catherine-de-Fierbois, I sent [a letter] to my king; then I went to the town of Chinon, where my king was; I arrived there about the hour of noon and found lodging at a hostelry.

—Joan's testimony at her Rouen trial

THE LETTER THAT JOAN SENT from Sainte-Catherine-de-Fierbois, the last stage of her journey to Chinon, has not survived. Since her arrival on territory obedient to the dauphin, she had no task more important than laying claim to what she called her "mission." At Fierbois, aware that she was no more than half a day's journey from the dauphin's residence, she dictated a letter to him. Among the "small company that escorted" her was a royal courier, Colet de Vienne, "in constant readiness" to deliver messages. Colet had guided his companions through the highways and byways and had shown them where to ford the rivers. His present assignment was to put spurs to this last stage of Joan's journey.

Sainte-Catherine-de-Fierbois was a historic and well-known site that became important to Joan of Arc's story. The chapel dates from the eighth century, indeed earlier than that; Charles Martel, the bellicose grandfather of Charlemagne, had left a sword there as a trophy of his victory over the Muslims in 732. The rectory in which Joan probably lodged was constructed around 1400 by Marshal Boucicaut, the hero of the disastrous crusade to Nicopolis. After his stay in Constantinople, where he assisted in the defense of the Byzantine capital from the Turks, the marshal had gone on a pilgrimage to Mt. Sinai to the tomb of St. Catherine. He brought back relics preserved in a silver reliquary, the only relics of that saint in France. Not long after Joan's death, the chapel was reconstructed: Hélie de Bourdeilles, the saintly archbishop of Tours, donated funds to build a new Flamboyant Gothic church that survives today. Before his promotion to the archbishopric of Tours, while still bishop of Périgueux, Bourdeilles was asked to provide an analysis of the trial that condemned Joan of Arc.

Two days after Joan's arrival at Fierbois (that is, according to tradition, March 4, 1428), her little company entered the town of Chinon and reached the crossroads of the Grand-Carroi. Who were these strangers? Where did they come from? This girl who seemed at ease in men's clothes and expressed her desire to be received by the dauphin—from where did she come? Questions such as these arose from the moment they dismounted onto the rim of a well at the corner of the square (a spot to this day pointed out to tourists).

There was already quite a story to tell. Of Joan herself, it was said that she came "from the marches of Lorraine," which conveyed the notion of a frontier. Her companions had met her not in her village of Domrémy but a short distance away in a place known as Vaucouleurs, whose name still evokes the great shadow of Jean de Joinville, seneschal of Champagne, companion and friend of St. Louis. Two hundred years earlier Joinville had granted the town a charter of municipal freedom.

The fortress of Vaucouleurs (II, 7) had been much on the minds of both the English and the French. This well-fortified strongpoint on the banks of the Meuse in the district of Toul, on the border between Champagne and the Barrois, maintained its allegiance to the dauphin even though it was surrounded by Burgundian territory. In 1428 the duke of Bedford, regent of France (II, 9) for his nephew the young Henry VI of England (II, 2), decided, at the urging of his chief captains, to rid himself of this pocket of resistance in a region where Anglo-Burgundian garrisons had been circulating freely. On June 22 Antoine de Vergy, the governor of Champagne, received instructions to besiege Vaucouleurs.

Vergy had at his disposal a contingent whose numbers we know exactly: 796 men. The squires and auxiliary troops who would have accompanied those men-at-arms would bring the force to a total of 2,500 combatants, reinforced by the troops of Pierre de Trie, captain of Beauvais, nicknamed Patrouillart, and by John, count of Freiburg and Neuchâtel, who had come from what was known as the county of Burgundy (the Franche-Comté).

The countrymen in the valley of the meandering river Meuse, crowded with men-at-arms, were agitated. The peasants of such villages as Domrémy, Greux, Coussey, and Burey abandoned their homes and, driving their cattle before them, sought refuge behind the walls of Neufchâteau, the only fortified city close by; from the ramparts, they soon saw their harvest burning in the distance. At Vaucouleurs, the royal captain, Robert de Baudricourt, stubbornly maintained his allegiance to the dauphin. He regrouped his garrison and reinforced his fortress, which had powerful defenses: probably twenty-three towers rising from the Meuse to the plateau whose escarpment served as the base of the fortified complex. These operations lasted most of July. Everyone waited for Baudricourt to surrender, as four years earlier Étienne de Vignolles, La Hire (II, 22), had surrendered at Vitry—a surrender that had brought in its wake the capitulation of several small strongholds in Champagne, such as Blanzy, Larzicourt, and Heilz-L'Évêque. The surrender of Vitry-en-Perthois was accepted by the man who had negotiated the Treaty of Troyes, Pierre Cauchon (II, 49); it had been a powerful signal for these fortresses of the eastern part of the kingdom, which the English rulers had come to count on as a reliable shield. Yet nothing decisive happened at Vaucouleurs. A compromise was reached near the end of July. Baudricourt did not surrender, and the attackers withdrew when he promised that he would forgo military action against the Burgundians. Thus neutralized, Vaucouleurs stayed free.

These events weighed on the minds of the little troupe that arrived at the Grand-Carroi. They had lived through them the previous summer of 1428. The little peasant girl in a red surcoat had first come to the attention of Baudricourt's fellow townspeople around Ascension Day (which in 1428 had fallen on May 13), as she strode along the high walls of Vaucouleurs, asking all she met where the lord Robert was and when he would be willing to receive her. This image of her animated the memory of Bertrand de Poulengy (II, 33), one of the two lords who soon took charge of escorting her as far as Chinon. Bertrand recounted that he had seen her speak to Robert de Baudricourt, the captain of Vaucouleurs; she had said that she came to him from her Lord so that he would tell the dauphin to stand fast and not to make war upon his enemies, for the Lord would bring him help before the next mid-Lent. Unperturbed by the laughter and the jeering she provoked, Joan said that the kingdom belonged not to the dauphin but to his Lord, that his Lord wished the dauphin to become king, and that he would hold the kingdom as a fief, whether his enemies wished it or not. She herself would lead him to be anointed. At the side of this peasant girl stood, somewhat sheepishly, a man whom she called her uncle (actually, her first cousin's husband), a certain Durand Laxart, from Burey-le-Petit. Robert had advised him to take the girl home with a slap or two to end her impertinence.

Two months later, in July 1428, Joan was on the road, hastening toward Neufchâteau with her parents, sister, and three brothers. For some time she had shared the lot of refugees crowded in an inn belonging to a woman named La Rousse (the Redhead), whom Joan helped from time to time with the dishes and the cooking, along with her good friend Hauviette. Hauviette was Joan's longtime friend; her family had fled home as well.

The red surcoat of the peasant girl of Domrémy was seen again in the course of that winter, at the beginning of Lent (which began early that year; in 1429, the first Sunday of Lent, known locally as Russet Sunday, fell on February 13). Robert de Baudricourt threw her out a second time. By then Joan had found lodging at Vaucouleurs, at the house of the wheelwright Henri Le Royer who with his wife, Catherine, had become her supporter. Joan continued to proclaim that it was necessary that she speak to the dauphin before mid-Lent, because she was bringing him help from heaven, help he would not get from anyone else. "Time wore on for her as for a woman great with child," in the familiar metaphor from the Psalms. The pressure was so great that she took to the road one morning with the devoted Durand Laxart and a resident of Vaucouleurs named Jacques Alain; they purchased her a horse for twelve francs. But they did not get far. Arriving at Saint-Nicolas-de-Sept-Fonts, on the route to Sauvroy, Joan realized that she had been precipitous to leave without achieving Baudricourt's approval; she declared that it was "not thus that they should depart," and they returned to Vaucouleurs.

Early every morning, this girl went to the castle's chapel, called Our Lady of the Vaults. "I frequently saw Joan the Maid come to this church with great piety; there, she heard morning mass and stayed a long time afterward to pray. I saw her under the vault of this church kneeling before the statue of the blessed Virgin, with her face sometimes downcast and sometimes gazing upright." So said Jean le Fumeux, then a young canon of Notre-Dame-de-Vaucouleurs, who like everyone else regarded the comings and goings of this little peasant of Domrémy with amazement.

One day, a messenger of the duke of Lorraine presented himself, carrying a safe-conduct for Joan. Duke Charles II (II, 26) had heard rumors about her in his castle at Nancy and wished to see her. Charles II, who had been hardly better than a highwayman, had grown old and sick. Perhaps he hoped to encounter some holy person through whom he could be healed. Joan, accompanied as always by Laxart, took the road armed with the duke's safe-conduct. She was brought before him: "He questioned me about the recovery of his health, and I said that I knew nothing about that. I said very little to the duke about my mission but did say nonetheless that he should give me his son and some men-at-arms for France and that I would pray to God for the restoration of his health."

She was not afraid to deliver a few admonitions about his conduct. He had abandoned his wife, Margaret of Bavaria, for a girl named Alison Dumay, by whom he had sired five bastards. In Neufchâteau, which had lodged a suit against him before the Parlement of Paris, such stories were common. The "son" Joan mentioned was in fact his son-in-law, René of Anjou (II, 5), the dauphin's brother-in-law.

Someone must have accompanied Joan during a part of this trip to Nancy—a journey that she converted into a pilgrimage, visiting shrines as distant as Saint-Nicolas-du-Port. Jean de Nouillonpont (also known as Jean de Metz; II, 30) accompanied her at least as far as Toul. Nouillonpont, a squire in the household of Robert de Baudricourt, later recalled how at first he teased the girl in the red dress. He had confronted her near the military headquarters, asking ironically: "Honey, what are you doing here? Shouldn't the dauphin be thrown out and all of us become English?" The Maid had answered, calmly as always:

> I came here to the king's chamber [that is, into royal territory] to speak to Robert de Baudricourt so that he would either bring me or have me brought to the king, but he pays no attention to me or to my words; nevertheless, it is important that I be at the king's side before mid-Lent arrives, even if it means I have to walk until my feet are worn down to my knees; there is in fact no one else, neither a king nor a duke nor the daughter of the king of Scotland, nor any other who can recover the kingdom of France, and he will have no help, if not through me, even though I would prefer to stay home and spin wool with my poor mother, for this is not my proper station, but I must go and I must do it, because my Lord wills that I do so.

He asked, "But who is your Lord?" And the Maid answered, "God."

> And so I promised the Maid, by placing my hands in hers as a sign of good faith, that I would with God's aid lead her to the king; and I begged her to tell me when she wanted to leave; she said "Better today than tomorrow, better tomorrow than later."

A practical man, the squire asked her if she expected to depart in the clothes she was wearing. She answered that she would prefer to wear men's clothes. He found among his servant's clothes something to dress her in: hose, jacket, and hat. Once she got back to the Le Royer house, Joan would find other apparel that the good folk of Vaucouleurs, now sympathetic to her cause, had made specifically for her: men's suits, hose, and all that was necessary, plus a horse worth about sixteen francs.

It was upon her return from Nancy that Robert de Baudricourt, tired of war and astonished by the enthusiasm that Joan the Maid left in her wake, resigned himself to giving her permission to go to the dauphin at Chinon. Her escort had already been formed. Jean de Metz was to accompany her, as was Bertrand de Poulengy, each with a servant: Julien for Bertrand de Poulengy and a certain Jean de Honnecourt for Jean de Metz.

Baudricourt added to their number the royal messenger Colet de Vienne, who knew the roads and could discern which men-at-arms and garrisons were loyal to the dauphin; a certain Richard Larcher went along as well, making a party of six men along with this girl who already rode like a man-at-arms. (Joan's riding ability is not surprising: The horse was then the primary mode of transport, and more than once she rode her father's plowhorses.)

As a precaution, Robert de Baudricourt had visited the Le Royers accompanied by the parish priest of Vaucouleurs, Jean Fournier, who, attired in his stole, pronounced an exorcism over Joan. Joan may well have been busy spinning with Catherine Le Royer (who later testified that she spun very well indeed) and quickly went up to the priest, throwing herself on her knees before him. But Joan later told Catherine that the parish priest had done ill: He had already heard her confession and knew perfectly well that she was a good Christian and did not need any exorcism. This (for Joan) pointless, indeed ridiculous scene probably took place before her first departure and bears witness to the uncertainties of the captain of Vaucouleurs, who took public precautions lest he be dealing with a sorceress. In the end, Robert himself traveled part of the way with the little group, all the way up to the Gate of France one evening, a little after Russet Sunday.

What were the feelings of these travelers who went to Chinon from so far away, after a journey of eleven days? Joan never stopped encouraging her companions. They passed their first night in the abbey of Saint-Urbain-lès-Joinville, but after that they traveled as much as they could at night, in order to avoid roaming bands of hostile Englishmen or Burgundians. Joan wanted to go to mass—"We would do well if we could hear mass," she was later quoted as saying—but that would have been too noticeable. Only in the friendly territory of Auxerre and Sainte-Catherine-de-Fierbois were they able to hear mass, twice in those eleven days. In the course of that journey, the young men who rode at her side (Jean de Metz was thirty-one, Bertrand de Poulengy thirty-seven), later declared that Joan had slept alongside them at every stop, keeping both her doublet and her hose closed and bound: they never felt any "carnal impulse" toward her. "Her words put me on fire, inspiring in me a love for her that was, I believe, divine."

The curious clustered around her at Chinon, as they had at Vaucouleurs. Joan had never stopped declaring to her companions that the "dauphin" (as she then called him) would receive her. Now messengers and sergeants buzzed about them, and her companions, who had been so intent upon their goal, felt some anxiety. For them, Joan had undergone a convincing test: During their eleven days together, they had found her without fault or weakness, exemplary in piety and charity, inflexible in resolve. Nonetheless, the final test still lay ahead: Did her words and her predictions correspond to any reality ahead?

Despite destruction in the seventeenth century, in the Revolution, and also under the Empire, the castle of Chinon with the pointed roofs of the little city at its feet still rises above the city like a cliff dominating the valley of the Vienne. During the long hours that stretched between the arrival of Joan and her escort toward noon until the evening of the following day, when she was finally admitted to the presence of the dauphin in the castle itself, there were constant comings and goings along the precipitous road today known as the rue Jeanne-d'Arc. "She was much questioned," declared Jean de Metz. According to Bertrand de Poulengy, she was questioned by the dauphin's noble counselors, whose perplexity was evident if Joan and her companions said nothing more about their origins and their goals than what Baudricourt's squire Nouillonpont reported earlier, including that disconcerting affirmation, "He will have no help if not through me."

At the nullification trial, Simon Charles, a man of great stature and president of the royal treasury, clearly recalled the unfolding of the subsequent events. He may not have been present at Chinon when Joan arrived, but having returned "to the court in the month of March" from his embassy for the dauphin to Venice, he discovered what had happened. Jean de Metz told him that the dauphin had sent his agents to question Joan in her hostelry: "What had she come to do and what did she want?" Joan had hesitated. She had no intention of divulging the specifics of her mission except to the dauphin, but finally she had answered that hers was a double mandate from the King of Heaven. She had first to raise the siege of Orléans, then to lead Charles to Reims to receive his crown and his anointing.

The dauphin's counselors were divided as they returned to him. One group, believing that the girl was mad, urged the dauphin to dismiss her without delay; the other thought that he should at the very least listen to her. It is likely that Charles was not convinced and did not agree to admit her to his presence until such time as he had received the message sent by Robert de Baudricourt shortly after the little escort had departed; his letter confirmed the report of Joan and her companions. Without this reassurance from a captain of tested loyalty, the dauphin, a suspicious and mistrustful man, most likely would never have received Joan. He must have reflected upon their long and perilous journey across an "occupied zone," fording rivers still swollen with the melting snows, past garrisons and enemy contingents that they had carefully avoided. The confirmation of these difficulties by the captain of a distant and sorely tried stronghold no doubt convinced him that Joan should at least be given an interview. One can understand then why Joan had earlier returned to Vaucouleurs, declaring "It is not thus that we should depart." Her stubborn solicitation of Robert de Baudricourt was justified because his support was essential to her mission.

"It was a high hour"—an evening hour. Nightfall in the first days of March then came at six-thirty or thereabouts at that latitude, so it could have been seven or seven-thirty in the evening when Joan, her companions, and most likely a messenger of the dauphin came together in the steep access road to the castle to which the Maid's name has since been given. "There were more than three hundred knights and fifty torches," she would later say, recalling that evening. The count of Vendôme had been charged with introducing her to those gathered in the castle's great hall. The "three hundred knights" may well be an exaggeration produced by the effect of such a spectacle on the peasant girl brought for the first time in her life into a vast hall where a multitude of torches and candelabra flared, illuminating the unfamiliar forms of great lords and noble ladies. Raoul de Gaucourt (II, 18) expresses the contrast between the thronging assembly, gathered perhaps with a slight purpose of intimidation, and Joan, whom he called the "shepherdess"—not a surprising term, since all peasant women were then more or less considered shepherdesses in the eyes of the great:

> I was myself present at the castle and the city of Chinon when the Maid arrived, and I saw her when she presented herself to his royal majesty; she showed great humility and simplicity of manner, this poor little shepherdess. . . . I heard her say the following words to the king: "Very noble lord dauphin, I have come and I have been sent from God to bring aid to you and to the kingdom."

This is a concise statement of the contrast between Joan's person and her message. The testimony of later trials and other reports amplify that contrast—as does, for example, the *Chronicle* of Jean Chartier, who was in some senses the official historian of the court:

> Then Joan, having come before the king, made the curtsies and reverences that customarily are made to a king as though she had been nourished at the court and, her greeting having been delivered, said in addressing the king, "God give

you life, gentle King," even though she did not know him and had never seen him, and there were many pompous lords there more opulently dressed than was the king. Wherefore he replied to Joan: "What if I am not the king, Joan?" Pointing to one of the lords, he said: "There is the king." To which she answered, "In God's name, gentle Prince, it is you and none other."

Simon Charles, who arrived at Chinon a little while afterward, says simply: "When the king knew that she was going to come, he withdrew slightly from the crowd; Joan nonetheless recognized him and made her reverence to him, speaking with him for some time. After hearing her, the king seemed radiant." Finally, the report made by Joan herself to Friar Jean Pasquerel, her confessor, eliminates accessory details but recalls her own words:

> When [the king] saw her, he asked Joan her name and she answered: "Gentle dauphin, I am Joan the Maid, and the King of Heaven commands that through me you be anointed and crowned in the city of Reims as a lieutenant of the King of Heaven, who is king of France." And after further questions asked by the king, Joan said to him anew: "I say to you, on behalf of the Lord, that you are the true heir of France, and a king's son, and He has sent me to you to lead you to Reims, so that you can receive your coronation and consecration if you wish it." This being understood, the king said to his courtiers that Joan had told him a certain secret that no one knew or could know except God; and that is why he had great confidence in her. All of that I learned from the mouth of Joan, because I was not present.

One thing seems beyond doubt. Whatever circumstances caused the legend of the first encounter between dauphin and maid to swell into a theatrical set piece, Joan did not allow herself to be disconcerted by the intimidating spectacle of this great hall rustling with the whispers of high society and ablaze with a brightness to which she was unaccustomed. She went straight to the dauphin and calmly delivered the message for which she had crossed half the country.

That message must have made a strong impression on the man who received it. Charles of Ponthieu, whom Joan called the dauphin, had lived as an exile since the English entered Paris in 1418. He was now twenty-six. For seven years after the death of his father, Charles VI, in 1422, he had awaited the anointing that would make him king. When he was twelve, his eldest brother, the dauphin Louis, died; that death was followed two years later by the death of the second dauphin, Jean, shortly after the Battle of Agincourt (October 25, 1415), which had cut huge holes in the French royal entourage. Some historians exaggerate when they say that his own mother had given rise to doubts of his legitimacy—a rumor circulated by his enemies—but Charles had been removed from succession to the throne in 1420 by the Treaty of Troyes, which had been ratified by both parties, including his mother. Yet despite his youth and a series of deceptions, defeats, and obstacles, he had never abandoned his claim. Charles, on becoming surviving son and thus dauphin, declared himself regent of France, but he did not use this title or act personally without the most dire consequences. The worst of them was the fateful outcome of that conversation on the bridge of Montereau, where John the Fearless, duke of Burgundy, had been assassinated by his own escort under a veil of mysterious circumstances. Ten years had passed since then, but that day, September 14, 1419, still weighed heavily in the dauphin's decisions. He would have no relief from that concern until the horror of its memory had been erased by formal reconciliation with his cousin, the duke of Burgundy.

What did Joan tell Charles? It is not known exactly, but the chronicle of Pierre Sala records that Guillaume Gouffier, the dauphin's chamberlain, alleged that:

> The king . . . went one morning alone into his oratory and there made a humble, silent request in prayer to Our Lord within his heart, in which he begged him devoutly that if it were true that he was His heir, descendant of the noble House of France, and that the kingdom should in justice belong to him, might it please God to protect and defend him, or at the very worst, allow him the grace of escaping alive and free from imprisonment so that he might find solace in Spain or in Scotland, which were from times long past brothers-in-arms and allies of the kings of France.

If Joan did indeed repeat to him anything like that prayer, "a sure secret that no one knew or could know except God," as Jean Pasquerel would later declare, the impact on Charles must have been enormous. This episode resounds with significance: It has a place in Joan's story and in history itself, a place that does not seem out of proportion to anyone who understands that it is the small event that can change life most radically.

The speculations of contemporaries, of historians, and of amateur commentators ever since generally have involved some more dramatic or salacious revelation: "proof" that Joan was, in fact, Charles's illegitimate half sister (III, 3), for example, or some password from a major field commander or leader of a court faction; perhaps even the knowledge of some private vice Charles had hoped was secret. The silent prayer that Pasquerel cited seems more plausible in that context, even though it poses a greater credibility problem for the rational modern mind.

In any case, this encounter produced in Charles an immediate decision. He would keep Joan in the castle and would entrust her to the wife of Guillaume Bellier, the bailiff of Troyes, who had authority over the personnel of the royal household. The Maid would move into royal quarters, the tower of Couldray. This castle to the west of the "middle castle," the principal building of the royal fortress, was a superb keep built two centuries earlier, the lower parts of which had housed the Knights Templar imprisoned there in 1308 on the order of King Philip the Fair. Whether that grim historical event was reported to Joan or not, she preferred the nearby chapel dedicated to St. Martin. From the moment Joan took up residence in the royal quarters, Louis de Coutes, a young boy of fifteen or sixteen, was assigned to her service; a bit later, he would officially become her page:

> A lodging was assigned to her in the castle of Couldray, and I lived there in that tower with Joan. All the time that she was there, I was with her continually during the day; at night, she had women with her; I remember well that from the moment she was in this tower of Couldray men of high rank frequently came to converse with Joan; what they did or said I did not know, for always, when I saw such men arrive, I went away, and I do not know who they were.

This recollection from a timid boy, just then learning the craft of arms as a member of the contingent of Raoul de Gaucourt, is completed by a detail that struck him as significant: "At that time, when I was with Joan in that tower, I often saw her on her knees praying, as it seemed to me; nevertheless, I could never hear what she was saying, even though sometimes she wept."

Joan's stay in the tower of Couldray was brief. Overwhelmed as the king may have been by the "sign" that Joan had given him, he needed to determine from whence she came and what sort of person she was. He sent her to Poitiers, where prelates, theologians, and masters of the University of Paris—the few who had remained faithful to him—were gathered. Poitiers had become the intellectual capital of the "king of Bourges." The royal household took to the road. Messengers went to Vaucouleurs and throughout that region to investigate the authenticity of this peasant girl.

For Joan the Maid, the moment to ride abroad had arrived. She who had never before left the countryside around her village now prepared to ride across a great part of France. She was to cover over 3,000 miles on horseback; the last phase of that long journey she would ride bound hand and foot to Rouen. But she knew nothing about that yet; she knew only that her career would be short. Had she not declared, upon arriving at Chinon, "I shall last one year, hardly more"?

For the moment, Joan delighted in riding across friendly territory. It was but a day's journey (thirty-one or thirty-seven miles, depending on the route taken) from Chinon to Poitiers, the capital city of the dukes of Aquitaine, the preferred residence of Queen Eleanor some 300 years earlier, and, even farther in the past, the city of Queen Radegund at the turn of the sixth and seventh centuries; that arrival at nightfall to a city bristling with belltowers must have been both solemn and joyous.

Before her trip to Poitiers, at Chinon, Joan had received an important visit from John, the duke of Alençon (II, 4), whom she would call "my fair duke" (the modifier 'fair' was much in use then; one said 'fair nephew' almost as we would say 'dear nephew'). He himself later recounted their first meeting:

> When Joan came to find the king, he was in the city of Chinon and I in the city of Saint-Florent [near Saumur]. I was out on a walk hunting quail when a messenger came to tell me that a maiden had arrived at the king's court who declared herself to have been sent by God to chase out the English and raise the siege the English had set around Orléans; that is why the next day I went to the king in the city of Chinon. I found Joan speaking with the king. When I came up to them, Joan immediately asked who I was, and the king answered that I was the duke of Alençon. Then Joan said, "You are very welcome; the more the blood of France is gathered together, the better it shall be."

The young duke of Alençon deserved the confidence the king placed in him. Close to Charles by blood, he was also close to him in age; born in 1406, he was three years younger than the dauphin. Above all, he had only recently returned from England, where he had been a prisoner: At twenty-three, he had been in captivity for five years. His comrades thought he was dead, but he had been found alive by the British among the heaped-up corpses on the field of battle at Verneuil in 1424. He had been imprisoned in the town of Crotoy, where his strong constitution had permitted him, against all expectations, to recover. Able to pay only a part of the high ransom that had been a condition of his release, he swore an oath not to fight against the English until the sum had been paid in full. He was thus a prisoner of his word of honor. We can imagine that he covered the distance that separates Saint-Florent-lès-Saumur from Chinon with particular haste, once he heard word of the astonishing promise this unknown girl had made. Joan's first response to him must have startled the duke, who remembered it sharply twenty-seven years later. In fact, Joan seems to have been at ease from that point, but she still had to explain herself to the dauphin, as the next section of the duke's report testifies:

> The next day, Joan came to the king's mass, and when she saw the king, she bowed deeply; and he led Joan into a chamber. The king kept the lord of La Trémoïlle [II, 25], and myself with him, saying to everyone else that they could retire. And then Joan made several requests of the king, among others that he give his kingdom to the King of Heaven, and that after that donation the King of Heaven would do to him as He had done to his predecessors and would bring

it back to its original condition; many other things that I do not remember were said until it was time for dinner; and after dinner, the king went for a walk in the fields, and there Joan ran about charging with a lance, and I, seeing Joan behave like this, carrying and running with the lance, gave her the gift of a horse.

The duke was dazzled. Joan already had acquired the ease with weapons necessary for a warrior; she clearly deserved that horse. This passage also allows us to understand how the duke of Alençon remained struck by Joan's presence for the rest of his life, as were so many others. His recollection continues:

The king concluded that Joan should be examined by churchmen; to this task were assigned the bishop of Castres, the king's confessor [Gerard Machet], the bishop of Senlis [Simon Bonnet, who in fact was not yet bishop of that city but would become so in time], the bishops of Maguelonne and Poitiers [the latter, Hugues de Cambarel], Master Pierre of Versailles, later bishop of Meaux, and Master Jean Morin; and many others whose names I do not remember.

This precious piece of evidence shows that there was a formal interrogation at Chinon conducted by churchmen, if not a trial like that held in Poitiers. As the duke made clear:

They asked Joan in my presence why she had come and who made her come to the king? She answered that she had come from the King of Heaven and that she had heard voices and a source of advice who told her what she had to do, and other things that I do not remember. Joan herself ate dinner with me and told me that she had been thoroughly examined, and that she both knew and also could say more than she had chosen to tell to those who interrogated her.

The duke of Alençon concluded: "The king, once he had heard the report of those who had been delegated to examine her, wished even more strongly that Joan go to the city of Poitiers to be examined once more; but I was not present at the Poitiers investigation."

The duke of Alençon's testimony reveals the character of this controversial "Poitiers Trial," which is the subject of contentious scholarly dispute, especially since its transcript has been lost. (This in itself is a surprising development. Many citations to and quotations from it have survived, but not the full transcript. See III, 13.) The ever-cautious dauphin wished to increase both the number and the quality of those responsible for her interrogation; at Poitiers, such men were readily available.

Joan was lodged there in the house of Master Jean Rabateau, an advocate of the Parlement of Paris, who had joined the dauphin two years earlier. While certain women secretly kept an eye on Joan's behavior, prelates were called together to form a tribunal of experts responsible for her interrogation. François Garivel, counselor of the king on the matter of feudal revenues, added several names to those provided by the duke of Alençon: Guillaume Aymeri, a theologian of the Dominican order; Guillaume Le Marié, bachelor in theology and canon of Poitiers; Pierre Seguin, described as a "specialist in holy scripture"; Jean Lambert, a Carmelite friar; Mathieu Mesnage; and, most of all, the Dominican who would become dean of the Faculty of Poitiers, Seguin Seguin. Garivel made it clear at a later date that Joan had been interrogated on several occasions and that her examination had taken about three weeks. He himself had asked her: "Why did she call the king 'dauphin' and not 'king'?" She answered that she would not call him "king" until he had been crowned and consecrated at Reims, where she intended to bring him. Garivel had been struck by the piety of this simple "shepherdess."

The deposition of Seguin Seguin at the nullification trial is most instructive. The Poitiers investigation must have been lively, for Joan, interrogated by well-intentioned judges, probably answered freely and forthrightly. Friar Seguin, when he recalled these moments, was an old man of around seventy years, yet he remembered certain of her answers vividly and transmitted clearly the impression Joan made upon him. He named master Regnault of Chartres, archbishop of Reims and chancellor of France (II, 13), as the cleric who presided over the king's council in this matter. He named another member of the University of Paris, also in exile in Poitiers, Master Jean Lombard, who had asked Joan why she had come. "She responded in great style," said Seguin. Joan's language always provoked admiration: "This girl spoke terribly well," Albert d'Ourches from the region of Vaucouleurs had said of her, adding "I would really like to have had so fine a daughter."

At Poitiers, we find for the first time the statement of what one might call Joan's "vocation," the calling that she always maintained she had answered. As Seguin reports:

> When she was watching over the animals, a voice revealed itself to her, which said that God had great pity on the people of France, and that she, Joan, had to go into France [from her home on the frontier]. Upon hearing that message, she began to weep, and then the voice bade her go to Vaucouleurs, where she should find a captain who would bring her safely into France unto the king and that she should have no uncertainty. And so she did, going to the king's court without delay.

What followed, according to Friar Seguin's report, has the tone of a formal interrogation. Witness her answer to Master Guillaume Aymeri: "You have said that your voice told you: 'God wishes to liberate the people of France from the calamities in which it now finds itself.' If He wishes to free it, there is no need to have soldiers, and then Joan answered: 'In God's name, the soldiers will give battle and God will give the victory.'"

"Master Guillaume was quite content with this response," Friar Seguin comments. Expertly trained theologians could hardly have given a better account of the delicate distinction between the action of grace and its temporal means. Friar Seguin was not afraid to report that he was in a small way a victim of Joan's humor, which was always sharp:

> I asked her what language her voice spoke. She answered, "Better than yours." Me, I spoke the dialect of Limoges; and then I asked her if she believed in God; she answered, "Yes, better than you." And I then said to her that God wouldn't want us to believe in her unless something made us think that we should do so. I could not advise the king simply on her assertion that he should entrust men-at-arms to her so that she might lead them into peril, unless she could at least tell him something further. And she answered, "In God's name, I did not come to Poitiers to produce signs." [This answer, like the one she gave above to Guillaume Aymeri, Seguin reports in French rather than Latin, having remembered Joan's own words.] "But lead me to Orléans, and I will show you the sign for which I was sent." Then she was given men-at-arms in such number as seemed good to her.

Then follows an exposition of Joan's mission, summarized in four points:

> And then she predicted to him and others who were present four things that would happen. They did indeed happen thereafter. First, she said that the English would be driven away and thus the siege they had laid to the city of Orléans would be lifted and that the city of Orléans would be free of the English but first she would send them an invitation to surrender. Next, she said that the king would then be consecrated at Reims. Third, she said that the city of Paris would return to the king's obedience, and [fourth] that the duke of Orléans would return from England. All these things have come to pass.

Joan had persuaded the first tribunal appointed to examine her: "We have reported all of this to the royal council, and we are of the opinion that given the pressing necessity and peril in which the city of Orléans stands, the king might accept her aid and send her to Orléans." The decisive step was taken. Until her arrival at Poitiers, Joan had been nothing more than a surprising peasant girl of obscure origin who had amazed the dauphin; by the end of her stay there, she had received permission to act.

An advocate of the Parlement, Jean Barbin, summarized in greater detail the impression Joan had produced on these clerics and prelates:

From the same doctors who had examined her and who had asked her all sorts of questions, I heard it reported that she had answered very prudently, as though she had been a good clerk [the term "clerk" then implied educated literacy], to the point that they marveled at her responses and believed that there was something of the divine therein, given the account of her life and her behavior; and finally, it was concluded by the clerks after their interrogations and their investigation that there was nothing evil in her, nothing contrary to the Catholic faith; and that given the great need in which both the king and the kingdom found themselves—since the king and his subjects were at that moment in despair and had no other hope of aid if it came not from God—the king should make use of her assistance.

This advocate then began to evoke certain older prophecies in connection with Joan associated with the famous visionary Marie, known as La Gasque d'Avignon:

> A certain Master Erault, professor in theology, mentioned that he had heard at another time from a certain Marie of Avignon, who had come to the king's court earlier, that the kingdom of France would have a great deal to suffer and that it would undergo numerous calamities. She said that she had had many visions concerning the desolation of the kingdom of France. Among these visions, she saw many suits of armor that had been presented to her, and Marie, frightened, feared being ordered to put on the suits of armor, but she was told that she should not fear because she should not bear these arms but that a maid would come after her who would carry the same arms and would free the kingdom of France from its enemies; and he believed firmly that this Joan was she of whom Marie of Avignon had spoken.

So much for popular rumor. The official decision, the conclusions of the doctors, reads as follows: "In her, Joan, we find no evil but only good, humility, virginity, devotion, honesty, and simplicity." Her hosts, Jean Rabateau and his wife, confirmed that every day after dinner and also during the night Joan prayed on her knees for a long time and that she often went into a little chapel in the house, praying there for a long time.

Finally, another kind of investigation was concluded. Jean Pasquerel, Joan's confessor, gives us an echo of it:

> I heard it said that Joan, when she came to the king's court, was examined by women to know what was in her, if she was a man or a woman, and if she was a virgin or corrupted. She was found to be a woman, and a virgin, and a maid. Those who visited her for this purpose were, from what I heard, the lady of

Gaucourt [Jeanne de Preuilly] and the lady of Trèves [Jeanne de Mortemer, wife of Robert Le Maçon].

Both of these ladies belonged to the household of the queen of Anjou and of Sicily, Yolanda of Aragon, the mother of the king's wife, Marie of Anjou.

This test of virginity has often been misunderstood. Our era, more interested in the history of witchcraft than was Joan of Arc's age, has seen in it a test designed to verify that she was not a sorceress, since sorceresses were always suspected of having had intercourse with the devil. The reality is simpler: Joan, who called herself "Joan the Maid" (III, 1)—the only name by which she was designated during her life—would have been discredited immediately if the examination had shown or claimed that she was not a virgin. A liar, she would have been sent home; her mission with its claims of authority and integrity would have ended. The test of virginity was above all a proof of sincerity. In Joan's time, those men and women who consecrated themselves completely to God showed their acceptance of the divine call by remaining virgin and hence autonomous, totally at the Lord's service in heart and body, without division of responsibility. Joan would have been convinced of this premise. She declared that she had dedicated herself to God from the moment that she had understood it was an angel's voice addressing her. There was never any question of devil worship or sorcery, nor did suspicion that she might have been involved in witchcraft gain currency until the twentieth century.

After she left Poitiers, Joan the Maid appeared to be exactly that, a maid, in the eyes of the French public. The initial astonishment that greeted her changed into devotion. It was expected that she would be put to the test—the test that she herself demanded, the liberation of Orléans by military action—but already she was surrounded by a kind of respectful aura. She had come to personify hope, the type of hope that (according to the witnesses of her time) the distressed kingdom no longer maintained—that is, the hope of divine assistance.

Some years earlier the poet Alain Chartier, who remained faithful to the dauphin as his legitimate king, had composed a work mixing prose and verse, entitled *Hope*. For someone with his loyalties to speak of hope in the year 1420, the year in which the Treaty of Troyes deprived the dauphin of his rights to the crown in favor of the English king, was most provocative. "This Lady Hope," he had written, "had a smiling and joyous face; she held her head high, her speech was indeed pleasant." For many of the dauphin's supporters, Joan now seemed to embody Chartier's optimistic prediction.

CHAPTER THREE

JOAN AND THE VICTORY AT ORLÉANS

The first test of Joan's mission was raising the siege of Orléans, which she accomplished in nine days and ten nights. On the way to her rendezvous at the besieged city with the Bastard of Orléans (see Part II, Section 16) and Duke John of Alençon (II, 4), a close relative of the dauphin and one of her staunchest partisans thereafter, Joan was equipped on the dauphin's orders with a full-fledged military household, heralds, banners, and a full suit of armor. On May 9, 1429, Joan left a delirious Orléans for the next stage of her mission, her next test.

Jesus-Maria,

King of England, and you, duke of Bedford [II, 9], who call yourself regent of the kingdom of France, you, William de la Poule [William de la Pole, earl of Suffolk; II, 41], Sir John Talbot [II, 40], and you, Sir Thomas of Scales [II, 39], who call yourself lieutenant of the aforesaid duke of Bedford, render your account to the King of Heaven. Surrender to the Maid, who is sent here from God, the King of Heaven, the keys to all of the good cities that you have taken and violated in France. She has come here from God to proclaim the blood royal. She is entirely ready to make peace, if you are willing to settle accounts with her, provided that you give up France and pay for having occupied her. And those among you, archers, companions-at-arms, gentlemen, and others who are before the city of Orléans, go back to your own countries, for God's sake. And if you do not do so, wait for the word of the Maid who will come visit you briefly, to your great damage. If you do not do so, I am commander of the armies, and in whatever place I shall meet your French allies, I shall make them leave it, whether they wish to or not; and if they will not obey, I shall have them all killed. I am sent from God, the King of Heaven, to chase you out of all of France, body for body [every last one of you]. And if they wish to obey, I shall have mercy on them. And have no other opinion, for you shall never hold the kingdom of France from God, the King of Heaven, the son of St. Mary; but King Charles [II, 1], the true heir, will hold it; for God, the King of Heaven, wishes it so and has revealed this through the Maid, and he will enter Paris with a goodly company. If you do not wish to believe this message from God through the Maid, then wherever we find you we will strike you there, and make a great uproar greater than any made in France for a thousand years, if you do not come to terms. And believe firmly that the King of Heaven will send the Maid more force than you will ever know how to achieve with all of your assaults on her and on her good men-at-arms; and in the exchange of blows we shall see who has better right from the King of Heaven. You, duke of Bedford, the Maid prays you and requests that you cause no more destruction. If you will settle your account, you can come to join her company, in which the French will achieve the finest feat ever accomplished in Christendom. And give answer, if you wish to make peace in the city of Orléans; and if indeed you do not do so, be mindful soon of your great damages.

—Written on Tuesday of Holy Week

THIS LETTER, in which Joan reveals the dynamic of her vocation, is dated exactly not only by the final reference to Tuesday (March 22) of Holy Week, 1429, but also by a witness who saw her in Poitiers and who reported the circumstances in which Joan dictated that letter. This royal esquire, Gobert Thibault, accompanied Pierre of Versailles and Jean Erault when they arrived at the house of Master Jean Rabateau to find Joan:

> When we arrived there, Joan came before us, and she clapped me on the shoulder, saying that she would very much like to have more men like me with her. And then Pierre of Versailles said to Jean that they had been sent to her by the king; she answered, "I believe that you have been sent to ask me more questions," and said, "Me, I don't know either A or B." And then he asked her why she had come; and she answered, "I come from the King of Heaven to raise the siege of Orléans and to lead the king to Reims for his coronation and his anointing." And she asked us if we had paper and ink, saying to Master Jean Erault, "Write what I shall say: You, Suffort, Classidas, and La Poule [Suffolk, Glasdale, William Pole], I summon you, by the King of Heaven, go away to England." And at that time, Versailles and Erault did nothing else that I can remember, and Joan stayed at Poitiers as long as the king made her do so.

Gobert Thibault was, like everyone else, curious to know who Joan was and what she wanted; he asked Jean de Metz (II, 30) and Bertrand de Poulengy (II, 33) and conveys to us the admiration of all of these men by describing how they had crossed the country west of Vaucouleurs "without any obstacles" even though it was under Burgundian control—a practical test that Joan had passed without flinching. This Gobert Thibault, whom one imagines to have been a solid man, was one of those people with a simple view of things who admired the purity of Joan's bearing. He analyzed the attitude of the soldiery toward Joan, at a time when all other women in the army were camp followers:

> In the army, she was always with the soldiers; I heard many of those closest to her say that they had never had any desire for her; that is to say, they sometimes felt a certain carnal urge but never dared to let themselves go with her, and they believed that it was not possible to desire her; often when they were speaking among themselves of the sin of the flesh and were saying things that might arouse desire, if they saw her or came near her, they were not able to continue such speech and suddenly their carnal impulses ceased. I have questioned several of those who sometimes slept the night in Joan's company about this, and they answered as I have, adding that they had never felt any carnal desire when they saw her.

Like the members of Joan's escort from Vaucouleurs to Chinon, all were struck by her purity. For them, as for the general public, the clergy, and the prelates who had examined her, Joan seemed to embody the virginal "Lady Hope."

Some historians have thought that the "Letter to the English" coincided with the end of the three-week "Trial of Poitiers." But in Gobert Thibault's account, Joan speaks like someone assured of success yet answers the Poitiers interrogators as if she is speaking to strangers. She came to know them well enough after three weeks of interrogation. Their visit was probably part of an interrogatory process that stretched out in several phases. Sometimes they surprised her where she was living; at other times, they report, she was summoned to the house of a certain La Macée, where larger numbers of her questioners probably gathered. It is likely that Joan spent Holy Week and Easter Day at Poitiers.

That very week was marked by an unusual event. In 1429 Good Friday fell on the same day as the feast of the Annunciation, March 25. The coincidence of two major feast days was the traditional occasion for a pilgrimage to Notre Dame at Le-Puy-en-Velay, a long-revered sanctuary. (In the nineteenth century, the eminent editor-historian, Jules Quicherat, refused to believe the records since he was certain that some copyist's error must explain the citation in the manuscript of the city of Le Puy as *villa Aniciensi*; he decided that it must be a misspelling of the Latin name for the city of Nancy in Lorraine.) Several of Joan's companions went there: perhaps the royal messenger, Colet de Vienne, or Jean de Metz, or perhaps his valet, Jean de

Honnecourt. We do not know exactly which of the six men who came with her from Vaucouleurs to Chinon went on that pilgrimage, but what does seem certain is that at least two of them did. Perhaps it was Bertrand and his servant, Julien, since it would have been quite natural for the royal messenger who knew the routes so well and also happened to know the lector of the Augustinian convent at Tours, Jean Pasquerel, to join the group of pilgrims from Lorraine. Joan's mother, Isabelle, was also among them; her surname, Romée—awarded to those who had successfully completed a pilgrimage—shows that she had experience of such sacred journeys.

The road from the banks of the Meuse all the way to Le-Puy-en-Velay was long and arduous. The journey from Lorraine to Le Puy must not have been much longer or much more difficult, however, than that of the pilgrims from Poitiers, who had to take a winding route through the mountains of Auvergne, following the valley of the Allier. Medieval people readily and steadily undertook such journeys. Even though the sheer number of pilgrims had declined considerably by the fourteenth century because of recurrent warfare, it continued to be significant. In any case, some of these pilgrims of 1429, including Isabelle, were in contact with the Franciscan friar Jean Pasquerel. They knew that he was attached to the convent of Tours, where the king often stayed; they recommended him to Joan, and he became her confessor. Joan's mother, who must have been intensely pious, had transmitted "her belief" to her daughter; in a sense, she also chose the man who would watch over her daughter's spiritual life during her incredible adventure.

Joan now entered the active phase of her public drama. After returning to Chinon from Poitiers, she was then brought to Tours, where the king commissioned for her "a harness that fitted her body"—that is, a suit of armor to her measure. (See III, 5.) Plate armor, which in Joan's time had been in use for less than a hundred years, had to be fitted exactly to protect its wearer without restricting movement.

At Tours, Joan was lodged in the house of Jean Dupuy; in that city, tourists are still shown the shop of the master armorer who cut and assembled her "harness." For the date of May 10, 1429, the account book of the royal treasurer Hémon Raguier lists the sum paid for that work: a hundred livres tournois. Joan herself ordered a standard and another banner for which the account books record the payment of twenty-four livres tournois to the painter Hauves Poulnoir. This standard was to play an active role in the Battle of Orléans; Joan "took the standard in her hand when she went to the assault, so as to avoid having to kill anyone." Jean Pasquerel is our witness that in designing the standard, Joan followed an order that she said she had received from her "voices," from her "counsel":

> She had asked the messengers of her lord, that is, God, who appeared to her,
> what she should do, and they had told Joan to take up the standard of her Lord;
> and for that reason, she had made for herself a standard on which was painted

the image of Our Savior, sitting in judgment in the clouds of heaven, and there was also painted an angel, holding in his hands a fleur-de-lys blessed by the image of the Lord.

Joan ordered yet another banner, to be carried by the priests who accompanied the army. This banner, bearing the image of the crucified Lord, served as the rallying point for the prayers to which Joan would summon the fighting men. Pasquerel remembered that priestly squad with approval:

> Twice a day, at evening and morning, Joan made me assemble all the priests. Once gathered, they sang antiphons and hymns to St. Mary. Joan was with them, and she did not wish any soldiers to join the priests if they had not gone to confession, and she exhorted all the soldiers to confess themselves in order to come to this gathering, and at the gathering all the priests were ready to hear all those who wished to confess themselves.

When the time came to complete her military equipment with a sword (III, 6), that instrument indispensable to any combatant, Joan expressed a startling wish: She asked that someone go fetch her sword at Sainte-Catherine-de-Fierbois, where she had stopped on the road to Chinon. When she was asked later, in her trial at Rouen on February 27, 1431, how she knew that this sword, "rusted, with five crosses engraved on it," was there, she answered:

> She knew from her voices that this sword was there, and she had never seen the man who went to find the aforesaid sword for her, and she wrote to the men of the church of that place that she hoped it would please them that she should have that sword, and they sent it to her. It was not very deeply buried underground, behind the altar; she did not know if it would be exactly before the altar or behind it. She said again that just after the sword was found the men of that church gave it a good rubbing, and thereupon the rust fell off without effort; it was an armorer of Tours who went to find it.

Joan already had a sword that Robert de Baudricourt (II, 7) had given her when she departed for Chinon. Later, she would have a third sword, a prize of war taken from a Burgundian. Joan would express a connoisseur's appreciation for this last weapon, declaring that "it was a good war sword, made for giving and taking good blows." For her second sword, that of Sainte-Catherine-de-Fierbois, the clergy of Tours offered her two sheaths, one of vermeil velvet and the other of cloth-of-gold; she herself ordered a sheath for it made of "good strong leather."

At Tours she was allocated the military entourage necessary for any commander. Her steward, Jean d'Aulon, is our chief source: "I was assigned that post, to guard and lead her, by our lord the king," he wrote. She had two pages, Louis de Coutes (mentioned above) and another named Raymond. She was assigned two heralds, Ambleville and Guyenne. Heralds, messengers wearing a livery by which they could be identified, exercised an official function. They bore messages and delivered challenges for designated persons of importance—kings, princes, or major commanders—and enjoyed immunity from attack. The king was beginning to treat Joan like a warrior of high rank with serious personal responsibilities. It has sometimes been asserted that she was used simply as a fetish to give courage to the soldiers whom she accompanied, but the official assignment of two heralds by the king himself challenges that interpretation. She also had the use of several horses and later would declare that she had had five coursers, "not counting the trotters, who were more than seven." Coursers were war-horses, also called destriers (horses that were controlled with the right hand); trotters served for the everyday coming and going of her entourage. This entourage would soon include her two brothers, Pierre and Jean, who seem to have joined her at Tours.

All the eyewitnesses report that Joan took great care in the spiritual preparation of the army. She exhorted her men to confess themselves; she drove away the ribaudes (the prostitutes who followed the soldiers). She forbade pillage, oaths, and blasphemy. The duke of Alençon related that "Joan became very angry when she heard the soldiers swear and she vehemently chided them, and myself as well, who would swear an oath from time to time. When I saw her, I restrained my swearing." The royal troops must have assembled at Blois, a fortress on the Loire more or less halfway between Tours and Orléans. Tours, like Blois, was in a region still controlled by the French, whereas upriver the right bank of the Loire was blocked by the English. Jean Chartier, the official chronicler of the reign of Charles VII, explains: "In the city of Blois, many supply wagons and carts were filled with grain and many oxen, sheep, cows, pigs, and other edible animals. And Joan the Maid took to the road along with the captains straight toward Orléans from the side of the Sologne" (that is, along the south bank of the Loire).

It was at Blois that Joan's banner was actually finished. Jean Chartier describes the livestock loaded onto the wagons to supply the needs of both the people of Orléans and the troops coming to free them. Joan's confessor, Pasquerel, was aware of the religious character of the army that was then put in motion:

> When Joan left Blois to go to Orléans, she had all the priests gather around the standard, and the priests went before the army. They marched out on the side of the Sologne assembled in that fashion; they sang *Veni creator spiritus* along with many antiphons, and they camped in the fields that night and the following day as well. On the third day, they arrived near Orléans, where the English had set up their siege along the bank of the Loire. And the king's soldiers came so close

to the English that Englishmen and Frenchmen could see one another within easy reach, and the soldiers of the king brought the food supplies there.

The duke of Alençon took an active part in these preparations. At the dauphin's request, he had visited the dauphin's mother-in-law, Yolanda, the queen of Sicily, who seems to have financed this new campaign against Orléans. The Bastard of Orléans gives us a detailed description:

> The king sent Joan in the company of the lord archbishop of Reims [Regnault of Chartres, at that time chancellor of France; II, 13] and the lord of Gaucourt, grand master of the king's household [II, 18], to the city of Blois, where those who had been leading the convoy of victuals had come—to wit, the lord Gilles de Rais [II, 34] and the lord of Boussac, marshal of France, with whom were the lord of Culant [Louis de Graville, admiral of France], La Hire [Étienne de Vignolles, soldier of fortune; II, 22], and Ambroise de Loré, later provost of Paris—who all together with the soldiers escorted the convoy of victuals; and Joan the Maid came in an army well arrayed up to the banks of the Loire on the Sologne side.

This long detour, made to avoid the English positions close to Orléans, was chosen without Joan's knowledge. Impatient to engage the enemy, apparently she was surprised to learn, as they approached the Loire, that they had in fact bypassed Orléans; hence there would be a stormy exchange between her and the Bastard, of which he preserved a vivid recollection. This girl, on whose account he had sent his companions to gather information a mere two months earlier, was now approaching, so he went swiftly to meet her and the vanguard of the army on the heights of Chécy to which she was leading her troops. A cunning strategist, the Bastard had already sent a few of his troops to cause a diversion around one of the *bastides* that encircled the city. The *Journal of the Siege of Orléans,* a priceless source of information on the rich events of these days, comments on that ruse: "The French made a sortie in great numbers and skirmished with the English before Saint-Loup-d'Orléans and pressed the English so hard that many were killed, wounded, and taken prisoner one place or the other, so much so that the French brought back to their city one of the English standards. As soon as this skirmish was over, the victuals and the artillery that the Maid had brought all the way up to Chécy entered the city."

On the bluffs overlooking that village dominated by a handsome Gothic church one can stand and paint anew the scene of Joan's arrival at Orléans. She lost no time. As the Bastard vividly remembered, she asked:

> "Are you the Bastard of Orléans?"
> "Yes, I am, and I rejoice in your coming."

"Are you the one who gave orders for me to come here, on this side of the river, so that I could not go directly to Talbot and the English?"

I answered that I and others, including the wisest men around me, had given this advice, believing it best and safest; then Joan said to me: "In God's name, the counsel of Our Lord God is wiser and safer than yours. You thought that you could fool me, and instead you fool yourself; I bring you better help than ever came to you from any soldier to any city: It is the help of the King of Heaven. This help comes not for love of me but from God Himself, who at the prayer of St. Louis and of St. Charlemagne has had pity on the city of Orléans. He has not wanted the enemy to have both the body of the lord of Orléans and his city."

Whatever annoyance the Bastard may have felt would soon be dispelled by what was about to happen. He was worried about the convoy of supplies, which was downriver at Blois, for it would have to sail up the Loire against the current. Worse, the wind had been blowing steadily from the east. Dunois (II, 16) reports: "All of a sudden, and as though at that very moment, the wind—which had been contrary and which had absolutely prevented the ships in which were the food supplies for the city of Orléans from coming upriver—changed and became favorable. From that moment I had good hope in her, more than ever before."

Dunois had the sails on his ships raised swiftly and begged Joan to cross the river from the French-controlled south bank and come with him into the city of Orléans, "where they deeply desired her." Joan hesitated; the soldiers surrounding her were ready for battle. She knew them well, they had confessed themselves, they had prayed with her; she hesitated to separate herself from them. Meanwhile, Dunois went to find her chief captains: "I begged and demanded that on behalf of the king they would agree that Joan herself enter the city of Orléans, while the captains themselves with their companies went to Blois, where they could cross the Loire so as to come to Orléans because no closer ford could be found. The captains granted this request and agreed to cross the river at Blois."

Joan's epic at Orléans began that Friday evening, April 29, 1429. As Dunois recalled the tale decades later: "Joan came with me, carrying her banner, which was white and on which was the image of Our Lord, holding the fleur-de-lys in his hand. [Contemporary descriptions of this banner disagree on details.] With me and La Hire, she crossed the river Loire, and together we entered into the city of Orléans."

The *Journal of the Siege* gives a more enthusiastic description of this entrance:

And so she entered Orléans, with the Bastard of Orléans at her left, very richly armed and mounted; afterward came other noble and valiant lords, squires, captains, and men-at-arms, as well as some from the garrison and bourgeoisie of Orléans who had gone ahead of her. From the city, other men-at-arms came to receive her, along with bourgeois of Orléans, carrying many torches and making such joy as if they had seen God Himself descend among them; and not without reason, for they had endured much difficulty, labor, pain, and fear of not being rescued and of losing all their bodies and goods. But they felt already comforted, as though freed of the siege by the divine virtue that they were told resided in that simple Maid, whom they regarded with strong affection, men as much as women and little children. And there was a marvelous crowd pressing to touch her or the horse on which she rode.

This encounter with the crowd signals Joan's vocation just as it evokes the hope placed in her by the inhabitants of the long-besieged city, which had been caught as in a vise for seven months. Here was someone who promised help from heaven. With Joan among them, they felt already freed from the siege. Joan must have been sure she could achieve this feat. She remained calm and, according to all appearances, entirely self-possessed.

> One of those bearing torches came so close that her standard caught fire, so she spurred her horse, turning him gently toward the pennant. She put out the fire as easily as if she had long war expertise; the men-at-arms considered this a great marvel, as did the citizens of Orléans, who accompanied her throughout the city, making great joy, and with a great deal of honor they conducted her up to the Renard Gate, to the residence of Jacques Boucher, then treasurer of the captive duke. There she was joyously received with her two brothers and two other gentlemen and their valets, who had come with her from the Barrois.

In Orléans today, Joan's path can be followed from the Burgundy Gate at the east of the city all the way to the other end of what was the old city, toward the Maison de Jeanne d'Arc on the square now known as Place Charles de Gaulle. The house was reconstructed after World War II, during which this quarter was leveled, with only the choir of the church of Notre-Dame-de-Recouvrance left intact, close to the Renard Gate and the residence of Jacques Boucher (II, 10).

Joan spent her first night in Orléans at Boucher's home. The city was filled with rumors and unfamiliar comings and goings. There followed a period of nine days during which events transpired with improbable speed, although the days seemed quite long to Joan.

She had arrived quivering with all the ardor of her youthful sixteen or seventeen years. Her life up to this point had been a series of tiresome preliminaries: interminable interrogations, the fitting of armor, and assembling her army. Now she had to wait again. On Saturday, April 30, she presented herself to the Bastard of Orléans. As Louis de Coutes reports it, "Upon her return, she was very angry because they had decided not to try an assault that day." The Bastard, who vividly recalled the defeat of the "Herrings," was unwilling to engage the enemy until the reinforcements marshaled by the king reached Orléans. Joan went out to survey the English positions, which at several places were within easy hearing distance of the city's defenders. At one such point, perhaps at the ramparts near her lodgings overlooking the Renard Gate, Joan indulged in a flare-up. Her page reports:

> She spoke with the English on the opposite embankment, telling them to go away in God's name, otherwise she would drive them out. One of them, named the Bastard of Granville [from the French point of view, a "renegade" Norman], traded insults with Joan, asking her if they really wanted them to surrender to a woman; he called the Frenchmen who were with Joan "worthless mackerels" [a sexual insult].

That evening Joan confronted more of the English on the bridge of Orléans where it joined the fortifications on the island of Belle-Croix. Beyond that point, two arches had been demolished. The rampart of the Tourelles, which prevented entrance into the city by way of the bridge, was solidly entrenched:

> From there, she spoke to Classidas [Glasdale] and to the other English in the Tourelles and told them that they should surrender for God's sake and that their lives would then be saved. But Glasdale and those of his company answered in a very ugly way, insulting her and calling her "cowherd," loudly shouting that they would burn her if they ever got hold of her.

A promise which would be kept.

The next day, May 1, was a Sunday. Joan observed the Sunday truce, but did not stay home. The *Journal of the Siege* records:

> The people of Orléans had such great desire to see Joan the Maid that they almost broke down the gate of her lodging in order to see her; therefore that day she rode on horseback throughout the city, accompanied by many knights and squires; there were so many city people in the streets through which she was riding that she was scarcely able to pass, for the people could not have their fill of seeing her. It seemed a great marvel to all that she could keep her seat on horseback as elegantly as she did. And in truth, she comported herself as well in every regard as if she had known how to be a man-at-arms following the wars since her youth.

Meanwhile, the Bastard of Orléans had gone to meet the reinforcements, and since he was commander of the defense, Joan did him the courtesy of undertaking no military action until his return. Two more days passed, Monday and Tuesday, May 2 and 3; on Tuesday, according to the city account books, there was a great procession in the city, "with Joan the Maid and other military commanders present." Finally, on Wednesday, May 4, the arrival of John the Bastard was announced. Joan hastened to meet him, accompanied by Jean d'Aulon, her steward, who reported that, after they dined, the Bastard told her that a new English army, commanded by the famous captain John Fastolf, had been sent toward Orléans and was already as close as Janville. Her steward then added her reaction:

> At these words, the Maid seemed to me full of joy, and she said to my lord of
> Dunois these words or others like them: "Bastard, O Bastard, in God's name, I
> order you, as soon as you know of Fastolf's coming, to let me know it, for if he
> should pass by without my knowing it, I promise you that I will have your head
> cut off!" The lord of Dunois answered that she should have no doubts on that
> score, for he would indeed let her know.

Provoked by the delays, Joan was fearful of being kept in the dark. Yet the moment to act was closer than she foresaw. A short skirmish occurred, after which the combatants returned to their quarters to rest. But not for long. Jean d'Aulon continues:

> Suddenly, the Maid got up from her bed, and noisily woke me up. When I asked
> her what she wanted she answered me, "In God's name, my advice has told me
> that I must go against the English, and I don't know if I should attack their
> fortifications or Fastolf, who is coming to resupply them."

After awaking her steward and her hostess, she proceeded to heap abuse on her page Louis de Coutes: "Ah, awful boy! You did not tell me that the blood of France had already been spilled!" Jacques Boucher's wife and daughter rushed to help arm Joan, while Louis de Coutes went to saddle her horse. He brought it to the gate of the Boucher home; Joan ordered him to bring her standard, which he then passed to her through the window; she wasted no time, "running in the direction of the Burgundy Gate." Around the outer entry to that gate the day's events would unfold. Louis de Coutes summarizes the opening action:

> There was then an attack—a skirmish—on the side of the Saint-Loup Gate, and
> in that attack the opposing embankment was taken, and on the way there Joan
> encountered many wounded Frenchmen, which saddened her. The English were

readying themselves for an active defense when Joan suddenly arrived before them, and as soon as the French saw Joan they began to raise a shout and took the *bastide* and fortress.

This was her first act of war—not terribly significant territorially, but nonetheless a major vitalizing victory. Joan knew how important it was to reverse the discouragement that had overcome the French soldiery. Her promise of renewal was found in her capture of the *bastide* of Saint-Loup, on the old Roman road to which the Burgundy Gate gave access next to the church of Saint-Loup, right on the Loire River to the east of the city. This event also marked Joan's first encounter with the cruelty of war. Her confessor, Jean Pasquerel, witnessed her experience, as did her page, who reported: "Joan grieved mightily . . . she wept for the men who died without confession. She went to confession herself, then exhorted 'all the soldiers to confess their sins publicly and to give thanks to God for the victory that He had granted.'"

The next day was Ascension Thursday. Joan declared that "she would not make war and would not even put on her armor out of respect for the feast day, and on that day she wished to confess herself and receive the sacrament of the Eucharist, which she did." But she took advantage of this enforced leisure to send the English her final summons. She sent three successive letters of demand, as was the custom, although we possess texts only of the first and third letters. The second letter may simply have repeated the text of the first one sent from Poitiers. The third letter of Ascension Thursday is more compact:

You, O English, who have no right to this kingdom of France, the King of Heaven orders and commands you through me, Joan the Maid, to leave your fortresses and return to your country, and if you do not so I shall make a *hahay* [uproar] that will be perpetually remembered. Behold what I write you for the third and final time; I shall write you no further.

Signed,
Jesus-Maria,
Joan the Maid.

Then follows a postscript that is not without wit:

I have sent you my letters honestly, but you have detained my messengers, for you have kept my herald named Guyenne with you. Please send him back to me and I will send you some of your men who were taken in the fortress of Saint-Loup, for they are not all dead.

Perhaps Joan's heralds Guyenne and Ambleville had been sent to bring the second summons. In defiance of the laws of war that protected heralds, one of them had been kept prisoner. So Joan used an untraditional method to send her third letter. As Pasquerel tells it:

> She took an arrow and tied the letter with a thread to the end of the arrow, and ordered an archer to shoot that arrow to the English lines, crying, "Read it, here is news!" The English received the arrow with the letter and read it, and having read it they began to raise a great shout: "Here's news from the whore of the Armagnacs!" At these words, Joan began to sigh and to weep abundant tears, calling the King of Heaven to her aid. Later she was comforted, she said, because she had received news from her Lord. That evening after dinner, she commanded me to get up earlier the next morning than I had on the day of the Ascension, because she wished to confess to me early in the morning, which she did.

The Friday after the Ascension was a day of surprises. Joan went to confession, heard mass, then, as she was getting ready for combat, she bumped into the governor of Orléans, Raoul de Gaucourt, who was keeping his eye on the gate and forbade her to make a sortie. Why? The captains had decided not to make an assault that day, but Joan "was of the opinion that the soldiers should make a sortie with the men of the city and attack the *bastide* of the Augustinians. Many of the men-at-arms and the people of the city were of the same opinion." Joan told the lord of Gaucourt: "whether you wish it or not, the men-at-arms will come and gain what they gained the other day." Joan's steward reports the events in detail; the victory was clearly the result of her initiative.

Joan made a sortie with her men "in good array" and crossed the Loire, always on the side of the Burgundy Gate, where, since the *bastide* of Saint-Loup had been taken, there was no reason to fear counterattack. She led her troops to the left bank, toward the quarter that is still called Saint-Jean-le-Blanc. There the English had erected another *bastide*, anchored on another small island in the Loire, the Ile-aux-Toiles. The French troops made a bridge of boats, crossed it, and found the *bastide* deserted: Its defenders had retired upriver, toward the much stronger *bastide* they had set up in the ruins of the old convent of the Augustinians at the south end of the fortified bridge called the Tourelles. This simple operation, an English withdrawal to regroup, put the French in a dangerous position. The retreat was under way, as Jean d'Aulon reports:

> As soon as the French began to return to the *bastide* of Saint-Jean-le-Blanc to enter the Ile [aux-Toiles], the Maid and La Hire went to the other side of that island, with a horse and a boat each, and mounted their horses as soon as they had landed, each with a lance in hand. And when they perceived that the enemy was coming out of

the *bastide* of the Augustinians to rush upon them, the Maid and La Hire, who were always in front of their men to protect them, immediately couched their lances and led the attack upon the enemy. Everyone followed them, and they began to strike the enemy in such a manner that they constrained them by sheer force to withdraw and to return to the *bastide* of the Augustinians. . . . Very bitterly and with great diligence, they assailed that *bastide* from all directions so that they seized it and took it by assault quickly. The greater part of the enemy were killed or captured, and those who could save themselves withdrew to the *bastide* of the Tourelles at the bridge's foot. The Maid and her company won a great victory over the enemy that day. The great *bastide* was taken, and the lords and their men remained before it all that night, along with the Maid.

Joan's determination had won an unexpected victory: In covering the French retreat, she provoked an assault and achieved the capture of an important fortification. Once again, however, the dauphin's longtime commanders and advisors—the party of inertia—reverted to their usual behavior. Pasquerel reports this development with a surprising, perhaps intentional, trace of amnesia that manages to avoid placing blame on Raoul de Gaucourt or perhaps the Bastard himself:

After dinner, a valiant and outstanding knight whose name I forget came to Joan. He told Joan that the captains and soldiers of the king had held council together and they observed that they were too few in comparison to the English and that God had granted a great favor already, adding: "Considering that the city is well fortified with food, we can guard it well while waiting for help from the king. It does not seem appropriate to the council that the soldiers make another sortie tomorrow."

Was Joan furious? Was she simply contemptuous of this council? The records allow us to say only that she saw her early success as simply a step on the road to ultimate victory and that she cared little for the counsel of the captains. Without delay, she gave her chaplain Pasquerel new instructions:

Get up tomorrow very early in the morning, earlier than you did today, and do the best you can; keep close to me, for tomorrow I will have much to do, more than I have ever done before; and tomorrow blood will leave my body above my breast.

Although he did not fight, Jean Pasquerel was also busy that following day, Saturday, May 7. Victory seemed close; during all that night, citizens of Orléans had crossed the Loire in boats to bring "bread, wine, and other victuals" to the men-at-arms holding the *bastide* of the Augustinians. The following morning at dawn, Pasquerel celebrated mass. An assault was made on the fortress of the Tourelles, which had been blocking the bridge since the previous October: It "lasted from morning until sunset." Convinced that the day would prove decisive, Pasquerel declared, "That very day, I heard men say to the Maid: 'In God's name, tonight we will enter the city by the bridge,'" which meant that communication between the two banks of the Loire, interrupted for seven months, would finally be reestablished.

Joan moved energetically and swiftly, showing just how much she could do, but near or shortly after midday she was wounded, apparently by an arrow above her breast, as she had foreseen. Weeping with frustration, she withdrew from the fight, and the arrow, which could not have penetrated very deeply, was removed. Someone suggested she "apply a charm to it," which she strenuously refused to do: "I would prefer to die rather than to do something I know to be a sin, or against the will of God." Instead, she received the usual treatment of an application of olive oil and bacon fat to protect the wound. She quickly returned to the assault.

The English defense of the fortress of the Tourelles was fierce and well organized, so the French decided to isolate the *bastide* by collapsing one of the arches of the bridge on which it relied for support. The city's account book hints that this decision was undertaken at Joan's suggestion: It gives the precise amount paid "to a certain Jean Poitevin, a fisherman by trade, who grounded a barge that was sent under the bridge of the Tourelles to burn them so that they might be taken." This barge, which must have been filled with fagots and tar, was set afire beneath the arch.

Toward evening the combatants grew discouraged once more. The Bastard of Orléans told Joan that he was going to give the order for the army to withdraw into the city. Joan had an alternative, sensible reaction—she understood better than experienced strategists what these men, who had been fighting since morning, needed: "Rest yourself a little bit, eat and drink," she advised—an instance of medieval women's mastery of the domain of food, its preparation and serving. She urged the Bastard to delay the withdrawal a little longer. She was seen mounting her horse and retiring alone "to a vineyard a little bit away from the mass of the men, and in that vineyard she remained in prayer for the space of a quarter of an hour," Dunois remembered.

Then came the decisive episode. Joan had handed her standard over to a squire named Le Basque. Jean d'Aulon ordered him to follow himself and Joan to the foot of the ditch. Joan caught sight of her standard, saw that the squire who carried it had entered the ditch, and grabbed it. Pulling with all of her strength, she "waved the standard in such a manner," said Jean d'Aulon, "that when she did so the others thought that she was giving them some signal. In short, all those in the army of the Maid rushed together and rallied themselves anew and with great ferocity assailed the breastwork, and shortly after this breastwork and the *bastide* were taken by them and abandoned by their enemies; and the French crossed the bridge and entered the city of Orléans.

To report simply that the Tourelles had been taken would have been monumental enough news for the day. But the fervor of Joan's soldiers had brought the greatest goal: total victory and liberation of the city of Orléans.

With planks they improvised a bridge over the arches that had been destroyed; over it passed some of the defenders who had stayed in Orléans. Communication was reestablished; the objective was won. The *Journal of the Siege* reports that everyone

> felt great joy and praised Our Lord for His gift of this great victory. And indeed they should have done so, for it was said that this assault, which lasted from sunrise to sunset, was so greatly fought on both sides that it was one of the fairest feats of arms that has ever been performed. . . . All the clergy and the people of Orléans devoutly sang *Te Deum laudamus* and rang all the city bells, very humbly thanking Our Lord for this glorious divine consolation. They expressed joy in every way, giving wondrous praise to their valiant defenders, and above all others to Joan the Maid. She spent that night, with the lords, captains, and men-at-arms with her, in the fields, both to guard the valiantly conquered Tourelles, and to learn if the English on the side of Saint-Laurent would sortie to aid or to avenge their companions. But they did not attempt it.

Joan was saddened because the English commander Glasdale, whom she called Classidas, "armed from head to toe, fell into the Loire and was drowned. Joan, moved by pity, wept for the soul of this Classidas and of the many others who drowned there, and that day all the English who were on the other side of the bridge were taken or killed."

Later Joan was brought back to her lodgings to rest her wound. She ate roast beef soaked in wine to restore her strength. The next day was Sunday, May 8, a day that ranks high in the annals of Orléans and later in those of all France. The *Journal of the Siege of Orléans* continues:

> The morning of the following day, a Sunday and the eighth day of May of this same year 1429, the English abandoned their *bastides* and raising the siege organized themselves in battle formation. . . . Therefore, the Maid and a great force of valiant men-of-war and citizens made a sortie from Orléans and arrayed themselves for battle before the English, and in that condition the French and the English were very close one to the other for the space of an entire hour without touching.

That hour when the French and the English were face to face beneath the ramparts of Orléans is one of the great moments of the two national histories. This time it was the French who were impatient to give battle. Galvanized by the extraordinary victories of May 6 and 7, the French had difficulty controlling their high spirits. Joan, however, again intervened. According to the *Journal of the Siege*: "The French chafed under their obedience to the Maid on one point. She forbade them . . . because of the honor of the holy Sunday . . . to attack the English; if the English assaulted them, they could defend themselves as strongly and bravely as they wished and they should have no fear: They would be the masters of that field."

Joan was firmly committed to the old rules of chivalry, which restricted the time within which warfare was allowed, imposing truce on Sundays and feast days. She had difficulty achieving even this limited time-frame. At a time when the organization of armies and practices of warfare were swiftly changing, Joan's point of view about honor and chivalry, in which the sword of the strong was yoked to the service of the weak, was profoundly conservative.

The *Journal of the Siege* continues: "Once an hour had passed, the English betook themselves to the road and went away in good order toward Meung-sur-Loire. They raised and totally abandoned the siege that they had laid to Orléans from the twelfth day of October 1428 up to this day."

Orléans had been liberated. The city was shaken by the shivers of joy, of exultation, and of astonishment that mark every individual or collective liberation.

> The Maid and the other lords and men-at-arms reentered Orléans to the great rejoicing of the clergy and the people, who together rendered humble thanks to Our Lord along with well-deserved praise for the very great aid and victories that He had given and sent them against the English, ancient enemies of the kingdom. . . . That same day and the following one, the men of the church made a great and solemn procession along with the lords, captains, men-at-arms, and bourgeois who normally lived in Orléans, and they all visited the churches with great devotion.

The compiler of the *Journal* noted one reconciliation that took place that day. The bourgeois and other citizens of Orléans had always feared the men-at-arms. Everyone knew the misdeeds of which armed men were capable when confronted with an unarmed population; these troops, mostly mercenaries recruited by captains who did not always maintain discipline, were as menacing in times of peace as in wartime. Their use by the kings and great lords caused much of the horror of what would later be called the Hundred Years War, a conflict that had little in common with the chivalric warfare of the twelfth and thirteenth centuries. Now, in the general joy, the bourgeois of Orléans no longer feared those who in principle had been their defenders but whose presence in their city had seemed rather like that of a worm in the fruit. Under the command of the Maid, even warfare had briefly changed its face back to a world of honor.

Messengers swiftly took to the highway en route to the castle of Chinon, where only a few weeks earlier Joan had exhorted the dauphin. At Orléans proof could be seen of what she had affirmed: that she had been sent by God to reestablish the kingdom of France. The dauphin dictated a letter to all of his "good cities," a letter to which he had to add a new paragraph twice before he finished because fresh messengers kept arriving:

> *From the king.* Dear and well-beloved subjects, we believe that you have been aware of the continuous efforts we have made to give every possible relief to the city of Orléans, for a long time now besieged by the English, the ancient enemies of our kingdom . . . and since we know that you cannot have greater joy and consolation as loyal subjects than to hear us announce good news, we inform you that by the mercy of Our Lord, from whence all good things come, we have just newly resupplied the city of Orléans powerfully twice in one week, in full view and knowledge of the enemy, who were unable to resist our action.

The dauphin was referring to the two relief convoys that had been able to reach the city by the Loire, the first under Joan's command and the second under that of the Bastard of Orléans. Charles then went on to report how on the previous Wednesday, May 4, "one of the most powerful fortresses of the enemy, that of Saint-Loup," had been taken. But then a new messenger arrived:

> While this letter was being composed, there came to us here about one hour after midnight a herald, who declared upon his life that last Friday our men crossed the river into Orléans by boats and besieged from the left bank of the river the *bastide* at the end of the bridge. And that the same day, they gained the *bastide* of the Augustinians, and that also on that Saturday they attacked the rest of the aforesaid *bastide*, which commanded the bridge, where there were a good six hundred English fighting men under two banners and the standard of Chandos [perhaps a textual error for Classidas/Glasdale]. And that finally, thanks to their great prowess and valor in arms, with recognition of the grace of Our Lord, they captured all of the aforesaid *bastide,* and all of the English who were in it were either killed or taken prisoner. . . . [The dauphin continued, exhorting his correspondents to] honor the virtuous deeds and wondrous things that this herald who was present reported to us, and also the Maid, who was present in person at the achievement of all of these deeds.

But that was not all:

> And once again, before the completion of this letter, there have arrived before
> us two gentlemen in the greatest haste, who have certified and confirmed it all,
> in fuller detail than had the herald. . . . After our men had last Saturday taken
> and discomfited the *bastide* at the end of the bridge, at dawn on the following
> day, the English, who had been staying there, decamped and set out to save
> themselves so swiftly that they left behind their bombards, cannons, and artillery
> and the greater part of their food supplies and baggage.

This missive, completed at Chinon on the night of May 9–10, 1429, testifies to
the messengers' breathless flurry of activity as they conveyed the story of Joan's
victory to her dauphin.

On May 10, the news from Orléans also reached Paris, where the Anglo-
Burgundian party held sway. The recording clerk of the Parlement, Clément de
Fauquembergue, was required by his office to record all judicial cases in his
register; in addition, he had grown accustomed to recording daily events that he
considered relevant to the concerns of Parlement. He made the following note:

> On Tuesday, the tenth day of May, it was reported and publicly said in Paris that
> on the previous Sunday, after many skirmishes continually undertaken by force
> of arms, a large number of the dauphin's men entered the *bastide* that William
> Glasdale and other captains with English men-at-arms held on the [English]
> king's behalf, along with the tower at the end of the bridge of Orléans [the
> Tourelles], from the other side of the Loire. And on that day, the other captains
> and men-at-arms who had been maintaining the siege . . . left these *bastides* and
> raised their siege to combat the enemy, who had in their companies a maid all
> alone who held her banner between the two enemy forces, according to what
> was said.

This imaginative clerk drew in the margin of his page a little sketch of that maid
of whom everyone was speaking on both sides of the Loire, at Paris as at Chinon.
Though he had not seen her, he drew her in profile, in a dress and with long hair.
His sketch emphasized her sword as much as her standard. Those two details
seem to have astonished him: a simple maid armed among men-at-arms, who
distinguished herself by a standard marked with the double name of Jesus-Maria.

These two contemporary testimonies, written from opposing sides, set
in sharp relief the impact of the extraordinary event that had just taken place.
Meanwhile, the Maid left Orléans and the residence of Jacques Boucher. Joan
of Arc was on the road again.

CHAPTER FOUR

HER DAUPHIN
ANOINTED KING
AT REIMS

Between May 9 and July 21, 1429, Joan won several kinds of victories. On June 18, she won a pitched field battle at Patay against a significant English force; the English estimated their casualties at two thousand, while the French lost miraculously few. Joan then persuaded the reluctant dauphin to march deep within enemy territory to Reims in order to be crowned and anointed properly. This daring feat required a high degree of military and diplomatic ingenuity: On July 17, Charles the dauphin became King Charles VII of France (see Part II, Section 1). Joan played a major and entirely unconventional role in that ceremony, standing close to her king in full armor and holding her banner; when reproached later for doing so, she answered that since her banner had worked hard to achieve this victory, it deserved some of the honor.

JOAN AND JOHN, the Bastard of Orléans (II, 16), went to Loches to meet the king after the siege was lifted. According to a well-informed German chronicler: "She took her banner in hand and rode to meet the king. The young girl bowed as deeply as she could before him, and the king promptly made her rise. From the joy he expressed, one thought that he might have hugged her. They met the Thursday before Pentecost, and she stayed near him until after the third day of June."

The date reported for this event and confirmed by her escort, the Bastard, was May 11, 1429. She had wasted no time in Orléans savoring her victory. Nor had the people of Orléans come to know her well, since she had worn a helmet and armor during more than half of her brief stay with them (a detail that would later prove important, when impostors presented themselves to the people of Orléans).

Her deed generated an instantaneous reputation throughout Europe. Eberhard von Windecken, treasurer of the Holy Roman Emperor Sigismund, was the author of the German chronicle just cited. The emperor, evidently showing a lively interest in Joan's exploits, had been sure to keep informed.

The swiftest transmitters of the news of Joan's victory at Orléans were probably agents representing great Italian merchant houses with branches in the most important international markets, especially Flanders and Avignon. In his journal, the Venetian Antonio Morosini kept a record of all the news reported by his firm's overseas agents. Since their business consisted in large measure of sales of arms and other military equipment, these Italian merchants had a vested interest in the state of the wars in France. One of the many exchanges was a letter sent from Bruges in the month of May that tells how a maiden born on the frontiers of Lorraine:

> went to the dauphin. She wished to speak to him alone, excluding all others . . . she told him that he should wage war vigorously, supply and stock Orléans, and challenge the English to battle; they would certainly be victorious and the siege before the town would be raised. . . . An Englishman named Lawrence Trent, an honest and distinguished person, seeing what so many pious and honorable men had said and reported entirely in good faith in their letters, wrote that "this has driven me mad." As an eyewitness, he notes that many of the barons hold her in high esteem, as well as many of the commoners. . . . Her uncontested victory . . . in conversations with the masters of theology makes her seem another St. Catherine [of Siena] come to walk the earth. Many knights, hearing her argue and discuss so many admirable things day after day, say that there is some great miracle to be found here.

A little later the same Morosini mentions another letter that he received in Venice from his Avignon correspondent: "This maiden said to Messire le Dauphin that he should go to Reims to bind about his head the crown of all France. We know that everything that she has said has come to pass, that her words are always confirmed by the event—she has in truth come to achieve great things in this world."

There was much interest in Joan throughout Italy. The duchess of Milan, Bona Visconti, wrote to Joan, insisting that the Maid come to take command of Visconti's own duchy. Another important personage, the royal counselor Perceval de Boulainvilliers, a French nobleman who had married the daughter of the governor of Asti, wrote a dithyrambic letter to the duke of Milan, Filippo-Maria Visconti. According to this poet, at Joan's birth at Domrémy on the night of the Epiphany, "the sixth of January," the cocks began to crow, awakening the entire village "like heralds of a new joy." Joan never lost a single sheep when she was keeping the flocks during her childhood; for the entire period of six days and six nights within the last year, she had been able to rest completely armed, astonishing everyone with the ease by which she could support plate armor and other heavy equipment. The poet Antonino d'Asti translated into verse modeled on the antique Latin eulogy this letter, which resonates with echoes of folklore arising around Joan's exploits.

Joan's achievements became exaggerated as her reputation spread Europe-wide among both partisans and enemies of the king of France. Close to the center of rumor diffusion, the *Journal of the Bourgeois of Paris*, the day-by-day record of a clerk of the University of Paris, amplifies Joan's deeds with mystic additions. In her earliest girlhood, as she kept the sheep, "the birds of the forests and of the fields responded to her call to eat their bread nestled in her bosom as though they were tame." Partisan contempt for the English soldiery emerges when the author notes that during "that time, the Armagnacs raised the siege of Orléans, whence they chased away the English," and the Maid foretold the death of an English captain: "And it was so, for he was drowned the day of the battle." This suggests that there was general discussion of the death of Glasdale during the attack on the Tourelles. The word had flown abroad: Joan had predicted that he would die "without bleeding."

These reports attest to the extraordinary emotional impact that the breaking of the siege of Orléans produced. The French, universally judged to be utterly defeated, had risen and countered the greatest military effort of their conquerors by throwing them into the Loire—and this feat was credited to a young girl of sixteen or seventeen. She was an inspired virgin from whom one could expect almost any miracle. The *capitouls* (municipal counselors) of Toulouse soon hoped for her aid, and they wrote to her explaining their financial difficulties. As far to the south as Montpellier, local legend declares that at that time the boulevard still called Bonne-Nouvelle (Good News) was so named because of the liberation of Orléans. The south of France was then adamantly loyalist; the sole surviving copy of the thrilling letter Charles the dauphin (II, 1) sent to all the "good cities" of the kingdom with the news of Orléans is from the archives of Narbonne. That "good city" was the only one that kept the original, although several other municipalities made mention of its arrival in their registers.

The supporters of the Valois claimant to the French crown were named "Armagnac" for good reason: The dauphin was supported most solidly in the south. Guyenne was an exception. That area lived under its familiar feudal law, whereas the occupied zone of the northern half of France found itself under English dominion by right of conquest—two very different modes of political dependency. Guyenne, with Bordeaux as its head, held for the king of England, since he was its legitimate hereditary lord. Behind this loyalty lay the economic agenda of Bordeaux's wine growers at a time when the English drank more wine per capita than is true even today. By contrast, in Normandy and the Ile-de-France the English conquerors had already aroused resistance that can be best compared to the French resistance against German occupation in the twentieth century.

No one gives a better idea of the public rumor growing up around Joan's exploits than her chaplain, Jean Pasquerel: "Never has anyone seen such a thing as we have seen in your deeds; in no book can one read of comparable feats." Joan returned to the dauphin's company with this aura of victory. Freeing Orléans as she had promised fulfilled the "sign" demanded of her. But her manner was not triumphant, for she believed that the most important part of her mission lay ahead of her. How much depended on her personal contribution to the combat? "I was the first to put the scaling ladder against the *bastide* on the end of the bridge at Orléans," she later declared. She triumphed then by courageously and emblematically exposing herself to danger, and she so exposed herself again. Three times her personal initiative was decisive in the victory at Orléans. At Loches, it had been the same: It was she who won the dauphin's assent to her mission.

How should the French have exploited the liberation of Orléans? From a strategic point of view, an offensive in the direction of Chartres, Normandy, and even Paris seemed to make most sense, especially with the ascendant spirit and high morale of the French troops. The duke of Brittany sent Joan a message that, since he could not come himself because he was "in a great state of infirmity," he was sending his son with reinforcements. Gobert Thibault later said of her men-at-arms: "There were an awful lot of them, for everyone followed her." Joan's victories had galvanized the country.

The Bastard of Orléans expressed himself unequivocally:

> I remember that after the victories of which I spoke [Orléans], the lords of royal blood and the captains wished the king to march into Normandy and not to Reims; but Joan was always of the opinion that we should go to Reims to consecrate the king. She argued that once the king was properly crowned and consecrated the power of his adversaries would continuously diminish, and that they would finally be rendered harmless both to him and to the kingdom. Everyone was persuaded by her.

That "everyone" did not include all the king's most intimate counselors, for Joan had to insist on this point quite forcefully in the royal council. The Bastard describes the moment in the dauphin's chamber in the castle of Loches when the dauphin held council with his advisors Christophe d'Harcourt, Gérard Machet, bishop of Castres, and Robert Le Maçon, chancellor of France: "The Maid, before entering the chamber, knocked on the door and as soon as she entered she dropped to her knees and embraced the legs of the king, saying these words or others like them: 'Do not hold a council meeting for such a long time, but come as quickly as possible to Reims to receive a worthy crown.'"

At that point, Christophe d'Harcourt interrogated her. Joan intrigued him; he did not doubt that she had been led there by divine inspiration, but he was perplexed: How could one follow the mysterious "counsel" to which she continuously referred? The dauphin then posed the same question. Joan blushed but answered with awkward confidence:

> Whenever something did not go well, because people were unwilling to accept and accede to what she had been told by God, she would withdraw a little and begin to pray to God, complaining to Him that those to whom she had spoken did not easily believe her; and when she had made this prayer to God, she heard a voice that said to her: "*Fille-Dé* [child of God], go, go, go; I will be at your aid, go." Whenever she heard that voice, she again felt a great joy and desired to remain always in that condition . . . and when she would repeat the message from her voices this way, she exulted in a wondrous fashion, raising her eyes toward heaven.

Joan won the argument, probably during those days at the castle of Loches. Her movements immediately thereafter related to the launching of her new campaign. Just after May 23, she went to meet the duke of Alençon (II, 4) at Saint-Florent-lès-Saumur. The duke finally had his hands free; his huge ransom had been paid. His duchess wás fearful of the repercussions of his political reengagement, and she begged her husband not to fight any more. "Jeannette"— little Joan—however, reassured her: "Lady, have no fear; I shall bring him back to you in good health and in better shape than he is now!"

With that comforting promise, the duke and duchess of Alençon separated once more. Joan is next cited at Selles-en-Berry, where the duke had also gone "with a very great company." After the duke played a game with Guy de Laval (a young lord who, with his brother André, had joined the royal army), Guy wrote his mother a letter that conveys the excitement of this moment: "They say here that my lord the constable is coming with six hundred men-at-arms and six hundred archers and that Jean de La Roche is also coming, and they say that the king has never had such a great army as the one expected here; and never has there been stronger will for the task that they undertake here."

This enthusiastic youth goes on to tell how he went to the castle at Loches to see the dauphin's son, the future Louis XI: "He is a very handsome and gracious lord; very well built, very agile, and clever for a seven-year-old." Joan also must have seen Louis during her stay there. The prince kept the memory of that childhood encounter with Joan all his life.

For Guy de Laval, too, the encounter with Joan the Maid was special. She had sent his grandmother Anne de Laval, who had been the wife of Bertrand Du Guesclin (II, 15), "a tiny ring of gold," even though she felt that it was too modest a gift, given the fame of that illustrious lady and of the valiant warrior who had been her spouse. Guy describes their conversation with an admiration close to fervor:

> The Maid gave my brother and myself a very good welcome. She was in full armor except for her head, and held a lance in her hand. After we had gone down to Selles, I visited her at her lodging. She had wine brought in and said that she would soon make me drink it in Paris. It all seemed entirely divine: her feats, and the chance for me to see and to hear her. . . . I saw her dressed entirely in white except for her head, a little ax in her hand, mount her horse, a great black charger, which reared up fiercely at the gate of her lodging and would not allow her to mount; and so she said, "Take him to the cross" before the church down the street. There she mounted him without any resistance, as though he had been tied. She then turned to the church door, which was very close: "You priests and men of the church, make a procession and pray to God." And then she returned the way she had come, saying, "Carry it before, carry it before," speaking of her unfurled standard, which a gracious page bore; she had her little ax in her hand, and her brother [Pierre or Jean?] who had come just eight days before, left with her all armed in white.

Everything was already under way on Wednesday, June 8, the day Guy's letter was written. Joan and her brother led them along the road toward Romorantin; at this point her Loire campaign began. Its objective was to dislodge the enemy from their entrenched positions on the banks of the Loire River and in the plains to the north, in order to protect the rear of the army when it departed for Reims. Guy and André de Laval were so eager to perform their first feats of arms that they could not hide their impatience. Their mother (driven from Laval, she had retired to the castle of Vitré in Brittany) had sent letters begging that her young sons not take part in combat so soon. Guy registered his humiliation and distress in a letter home: "I don't know what kind of a letter you have sent to my cousin of La Trémoïlle [II, 25], but as a result the king has made a point of keeping me with him. Thus the Maid will be in front of all the English positions around Orléans, where we are going to besiege them, and the artillery has already been provided for that purpose; this does not bother the Maid at all, and she says that when the king takes the road toward Reims, I shall go with him."

Events went quickly—as they tended to do whenever Joan had liberty to act. She had already moved swiftly to Selles and Romorantin and then returned to Orléans. Having been driven from Orléans, the remnants of the English army, under the command of the earl of Suffolk (II, 41), retreated to Jargeau. Elsewhere, Suffolk hastened to assemble a reinforcement of troops under the command of John Fastolf.

The dauphin entrusted the command of the Loire campaign to the duke of Alençon. He allotted 600 knights—close to 2,000 men in total—to the army, which he sent against Jargeau first. Their number was doubled the following day when they were joined by the companies of the Bastard of Orléans and of Florent d'Illiers, the captain of Châteaudun. Predictably, the captains debated whether to attack Jargeau, since they assumed that the English within were numerous. Joan was, once again, forced to provoke action. As Alençon recalled, "Joan, seeing that there was dissent, told them that they should not fear being outnumbered nor worry about attacking the English, for God would be leading that action. She said that, had she not been sure that God was directing this business, she would have preferred to watch the sheep than to expose herself to such peril."

And so they marched toward Jargeau, intending to march into the suburbs and camp there overnight, as the duke of Alençon later said:

> Aware of this, the English came to meet them and in the first encounter drove back
> the king's men. Seeing this, Joan seized her standard, rode into the fray and found
> the soldiers displaying great courage. They did so well that by nightfall the king's
> soldiers lodged in the suburbs of Jargeau. I think God did indeed direct this matter,
> for that night there was no posting of the guard. If the English had made a sortie
> from the town, the king's soldiers would have been in great peril.

Once again on the following morning, rather than letting the council run on inconclusively,

> Joan herself said to me, "Forward, gentle duke, to the assault!" It seemed
> premature to me to start the attack so rapidly, but Joan said, "Have no doubt, the
> hour that pleases God is at hand." She said that we must act when God wished
> it: "Act and God will act!" She said to me later, "Are you afraid, gentle duke?
> Do you not know that I promised your wife to bring you back safe and sound?"

The duke of Alençon reckoned that Joan had saved his life during the attack on Jargeau:

> At one point, when I was attempting to hold a certain position, Joan told me to
> retire from that place, because if I did not, "that machine"—and she showed me

a machine that was in the city—"will kill you." I withdrew, and a little later at the very spot from which I had withdrawn, someone name Monseigneur du Lude was killed; that struck great fear in me, and after these events I marveled greatly at anything Joan said.

Alençon then recounts Suffolk's unsuccessful effort to obtain a truce in the midst of combat. It was June 12, 1429. Suffolk was taken prisoner. The assault finally ended, but not before Joan—on a scaling ladder with her standard in her hand—was cast down to earth by a stone that broke apart on her helmet (*chapeline*). She swiftly stood up and cried to the soldiers: "Up, up my friends! Our Lord has condemned the English, at this very hour they are ours; take courage!"

The French immediately moved on to Meung and Beaugency. They quickly took the town of Beaugency when the English retreated into the castle. The duke of Alençon received unexpected reinforcements commanded by the constable Arthur de Richemont (II, 36), who was then in disgrace. Richemont had enjoyed influence with the dauphin Charles but had found himself displaced in favor by his own former ally, now enemy, La Trémoïlle. Was the campaign going to be disrupted by these power struggles? Alençon told Joan "that if the Constable came, [he] would go away." To which she remarked "that he had need of help." They had in fact just learned that "the English army was approaching, and in its company was the lord Talbot," (II, 40) a seasoned warrior, the mention of whose name must have calmed the discords in the French camp for a time. The duke of Alençon negotiated the surrender of the castle of Beaugency and granted its garrison safe-conduct. "As soon as the English had withdrawn, someone from the company of La Hire [II, 22] came to see me. He said, as did the king's captain, that the English were coming, that we would soon be face-to-face, and that they were about one thousand men-at-arms."

On June 17, the two armies came swiftly within view of each other. Jean de Wavrin, known as the Bastard, fighting in the English ranks, recalled:

> From every direction across the wide and ample Beauce, you could see the English riding in handsome array. They then merged one league away from Meung, fairly close to Beaugency. The French, alerted to their arrival, had about six thousand combatants whose commanders were Joan the Maid, the duke of Alençon, the Bastard of Orléans, the marshal of La Fayette, La Hire, Poton [II, 44], and others; they fell into formation and positioned themselves on a little hillock, in order to disconcert the English.

The English halted their march and arranged themselves in battle formation. As was their custom, the archers formed the first lines, "their stakes in front of them." These pikes fixed in the earth were designed to hinder any cavalry charge.

The English sent two heralds to the French to say that it was up to them to descend and join combat. "An answer was given them by the men of the Maid: 'Go find yourselves lodging, for it is already late in the day, and tomorrow, at the pleasure of God and Our Lady, we will take a closer look at one another.'"

The night of June 17–18 passed with that challenge still in effect and with positions maintained. The English were in Meung, the French in Beaugency, which was disquieted by the knowledge that English reinforcements were in the field. The Bastard of Orléans reported that an uncertain duke of Alençon consulted Joan: "She answered him in a loud voice, saying, 'Everyone be sure to have good spurs!' Hearing this, those present asked Joan, 'What do you mean? Are we going to turn our backs on them?' Joan answered, 'No, it is the English who will not defend themselves and who will be conquered. You will have need of good spurs as you chase after them.' And it was so, for they took flight and we took more than four thousand of them, as many dead as captive."

June 18 was to be the greatest victory Joan would ever achieve, and she won it in the open field. The Battle of Patay was a mirror image of Agincourt. If the October 25, 1415 victory of Henry V at Agincourt decided the third phase of the Hundred Years War in favor of the Plantagenet party, then the victory of Patay reversed its results for the fourth phase in favor of the Armagnacs. One participant, Jean de Wavrin, described that extraordinary feat. Behind the vanguard, the main body of English troops was commanded by Fastolf, Talbot, and one Thomas Rameston.

A series of accidents shattered the English array. The vanguard gave warning of the French approach and then assumed its position among the support wagons and artillery "all along the hedges that were near Patay." Talbot then posted himself where he thought the French would pass, "guessing that he would be able to hold that passage until the arrival of troop reinforcements." But he was wrong, as Wavrin remarked: "The French held tight formation and pursued their enemies, whom they could not yet see, nor did they know their positions, until by luck the scouts in front saw a stag leap from the woods and take the road toward Patay. It jumped into the English formation, whereupon it uttered a great cry. The French had not known that their enemies were so close to them."

The scouts ran to inform their companies. The engagement began before the major units of the English force could come together, even in a disorderly fashion. The men of the vanguard saw Captain Fastolf arrive in haste and thought "that everything was lost, and that their divisions were in flight. Believing this, the captain of the vanguard took flight with his white standard and abandoned the hedge." Fastolf and his men were also seized by panic. "It was said in my presence," Wavrin declares, "that he should take care of himself, for the battle was lost." In another unit of troops, Talbot had just been taken prisoner:

confusion had led to a rout. The Bastard of Wavrin shared the lot of Fastolf, who fled in the direction of Étampes and Corbeil.

On the French side, three men were dead; on the English side, the Burgundian chroniclers estimated the casualties at two thousand. Wavrin concluded: "Thus the French gained victory at the place called Patay, where they spent the night, thanking Our Lord for their fine adventure. . . . Because of its location, that battle will forever be called 'The Day of Patay.'"

The unexpected outcome of this encounter provoked panic all the way to Paris. As soon as they heard about "The Day of Patay" the Parisians became convinced (according to the *Journal of the Siege of Orléans*) that "the Armagnacs were coming to assail them, and so they reinforced the watch and began to make preparations to fortify the city defensively."

But it was not against Paris that Joan intended to direct the royal army, which, assembled at Gien, may have amounted to some 12,000 combatants. In the aftermath of combat, the dauphin agreed to head for Reims. He sent a formal letter of convocation to the cities in his kingdom and to the peers of France, both lay and ecclesiastical, who were to participate in his coronation. Among these, of course, was the duke of Burgundy. It is known that Joan herself sent the duke a letter, unfortunately lost, inviting him to swear fealty to the king of France. Another letter that she dictated invited the inhabitants of Tournai to Reims for the coronation; it remained in the archives until it was destroyed in World War II. She proudly announced that: "by my baton, I shall lead the gentle lord Charles and his company safely, and he will be consecrated at Reims."

According to Perceval de Cagny, the chronicler of the duke of Alençon, Joan was vexed by the delay of eight days between the victory of Patay and the departure from Gien. The dauphin did not, in fact, begin the march until June 29. "In her impatience, the Maid left her lodgings in town, staying in the fields for two days before the king departed." The march to Reims was a strategic absurdity: It led deep into territory under Burgundian control. On June 20, at Auxerre, the end of the first stage of the journey, the dauphin's party ran into a Burgundian garrison. Delegations went back and forth between the king and the bourgeois of the town, who finally provided the army with food and publicly declared that they would give "the king such obedience as would the cities of Troyes, Châlons, and Reims."

It was at Troyes that Henry V of England had been declared regent of France; his marriage to Catherine of France made him the son-in-law of the unfortunate Charles VI and of Isabeau of Bavaria (II, 23), and his descendants were promised the crown of France. On July 4 the French forces reached Saint-Phal, a little more than fifteen miles from Troyes. Joan prudently addressed a letter to the inhabitants; Charles did likewise. He promised complete amnesty, as did Joan:

Loyal Frenchmen, come before your lord Charles. Since there is no question of fault, have no fear for your bodies, nor your goods, if you do so; and if you do not do so, I promise you on your lives that we shall take all of the cities that should belong to his holy kingdom with God's aid, and—no matter who presumes to come against us—we shall make a good solid peace. I commend you to God; may He guard you if it please Him. A swift reply is expected.

In response to these stern words, the men of Troyes, like those of Auxerre, were anxious to learn how people in Reims and other places felt. Messengers were sent back and forth, among them Friar Richard (II, 35), a Franciscan with a reputation for sanctity. Joan would later remember his arrival with a certain irony: "When he came toward me, he made the sign of the cross and tossed holy water around; and I said 'Be brave and approach, I won't fly away!'" She was becoming accustomed to the rituals of exorcism.

The army's situation was critical. Their food supplies were exhausted, a strong Burgundian garrison held the center of the city, and, as always, the French captains were divided about their preferred course of action. The Bastard of Orléans tells us how Joan intervened once again:

And so the Maid went and entered the council of the king, saying these words or nearly so: "Noble dauphin, command your people to come and besiege the city of Troyes, and do not waste more time in long councils, for in God's name, within three days I shall lead you into the city of Troyes, by love or by force and either way with courage: Burgundy will be stupefied by it."

Joan posted troops along the ditches outside the wall and strengthened them with artillery; "and she worked so well that night and the next day that the bishop and townspeople, shaking and trembling, made their obedience to the king." Simon Charles, another eyewitness to these events, adds the important detail that Joan took her standard on this maneuver:

A large number of foot soldiers followed her, and she ordered them to make bundles of sticks to fill the ditches. They made many, and the next day Joan issued a call for the assault, giving the order to put the bundles in the ditches. Seeing this, the inhabitants of Troyes, fearing an assault, sent to the king to negotiate their surrender. The king reached an agreement with the inhabitants and he entered Troyes with great ceremony, and Joan carried her standard near him.

This processional entry into Troyes took place on Sunday, July 10. On Tuesday, July 12, the army resumed its march; two days later it stood before Châlons-sur-Marne. The royal herald Montjoie announced himself with the dauphin's letter, which as elsewhere promised amnesty. The bishop, Jean of Montbéliard, imitating his colleague Jean Léguisé, bishop of Troyes, promptly presented the keys of the city to the dauphin. Little by little, as the dauphin's forces approached Reims, negotiations grew less lengthy and the French army's progress more self-assured.

The army's stop at Châlons was marked by a significant event. The dauphin had decided to inform his subjects that he was going to receive his anointing to Reims by inviting them to attend. He ordered the public criers to repeat this invitation in any region that had remained faithful to him. The people responded, as they traditionally had, by setting out on the road to Reims: The coronation of a king was a popular celebration. Though solemn, the ritual was not yet the closed official ceremony of later centuries.

Joan met several people on the road who called her "Jeannette," among them villagers from Domrémy, for whom the coronation held special significance. One of these was her cousin Jean Moreau, who would later emotionally recount that when they met Joan made him the gift of "a red dress that she was carrying." (Although dressed in male attire, Joan seems to have brought women's clothes along with her as well.) Jean Moreau was one of a group of five men from Domrémy who traveled together. To them, Joan confided, as Gérardin d'Épinal recalled, "that she feared nothing except treason." Joan's father and mother, Jacques d'Arc and Isabelle Romée, were also present at the coronation. (See III, 1.)

On July 16, at the castle of Sept-Saulx, Charles the dauphin received a deputation of the bourgeois of Reims, who offered him full and complete obedience. This was the first time that loyalty to the dauphin from a city in Burgundian territory was so openly expressed. On that same day, a number of "renegade Frenchmen" who had collaborated with the English left the city. Among them was the former rector of the University of Paris, a native of Reims named Pierre Cauchon (II, 49), who had been one of the principal negotiators of the Treaty of Troyes. That evening, Charles made his formal entry into the city of Reims to cries raised by the general populace of "Noël [Christmas], Noël!" for Christmas had been associated with coronations ever since Charlemagne was crowned in Rome on Christmas Day of the year 800.

The following day, Sunday, July 17, 1429, after swift preparations, Charles VII was anointed according to traditional rites. Although most of the traditional coronation regalia seems to have been in the cathedral of Notre Dame in Paris—and was used later when England's young king Henry was there crowned "king of France"—only the dauphin Charles's coronation invoked the irreducible symbol (the *saint ampoule*, or holy oil, that was kept in the abbey of Saint-Rémi in Reims) and the most traditional elements (Reims as the place; its bishop as the officiant). The dauphin became the king of France, consecrated with the sacred oil. Doubts about his legitimate title were put to rest among his adherents.

Little is known about the actual ceremony. Since the *Ordo coronationis* changed little over time, this coronation may well have resembled that of St. Louis in 1226. On the other hand, some historians (see Richard Jackson's argument in *Vive le roi*) think that this ritual might have followed an *ordo* probably composed during the 1250s, when St. Louis was held as a prisoner by the Turks at Damietta in Egypt; the French feared they might need to crown another king. The man whom Joan up to this point had called the dauphin—"she said she would not call him king until he was crowned and anointed at Reims, where she had decided to lead him," according to the royal counselor François Garivel—had probably appeared before the cathedral on the previous evening, to "pray to God and to keep the vigil while praying as much as seemed right to him and as his devotion compelled him."

In the morning the four knights known as Guardians of the Holy Vial made their way to the abbey of Saint-Rémi to take possession of the precious flask of oil. Legend affirmed that angels brought it on the occasion of the baptism of Clovis, the first king of the Franks, traditionally dated 496. Custom required that a drop of it be mixed with the Holy Chrism used to anoint the new king. It seems that the Holy Vial was the only traditional coronation item that the English forces had not removed from Reims to Paris. The four Guardians were the marshal de Boussac, the admiral Culant, the lord of Graville, and—to increase his visibility—Gilles de Rais (II, 34). This last figure, a rich nobleman from Brittany, was not yet known for anything other than military valor. He had taken part in the raising of the siege of Orléans and in the campaign of the Loire. Two months later (in a charter still preserved in the Archives Nationales), Charles VII granted him the right to carry the fleurs-de-lys on the bordure of his coat of arms.

At their return, escorting the Holy Vial, which the abbot Jean Canard had put in their charge, the four Guardians encountered a long procession of canons, bishops, and prelates surrounding the king, who had spent the night at the archbishop's palace before entering the church to the singing of psalms. The main door of the cathedral had been thrown open; the clatter of resounding hooves mixed with the shouts of the crowd that had gathered in and around the cathedral, for the four knights who escorted the Holy Vial entered the church on horseback.

The ceremony of coronation included the oath of loyalty required by the king, the singing of the *Te Deum*, and the benediction of the royal insignia: crown, golden spurs, scepter, and (since the beginning of the fourteenth century) the "hand of justice," a second scepter sculpted in ivory. At the core of the rite was the anointing itself, the essential element considered comparable to a sacrament like confirmation or holy orders. The king prostrated himself on the steps of the altar, while litanies of the saints were chanted. The archbishop, who had prostrated himself at the king's side, marked the king with holy oil on the head, chest, shoulders, elbows, and wrists. The king, dressed until that point only in his shoes and a loose shirt, then put on a tunic and a coat of silk. Once anointed afresh on his hands, he pulled on gloves; the ring that was the symbol of the union between the king and his people was slipped on his finger. The crown was taken from the altar and placed on the new king's head, but not before the ten of the twelve peers of France who were actually present—five laymen and five ecclesiastics—had held it above his head as he was led from the altar up to the dais on which was placed the throne. It was then that, as depicted on the seals of the time, the new king appeared in royal majesty. Three gentlemen from Anjou who were charged with reporting the ceremony to the queen, Marie of Anjou, and her mother, record the scene:

> And at the hour that the king was consecrated and also when they had placed the crown on his head, every man cried out: *Noël!* And the trumpets sounded so that it seemed as though the walls of the church should have crumbled. During the aforesaid mystery, the Maid was always at the king's side, holding his standard in her hand. It was fine to see the elegant manners not only of the king but also of the Maid, and God knows that you would have wished them well.

After the archbishop and the peers pledged homage, Joan went to kneel before the king. The chronicler of the *Siege of Orléans* captured the general emotion of this moment: "And she evoked great pity in all who beheld her." Embracing the new king's legs, she wept and said:

> Gentle king, from this moment the pleasure of God is executed. He wished me to raise the siege of Orléans and bring you to the city of Reims to receive your anointing, which shows that you are the true king and the one to whom the kingdom should belong.

Some felt that it would have been more appropriate to place Joan among the other captains, even though all recognized the essential part she had played in this event. Her enemies would later ask this question: "Why was your standard carried to the anointing of the king in the church of Reims, rather than the standards of the other captains?" To which she then responded: "That standard had gone to great pains; it was fair that it should share the honor."

Anointing was the paramount symbol of a sovereign's capacity to unify his subjects around his body, his person. The list of those absent from the ceremony at Reims is therefore quite instructive. Paramount among those absent was Charles's wife, Marie of Anjou. When the army set off for Reims, and Charles was at Gien, he sent her instructions to return to Bourges, since the operation he was launching was a dangerous one. In addition, Marie was not at

Reims because the royal entourage judged that it was the king alone whose coronation then mattered. Lesser importance was attached to her coronation as queen, a ceremony that took place later at Paris. The time of such formidable queens as Eleanor of Aquitaine and Blanche of Castile was over. The role of the queen continued to diminish until even coronation rites were eliminated: the last French queen to be crowned at all would be Marie de Médicis in 1610.

Another notable figure who was absent from the coronation was the constable Arthur de Richemont. He should by custom have had the honor of carrying the ceremonial sword after the benediction, but the lord of Albret was appointed to hold it in his place. The chronicle of Guillaume Gruel, one of the constable's friends, reports that Richemont, who had so recently taken part in the brilliant victory of Patay, wanted intensely to accompany the king to Reims, but the king had adamantly refused, despite the urging of Joan, "who was very displeased about it." Guillaume adds that the king declared that "he would rather never be crowned than have my lord [Arthur] in attendance." The powerful influence on Charles VII of Richemont's enemy La Trémoïlle is discernible in this action. The dauphin's insecure court was long dominated by the sway of rivalries among such overmighty factions.

There were two other noteworthy absences: Pierre Cauchon, the bishop of Beauvais, one of the six ecclesiastical peers, whose absence is explained by his longtime devotion to the Anglo-Burgundian faction, and Philip the Good, duke of Burgundy (II, 3), one of the six lay peers. Joan had written the duke on the Sunday morning of the coronation, July 17; her letter is preserved in the archives of Lille:

> Jesus Maria. High and dread prince, duke of Burgundy, the Maid calls upon you by the King of Heaven, my rightful and sovereign Lord, to make a firm and lasting peace with the king of France. You two must pardon one another fully with a sincere heart, as loyal Christians should; and if it pleases you to make war, go and wage it on the Saracens. Prince of Burgundy, I pray you, supplicate, and humbly request rather than require you, make war no more on the holy kingdom of France. Withdraw at once and swiftly those of your men who are in certain places and fortresses of the aforesaid holy kingdom. As for the gentle king of France, he is ready to make peace with you, saving his honor, if it has to do with you alone. And I must make known to you from the King of Heaven, my rightful and sovereign Lord, for your good and for your honor and upon your life, that you will win no more battles against loyal Frenchmen and that all those who wage war against the aforesaid holy kingdom of France are warring against King Jesus, King of Heaven and of all the earth, my rightful and sovereign Lord. And I pray you and call upon you with hands joined not to seek any battle nor war against us, neither you nor your men nor subjects, and believe firmly that

no number of men that you bring against us will win, and that there will be great pity for the battle and the bloodshed there of those who come against us. And it is three weeks since I wrote that you should be at the anointing of the king, which today, Sunday the seventeenth day of this month of July, is taking place in the city of Reims: to which I have had no reply, nor have I ever heard any news of that herald. I commend you to God; may He guard you, if it pleases Him; and I pray God that He will establish a good peace. Written in the aforesaid place of Reims, on the aforesaid seventeenth day of July.

This letter evokes the grandeur of Joan's Christian, martial, and chivalric mentality at the same time that it masks the increasing irrelevance of these qualities to her world and moment. The letter reveals that Joan expected the fate of her king and kingdom to be determined by submission or by battle. She was not of her king's council. She was ignorant of the swarming diplomatic activity then under way among French, English, and Burgundian diplomats.

CHAPTER FIVE

INTRIGUE, FRUSTRATION, AND CAPTURE

From mid-July 1429 to May 23, 1430—from the days following the coronation of Charles VII at Reims (see Part II, Section 1) to her capture by a Burgundian force at Compiègne—Joan experienced nearly constant waves of disillusionment. She had made Charles king but was forced to accept the consequences: evasive and suspicious, Charles preferred delay and negotiation to the swift, decisive action to which Joan was naturally inclined. Her loyal partisans (such as Duke John of Alençon; II, 4) shared her desire to make the most of the wave of patriotic enthusiasm that her triumphs had aroused, but the king, probably obsessed by his guilt for the murder of the duke of Burgundy's father, listened to counselors like Georges de La Trémoïlle (II, 25) and the archbishop of Reims (II, 13), who resented Joan. In September 1429, she was ordered to abandon the effort to take Paris; in October, after the royal army was disbanded, Joan was sent to deal with a minor bandit chief in central France; after a frustrating winter, she was allowed to lead only a small mercenary band against the English and Burgundians northeast of Paris. On May 23, while retreating to the supposedly pro-French town of Compiègne, she was left outside a suddenly closed gate and promptly captured by some Burgundians scarcely able to credit their luck: an accident or an act of treason?

ALTHOUGH THE CORONATION AT REIMS WAS HASTILY ORGANIZED, it was undertaken with customary pomp. So that he could perform the traditional ritual

at the nearby abbey of Saint-Marcoul-de-Corbény of "touching for scrofula"—
exercising the healing power believed to be granted the king by his coronation—
Charles (II, 1) did not leave the city until July 21.

The coronation produced an extraordinary perception of Joan of Arc in
France and beyond. Even before the king's consecration, a verbal duel about
Joan had taken place. Two pamphlets had appeared at Paris (as well as a treatise
written by Jacques Gélu [II, 19] in her favor); the first, an attack now lost, was
the opening salvo of many assaults on Joan by members of the University of
Paris. The other, a defense against this attack, probably came from the pen of
Jean Gerson (II, 20), a respected authority on legal and religious matters. Gerson,
previously the university's chancellor, knew the reigning academic temperament
well. He himself had been expelled from the corporation of the university
because of his pro-Valois sentiments. From July 6, 1418, his absence from the
university was recorded on its registers. In fact, while attending the Council of
Constance, he learned that Paris had fallen into the hands of the Anglo-
Burgundians and refused to return. After living for some time in Austria, he
joined one of his brothers, a friar at the Celestine convent in Lyons. The pamphlet
in defense of Joan, which he probably composed in June 1429, might have been
his last work; he died on July 12, five days before the anointing at Reims.

When he supported Joan's cause, Gerson could not have known that he
was once more on the side of his old ally, Christine de Pisan (II, 32). A well-
known public personality, a poet, and a historian whom Duke Philip the Bold
of Burgundy (II,3) earlier had asked to compose the history of his brother "the
wise king, Charles V," Christine de Pisan never ceased to champion peace and
to defend women. Gerson had joined her in those efforts. When the English had
first entered Paris, Christine de Pisan retired from the city, probably to the
convent of Poissy, where her daughter was a nun. She kept silent for eleven
years, ceasing to write except for some poems that are really prayers. Christine
de Pisan was then dazzled by Joan's exploits; all of a sudden, she beheld an
unexpected dawn. In July 1429 she took up her pen again to celebrate this girl
who had just achieved victories that would have been considered impossible
even for any man: Her famous poem of fifty-six strophes, the *Ditié de Jehanne
d'Arc,* comprises 448 lines sketching Joan's story. She reminds her readers how
Joan had been examined by the prelates and how she had given proof of her
claim at the siege of Orléans. Above all, she speaks with awe about the anointing
and coronation. The cry that she had raised at the news of these events is well
known:

> In the year one thousand four hundred twenty and nine
> the sun began to shine again. . . .
> Behold this woman, a simple shepherdess,

more valiant than was ever any man at Rome. . . .
During the siege of Orléans
her force first appeared. . . .
With great triumph and power
Charles was crowned at Reims . . .
never have we heard
speak of so great a marvel.

In this poem, her final work, Christine de Pisan once more balanced her roles as historian and poet. In July 1429, the writer Alain Chartier also exalted Joan in poetic prose:

Behold her there, she who does not seem to have come from any place in the world, but to have been sent from heaven to raise up the head and the shoulders of a Gaul beaten down into the earth. . . . O singular virgin, worthy of all glories, of all praises, of divine honors, you are the greatness of the kingdom, you are the light of the lily, you are the brilliance, you are the glory, not only of the French, but also of all Christians.

These poets were quick to praise the Maid's exploits. Commentaries and contemporary historical documents in many genres provide multiple, often contradictory, opinions of Joan. No assessments are less guarded or more enthusiastic than these poetic voices as they record Joan's victories and Charles's coronation as events, in Christine's words, "above all others to be marveled at."

Despite the difficult situation in which events had placed him, one man was methodically setting things in order to counter the disastrous effects of Joan's victories—John, duke of Bedford, regent of France (II, 9). One of his best captains, John Talbot (II, 40), had just been made prisoner by Joan and Duke John of Alençon at Patay (II, 4). The other, John Fastolf, suffered reproach for having fled in that same battle, although his retreat had permitted him to save his unit of troops. Bedford also knew that he had at his disposal 350 men-at-arms, as many of them horsemen as archers, who had just disembarked at Calais on July 1. They were an army recruited by Cardinal Henry Beaufort (II, 8), bishop of Winchester and the natural uncle of the duke of Bedford (he was a bastard son of Bedford's grandfather John of Gaunt, duke of Lancaster), to fight the Hussites in Bohemia. The recruitment and supply of this army had been financed by special tithes raised with papal authorization and supplemented by papal finances; uncle and nephew had decided with one mind to deflect this force from its intended target. On July 15 the troops left Calais for Paris, where they arrived ten days later as a fresh body of reinforcements for the struggle against the newly crowned King Charles VII of France.

Not content with diverting for personal profit a military force that the English people believed had been raised for the good of Christianity, Bedford was also carrying on a wide-ranging diplomatic offensive. His brother, Henry V, had been a warrior, but Bedford was an administrator. He had married Anne of Burgundy, Duke Philip's sister and (in the words of the Bourgeois of Paris) "the most agreeable lady who was then in France, being beautiful, young, and good." Bedford relied on this family connection to obtain, from an ally whom he did not always find reliable, the guarantees that were indispensable in his effort to avert these new threats to the English conquest. Cleverly, he had invited the duke of Burgundy to spend several days in Paris. Between July 10 and 15, a series of festivals and spectacular demonstrations of support, with a general procession and a sermon at Notre Dame, resulted in a promise from the people of Paris that "all would be good and loyal to the regent and to the duke of Burgundy."

Christine de Pisan protested:

> O Paris very ill advised!
> Foolish and untrustworthy citizens!

The duke of Burgundy returned to his territory without his jewels, which he left with Bedford for a sum of 20,000 livres and a promise that the gift would be returned to him at the end of the month, in return for which Bedford had promised to recruit an army. Through the agency of his herald Jarretière (the Garter Herald), Bedford pressed the city of London to send him a subsidy, emphasizing that without the Burgundian alliance English power in France could disappear "at a single blow."

A more serious aspect of this diplomatic game involved the negotiations that Georges de La Trémoïlle (II, 25) had begun on June 30 with the court of Burgundy. These had gone so well that the Burgundian Jean de Vimeu left Dijon for Arras on July 16 in order to report the progress of these negotiations to Philip the Good when he returned from Paris. An embassy led by David de Brimeu arrived at Reims while the king was there; a letter bringing Queen Marie of Anjou and her mother, Yolanda of Sicily, news about the coronation ceremony expressed the hope that the king would conclude "a good treaty . . . before he leaves." The same letter made a reference to Joan: "She leaves no doubt that she will bring Paris under her control."

Joan was preoccupied with following up a fruitful military offensive, the king with negotiating. Instead of achieving a "good treaty," Charles concluded a truce of fifteen days. After just one triumphal day at Reims, the French party found itself in a state of mutual misunderstanding.

As she had already said, Joan feared only treason. It is difficult to determine whether, exactly why, or by whom Joan was finally betrayed. (See III, 10.) Some surmise an early shadow of treachery during the coronation banquet. Thereafter, all her initiatives would have to deal with insecure or inadequate support. At the very moment when her father, mother, and "uncle" Durand Laxart were returning to Domrémy overwhelmed with the unexpected glory of their "Jeannette," a time of uncertainty, of reversals, and even of final torment was beginning for her. The Bastard of Orléans (II, 16) reported Joan's sorrowful exclamation on the road between La Ferté-Melon and Crépy-en-Valois: "May it please God my creator that I now withdraw from arms, and so serve my father and my mother by taking care of the flocks with my sister and my brother, who would be so happy to see me again!" This remark is atypically poignant; it resonates how disarmed Joan was by the possibility of treason, "which at every step went before her."

The changing mood is reflected in the king's itinerary. In contrast to the swift march to Reims, he now took thirty-six days to cover the ninety miles from Reims to Paris. This funereal pace must have been torture for any warrior, especially Joan, who expected to enhance the élan that the French troops shared. "One Frenchman could have defeated ten Englishmen then," Jean Chartier wrote in his *Chronicle*. Impelled toward the conquest of Paris, Joan did not know that Charles VII already had committed himself to avoiding a battle for the city. She must have felt some hope during the first stages of the advance, at Vailly, then at Soissons: "The king went to Soissons, where he was received with great joy by all, and many loved him and desired his arrival." The coronation had made him a true king, and the cities—Laon, Château-Thierry, Crépy, Provins, Coulommiers—expressed their joy and their wish to recognize him. From Crépy-en-Valois he sent his envoy to Compiègne, demanding that its inhabitants "place themselves in his obedience," to which they responded that they "were very willing to do so." Even the city of Beauvais, whose bishop was Pierre Cauchon (II, 49), sang a *Te Deum* for the king of France.

During his stay at Château-Thierry, on July 31, Charles VII at Joan's request exempted in perpetuity the inhabitants of Domrémy and Greux from taxation. This was the Maid's only such request; the exemption was maintained up to the reign of Louis XVI (III, 9).

Bedford the regent profited from Charles's unexpected delay and reinforced the defenses of Paris. Leaving the city on August 4 at the head of a powerful army, he marched up the left bank of the Seine. Three days later he sent the king of France a challenge from Montereau: "You seduce and abuse the ignorant and rely upon the assistance of the superstitious and reprobate, and even of that deranged and infamous woman who goes about in men's clothes and is of dissolute conduct." Bedford proposed to take up positions in the Brie and Ile-de-France. The English army set out in the direction of Senlis and halted on August 14 near the village of Montépilloy. During these maneuvers, Bedford named the duke of Burgundy governor of Paris, so that a prince of the blood royal could be said to exercise political authority over the capital of France.

It seemed for a while that a decisive battle would take place at Montépilloy. The peaceful course of the Nonnette, a little stream that crisscrosses the countryside, had become a base for Bedford's army, now reinforced by 700 Picards sent by the duke of Burgundy. The French troops that came from Crépy-en-Valois were divided into "battles," of which the first, commanded by the lord of Albret, included Joan herself, the Bastard of Orléans, and La Hire (II, 22).

It was a moment of high suspense. An entire day, August 15, was spent in dust clouds under a burning sun ("such great powder," says Perceval de Cagny, "that one could recognize neither French nor English"). Each side was expecting an engagement that might prove decisive. The English in their usual fashion entrenched themselves behind rows of sharpened stakes and wagons that served as a rampart. Charles VII rode about the battlefield with the duke of Bourbon (II, 11) and La Trémoïlle; Bedford did not show himself. On the afternoon of August 16, the English began retreating toward Paris. The Berry Herald, an eyewitness, wrote that "all the day, they stood one facing the other, without hedges or bushes, as close as the shot of a culverine, and they did not fight. And on the evening, the king went away to Crépy and the duke of Bedford went to Senlis." Meanwhile, on that same August 16, Philip the Good, duke of Burgundy, had reason to feel in control of the situation. A French embassy led by Regnault of Chartres, archbishop of Reims (II, 13), and including many notables, among them Raoul de Gaucourt (II, 18), came as beggars to "the grand duke of the west," as one witness remarked, presenting him with "greater offers of reparation than the royal majesty actually possessed." In reparation for the assassination of John the Fearless at Montereau, the king asked the duke to accept every possible guarantee "by hostages, corporal punishments, or pecuniary penalties, obligation and submission to the church and to secular courts, as strongly as can be devised." All this was offered simply in exchange for Burgundy's neutrality in the conflict between the French and the English. At Arras, the English negotiated through Hugues de Lannoy, the Burgundian diplomat who was also a member of the royal council of England. The duke of Burgundy let it be understood that he would participate in a peace conference proposed by Amadeus VIII of Savoy.

With the departure of the king of France, the bourgeois of Reims found themselves isolated in Burgundian territory, and impinging troop movements gave them cause for worry. They appealed to Joan, who responded in a disquieted letter:

> I promise and certify that I shall never abandon you as long as I shall live. And
> it is true that the king has made a truce with the duke of Burgundy, lasting fifteen
> days. . . . However many truces may be made in this fashion, I am not content,
> and I do not know if I will hold to them. But if I do hold to them, it will be only
> to maintain the honor of the king.

She urged Reims to "keep good watch and guard the king's good city." The place
and date of this letter are significant: "written on Friday, the fifth day of August,
near Provins, from a residence in the fields, on the road to Paris." This letter,
like the one she sent to the duke of Burgundy, does not bear her signature, but
it does bear the mark of Joan's personality and intentions: "On the road to Paris"
is itself a challenge.

The atmosphere of misunderstanding persisted. Joan thought only of
profiting from the general enthusiasm and the strong army that had now
assembled; the king had nothing in his head but negotiations and truces. On
August 17 the keys of Compiègne were brought to him at Crépy, where he had
retired. The following day, he made his formal entry through the Pierrefonds
Gate and was received by the notables of the city, including Guillaume de Flavy,
a mercenary captain on whom the defense of Compiègne depended (III, 10).

On August 21, a Burgundian embassy arrived led by John of Luxembourg
(II, 28). After a week of laborious negotiations, another truce of four months
was signed, this time applying to all the territory on the right bank of the Seine
from Nogent-sur-Seine to Honfleur. During that period, neither Burgundy nor
France would be allowed to take the cities situated within those defined areas
nor to receive their obedience. Firmer guarantees were given orally by Charles
VII, who was engaged in returning to the duke of Burgundy important cities
along the river Oise: Compiègne, Pont-Sainte-Maxence, Creil, Senlis. Bedford
could be content, having returned to Paris with an intact army, and the duke of
Burgundy was more than ever master of the situation.

About this same time, Hugues de Lannoy drafted two memoirs outlining the
Anglo-Burgundian strategy. Before the expiration of the truces—that is, before
Christmas—a strong English army, "a good and great power of men-at-arms and of
armies," would be brought into France. More than ever before, it would be
indispensable for the English to cultivate their alliance with the duke of Burgundy,
because without him "no good, durable exploit can proceed." After January 1, 1430,
when the truce ended, England was to provide the duke with 2,000 men, for whom
he would pay, requiring in return whatever would be necessary to defend Paris. But
the English understood that it would be necessary to compensate the duke, "granting
him great and notable authority" as well as the gift of "some great lordship." These
two points would be observed to the letter by the duke of Bedford, who was expert
at maintaining alliances. On October 13 Philip the Good would be granted the

lieutenant generalcy of France; on January 12, 1430, the English gave him the counties of Champagne and of Brie.

An English alliance with the duke of Brittany was ensured by the offer of the county of Poitou: The constable Arthur de Richemont (II, 36) was courted by the offer of appointment to constable in the king of England's name and by the promise of Touraine, Saintonge, Aunis, and La Rochelle. The partition of France to suit English interests progressed steadily. Plans were made for an offensive against Berry, now once more the king of France's favorite zone of retreat. Troops were sent into Guyenne to contain the counts of Armagnac (II, 6) and Foix, allies of the king. Every effort was made to relieve "the very great necessity now in France" and to reverse recent French successes. All of this was proposed along with a series of later truces that were useful exercises in the implementation of the grand plan. Hugues de Lannoy, the Burgundian courtier and chronicler, advised that embassies be sent to the kings of Castile, Aragon, and Portugal, to the duke of Milan, to Lorraine, and above all to Scotland, "the allies in which the enemies have great hope, and among whom they boast that they are very strong."

While the scaffolding for these projects was being erected in the shadows, Joan's impatience mounted, according to Perceval de Cagny: "When the king found himself at Compiègne, the Maid was deeply grieved that he wished to extend his stay. She called on the duke of Alençon and said to him, 'My fair duke, equip your men and those of the other captains. By my banner, I want to go see Paris from closer than I have ever seen it.'"

On the English side, Bedford left Senlis for Rouen. The news he heard from Normandy was alarming, for the province was being scoured by "partisans," (resistance fighters). As the chronicler tells us: "On the Friday following the 26th day of August, the Maid, the duke of Alençon, and their company were lodged in the city of Saint-Denis. And when the king knew that they were lodged in the city of Saint-Denis, with great regret he came as far as the city of Senlis. And it seemed that he was counseled against the will of the Maid, of the duke of Alençon, and of their company."

The days that followed were spent in skirmishes. Joan examined the ramparts of Paris, where the population was in a state of high anxiety, organizing its defense under the orders of the Burgundian Louis of Luxembourg (II, 29), bishop of Thérouanne and chancellor of France for the English crown. The duke of Alençon shuttled between Saint-Denis and the king, first at Senlis and then at Compiègne: "And there was no one of any estate who did not say 'She will put the king in Paris, so long as he has nothing to do with it.'"

An attack was finally made on Thursday, September 8. Leaving La Chapelle to the north of the city, Joan, Marshal Gilles de Rais (II, 34), and the lord of Gaucourt attacked the Saint-Honoré Gate. The king, who had arrived the previous evening, was impressed by the enthusiasm of his entourage, but, as subsequent events demonstrated, did nothing.

Clément de Fauquembergue, the clerk of the Parlement of Paris who, four months earlier, had recorded the liberation of Orléans, noted these recent activities in his register:

> Thursday, the eighth day of September, feast of the Nativity of the Mother of God. The men-at-arms of my lord Charles of Valois assembled in great numbers near the wall of Paris, toward the Saint-Honoré Gate, hoping to grieve and damage the inhabitants of the city of Paris, more by upsetting the people than by power and force of arms, and at about two hours in the afternoon began to make a show of attacking the city of Paris . . . and at that hour there were in Paris confused and corrupted men who raised their voice in all parts of the city on both sides of the bridges, crying that everything was lost, that the enemies were inside Paris, and that everyone should withdraw and make every effort to save himself.

A significant portion of the population must have hoped that the king of France would enter the city; these movements of panic reveal the Parisians' indecision. Between the Saint-Honoré Gate and the Saint-Denis Gate, the attack was pressed in a lively fashion, according to Cagny:

> The Maid took her standard in hand and with the first troops entered the ditches toward the swine market. The assault was hard and long, and it was wondrous to hear the noise and the explosion of the cannons and the culverines that those inside the city fired against those outside, and all manner of blows in such great abundance that they were beyond being counted. The assault lasted from about the hour of midday until about the hour of nightfall. After the sun had set, the Maid was hit by a crossbow bolt in her thigh. After she had been hit, she insisted even more strenuously that everyone should approach the walls so that the place would be taken; but because it was night and she was wounded and the men-at-arms were weary from the day-long assault, the lord of Gaucourt and others came to the Maid and against her will carried her out of the ditch, and so the assault ended.

They took Joan to the camp of La Chapelle, where she had prayed and rested part of the previous night. The following day, despite her wound, she went to find the duke of Alençon, but "the duke of Bar and the duke of Clermont arrived from the king" with the royal order to retreat. The duke of Alençon had built a bridge in hopes of resuming the offensive; the king forced him to destroy it during the night.

Then, staying at Saint-Denis until Tuesday, September 13, Charles gave the order to "return to the banks of the Loire, to the great displeasure of the Maid." More than ever, according to Poton de Xaintrailles (II, 44), those "sitting in the council of the court had won out over those performing exploits in the field."

Before withdrawing, Joan went to the basilica of Saint-Denis, where as a votive offering she hung "an entire suit of white armor, of the sort for a man-at-arms, with a sword won before the city of Paris"—the sword of a prisoner Joan had captured in the assault (III, 6).

Joan "feared nothing but treason," and treason was everywhere in the aftermath of the coronation. The Berry Herald reports that during her stay at Compiègne, even before the attack on Paris, the king had received John of Luxembourg, "who made many promises of peace between the king and the duke of Burgundy, about which he did nothing besides deceive the king." Duke Philip the Good sent Charles-Pierre de Bauffremont, of Charny, to convey the message to the king "that he would give him Paris . . . and that he would come to Paris to speak to his partisans; for that reason, he needed a safe-conduct. And the aforesaid duke was granted a safe-conduct from the king, but when he came up to Paris, the duke of Bedford and he made a stronger alliance than the one he had made previously with the king."

Even before Charles VII returned to Gien on September 21, Joan realized that the great army of the coronation, unified by a common hope, was drifting apart. The very moment of triumph—the anointing at Reims—marked an inversion of the political situation: Charles, now established as king, intended to direct his own policy. This policy slighted "exploits in the field" and remained fixed on possible reconciliation with the duke of Burgundy, no doubt in an effort to efface the memory of Montereau, where John the Fearless had died. As Perceval de Cagny judged, "He was content at that hour with the grace that God had given him, without the need to undertake anything else." Yet an awareness that Charles could be perceived as deceiving the mass of his subjects, now won to his cause, penetrates the circular letter sent out from the royal chancery under the date of September 13. The copy sent to the citizens of Reims is the only one that has survived. The king tried to reassure his subjects. He was going to "make an inspection tour beyond the banks of the Seine," but only because a truce had been concluded with the duke of Burgundy, and he was preparing the peace; if he leads his army away, he says it is because leaving the army longer in the field "would have caused the total destruction of our country on this side of the Loire." The king wished his subjects to be reassured: If the duke of Burgundy does not hold to his promises, the king will return "with a great army."

What was then possible? The Berry Herald writes: "With the king at Gien, the duke of Alençon wished to bring the Maid and the men-at-arms to Normandy, but the lord of La Trémoïlle did not agree." The chronicler of the duke of Aléncon adds: "And the Maid remained much annoyed at the king for leaving." Joan would never see her "fair duke" again: "[the counselors] never wished to agree," says Perceval de Cagny, "nor to allow the Maid and the duke to be together, and thereafter he never regained her company."

Charles VII was well described by the Burgundian chronicler Georges Chastellain, who sketched unforgettable portraits of the principal figures of his time: To Charles, he attributed three vices: "changeability, defiance, and above all, envy." And he added: "There were frequent and diverse changes all around his person, for it was his habit . . . when one had been raised high in his company even to the summit of the wheel, that then he began to be annoyed with him, and at the first occasion that could provide some sort of justification, he willfully reversed that person from high to low."

This was the experience of all who were close to Charles VII; it was so public that rebellions seethed around him. The duke of Aléncon, whom he separated from Joan for fear of what their joint enthusiasm might produce, would one day come to ally himself with the English. The wise and faithful Dunois (II, 16) would join one of the later revolts of the nobility. The king's conduct even toward his own son was capricious: Every time that the dauphin Louis (the future Louis XI) won a victory, Charles would recall him to court immediately in order to neutralize his power.

For the moment, Charles went in rapid succession to Selles-en-Berry and then to Montargis, savoring his victories and receiving the homage of his subjects; he did the same at Loches, Vierzon, Jargeau, and Issoudun before settling down around November 15 in one of his favorite residences, the castle of Mehun-sur-Yèvre.

Joan, in the meantime, had been entrusted to the lord of Albret, the half brother of La Trémoïlle, lieutenant general of the king in Berry. He brought her first of all to Bourges, where she rested for three weeks at the house of René de Bouligny, the king's general counselor for finance. His wife, Marguerite La Touroulde, later recalled Joan's stay and her conversations, and even her bursts of laughter when she was asked to hallow rosaries or other devotional objects: "Touch them yourselves," she said to Marguerite; "your touch will do as much good as mine!" Marguerite attested not only to Joan's piety—she had gone more than once with her to mass and to matins—but also to her purity and her behavior in general. The two women often went together to the baths and to the sweating rooms; at night they shared a bed. A little before her departure, Joan met with a "clairvoyant," Catherine de La Rochelle (II, 37), who had been sent by the same Friar Richard (II, 35) whom Joan had met during the siege of Troyes. Catherine claimed that every night a White Lady covered in gold appeared to her ordering her to go to the king to tell him that she would discover hidden treasures, thanks to which he could afford armed men for his future combats.

Joan received this visionary at Montfaucon-en-Berry (later renamed Ville-quiers), some distance from Bourges, near Baugy. She kept vigil with Catherine for two nights in a row without seeing the White Lady. Joan then advised Catherine "to return to her husband, to run her household, and to nourish her children" and wrote to the king that she thought "the business of this Catherine is nothing but folly."

One idea, probably La Trémoïlle's, was advanced to keep Joan usefully occupied but removed from any possible interference with royal negotiations. In that era of insecurity, bandit chieftains had been able to establish themselves in castles or donjons, holding merchant and warrior alike for ransom and sowing terror among the populace. One of them, Perrinet Gressart (II, 21), was already famous in the center of France. Installed at La Charité-sur-Loire, he sold his services now to the duke to Burgundy, now to Bedford, who knew how to control Perrinet by showering him with favors and money. La Trémoïlle was held prisoner by Perrinet and freed himself only by paying a heavy ransom of 14,000 écus "of good weight." Increasingly committed to act as an agent of the English cause, Perrinet proceeded to fortify new strongholds in the Nivernais. Besides La Charité, he held Saint-Pierre-le-Moûtier, Dompierre-sur-Besbre, and La-Motte-Josserand, of which he called himself seigneur. His position eventually made him a source of concern to the Burgundians as well as to the French.

Although attacking such a person was not what Joan considered her mission—she would have preferred to pursue the invaders in the direction of the Ile-de-France or Normandy, so as to dislodge them for good—she accepted this lesser assignment. She was accompanied by her steward Jean d'Aulon and by men-at-arms granted to her by the court. Following the advice of the royal council, she prepared to invade the stronghold of Saint-Pierre-le-Moûtier; halfway between Nevers and Moulins, in the hands of mercenaries, it had become a dangerous way station. The siege of Saint-Pierre-le-Moûtier proved difficult. The expedition was under the command of Albret, with Marshal Boussac and the count of Montpensier; the royal army's assault was repulsed. The retreat was already under way when Jean d'Aulon saw the Maid

surrounded by a very small group of her men and a few others. Riding toward her, he asked what she was doing alone and why she did not withdraw like the others. She removed her sallet [flat-topped helmet] from her head and answered that she was not alone and that she still had in her company fifty thousand of her men and that she would not depart from there until she had taken the city. At that time, despite what she said, she did not have with her more than four or five men. . . . I said to her directly that she should leave and retire as the others had done; and then she said that I should bring some bundles of sticks and wicker hurdles to make a bridge over the town moat so that they could approach better.

Having just given me that instruction, she cried out in a loud voice: "To the bundles and the hurdles, everybody, make the bridge!"—which was prepared swiftly and then accomplished. I was entirely amazed, for the city was taken all at once by her assault, without finding therein very much resistance.

This occurred in November of 1429. The town was taken and Joan's troops headed north to attempt the siege of Perrinet Gressart's capital, La Charité-sur-Loire. Winter came early that year, and the small force had nearly exhausted its munitions at Saint-Pierre-le-Moûtier. Joan sent two letters from Moulins to the cities of Clermont and Riom, demanding their assistance in obtaining "the necessities of war," such as powder, saltpeter, sulfur, and crossbow bolts. A letter addressed to the citizens of Clermont is known only from its mention in the register of the town, which hastened to respond with two quintals of saltpeter and two cases of bolts. The people of Riom sent money, which arrived too late; however, they preserved the original of Joan's letter, dated November 9. Unlike any previous letters, this one carried the signature Jehanne, written in an awkward fashion (five downstrokes instead of four to form the double n). This is plausible evidence that Joan had learned to sign her name and perhaps to read and to write.

The siege of La Charité, begun on November 14, was unsuccessful. "In the hardest part of winter and with few men at La Charité to besiege it . . . [after] about one month they had to lift the siege shamefully, even without any relief having come to the aid of the besieged, and they even lost their bombards and artillery," the Berry Herald wrote. Another witness, Perceval de Cagny, added an important comment: "Because the king did not raise funds to send her either supplies or money to maintain her company, [Joan] had to raise the siege and withdraw in great displeasure."

Joan, at Jargeau for Christmas, was not likely to find consolation in the letters conferring nobility that the king sent her at the end of December at Mehun-sur-Yèvre:

> Wishing to give thanks for the multiple and striking benefits of divine grandeur that have been accorded us through the agency of the Maid, Jeanne d'Ay de Domrémy . . . considering also the praiseworthy, graceful, and useful services already rendered by the aforesaid Joan the Maid in every way, to us and to our kingdom, which we hope to pursue in the future. . . .

The king proceeded to ennoble her parents and her brothers; he went so far as to grant the special favor that, for Joan and her family, nobility would be transmitted not only in the male line, which was customary since the reign of King Philip the Fair (1285–1314), but in the female line as well (III, 2). Charles

VII, baring his administrative soul, acted like a minister of state granting a decoration to a functionary he is about to send into retirement.

A somber winter was setting in for Joan. She probably spent the greater part of it at Sully-sur-Loire, in the castle belonging to the family of La Trémoïlle. On January 19, she was invited to a banquet by the city council of Orléans. Among the guests was the man into whose house she had been welcomed at Poitiers, Jean Rabateau, the procurer general of the royal treasury, the Chambre des Comptes. The municipal registers attest that at least one of Joan's brothers, who had been with her on all of her campaigns, was invited also. Another event during that winter was the marriage of the daughter of Hauves Poulnoir the painter, who had made Joan's standard. At the end of January 1430, Joan wrote to the treasurer of the city of Tours, requesting the sum of 100 écus to permit the bride-to-be to buy her trousseau. The city council, however, offered only to pay for the wedding party's bread and wine, which amounted to 4 livres and 10 sous.

Another wedding, but one in high pomp, was celebrated at Bruges. Duke Philip the Good, at the peak of his glory, married Isabelle of Portugal (II, 24) on January 8, 1430. In the midst of these festivities marked by extreme luxury, he created the Order of the Golden Fleece, a chivalric order for the Burgundian nobility, and thus gathered knights around him on the model of the Arthurian Round Table. Philip named Hugues de Lannoy, the man who prepared a military campaign that would soon be launched against the king of France, as his negotiator during the truces concluded with Charles VII.

On February 15 Charles VII left Mehun-sur-Yèvre for Sully-sur-Loire, where Joan rejoined him at the beginning of March. The optimism with which the king concluded the truces crushed the élan of the royal army, which began to show signs of discontent. The attitude of the duke of Burgundy was more than provocative. He consistently postponed the commencement of the peace conference that was supposed to be the goal of the truces, all the while demanding that the cities of the Oise, promised him as a guarantee, be handed over without delay; at the same time, he did not hesitate to launch an offensive in Champagne. Yet the activity of royalist "partisans" was seen everywhere. Popular uprisings chased the Burgundian garrison from Saint-Denis and the English troops from Melun. In Paris a broad-based conspiracy of popular bourgeois factions plotted during March: Clerks, artisans, and merchants, led by a certain Jacques Perdriel, were assisted by the monks of the Carmelite convent, where they assembled disguised as plowmen. The arrest of one of them, Friar d'Allée, aborted the uprising. Under torture, he gave the names of fellow plotters. There were more than 150 arrests and 6 public executions in Paris on April 8; others were thrown into the Seine, and some managed to avoid death by paying a ransom.

The resistance was more lively in Compiègne. In executing the truces, the count of Clermont had arrived with the king's demand that the inhabitants surrender to the duke of Burgundy because their city was part, along with Creil and Pont-Sainte-Maxence, of the truce guarantees. But the people of Compiègne vehemently refused to obey; the captain of the French garrison, Guillaume de Flavy, put the fortifications in a state of readiness. Charles de Bourbon was able only to protest to the duke of Burgundy that he could not force the city to obey. The inhabitants had made their choice and were "resolute to undergo every risk for themselves, their children, and their infants, rather than be exposed to the mercy of the duke."

Joan used the month of March 1430 to prepare for war. She knew, as she had declared to Catherine de La Rochelle, that there would be no fair reckoning from the enemy "except at lance point." During March she wrote two letters to the inhabitants of Reims, who sensed their increasing danger: "Very dear and well beloved friends whom I wish greatly to see again, Joan the Maid has received your letters, which mention that you fear that you will be besieged." Without naming the enemies everyone had clearly in mind, she added: "Know well that you should not be at all distressed if I can confront them. If they come near, shut your gates, for I will be very direct with you: if they come there, I will make them fasten their spurs so fast that they will not know how to put them on and get out of there, and very quickly at that. I will write you nothing more at present, but pray remain good and loyal. I pray God to keep you safe."

This letter, very much in her style, is dated March 16. On the twenty-eighth, Joan dictated another. Between those two dates, the king's court had learned that a plot was developing in Reims among citizens who wanted to surrender to the duke of Burgundy: "Very dear and good friends, it has been reported to the king that in the good city of Reims there are also many wicked people," but she said that the king knew the great majority of Reims were faithful to him: "Believe that you are well in his grace, and if you have to fight, he would assist you in the event of any siege; and he knows very well that you would have much to suffer because of the hardships that these treasonous Burgundian adversaries have imposed on you." Both of these letters carry her signature; on the originals, which have been preserved, her signature is now handsome and firmly written.

There is, however, no signature on the text of another recently discovered letter addressed to the Hussites of Bohemia in Joan's name by her chaplain, Jean Pasquerel (appendix I, letter 16). This letter, in Latin, is in line with the rapprochement that Charles VII was working toward with the German emperor Sigismund and with Frederick IV, duke of Austria. Disciples of Jan Hus, the Hussites were part of a religious movement with political repercussions, which the emperor had been trying to control by force for ten years. He had sought papal approval for a crusade against them; troops raised in England, thanks to the subsidies approved for that crusade, had been deflected once they arrived at Calais by Cardinal Henry Beaufort, the bishop of Winchester (II, 8). The French king was now trying to shore up alliances to the east.

In contrast, Philip the Good was not content with a merely diplomatic offensive. On April 4, 1430, he was at Péronne, where he had given orders for a rendezvous with all available troops. His vanguard marched under the command of John of Luxembourg. On the twenty-second, the duke himself left "with his entire force." By April 23 Bedford was at Calais awaiting the arrival of the young English King Henry VI (II, 2), who had been crowned at Westminster on November 6, 1429. Henry soon landed with 200 men and "a great supply of livestock and other foodstuffs." The duke of Bedford encountered difficulties in recruiting this contingent. On two occasions, as he claimed in one of his letters, he delivered personal threats and sent instructions drafting men who refused to go to France "through fear of the devices of the Maid."

The planning of this Anglo-Burgundian operation had been carefully coordinated. Philip the Good wanted above all to take possession of the cities that commanded the crossings of the river Oise, especially those that had refused his dominion, such as Creil and Compiègne. Bedford supported this goal in order to protect the Ile-de-France and, most specifically, Paris, "heart and principal head of the kingdom." The duke of Burgundy began operations in May. By the sixth he was at Noyon; the fortress of Gourney-sur-Aronde, to the north of Compiègne, had surrendered without a blow. He then attacked Choisy-au-Bac, which commanded an important passage across the Aisne; he personally accomplished that the following day.

It was not until May 6 that Charles VII acknowledged his error and admitted that he had been duped by his cousin of Burgundy. The chancellor, Regnault of Chartres, relates: "After he [the duke of Burgundy] had amused himself and deceived us for a certain time through truces and otherwise, under the pretense of good faith, for he affirmed that he wished to come and to make peace for the relief of our poor people, who, to the displeasure of our heart, have already suffered and now suffer every day the fact of war . . . he set himself with certain forces to make war against us, our country, and our loyal subjects."

But while the duke of Burgundy was setting in motion a carefully conceived battle plan and could count on the reinforcement of the English army, Charles VII had prepared nothing. His greatest resource was Joan the Maid, whom he had deprived of any effective means of action. It is nevertheless true that the news of her activity spread rapidly, producing panic in the Ile-de-France: "There was a great voice and a great noise at Paris and other places hostile to the king about her coming," writes Perceval de Cagny. According to Perceval, at the end of March or early in April Joan left Sully-sur-Loire with a small company of volunteers composed of the troops of the mercenary Barthélemy Baretta as well as some 200 men from the Italian Piedmont. The chronicler maintains that they departed without the king's knowledge and that Joan, without taking his leave, intended to "go disport herself" at war and, without returning to Reims, proceeded to Lagny-sur-Marne.

This implausible scenario may be one of Perceval de Cagny's habitual exaggerations, since it seems more likely that the king and his counselors let Joan take her own risks now. In the Battle of Orléans she had been a major military commander, but now at her departure from Sully she commanded only a small band. Her steward Jean d'Aulon and her brother Pierre accompanied her, but she no longer had a military household, pages, or, above all, the heralds who in some sense made a mission official. She was more of a captain, like many who recruited paid troops.

Joan headed for the Ile-de-France. She was at Melun, according to her own testimony, during Easter, which fell that year during the week of April 22. The city must have been sympathetic to her: She had just recently driven away the English garrison. From there Joan went to Lagny. In his *Chronicle*, Enguerrand de Monstrelet affirms that "the men of that place waged good war against the English of Paris and elsewhere"—along with captains Jean Foucault, Geoffroy de Saint-Aubin, and "Canede," Hugh Kennedy, a Scotsman.

She then clashed with a band of Anglo-Burgundians commanded by a famous mercenary, Franquet d'Arras, whose companions were put to flight; Franquet himself was taken prisoner. He was claimed by the bailiff of Senlis, who intended to prosecute him for what we would now call war crimes against humanity. Instead Joan wanted to keep him and possibly exchange him for her partisan, Jacquet Guillaume, who had been captured in the plot recently hatched at Paris—which shows that she was kept up-to-date on the acts and intentions of the Armagnacs in the capital. When she learned of the death of Jacquet Guillaume, who probably was condemned and executed along with the rest of his companions, she surrendered Franquet d'Arras to justice in Senlis. After a trial of fifteen days, he met an end appropriate, in the public's eyes, for such a mercenary: He was sentenced to death as "a murderer, a thief, and a traitor."

One day in Lagny a family begged Joan to aid a newborn baby on the point of death who had not yet been baptized. The child had seemed dead for three days; "he was as black as my coat of mail," Joan later declared. "I was with the girls on my knees before Our Lady to pray," she said, when the infant suddenly awoke. He yawned three times, received baptism, died, and was buried in Christian earth.

Every inch of Joan's journey can be tracked up to Senlis, where she arrived on April 24. The record goes blank until May 14, when the city authorities of Compiègne offered her a reception. Two other important individuals also attended: Regnault of Chartres, the archbishop of Reims, and Louis de Bourbon, the count of Vendôme. Joan took part in a maneuver designed to assist Choisy-au-Bac, which was under the command of Louis de Flavy, the brother of Guillaume de Flavy, who was defender of Compiègne. Later, a surprise attack on Pont-l'Évêque was rebuffed due to the intervention of a Burgundian lord, Jean de Brimeu, to whom the duke of Burgundy had entrusted the command of the city of Noyon. Some days later, in the course of an ambush, Brimeu was taken prisoner by Poton de Xaintrailles. The troops at Choisy nevertheless were forced to surrender to the powerful artillery of the duke of Burgundy. On May 16, Louis de Flavy and his men abandoned Choisy and took refuge in Compiègne.

Two days later, Joan, with Regnault of Chartres and the count of Vendôme, left Compiègne heading toward Soissons in an attempt to cross the Aisne River and surprise the Burgundians from the rear on the heights of Choisy. Although the captain of Soissons, Guichard Bournel, allowed the Maid and the two great lords to enter his city, he refused entry to her men-at-arms, alleging that the inhabitants had no wish to entertain soldiers. The following day, says the Berry Herald, "the aforesaid lords left Senlis and the aforesaid Maid went to Compiègne, and, unhappy that they had abandoned Soissons, Guichard sold the city to the duke of Burgundy and put it in the hand of my lord John of Luxembourg: which he did foully and against his honor."

When she returned to Compiègne from Crépy-en-Valois, Joan and the reduced force that then accompanied her—300 to 400 combatants—traveled through the night across the forest and entered the city by the Pierrefonds Gate "at a secret hour of the morning." On the following day she prepared a surprise operation with Guillaume de Flavy against one of the Burgundian posts called Margny, which was installed along the valley of Oise to the north of the city and commanded by Baudot de Noyelles. The Burgundian chronicler Chastellain, who was not present at those events but who was nonetheless well informed about them, describes Joan at that point and provides the final image of her as warrior:

> She mounted her horse armed as would a man, adorned with a doublet of rich cloth-of-gold over her breastplate; she rode a very handsome, very proud gray courser and displayed herself in her armor and her bearing as a captain would have done . . . and in that array, with her standard raised high and fluttering in the wind, and well-accompanied by many noble men, she sallied forth from the city, about four hours past midday.

The attack failed to attain its objective. At Margny, the defenders were dispersed but managed to reassemble, though not without losses, while John of Luxembourg and the lord of Créqui, who were riding about to inspect the terrain, took warning from the tumult and alerted their troops, who were lying in ambush at Clairoix; "by force of spurs" they reached the scene of battle. "The noise that arose all about and the great din of the voices crying out caused men to gather from all sides and more assistance flowed toward the Burgundians than they needed." The alarm was sounded as near as Venette, where English troops had come to reinforce those with the duke of Burgundy, and as far as Coudun, where the duke himself then marched toward Margny.

Joan declared later that she had twice driven the enemy from their positions and that she had a third time forced them into the middle of the battlefield. Nevertheless, seeing the reinforcements arriving from Venette and Clairoix, the French began to withdraw toward Compiègne. Fearing that they would be overwhelmed, many of them rushed onto the bridge of boats that Guillaume de Flavy had strung out across the Oise, and Joan, who never withdrew without regret, protected their retreat. Perceval de Cagny attempted to explain the strange turn of events as the battle at the foot of the bridge became furious:

> During that time, the captain of the place, seeing the great multitude of Burgundians and Englishmen ready to get on the bridge, out of fear that he would lose his position, raised the drawbridge of the city and closed the gate. So the Maid remained outside and only a few of her men were with her.

Other details are etched in Chastellain's description of Joan fighting with her back to the wall:

> The Maid, going beyond the nature of womankind, performed a great feat and took much pain to save her company from loss, staying behind like a chief and like the most valiant member of the flock. . . . An archer, a stiff and very harsh man, angry that a woman of whom one had heard so much should have surpassed so many valiant men . . . laid hold of her from the side by her cloth-of-gold doublet and pulled her from her horse flat upon the ground.

This version of the events at Compiègne is suspicious (III, 10), since it was not the main gate of the city that had been closed but a gate in the curtain wall, which was not vital to the defense of the city proper and which prematurely cut off the combatants' retreat. This is why—though reasonable skepticism persists—some believe that Joan's fear of betrayal was fulfilled.

Chastellain's report replicates what Jean Glénisson has called "the ritual of surrender in fifteenth-century warfare." In the midst of enemies who pressed her and demanded, each competing with the others, "Surrender to me and tender faith" (give me your promise), Joan cried out, "I have sworn and tendered faith to another than you, and I shall keep my oath." The archer who pulled her by her doublet threw her to the earth just as Lionel, the Bastard of Wandomme (II, 42), presented himself to receive her "faith." The Bastard was a lieutenant of John of Luxembourg, whose prisoner she officially became. Wandomme was not the only one who hastened to witness her capture: "The Bastard, more joyous," Monstrelet tells us, "than if he had held a king within his hand, swiftly brought her to Margny and kept her under guard until the end of the engagement." Not far from there, at Coudun, was Philip the Good, who hurried, having been alerted by the "great cries and lively noise caused by the capture of the Maid." The Burgundian chronicler Enguerrand de Monstrelet claimed "not [to] remember very well, although [he] was present there" what Philip the Good actually said to Joan, or what she said to him at this memorable moment. Monstrelet, chronicler of the House of Luxembourg, frequently glides over matters that might not reflect glory on that famous family. There are some notable gaps in his account. Not only does he not mention the sale of Joan to the English, but he also suppresses references to her trial, although he does quote the king of England's letter to prelates and princes announcing the sentence of guilt and Joan's execution. Monstrelet ends his often sharply detailed recollection with this curious spurt of amnesia:

> The Burgundian and English partisans were very joyous, more than if they had taken five hundred combatants, for they did not fear or dread either captains or any other war chief as much they had up to that day this maid. . . . The duke went to see her in the residence where she was held and said some words that I do not remember very well, although I was present there.

Joan was to be a prisoner for the remaining year of her life.

CHAPTER SIX

JOAN
THE PRISONER

Taken prisoner at Compiègne on May 23, 1430, Joan did not reach Rouen, the place appointed for her trial, until Christmas Eve of that year. The seven intervening months were filled with negotiations concerning her ransom, which turned into a sale price—anything but a ransom—of 10,000 pounds paid by the English crown. The primary agent of that negotiation was Pierre Cauchon, formerly rector of the University of Paris and bishop of Beauvais (see Part II, Section 49)—and hence an exile, since Beauvais had welcomed Charles VII (II, 1). Single-minded and tireless, Cauchon arranged to have himself appointed chief judge of Joan's ecclesiastical trial. Charles VII made no effort to ransom or free Joan. Hostile as they must have been to her, her captor, John of Luxembourg (II, 28), and his lord, Duke Philip of Burgundy (II, 3), seem to have hesitated to hand Joan over to the English and the Paris university faction: the influence of three ladies named Joan with whom Joan spent over three months in the fortress of Beaurevoir (and perhaps also that of the Duchess Isabelle of Burgundy [II, 24]) may account for the delay. Joan tried several times to escape but was chided by her 'voices' for those efforts.

Easter week had just passed when I found myself in the moat at Melun, and my voices, that is the voices of Sts. Catherine and Margaret, told me that I would be captured before St. John's Day, that it had to be so, that I should not be amazed thereat but that I should take it favorably and that God would aid me.

BETWEEN APRIL 17 AND 22, 1430, Joan learned she would become a prisoner before St. John's Day (June 24). From the trial records, we know what that revelation was about and how much it cost her to accept what "her voices told her":

> "From that place at Melun, was it not said to you by your voices that you would be taken?"
>
> "Yes, often and almost every day, and I asked my voices [if, when I was taken, I might die quickly], without long torment in prison, and my voices said that I should take it all well and that it was necessary that it be so; but they did not tell me the hour, and if I had known the hour, I would not have gone there. I had asked my voices many times to know the hour of my capture, but they would not tell me."
>
> "If your voices had ordered you to sally forth from Compiègne, telling you that you would be captured, what would you have done?"
>
> "If I had known the hour and that I should be captured, I would not have gone willingly. Just the same, I would have obeyed the command of the voices, whatever was to happen."
>
> "When you left Compiègne, had you received a voice or a revelation to leave and make that sortie?"
>
> "I did not know that I would be taken that day, and I had no other command to make the sortie, but it was always said to me that it was necessary that I become a prisoner."

What Joan's capture represented for her contemporaries is shown in three letters. The first, in a circular letter from the duke of Burgundy (II, 3), expressed his exultation announcing Joan's capture to the "good cities" of his realm, a theme he developed in a message to the duke of Savoy:

> By the pleasure of our blessed Creator, the woman called the Maid has been taken; and from her capture will be recognized the error and mad belief of all those who became sympathetic and favorable to the deeds of this woman . . . and we write you this news hoping that you will have joy and consolation in it and that you will render homage to our Creator, who through His blessed pleasure has wished to conduct the rest of our enterprises on behalf of our lord the king of England and of France and for the comfort of his good and loyal subjects.

Another letter—composed on May 26, three days after Joan's capture, which took place about six-thirty in the evening—came from the University of Paris, which probably had learned the news from criers in the streets of the capital only on the twenty-fifth, the day it was recorded on the register of Parlement.

No time had been lost. The university wrote the letter to the duke of Burgundy in the name of Jean Graverent, the Inquisitor of France (II, 53), urging that Joan be surrendered to him:

> Since all loyal Christian princes and all other true Catholics are held to the duty of extirpating all errors against the Faith and the scandal that follows such errors among the simple Christian folk, and since it is a matter of common repute that diverse errors have been sown and published in many cities, good towns, and other places of this kingdom by a certain woman named Joan, whom the adversaries of this kingdom call the Maid, . . . we beseech you with good affection, you, most mighty prince . . . that as soon as it can be done safely and conveniently, the aforesaid Joan be brought under our jurisdiction as a prisoner since she is strongly suspected of various crimes smacking of heresy, so as to appear before us and a procurator of the Holy Inquisition.

These agents of the University of Paris, leaders of the intellectual elite, needed no time to reflect on the merits of this case. As early as May 1429, they had smelled heresy in Joan's victories. Once captive, she was thought guiltier than ever of "many crimes smacking of heresy." During the whole of Joan's second year of public life, they would be the zealous and effective instruments of a vengeance whose bitterness outstripped even that of the duke of Burgundy.

A third message, from Regnault of Chartres, the archbishop of Reims (II, 13), to its inhabitants, explained that Joan had been taken prisoner at Compiègne because "she did not wish to pay attention to any counsel and did everything at her own pleasure." He retrospectively found faults in her: "She had become full of pride due to the rich garments she had begun to wear. She had not been doing what God had commanded her but her own will." The archbishop had in fact already sought out, as Joan's replacement, "a young shepherd of the mountains of the Gévaudan, whom he said to be neither more nor less than the Maid"— this was an unfortunate shepherd named Guillaume who believed himself to be inspired and would soon pay for that illusion by being drowned in the Seine.

Once more the voice of the "council of the court" triumphed over those performing "exploits of the field." Regnault of Chartres had spent time with Joan during May; it was with his aid and that of the count of Vendôme, Louis de Bourbon, that they had made the move toward Soissons that was checked by the treason of Guichard Bournel. But these two great lords had withdrawn when they learned of the surrender of Choisy-au-Bac. They had decided to return to the valley of the Marne, while Joan had, with her small troop of mercenaries from the Piedmont, turned back toward Compiègne in an effort to comfort its inhabitants and to prevent an imminent siege. The party of prudence continued to dominate the entourage of Charles VII (II, 1).

Now a prisoner of John of Luxembourg (II, 28), Joan was taken, with her brother Pierre, her steward Jean d'Aulon, and his brother Poton the Burgundian, to the fortress of Clairoix. Pierre Rocolle, author of *Jeanne prisonnière*, places the departure from Clairoix on May 26, since May 25 was the feast of the Ascension and therefore a day of truce. On May 26th, new positions were taken by the Burgundians around Compiègne: Philip the Good (II, 3) wanted to establish his headquarters at the abbey of Saint-Corneille. John of Luxembourg set up his headquarters at Margny. He had decided to sequester his prisoner, for whom he expected a heavy ransom, in the castle of Beaulieu-lès-Fontaines, which he had taken early in 1430; its castellan was to be Lionel de Wandomme (II, 42). Joan, with Jean d'Aulon and her brother Pierre, was transferred to Beaulieu, to the north of Noyon. Tradition has it that she stopped in the course of that twenty-five-mile route at the castle of Beauvoir, near the village of Elincourt, where there was a priory dedicated to St. Margaret; while there, she received permission to go and kneel in veneration of the one whose voice she said she heard.

Today at Beaulieu, visitors can see the underground rooms that in the fifteenth century constituted the basement quarters of the tower in which Joan was briefly lodged. On June 6, Philip the Good arrived at Noyon with his wife, Isabelle of Portugal (II, 24), who had asked to see the prisoner. Joan was brought into the presence of the duke and duchess in the elegant setting of the episcopal palace near the cathedral. The bishop of Noyon, Jean de Mailly (II, 61), had rallied to the Burgundian cause. Although no report of the exchange between the two women survives, Pierre Rocolle argues that Isabelle was sympathetic to Joan. It is possible that the young duchess influenced the choice of a more suitable residence for the prisoner, the castle of Beaurevoir, a larger and more inhabited site rather than a mere fortress made especially dangerous for a woman by the comings and goings of soldiers.

The stay at Beaulieu-lès-Fontaines was marked by Joan's first attempt to escape. This probably took place after she had returned from Noyon; the prisoner learned that she was going to be transferred to a much more distant site and also separated from her steward and her brother. At her trial, an attempted escape "between two pieces of wood" is mentioned. She said: "I was in the castle and I shut my guard in the tower; if only the porter had not seen me and stopped me!" She may have hoped to liberate her two companions once her guard was shut up in the tower, but the effort failed, and her transfer to Beaurevoir probably took place in the first fortnight of June 1430.

No contemporary chronicler has left an account of the second meeting at Noyon between Joan and the duke of Burgundy, accompanied by the duchess, although it is known that John of Luxembourg and his wife, Joan of Béthune, were there as well. On June 22, the University of Paris wrote once again to the duke of Burgundy to demand that he deliver the prisoner into its jurisdiction. This time the university was represented by someone who would become well known to Joan: the bishop of Beauvais, Pierre Cauchon (II, 49), who was then in exile from his diocese since Beauvais had gone over to the side of the French.

Pierre Cauchon was at Calais on May 26, the day the news of Joan's capture arrived. Since he was one of the counselors and intimates of the duke of Bedford (II, 9), plans were doubtless afoot for the prisoner to be handed over as quickly as possible both to the English and the members of the university, but Philip the Good was in no hurry to accede to this request. His attitude contrasts with the joy that he had shown when Joan was brought to him after her capture: It may be that the two ladies with him at Noyon influenced him to consider showing clemency. Later, Joan herself would bear witness to the sympathy the wife of John of Luxembourg had shown her when they met again at the castle of Beaurevoir.

The stages of Joan's thirty-seven-mile journey from Beaulieu-lès-Fontaines to Beaurevoir can be reconstructed with some precision. It is likely that she paused at the castle of Ham (where much later another famous prisoner, the future Napoleon III, would be held). She must then have passed by Saint-Quentin and may well have seen its admirable collegial church.

Nothing remains of the castle of Beaurevoir aside from one tower and fragments of its walls. In Joan's time it was a mighty fortress that had belonged to the domains of the family of Luxembourg since 1270, when Joan of Beaurevoir had married Waleran I of Luxembourg and thus founded that famous lineage. The great-great-grandson of Waleran I, Guy of Luxembourg, had four children, one of whom, Joan of Luxembourg (II, 27), born in 1363, played a role in the remaining story of Joan of Arc. Her brother, John II, had three children, Peter, Louis (II, 29), and John III of Luxembourg, who held Joan as his official prisoner. John III had married Joan of Béthune, who by a first marriage had a daughter named Joan of Bar—her father was Robert of Bar, who had been killed at Agincourt.

Joan of Arc was imprisoned in the tower of the keep of Beaurevoir, where lived three other Joans: Joan of Bar, Joan of Béthune, and Joan of Luxembourg, aunt of the John on whom the prisoner's fortune depended. She was there, according to her own testimony, for about four months. The hardship of her captivity was evidently somewhat alleviated by these three other Joans. As her trial testimony later affirms, they offered her women's clothes or the material to make some, and Joan allowed that: "I would have dressed in women's clothes more willingly at the request of these women than of any other woman who might be in France, except for my queen." On a graver matter, she said: "The lady of Luxembourg asked my lord of Luxembourg that I not be delivered to the English."

The attitude of the "three Joans," much more than that of John of Luxembourg, was dictated by a careful recognition of the issues that were forcing them to choose between the conqueror and their conquered country. John of Luxembourg was a vassal of Philip the Good, duke of Burgundy, and his conduct was dictated by his fealty to his lord. Philip had showered honors upon him, awarding him one of the original twenty-four collars at the foundation of the Order of the Golden Fleece on June 7, 1430. John had sworn fealty to Philip and could expect reprisals should he not conform. The ladies of Beaurevoir had the luxury of freer judgment. John's wife was the widow of one of those French knights who had fallen at Agincourt fighting Henry V. His aunt was a lady-in-waiting to Isabeau of Bavaria, queen of France (II, 23), and stood as a godmother to Charles VII (II, 1) when he was born in 1403.

John of Luxembourg might well have found himself in a state of indecision during the month of August 1430: He had solid reasons to displease neither his lord nor his aunt. While Joan of Arc was imprisoned at Beaurevoir, the lady of Luxembourg—by then "very ancient," in Enguerrand de Monstrelet's view (she was sixty-seven)—herself went to receive the inheritance of her great-nephew Philip of Brabant, who had died at Louvain on August 4, 1430. The counties of Saint-Pôl and of Ligny, the lordships that had belonged to her brother Waleran, then came to her in the absence of any other successor. Monstrelet reports that the lady of Luxembourg either made a will or promised to make one in favor of John: "Inasmuch as she loved her nephew John of Luxembourg well, she gave him a great part of her lordship after her passing; his elder brother, the lord of Enghien, was most displeased by this"—John of Luxembourg's brother Peter was apparently not in their aunt Joan's good graces.

There was intense activity all around Beaurevoir, although not among the French royal entourage at Bourges, where one might most expect it. In contrast, the University of Paris expended energy in its fear that the king of France would try to rescue Joan and so deprive it of the opportunity it had been demanding ever since the liberation of Orléans. Pierre Cauchon, former rector of the university and now bishop of Beauvais thanks to the duke of Burgundy, was on the road from one negotiation to the next all that summer of 1430.

Joan was to remain in the fortress of Beaurevoir until the end of November 1430. In the meantime the English agitated to have the prisoner handed over to them. Cauchon was particularly apt at handling these negotiations. In 1430 he was about sixty years of age, and he had had a brilliant career both as a diplomat and as a university man. He had been rector of the University of Paris as early as 1403, and he had played a leading role throughout the troubles as a result of which the university had taken the Burgundian side against the Armagnacs. In 1419, when the theory of the double monarchy, which placed the two kingdoms of France and England under the single crown of England, was being worked out at the university, Cauchon was conservator of the university privileges. He was one of the negotiators appointed for the Treaty of Troyes, and immediately thereafter, on August 21, 1420, he was made bishop of Beauvais. In 1424 he received the capitulation of the town of Vitry on behalf of the king of England; the town had succumbed despite the defense put up by La Hire (II, 22), one of the captains who was to find himself fighting at Joan's side five years later. It is not difficult to imagine what Cauchon must have felt about the year 1429, in which he had been forced to flee first from Reims, where he was living just before the coronation and where he had conducted the *Fête-Dieu* ceremonies, then from Beauvais when that town opened its gates to Charles VII. The negotiations entrusted to him would enable him both to avenge himself for that double humiliation and to vindicate political theories dear to the heart of the faculty of the University of Paris, and which he maintained throughout his life. Checked in his progress by Joan's dazzling campaign and by the sacring of Charles VII at Reims, Cauchon's favored double-monarchy theory might recover all its prestige if it could be shown that Joan, an instrument of the French cause, was nothing but a despicable heretic and a witch. There was another and still-secret stimulus to his activity as a negotiator: the archbishopric of Rouen had recently fallen vacant, and he, driven out of his own diocese, had hopes of obtaining the preferment as a reward for his good offices.

Cauchon spent June in Paris, from which he sent the university's letter to Philip the Good and John of Luxembourg quoted earlier, begging them "to see that this woman is given to the reverend father in God, my lord the bishop of Beauvais." Cauchon then went to Calais, where the duke of Bedford was with Henry VI (II, 2), the anointed king of England who still hoped also to be anointed king of France. The conditions for the prisoner's purchase then were set: A ransom of 6,000 pounds was to be offered, with the understanding that it might be raised as high as 10,000 pounds, following the rules of normal commercial exchange. In addition, Lionel de Wandomme, the man who had captured Joan, was granted a pension of 300 pounds. Reaching Compiègne on June 27, Cauchon again wrote to Philip the Good and to John of Luxembourg detailing new conditions, although the duke of Burgundy had still not answered his previous letters.

Cauchon left Compiègne on July 7 and on the fourteenth had a conversation first with Philip the Good and then with John of Luxembourg, who was waiting in a neighboring room for the results of the first encounter. Apparently, Cauchon was persuasive; shortly thereafter, he and Joan of Luxembourg left for Beaurevoir. We do not know the details of the conversation between the bishop and the lady of Luxembourg with the prisoner, but it seems that Cauchon did not obtain Joan's transfer to his authority at that time. On the other hand, it may be true that Cauchon's visit drove Joan of Arc to her second effort to escape.

"What was the reason you jumped from the tower of Beaurevoir?"

"I had heard that all the people of Compiègne beyond the age of seven would be subjected to fire and sword, and I preferred to die rather than to live after such a destruction of good people, and that was one of the reasons why I jumped; and the other was that I knew that I had been sold to the English, and I would have preferred to die rather than to be in the hands of the English, my enemies. . . . After I fell from the tower, I was for two or three days without desire to eat, and I was so wounded in that jump that I could neither eat nor drink; but nevertheless, I had comfort from St. Catherine, who told me to confess myself and ask pardon from God for having jumped and that without fail the people of Compiègne would have help before the feast of St. Martin in the winter. And so I began to return to health; I began to eat and soon I was healed."

Since the feast of St. Martin falls on November 11, the "leap of Beaurevoir" must have been attempted well before that date.

Military action was beginning to resume at the end of July. Cauchon returned to Rouen, where he met once more with the duke of Bedford and his nephew, the young king. While the bishop was busy raising a tax voted by the Estates of Normandy for the king of England, the duke of Burgundy decided to lay siege to Compiègne, still held by French partisans; he put John of Luxembourg in charge of that siege on August 15. But it was not a military operation that decided the fate of Joan of Arc. At the beginning of September, the lady of Luxembourg got ready to leave for Avignon. She probably had left Beaurevoir by late August, since her advanced age would have required her to travel in short stages. Upon arrival in the papal city on September 10, 1430, she drew up her will. She died on September 18. John of Luxembourg, no longer subject to his aunt's influence, now fell under the sway of his brother Louis, bishop of Thérouanne and a partisan of the English. Named archbishop of Rouen in 1436, Louis died in England as bishop of Ely in 1443.

Compiègne was to be liberated from its besiegers. On October 24, a decisive assault was made by Marshal Boussac, who had come to reinforce the pro-French garrison and citizenry. John of Luxembourg fell back on Noyon and left Compiègne "shamefully," according to Monstrelet, abandoning his bombards and artillery. On the following Saturday, October 28, the little fortresses around Compiègne surrendered to the French. John of Luxembourg returned to Beaurevoir, where thereafter his decisions would be law. Joan could find reassurance about the fate of "her good friends of Compiègne," but, ever more certain of her fate, she would declare later:

St. Catherine told me almost every day that I should not try to jump and that God would aid me and also the people of Compiègne. And I said that if God aided those of Compiègne, I myself would wish to be down there. And so St. Catherine said to me, "Without any fault you must accept this willingly and you will not be delivered until you have seen the king of the English." And I answered her, "Truly I would not like to see him; and I would rather die than be put in the hands of the English."

For 153 days "Pierre Cauchon took leave of the king, our lord, to do his business, as much in the city of Calais as in many trips to my lord the duke of Burgundy or to my lord John of Luxembourg in Flanders, to the siege before Compiègne, and at Beaurevoir in the matter of Joan called the Maid." For those services the receiver general of Normandy, Pierre Surreau, paid him the sum of 765 livres tournois. The receipt dates from the last day of September. By October 24, the day of the liberation of Compiègne, the English treasurer, Thomas Blount, had amassed the remaining 5,000 pounds that were necessary for the sale of Joan of Arc. Cauchon probably departed from the castle of Beaurevoir around that time.

Philip the Good's receiver general of finances, Jean de Pressy, may have accompanied Cauchon. His presence is mentioned several times subsequently at Arras, where Joan also appears in the records. Philip the Good arrived there on November 2; Joan arrived a week later. In Arras she received the humble parting gift that she had earlier requested from the bourgeois of Tournai, twenty-two gold crowns "to use for her necessities." Tradition alleges that a Scotsman painted her portrait in that city; but it is more likely, as Père Doncoeur argues, that "Arras" was a scribal error for Reims; the portrait (see III, 15) was most likely executed there, at the coronation.

On December 6 John of Luxembourg was paid for the transfer of Joan the Maid to the English; a receipt of Jean Bruyse, a squire, attests that he received "the 10,000 livres tournois [for] Joan, who is called the Maid, a prisoner of war." This sum was delivered to him by the Norman receiver general, Pierre Surreau. The University of Paris had done everything possible to speed up the negotiations: On November 21, it sent a letter to Pierre Cauchon: "We note with extreme amazement that the delivery of this woman popularly known as the Maid is long postponed to the prejudice of the Faith and of ecclesiastical jurisdiction."

Rumor carried news of Joan's sale far afield. A letter dated November 24, recorded in the journal of the merchant Niccolò Morosini and sent from the family firm's Bruges branch to Venice by a well-informed observer, makes this clear: "It is certain that the Maid was sent to Rouen to the king of England and in that negotiation my lord John of Luxembourg (II, 28), who had made her prisoner, was paid 10,000 crowns to deliver her to the English." Yet more directly, Morosini, who had left Bruges on December 15, wrote to Venice as recorded in his *Journal*: "One heard first that the lady had been in the hands of the duke of Burgundy, and many men said that the English would buy her for money, but at that news Charles sent them an embassy to alert them that he would never consent to such a deal; if they persisted, he would give similar treatment to those of their men whom he held hostage."

The slight tremor in a rumor of this passage is the sole piece of evidence for the suggestion that Charles VII (II, 1) made any effort on Joan's behalf. Even here there is no claim that he himself attempted to ransom Joan, but only to prevent her delivery to the enemy. No documentary evidence suggests that the king offered a ransom or made any effort whatsoever to free Joan of Arc. Although the English government was active, and spared neither time nor money, the king of France seemed stricken with complete inertia in regard to a ransom for Joan. Only the hint in Morosini's *Journal* suggests he had any interest in the matter. And in the university's letter to John of Luxembourg we read that they fear "that this woman be delivered or lost, for it is said that some of the adversaries [i.e., of the King of England] are doing all in their power to accomplish and apply to that end all their understanding by extraordinary means and what is worse by money or ransom." These are the only allusions, remote and indirect, to any effort the king of France might be making to save the girl to whom he owed his crown.

But need we be surprised? Contemporary accounts of Charles VII suggest that he was weak in character and of a changeable temperament: "There were frequent and diverse changes all around his person, for it was his habit . . . when one had been raised high in his company even to the summit of the wheel, that then he began to be annoyed with him, and, at the first occasion that could provide some sort of justification, he willfully reversed that person from high to low." The historian Georges Chastellain, to whom we owe this portrait, adds that Charles VII furthermore "savored all the fruit all he could suck" from such abusive treatment. Moreover, the king was very careful to foster his own fame at every possible opportunity: After recovering the kingdom from the English, he had innumerable medals struck on which he is called "Charles the Victorious." It may be, after all, that contrary to all expectations, once he had received that crown and sacring that made him king of France, he was not sorry to see Joan—to whom he owed them—put out of the way. Bonnie Wheeler argues that there are several explanations for Charles's abandonment of Joan. First, Joan was always a challenge to Charles VII; they were never cozy or comfortable companions, and his abandonment of Joan was a gradual process that culminated at Compiègne but began at least from the time of his coronation. Next, once captured, Joan may have become a serious public liability, and thus the king did not try to arrange to relieve her troops or to rescue her. It may be that Charles VII feared that he and his legitimate rulership would be tainted by Joan's failure to take Paris and by her capture at Compiègne, for these events left her susceptible, in the eyes of some—such as readers of Christine de Pisan's

Ditié de Jeanne d'Arc—to charges that she was a false prophet. Furthermore, the window of opportunity in which it was possible for Charles VII to rescue Joan was very narrow: Once she was in the custody of ecclesiastical authorities and officially suspected of heresy, no transfer back to the secular arm would have been possible. In addition, within the context of chivalric society and chivalric ransom, Joan was an anomaly. It is impossible to gauge the impact of her birth status (although she and her family had recently been ennobled) on the issue of ransom by Charles VII or any of Joan's noble and well-endowed friends, for (again as Wheeler argues) there was no legal or social context upon which Joan could naturally depend, no noble blood relations whose shifting political allegiances and ample resources made chivalric ransom so attractive a common enterprise and class commitment.

There were envious persons in Charles's entourage who might rejoice at Joan's capture. Most notable among these was the archbishop of Reims, Regnault de Chartres, who was hand-in-glove with LaTrémoïlle and who, as the head of the delegation that had presented itself to the duke of Burgundy at Arras exactly one month after the sacring, had (without Joan's knowledge) signed the truces that betrayed Joan's goals. Events had revealed the folly of these policies; might the archbishop have borne Joan a grudge because he had been forced to recognize that he had been duped in those negotiations? Reference exists to a letter he had written to his diocesans in which he insinuates that "God had suffered that Joan the Maid be taken because she had puffed herself up with pride and because of the rich garments which she had taken it upon herself to wear, and because she had not done what God had commanded her, but had done her own will." But this archbishop of Reims was finally converted to her view later, when it again became apparent that only the use of armed force would be effective.

As far away as Constantinople, Bertrandon de La Broquière, an intimate of the duke of Burgundy, produced astonishment when he confirmed that the Maid had become a prisoner of the English. People there refused to believe him. Morosini's informant reports that in the month of August: "It is said that that damsel had been imprisoned with many damsels in a fortress under very strong guard, but since she could not be so well guarded that God could not do with them as He pleased, she escaped and returned to her people without having been molested in her person."

The belief that Joan could not have been captured or kept in captivity— her power was too great, and God would help her to escape—was almost universal. In regions that adhered to the French cause, the clergy ordered prayers for her liberation: At Embrun in the Alps, the diocese of Jacques Gélu (II, 19), three prayers besought the Lord "that the Maid kept in the prisons of the enemies may be freed without evil, and that she may complete entirely the work that You have entrusted to her." At Tours, at Meaux, and at Orléans, liturgical hours were celebrated with these prayers of intention.

Joan probably left Arras about November 15. A local tradition there claims that she was imprisoned in one of the turrets that rose above the Ronville Gate. On the twenty-first, in a letter addressed "to the Most Excellent Prince, the King of France and of England," the faculty of the University of Paris exulted: "We have recently heard that into your power has now been delivered this woman called the Maid, at which we greatly rejoice, confident that by your good command this woman will be sent to justice to repair the great wickedness and scandals that have arisen notoriously in this kingdom on her account, to the great prejudice of the divine honor of our holy Faith and of all your good people." The professors demanded that the prisoner be entrusted to their hands and that the bishop of Beauvais judge her at Paris. This latter request was denied by the English king. Joan's transfer from Arras to Le Crotoy took place about the same time, the middle of November; it was then that the transfer money was to be exchanged. The principal stages of that journey, approximately sixty-two miles, no doubt included the castle of Lucheux and then the abbey of Saint-Riquier. It is likely that Joan was also brought to the castle at Drugy. Two monks of Saint-Riquier, the provost and grand chaplain, came to greet her as she passed by. As in many other abbeys of the Norman region—such as Fécamp and Mont-Saint-Michel—the abbot, Hugues Cuillerel, had embraced the Burgundian cause, but the monks did not uniformly share his sentiments. Surrounded by her armed escort, after passing through the great forest of Crécy, Joan must have reached the estuary of the Somme on the following day. There, she would have seen the sea for the first time. Beyond it lay England.

Negotiations about the disposition of the prisoner made rapid progress. Pierre Cauchon was active during December, obtaining from the duke of Bedford an agreement about the place where the prisoner would be judged and then ensuring the conditions of due process acceptable to ecclesiastical jurisdiction, for the trial had to take place in a safe location and be correct in procedure.

To serve as Joan's judge within the requirements of technical propriety, Cauchon should have arranged for the trial to take place somewhere in the diocese of Beauvais, since the prisoner's capture on the right bank of the Oise might have validated his jurisdictional competence. According to the rules of tribunals of the Inquisition, a person must be judged either by the bishop of his or her birthplace or in the diocese in which the crime of heresy was committed. But since Compiègne was in the diocese of Beauvais, and Beauvais had surrendered to the king of France, Bedford decided that the trial would take place at Rouen, the Norman capital, where English power had been securely established for twelve years. Cauchon, as bishop of Beauvais, had no right to act as a judge in Rouen, but Bedford had previously asked the ecclesiastical authorities of Rouen to grant Cauchon a "commission of territory" in order to circumvent the rule. A delegation of venue was formally requested by the chapter of Rouen and obtained by an act dated December 28, 1430. Cauchon immediately surged into action. He sent an agent to Lorraine charged with gathering information about Joan's childhood and youth. The envoy, whose name is not recorded, went to Chaumont, where both Nicolas Bailly, a notary, and a clerk competent in juridical matters named Gérard Petit became his assistants. The three men must have successively visited Domrémy, Vaucouleurs, and Toul; the results of their query would not reach Rouen before the end of January 1431. In the meantime, at Cauchon's request, an escort of some fifty men-at-arms left with him to ensure Joan's final transfer from Le Crotoy to Rouen. This group was composed of two "furnished lances," or ten men-at-arms with twenty-five archers and the men necessary to take care of the baggage and the transport of the transfer ransom, which must have been paid around December 15. This last stage of the journey must have taken place swiftly.

In Pierre Rocolle's reconstruction of her itinerary, Joan must have been led in a boat from Le Crotoy to Saint-Valéry-sur-Somme, following the channel that the Somme traces in its estuary at high tide, while the knights and their mounts—the bulk of the troop—crossed the Somme by the bridge at Abbeville, since the transport of fifty horses and horsemen on boats would have been difficult. There was probably a halt at Saint-Valéry and perhaps also in the little town of Eu, fifteen miles away, if the crossing of the estuary was swift. Joan's itinerary thereafter probably followed for some time the route of the ancient Roman road through Arques and Bosc-le-Hard. Without having to pass through the city of Rouen, the escort reached the castle of Bouvreuil, constructed in the thirteenth century by King Philip II Augustus and now the residence of Richard Beauchamp, the earl of Warwick (II, 43), guardian of the young English king Henry VI.

It was Christmas Eve, 1430.

CHAPTER SEVEN

JOAN'S TRIAL
AND EXECUTION
AT ROUEN

This chapter reports the extraordinary record of Joan's trial by an inquisitorial court composed of dozens of professional experts directed by the hostile presiding judge, Pierre Cauchon (see Part II, Section 49). From January 9 until the end of May 1431, they tried to confuse and entrap this barely literate peasant girl, against whom they had not formulated a charge—a procedural flaw that would later make this trial easy to nullify. She stood them off until the very end, finally confused by her judges' decision that she had refused to submit to the Church Militant on the matter of wearing men's clothes. Joan had agreed to sign a document abjuring her "voices" on the understanding that she would be transferred to an ecclesiastical prison in the custody of women, rather than remain in a military prison guarded by hostile English soldiers who threatened her virginity. Betrayed on this point by Cauchon, she resumed men's clothes, was thus declared a 'relapsed heretic,' and was burned at the stake in the public marketplace at Rouen on May 30, 1431. Her ashes were scattered to the wind. She was nineteen years old.

IT TOOK FIVE MONTHS TO COMPLETE THE PROCEEDINGS that culminated in Joan's conviction. The proceedings, from January 9 to May 30, 1431, can be separated into three phases: from January 9 through March 26, the "procès d'office," or the judge's investigations before the official trial in court; from March 26 through May 24, the "ordinary" trial that culminated in Joan's recantation, or "abjuration"; and finally, on May 28 and May 29, the brief relapse trial.

The tower in which Joan was held was still standing at the beginning of the nineteenth century. Several witnesses said that the Crowned Tower, one of seven that enclosed a "vast lower court" in the fortress of Bouvreuil, faced the fields; it is thought that Joan's cell was on the first story looking toward the exterior of the fortress. Recent excavations have led scholars to modify their views of the layout, but one thing is certain: What is today called the Joan of Arc Tower represents the heavily restored remains of the ancient keep, not the site of her detention.

Her cell and its neighboring wings probably rose above three indentations in the thickness of the wall foundation. One of them corresponds to the window, no doubt provided with bars; a second would have been the latrine—with which all towers of that type were equipped; and the third space must have communicated directly with the staircase; it probably gave access to some sort of tunnel that permitted anyone standing there to hear what was said in the prisoner's cell without being seen. Such surveillance, which also could have been exercised through the flooring that separated the cell from its counterpart on the story above, was the primary responsibility of a royal squire, John Grey, who was assisted by two other Englishmen, John Berwoit and William Talbot. All three had been required to swear on the Bible that they would be vigilant and forbid any visitor who was not authorized in advance and in person by Pierre Cauchon (II, 49) or by Richard Beauchamp (II, 43), the earl of Warwick and the governor of the castle. They were assisted in their jobs by "five Englishmen of the lowest rank, those who are called in French *houssepaillers,*" a word that in modern French has come to mean 'abusers.'

Joan was spared no humiliation. "I saw her in the prison of the castle of Rouen, in quite a dark room, chained and with leg irons," declared Isambart de La Pierre, a Dominican of the convent of Saint-Jacques at Rouen and an assessor at her trial. A certain Pierre Daron, lieutenant of the bailiff of Rouen, recalled that he saw her "in a tower of the castle, with leg irons attached to a large piece of wood: she had several English guards." The most complete details were given by the usher Jean Massieu (II, 63), whose responsibilities included accompanying the prisoner from the place where she was detained to the place where the tribunal met. She was, he said, in the hands of "five Englishmen," of whom three spent the night in her cell and two outside it at the door. "And I know for certain that at night she slept with two pairs of irons on her legs, attached by a chain very tightly to another chain that was connected to the foot of her bed, itself anchored by a large piece of wood five or six feet long. The whole contraption was fastened by a key."

Joan thus wore leg irons during the day, and at night her jailers attached to this fetter a chain that connected the foot of her bed to a piece of wood that she could not possibly have moved. Massieu testified: "Whenever I led her from her cell or back to it, she was always in leg irons." She could not, in fact, have walked in leg irons from her prison to the hall of judgment without assistance. From her first appearance before the tribunal, Joan complained "of being held and chained and in these iron hobbles." Cauchon had taken even stronger precautions: Fearing that Joan might escape, he had a certain Étienne Castille forge an iron cage in which she could have been kept standing upright "fastened by the neck, the hands, and the feet." The cage does not seem to have been used. Physical restraint, however, must have seemed inconsequential compared to the mental torture to which Joan had to submit: the mockery of the guards, the hostile shouts, the obscenities and insults whenever she appeared in the courtyard of the castle.

How in these conditions could she have preserved her virginity and remained "Joan the Maid"? According to the principal notary of the trial, Guillaume Manchon (II, 62), the young girl feared "that at night her guardians would do her some violence," and "one or two times she complained to the bishop of Beauvais, to the subinquisitor, and to Master Nicolas Loiseleur [II, 60] that one of the guards had wished to violate her."

Someone seems to have intervened on her behalf. At Rouen, while several inquests were still under way in her home country, she had to undergo once more that examination of virginity to which she had already been subjected at Poitiers; this time it was conducted under the auspices of Anne of Burgundy, duchess of Bedford. The examination took place before January 13, 1431, since the duchess and her husband left Rouen on that date. The name of one of the matrons who examined her, Anne Bavon, is known. Joan's virginity was duly attested. Anne of Burgundy may well have forbidden Joan's guards to molest her.

The ambiguity of Joan's situation was evident from her first days in the prison at Rouen. Pierre Cauchon and the University of Paris intended to try her for heresy, so this had to be a church trial. According to normal canon-law procedure, Joan should have been detained in an ecclesiastical prison, guarded by women; and thus she would have received moderately humane treatment. Yet throughout the trial Joan was treated as a prisoner of war, chained and guarded by soldiers. To disguise this legal inconsistency, the bishop of Beauvais and the duke of Bedford (II, 9) had recourse to a legal fiction: The lock of the door of her prison cell was secured by three keys, of which one was to be kept by Cardinal Henry Beaufort, bishop of Winchester (II, 8), who was to be present during the trial's entirety, and the two others were to be held by the judges, Cauchon himself or the *promotor* (prosecutor, more or less), Jean d'Estivet (II, 52), and by the vice-inquisitor, who was to be designated by Jean Graverent, the Inquisitor of France (II, 53). Since all three were clerics, the fiction could be maintained that she was entirely subject to ecclesiastical custody. This procedural trick had no more validity than the prohibition that Cauchon tried to impose on Joan during her first appearance before the tribunal: "We forbid you to leave without our permission the prison cell that has been assigned you in the castle of Rouen, under the penalty of being convicted of the crime of heresy." But this did not fool the prisoner, who immediately replied: "I do not accept that prohibition; if I were to escape, no one would blame me for having either offended or violated my faith." Her drama and her life now turned on that ambiguity: Was she a prisoner of war or an alleged heretic?

Joan reveals here as elsewhere that she considered herself an archetypal political prisoner—persecuted because she threatened and annoyed her captors and their ideology—and not a deliberate heretic. This accusation of heresy permitted her judges also to impugn the king of France: Since he owed Joan his crown, the legitimacy of his authority would be thoroughly tainted if she were found guilty. This conflation of ideology with politics and religion was already well established in Paris. Joan had not yet been born when the faculty of the University of Paris, in a densely argued dossier written by one of its members, Jean Petit, defended the political assassination of Louis of Orléans by his cousin John the Fearless. This was the first time since antiquity that intellectuals had extolled political assassination. What was the impact of this intellectual climate on Joan's trial?

Philip of Burgundy (II, 3) was skillful at manipulating both ideological theory and the more turbulent sectors of public opinion. He knew how to gain the support of the university professors on one hand and on the other that of the High Boucherie, the masters of the Paris butchers' guild, who had at their disposal practically an army of cutlers and skinners, and who had already joined the Parisian revolt led by the eloquent skinner Simon Caboche in 1413. They controlled the city for five months armed with the lethal blades that they, as butchers, had a right to own. Caboche and the Burgundian faction in Paris introduced a program of social reform, which finally made the wealthier bourgeoisie so nervous that they called in the troops of the Armagnac faction, who put an end to Simon Caboche and his revolt.

Among the supporters of that revolt was an intellectual faction entrenched in the University of Paris. Caboche's quasi-revolutionary coup had seemed to them a convenient way to take power in the capital, and this was a key element in their grand scheme to win mastery of the entire kingdom, as eventually of the Universal Church.

The Catholic church was then deeply divided by the Great Schism (1378–1415; see "Prelude"). To bind that rift, the Paris intellectuals strongly supported empowering the institution of the General Council, so that it would act as coruler of the church along with the papacy, in a situation loosely parallel to the way that the kingdom of England was ruled by Parliament and the crown. The English Parliament had assumed increasing power during the reigns of the last four

Plantagenet kings—Edward I (1272–1307), Edward II (1307–1327), Edward III (1327–1377), and Richard II (1377–1399); the Lancastrian kings Henry IV (1400–1413) and Henry V (1413–1422) were even more beholden to Parliament.

The University of Paris intellectuals probably hoped to make the French national assembly, the Estates-General, as powerful as the English Parliament had become. If France became part of a dual monarchy reigned over by Henry VI (II, 2), a boy-king likely to stay weak even after he had outgrown his regency, the French part of his kingdom might become a realm ruled by the Estates-General, which the Paris intelligentsia thought it could control. Since they saw the Great Councils (Constance, Basel, and their successors) as the dominant institution of their future church, this group of university professors must have dreamed of their eventual mastery over Western Christendom as well as its largest and most populous constituent kingdom, France. The eventual success of their plan seemed inevitable to them. The Treaty of Troyes, which Cauchon, the former rector of the University of Paris, had indefatigably negotiated, established a new polity founded on feudal conquests and justified by the clergy. But Joan of Arc, a peasant girl from nowhere, endangered this new, progressive structure by her victories in war and her crucial insistence on the traditional sacramental anointing of Charles VII's coronation (II, 1).

For the University of Paris, Joan's trial was also a chance to claim the prestige of the Universal Church, even before the General Council had achieved maturity. Although by now Pope Martin V was the sole pope—the Great Schism ended in Joan's youth, in 1415—and although he upheld papal authority against supporters of conciliar supremacy, it was not yet clear that he could contain the challenge to papal power of the General Councils. Even before the great councils of Constance and Basel, the University of Paris had exercised decisive influence over the whole church by dominating the periodic councils called at the behest of the Avignon popes. By the adroit exploitation of highly visible heresy trials, might not the university regain the effective regency of Christendom that it had enjoyed in the days of the Avignon papacy? The leaders of the Council of Constance had profited greatly (at least in the short run) from their condemnation of Jan Hus as a heretic in 1415: to Cauchon and others, that must have seemed a precedent for the case of this ignorant girl whose insolence would surely be easy to crush.

The exemplary trial on which that faction counted began badly. The virginity test, which could have convicted the Maid of falsehood, had turned to her advantage. The inquest into her habits and virtue that was undertaken in her homeland failed to produce compelling evidence against her. Having interrogated twelve or fifteen witnesses at Domrémy and in five or six neighboring parishes, Cauchon's representative Nicolas Bailly "had found nothing about Joan that he would not wish to find about his own sister." An exchange of information among the investigators confirmed this impression. Although the bailiff of Chaumont abused them as "treacherous Armagnacs," the investigators brought back nothing that could be used as a heresy charge against Joan.

As a consequence, the judges could find no grounds on which to formulate an accusation. In his punctilious analysis of the condemnation trial, the modern scholar Pierre Tisset argues that, through a striking procedural flaw, Joan was condemned only on the basis of the interrogation to which she was subjected at Rouen. Nothing was proven against her; it was on the basis of her words alone, as they were interpreted by her enemies, that she was condemned. Ironically, by preserving so carefully her words and the minutes of her trial (see III, 13), Cauchon erected the most lasting monument to Joan of Arc.

The difficulties that Cauchon and Bedford faced were aggravated by the reticence of the vice-inquisitor, a Dominican friar of the convent of Rouen, Jean Lemaître (II, 59), who should have been the chief of the two judges required in a properly conducted inquisitorial trial. Lemaître had responded to Cauchon's invitation by saying that "as much for the serenity of his conscience as for a more certain conduct of the trial, he did not wish to be involved in this present affair." He alleged that he did not have the authority, because his jurisdiction extended only over the cities of the dioceses of Rouen, and "this trial had been launched on borrowed territory"—borrowed from Rouen, that is, by the bishop of Beauvais on what had been declared his own jurisdiction by means of a legal fiction. Cauchon insisted on preserving this element of inquisitorial judicial protocol, and he demanded that Jean Graverent, as Inquisitor of France, require Lemaître's presence. It was only on February 22, after the preliminaries had been completed and the trial's second session was beginning, that Lemaître appeared. Despite the care Cauchon took to respect the forms of an inquisitorial trial, it began with several irregularities: The inquisitor was absent; the "preliminary information" prejudicial to Joan's religious conformity was anonymous, from undisclosed sources; and no formal charges were brought against the prisoner. Tisset argues that it was an "entirely exceptional phenomenon" for this trial to have been based exclusively on the interrogation of the accused without anyone, including the accused herself, knowing what charge was being brought against her.

Although Cauchon had assembled an imposing tribunal, he tended to preside alone, except on those occasions when he could get the inquisitor to join him. He wrote letter after official letter and made a special appeal to the cathedral chapter of Rouen, which the king of England had informed of the change of venue in a "Commission of Territory" permitting the bishop of Beauvais to exercise jurisdiction at Rouen. In one letter, Cauchon explicitly mentioned the demand of the University of Paris that he be appointed to conduct the trial. The terms of this last document underscore the trial's political nature: "Our intention is to recover the aforesaid Joan and get her back under our control on one or another of the charges regarding our Faith if it should happen that she should not be convicted or attainted with the charge of heresy."

The first public session of the trial was held on Ash Wednesday, the first day of Lent. On that Wednesday, February 21, 1431, about 8 o'clock in the morning, Joan found herself facing forty-four imposing persons listed in that day's transcript. Among them were nine doctors of theology, four doctors of canon law, one doctor of "both laws" (the civil and the canon)—a holder of the degree of J.U.D. (Juris Ultriusque Doctor) from Bologna—seven bachelors of theology, eleven licentiates in canon law and four in civil law, as well as the *promotor*, Jean d'Estivet. Contrary to the traditional procedures of the Inquisition, Joan stood alone, without a lawyer to represent her. Her detention does not seem to have weakened her will or resistance, of which Cauchon became aware from the first formality, when she resisted the swearing of an oath: "I do not know about what you wish to interrogate me," she answered, "and perhaps you will ask me things that I will not tell you." This was followed by a new and more urgent exhortation by the bishop:

> "Swear to tell the truth concerning whatever will be asked you that has to do with the Catholic faith and with anything else that you know."

> "About my father and mother, and everything that I have done since I took the road to come to France, I shall willingly swear; but never have I said or revealed anything about the revelations made to me by God except to Charles, my king. And even if you wish to cut my head off, I will not reveal them, because I know from my visions that I must keep them secret."

This line of questioning persisted, and Joan continued to answer in this vein in successive encounters. Finally, Joan, on her knees with her two hands on the missal, swore to tell the truth about whatever would be asked her concerning matters of religious belief.

Then the interrogation proper began. Every detained or accused person had to begin by stating name, forename, and social class: "In the country where I was born, I was called Jeannette, and in France Jeanne [Joan]. . . . I was born in a village that is called Domrémy-Greux; the main church is in Greux. My father is named Jacques Darc, and my mother Isabelle." She then named her godfathers, godmothers, and the priest Jean Minet who had baptized her; finally, she gave her age: "as best as I can tell, around nineteen years."

Another obstacle arose. The bishop instructed her to say the *Pater Noster* (Our Father) to which Joan answered: "Hear me in confession and I will say it to you willingly." Joan's wish that the bishop hear her confession—evidently not in conformity with the customs of an inquisitorial trial—was clever, in that it invoked Cauchon in his priestly role, which required him to accord the sacrament of penance as much importance as did Joan. Despite the bishop's insistence, she refused to recite this basic Christian prayer unless he agreed to hear her confession. She then spoke about the fashion in which she was held in prison by "five Englishmen of the lowest rank." She was instructed to appear the following day at the same hour.

On the following day she appeared for the second time. The previous day's exchange regarding the oath was reenacted: "I gave you that oath yesterday; it should be enough for you. You are burdening me too much." Joan consented, nevertheless, "to tell the truth on any points touching the Faith."

Jean Beaupère (II, 47), one of the assessors, was put in charge of the interrogation. Like Cauchon, he had been rector of the University of Paris (in 1412 and 1413); he achieved the confirmation of the university's privileges from the queen of England and the duke of Gloucester in 1422; the university had sent him to Troyes to assist Cauchon during the negotiations for the treaty of 1420. Subsequently named a canon of Rouen, Beaupère continued to act as an English agent and later was sent as the official ambassador of the king of England to the Council of Basel, where he arrived on May 28, 1431, just before Joan's execution. In 1435, King Henry VI awarded him an annual payment of 100 pounds "for his good services in France and at the Council of Basel." Beaupère collected benefices—becoming canon not only at Rouen but also at Besançon, Sens, Paris, Beauvais, Laon, Autun, and Lisieux—despite the fact that he could not physically celebrate mass: His right hand had been crippled during an encounter with brigands.

Beaupère asked Joan questions about her youth, about what she called her "voices," and about her activities between the time she left Vaucouleurs and her arrival at Chinon. He asked her hardly anything about her exploits at Orléans and Patay but concentrated on Saint-Denis, "the skirmish before the city of Paris":

> "Was that not a feast day?"
> Joan answered, "I think it was a feast day."
> "Was that well done?"
> "Move on with your questioning."

This line of interrogation swiftly reviewed her activities, concentrating only on the attack she led on September 8, 1429, the feast of the Nativity of the Virgin Mary, when Joan had tried to take the Saint-Honoré Gate at Paris. After lengthy questioning, Joan was instructed to appear the next day, on Saturday, February 24.

A surprise awaited her, for among the assessors was the priest Nicolas Loiseleur, who had more than once come to visit her in her prison cell, pretending that he was Joan's fellow countryman from the banks of the Meuse and her fellow prisoner. As a priest, he had offered to hear her confession; once he won her confidence, he did so. It was revealed much later in the trial that Guillaume Manchon, one of the assigned notaries, along with his assistant Boisguillaume (II, 48) ("and other witnesses," Manchon added), was ordered to hide near the nook that opened onto Joan's cell, in order to overhear what "she was saying or confessing to the aforesaid Loiseleur."

From the beginning of the interrogation, Joan grew increasingly restive and more stubborn in her refusal to swear oaths. Cauchon with several other assessors eventually demanded that she swear another oath, because Joan had answered in annoyance at one point: "Let me speak." The usher Jean Massieu reported later that in these interrogations, which generally lasted from 8 to 11 o'clock in the morning, it was standard for several judges to ask their questions all at once, so that "many times she said to those who were interrogating her: 'Fair sirs, ask me one after the other.'" In any case, when she finally said: "I am ready to swear to tell the truth concerning what I shall know about this trial," the minutes carry a significant addition: "But I shall not ever say everything that I know."

Throughout her interrogation, Joan placed herself in a dangerous position by claiming to be in communication with the world beyond, to which she referred by the general designation of her "voice" or "voices." She was clear about her sense of the supernatural character of her mission. When Beaupère asked if her voice had forbidden her to say anything about what would be asked of her, she reserved the right to answer later. Joan countered the question "Did he forbid you to make his revelations known?" by asking: "If the voice forbade me to, what would you have me say about it?" She added, "Know for certain that these are not men who have forbidden it!" She insisted on the distance between the world with which she claimed to communicate and that which surrounded her: "I have greater fear of failing my voices in saying something that displeases them than I have of answering you." Her tone, never that of an ecstatic or a mystic, is sometimes amused, even blustering: "This last night, my voices told me many things for the advantage of my king, which I dearly wish my king knew at this moment, even if as a result I had to fast from wine until Easter, though it would be joyous to feast!" Her bravado provoked a devious question: "Has your voice revealed that you will escape from prison?" To which she responded: "Do I have to tell you that?"

Her speech was often eloquent. When she said: "If it were not for the grace of God, I would not know how to do anything," Joan provoked the interrogator to ask the famous question: "Do you know if you are in the grace of God?" Her answer: "If I am not, may God put me there. And if I am, may God keep me there, for I would be the most sorrowful woman in the world if I knew that I was not in the grace of God." The notary Boisguillaume later declared, in the nullification trial of 1455–1456, that "Those who were interrogating her were stupefied." Joan's answer here echoes a prayer found in three fifteenth-century manuscripts. Was Joan inspired by that prayer? Or could her response, sublime in its simplicity, have influenced its composition? The latter is more likely, for the assessors would hardly have been so astonished if Joan had merely repeated a familiar formula.

The notary asked that the questioning stop at that point. Stenographers had written the questions along with Joan's answers in French; their record was later amplified and translated into Latin (III, 13). But from this point forward, Joan's replies were recorded in indirect discourse, rather than in the direct quotations recorded until her simple, sublime reply. For instance: "She said that if she had been in sin, she thinks that the voice would not have come to her, and she wished that everyone could hear it as well as herself." Why was this change in record-keeping technique made? Some speculate that Cauchon and his associates wanted two contradictory outcomes: they wanted to preserve the transcript, but they did not want Joan to seem so persuasive, and the force of her personality could be muted in indirect discourse. Their worried reaction to her replies is attested even more strikingly by the presence of several erasures in the French stenographic record. One such erasure occurs at this point, when Joan's replies began to be recorded in indirect discourse. Hereafter, we have converted the transcript's indirect discourse to the direct discourse that it is reasonable to assume was actually spoken.

Impressed as they seem to have been at Joan's reply, the tribunal remained hostile. Jean Beaupère moved to the question of the Fairy Tree at Domrémy. The inquest made at the village had probably revealed to him that most of her fellow villagers thought that Joan had "received her mission at the Fairy Tree." Some of the witnesses at the inquest had said so, her own brother had assumed so, and she had needed to "tell him to the contrary." Through this line of questioning Joan evokes a village feast:

> Close to the village of Domrémy, there is a tree called the Tree of the Ladies; others call it the Tree of the Fairies; near it is a spring. I've heard it said that people sick with fever drink at that spring and go there to get water to regain their health. I've seen people do that myself, but I don't know if they get well or not. . . . It's a big tree called a beech—from it comes the maypole that people say belongs to Monseigneur Pierre de Bourlémont, a knight. Sometimes I used to walk around there with the other girls, and from that tree I made garlands for the image of Our Lady of Domrémy. I've seen these garlands hung on the

branches of the tree by young girls, and sometimes I did that along with the
others; sometimes we took them away with us afterward and sometimes we left
them there. . . . I don't know if I danced around that tree after the age of reason;
I might have danced with the children, but I sang more than I danced.

She continued with a description of the Bois Chesnu, the Oak Grove ("You could
see it from the door of my father's house, and it's only half a league away"). She
was not afraid to admit that she had been asked about prophecies claiming that
from the neighborhood of that grove would come a maid who would do noble
things; "but," she said, "I never believed it."

This rich line of questioning terminates at this point. A new direction
was set on the following Tuesday, February 27. On that day, Joan revealed the
names of the saints from whom she said she received revelations: St. Catherine
and St. Margaret. Jean Beaupère directed the interrogation on this topic as well.
Having asked, apparently casually, if Joan were fasting during the current Lent,
he resumed questioning about the voices: "Had Joan heard that voice last
Saturday?"

"I did not understand the voice very well, and I did not understand anything that
I can repeat to you until I returned to my room [cell]."
"What did the voice tell you when you returned to your room?"
"It told me that I should answer you bravely."

"Is it the voice of an angel?" Beaupère persisted a little later. Joan then named
the two saints who would return thereafter in her statements as specific members
of the invisible entourage that she claimed for herself: St. Catherine and St.
Margaret. Although there is lively contention about which saints with these
names are the ones to whom Joan refers, it is probable that her St. Catherine
was St. Catherine of Alexandria, a popular medieval saint who was patron of
young girls and also patron of the parish of Maxey-sur-Meuse, near Domrémy;
her St. Margaret was probably St. Margaret of Antioch, who was widely invoked
on behalf of women in childbirth and whose statue, which Joan probably saw,
is still in the church at Domrémy. Insistent questioning was directed toward the
apparitions of those two saints, to whom, on that same Tuesday, Joan added St.
Michael. It was, she said, St. Michael who came first. She became insistent on
that point: "It was St. Michael whom I saw before my eyes, and he was not alone
but was well accompanied by angels of heaven. . . . I saw them with the eyes of
my body as well as I see you; and when they left me I wept and wished that they
would have taken me with them."

Also during that interrogation session, Joan mentioned for the first time
the "Book of Poitiers": "If you have doubts about that, send to Poitiers, where

I have already been examined." The Poitiers investigation must have dealt with Joan's apparitions, and there she may well have given testimony in which she named the saints from whom she claimed revelations. The interrogation followed that line of questioning up to the moment when Joan answered: "I've told you enough about it: they are St. Catherine and St. Margaret, and believe me or not as you wish." She then restated with force what she would maintain throughout the trial: "I came into France only at God's command. . . . I would have preferred to have been torn apart by four horses than to have come into France without God's permission. . . . everything was done at the command of the Lord. . . . I have never acted except at God's command." (In medieval French, the term "France" referred to the core of the kingdom, not its periphery.)

In the course of that interrogation appeared a question to which Joan at first seems to have attached no importance:

> "Is it God who commanded you to wear men's clothes?"
>
> "The clothes are a small matter, the least of all things; and I did not take up men's clothes on the advice of this world. I neither put on these clothes nor did I do anything except by the commandment of God and his angels."

Other questions about her mode of dress provoked only repetitions of these answers: She had done nothing that was not by the commandment of God. Probably not even Cauchon could then have guessed the importance that her mode of dress would come to assume.

The judges then tried to surprise her into telling about her revelations regarding the king of France: "Was there an angel on the head of your king when you saw him for the first time?" "By St. Mary! I don't know and I certainly didn't see any." She would later allude to a "sign" that the king received, permitting him to have faith in what she said; she made clear that the sign had come to her "from the clerks."

The question led her back to the encounter at Chinon and to the Poitiers investigation. Asked how she knew a sword could be found buried in the church of Sainte-Catherine-de-Fierbois, Joan retold the startling story about "that rusted sword with five crosses engraved on it":

> She knew from her voices that this sword was there, and she had never seen the man who went to find the aforesaid sword for her, and she wrote to the men of the church of that place that she hoped it would please them that she should have that sword, and they sent it to her. It was not very deeply buried underground, behind the altar; she did not know if it would be exactly before the altar or behind it. She said again that just after the sword was found the men of that church gave it a good rubbing, and thereupon the rust fell off without effort.

"Had she had anyone bless it?" "I never requested a benediction of any kind, and I would not know how to do that." The judges dropped the subject of this marvelous sword (III, 6) and they passed swiftly to the description of the standard, which provoked another of Joan's famous responses: "Would you prefer your standard or your sword?" "I would prefer, maybe forty times, my standard to my sword." A little later: "I carried my standard in my own hand when we went to the assault, to avoid having to kill anyone. I have never killed anyone." The session closed with questions referring briefly to her military exploits at Orléans and at Jargeau.

The tribunal convened again on Thursday and Saturday, March 1 and 3, for more public interrogation. The Thursday session may have been directed by Cauchon himself. He opened with a confusing point that was a lively preoccupation for university professors: the pope. A letter was read stating that John, the count of Armagnac (II, 6), had written the Maid on the question that had long divided Christendom: "Who is the true pope?"

"As far as I know, I believe in the lord pope who is at Rome," Joan declared. This unambiguous answer might well have offended the men of the university, who had taken for so long the side of the Avignon pontiff and who were still far from reconciled with the pope at Rome, Martin V; they would soon raise an antipope against him at the Council of Basel, which would meet for the first time two months after Joan's death. Joan gave no more than a dilatory reply about her letter from the count of Armagnac. Since this trial session concentrated heavily on her correspondence, Joan's first ultimatum to the English at Orléans was read. She acknowledged that text, with the exception of a few details. She provoked her judges: "Before seven years are over, the English will suffer more severe losses than they did at Orléans, and they will lose everything in France . . . and this will be accomplished through a great victory that God will send the French."

In striving to establish precisely (which she refused to do) the day, the hour, and the year of that victory, the interrogators wanted to know what she had said to her English guard, John Grey, concerning the winter feast of St. Martin. Her guards filled their classic trial role, and their daily reports were used in preparing the interrogations.

After a brief digression, the interview returned to the saints to whom Joan attributed her voices: She revealed nothing useful about their appearance and was amused when asked if the saints had hair: "That's an important point!" Cauchon persisted: "Did St. Margaret speak the language of the English?" "How should she speak English, since she is not of the English party?"

The transcript shows that Cauchon repeatedly tried to confound Joan with questions about sorcery. Joan would be answering questions about the events at Reims, for example, when the interrogators would suddenly return to the Fairy Tree and the spring at Domrémy. Or: "What have you done with your mandrake?" "I don't have a mandrake and I never had one!" And since they insisted: "I heard that it is something done to get money, but I don't believe it at all," adding "My voices have never said anything to me about that." Joan's voices had nothing to say about the judges' preoccupation with mandrakes, good-luck rings, or popular magic formulae. Witness her robust humor in the interrogation session of March 1:

> "What did St. Michael look like when he appeared to you? . . . Was he naked?"
>> "Do you think that God doesn't have the wherewithal to give him clothes?"
>> "Did he have hair?"
>> "Why would it have been cut off?"
>> "Did he have a scale?"
>> "I don't know anything about that. I have great joy when I see him."

A frustrated Cauchon returned from that exchange to the "king's sign": "I have told you that you would not drag that out of my mouth. Go ask him!" The symbolism of the royal crown was raised. Almost taking the offensive, Joan specified that, in addition to the crown the king had received at Reims, "if he had waited, he would have had a crown a thousand times richer." The questioning would return many times to that crown.

The session on the following Saturday was longer and touched on diverse subjects—first of all, on the saints who appeared to her: "I have told you what I know and will not answer anything else." Jean Beaupère, directing the interrogation that day, raised the question of the fate awaiting Joan:

> "Did you know through a revelation that you would escape?"
>> "That has nothing to do with your trial; do you want me to speak against myself?"
>> "Have your voices told you something about that?"
>> "Yes, indeed, they have told me that I would be delivered, but I do not know the day or the hour, and they said that I should bravely maintain a good face."

Did her idea of deliverance here refer to the spiritual deliverance of death and the afterlife, or was Joan the warrior thinking of escape? It is least likely that Joan the prisoner imagined that she would be exonerated and liberated by her judges.

Changing his tactics, Beaupère questioned her again about her male attire: "I've answered you about that already." She added: "It was written down at Poitiers," thus proving that the theologians who originally questioned her at Poitiers and whose king "found nothing but good in her" had raised the issue of Joan wearing men's clothes without finding it an offense. This point, first raised in early March, steadily assumes greater significance: Lacking any other solid charge, her judges eventually would rely on her cross-dressing as the visible basis for the accusation of heresy.

The judges returned to questions of sorcery, asking about the pennons or badges adopted in the French army by the Maid and her followers: "Did anyone sprinkle them with holy water? . . . Did anyone carry these cloths to an altar or a church in any kind of procession, so as to make badges of them?"

More insidious were questions about the infant whom Joan had supposedly restored to life at Lagny, who lived long enough to be baptized, and questions concerning Catherine de La Rochelle (II, 37). In both cases, Joan responded with clear simplicity, as she did when asked about her jump from the tower at Beaurevoir. Her reply was memorable: "I would prefer to surrender my soul to God than to be in the hands of the English."

These sessions of public interrogation had now lasted eleven days. Eight days later, on Saturday, March 10, Pierre Cauchon himself entered her cell accompanied by three individuals who had already appeared several times among the assessors: Nicolas Midy (II, 65), Gérard Feuillet, and Master Jean de La Fontaine (II, 58), who had from time to time been designated by Cauchon to take his place during interrogation. The same role was played by the usher Jean Massieu, who accompanied Joan from her cell to the courtroom, and also by Jean Secard, a canon of Rouen and an ecclesiastical lawyer who appears infrequently in the hearing reports.

Nicolas Midy and Gérard Feuillet were among the six professors sent by the University of Paris as special envoys to follow the trial; they had been escorted to Rouen by Jean de Rinel (II, 67), an agent of the king of England and husband of Pierre Cauchon's niece, Guillemette Bidault. Jean de La Fontaine, also a member of the university, a master of arts and licentiate in canon law, was not officially part of that delegation. Cauchon must have recognized in him a conscientious man: He conducted his interrogations with rigor, but also with a certain reticence. According to the later testimony of the notary Guillaume Manchon, Jean warned Joan that, if she did not declare her submission to the pope and to the Council, she would put herself "in great danger." When the bishop heard of that sympathetic admonition, he "was strongly annoyed." Weighing the danger of Cauchon's displeasure, Jean de La Fontaine left Rouen discreetly. He conducted no interrogation session thereafter and disappears entirely from the transcript on March 28.

During that first interrogation behind closed doors, Jean de La Fontaine began by questioning Joan about the circumstances of her capture and about the warnings that her voices might have given her at that point: "If I had known the hour that I was going to be taken, I would never have gone willingly; nevertheless, I would have obeyed the command of my voices, whatever happened." And she recalled "that it had always been said that she must be taken prisoner."

She was asked for precise figures on the horses and money at her disposal. She also spoke again of the "king's sign," a symbolic royal crown to which she would return several times. It was for her an image, almost a parable, that seemed to please her and that became richer in her responses to questioning throughout March. On March 1 she had alluded to a crown "a thousand times richer" than that which the king had received at his anointing. Her final thought on this point was summarized in Article 51 of the accusation drawn up by the *promotor*, Jean d'Estivet:

> An angel gave the sign to her king . . . Joan had sworn to St. Catherine that she would say nothing about this sign. . . . In bringing him the crown, the angel had promised the king that he would have the whole kingdom of France with the aid of God. As to the crown, it had been given to the archbishop of Reims, who had received it in person and had handed it to the king in Joan's presence. . . . The angel came by the commandment of God . . . He came before her king and made reverence, bowing before him. . . . There were many other angels in his company and also St. Catherine and St. Margaret, who were with the angel even in the chamber of her king. . . . As for the crown, it was brought from God, and there is no goldsmith in the world who knows how to make one so beautiful and so rich.

In reply to another question, Joan remarked that the crown "will have a good odor," provided that it be well guarded.

The majority of these details came out during the interrogation session of March 13, in the course of which Joan uttered another famous reply. When Jean de La Fontaine asked, "Why you, rather than another?" she said, "It pleased God to do so through a simple maiden, to humble the king's enemies."

Joan's symbolic language about the angel and the crown has disconcerted historians. These symbols, richer in meaning than mere abstract formulations, were standard instruments of exchange and communication entirely in line with the spirit of the late age of medieval heraldry. Heraldry is a language of encoded signs and colors, the rules of which were not yet frozen. Joan herself provided a key to her symbolic narrative when she later declared that she saw her mission in this figure; the crown that the king received was her coming at God's command to establish him in his kingly power. At that time symbolic memories were deep, preserved for example in the image of a clump of earth handed over to signify the sale of a field, with any written act serving only as a memorandum. But long before Joan's generation this symbolic mentality was out of intellectual favor. The University of Paris, like universities today, preferred modes of logical thought expressed in the language of deduction, definition, and analysis.

The record reveals when Joan was next questioned and by whom, but her interrogation now took place behind closed doors. It continued on Saturday, March 10; Monday, the twelfth, in the morning and afternoon; Tuesday, the thirteenth; Wednesday, the fourteenth, in the morning and afternoon; Thursday, the fifteenth; and Saturday, the sixteenth, also in the morning and afternoon. Jean de La Fontaine was the inquisitor. Various university professors, including Pierre Cauchon himself, returned to get more precise information on several points on Saturday, March 24. The bishop returned on Palm Sunday, March 25, along with Jean Beaupère, Nicolas Midy, and two others whose names recur frequently in the transcript: Pierre Maurice and Thomas de Courcelles (II, 50). It is noted that they tried to convince Joan to stop wearing men's clothes—an issue that surfaces increasingly—under the pretext that she would not be permitted to hear mass or receive the Eucharist on Easter if she persisted in wearing them.

During the first part of the trial, which was now at an end, no regular accusation was found with which to charge her; none of the inquests Cauchon had launched in January and February provided material useful for proceeding against her. Her interrogators' dilemma is revealed by their insistence on returning, over and over again, to the answers she had given during the preliminary interrogations of February 21 to March 24, but their doggedness did little but establish a clear sense of Joan's attitudes. On Monday, March 26, the "ordinary" trial began. (Nothing in Anglo-American court procedure or terminology corresponds to this Roman law distinction between the preliminary trial "of instruction" and the subsequent "ordinary" trial, normally followed by judgment and sentencing.) When Joan's answers to the preliminary interrogation are compared to those in the "ordinary trial," her views on such matters as filial piety can be clarified and both her earthy pragmatism and her closeness to the spirit world can be glimpsed.

Jean de La Fontaine asked Joan about leaving her village, about her father, and about her mother. She replied: "Since it was God who commanded it, if I had a hundred fathers and a hundred mothers, or if I had been the daughter of a king, I would have left." She would insist, when the interrogation returned to this point, which had first arisen on the afternoon of Monday, March 12, that she "obeyed her father and her mother in everything, except in regard to the suit that she had in the city of Toul on the issue of marriage." It seems that Joan had rejected a betrothal arranged by her parents, and she had to defend herself in a breach-of-promise suit in the ecclesiastical court of her diocese at Toul. She claimed that "she had not made any man any promise." Nothing is known about this trial at Toul except that Joan's cause succeeded. Her father frequently dreamed that his daughter Joan would go away with men-at-arms; he found this prospect terrifying. She explained herself in this fashion: "I heard from my mother that my father had said to my brothers, 'Truly, if I thought that what I fear for my daughter would come to happen, I wish that you would drown her, and if you do not do it, I will drown her myself.'"

The interrogators then returned to her leap from the tower of Beaurevoir; Joan explained it with her usual common sense:

> "I did not do it out of despair, but in the hope of saving my body and of going to assist many good men who were in need. And after the jump I went to confession and asked pardon of the Lord."
>
> "Was any penance imposed on you because of that?"
>
> "I bore part of the penance in the damage I did myself by falling!"

Elsewhere in the course of these repetitive interrogations Joan mentions Franquet d'Arras, the mercenary captain she had handed over to justice at Lagny in April of the previous year (1430). She experienced no qualms of conscience about his subsequent execution, for he was a rapist, a traitor, and a murderer. Her common sense emerges in her response to the questions about a certain hackney she was accused of stealing, but which she insisted she had bought from the bishop of Senlis: In any case, it was "worthless as a mount," she declared. Of far greater importance to Joan's judges is the question of her otherworldly spirituality. During the interrogation of Tuesday morning, March 14, Joan had explained her relationship with her voices:

> St. Catherine told me that I would have help; and I do not know if this will be deliverance from prison or deliverance when I face judgment. Some upheaval may suddenly arise through which I can be delivered, but I think that it will be one or the other. But most often my voices tell me that I will be delivered by a great victory, and then my voices say, "Take everything serenely, do not shrink from your martyrdom; from that you will come finally to the kingdom of paradise." And my voices say that simply and absolutely, without fail. I call this a martyrdom because of the pain and hardship that I suffer in my imprisonment. I do not know if I will have to suffer worse, but I defer in this as in everything to Our Lord.

However hard she was pressed later on, Joan would never go further in her confidences about her voices than this declaration, in which she transcended her own desires to acknowledge the destiny that awaited her. She began to foresee her fate despite herself when she mentioned martyrdom. She wished to give the word another interpretation, but the caution her voices gave her brought her beyond herself. When she was asked if she was sure of being saved, she answered:

"I believe firmly what my voices have told me, that is, that I shall be saved, as firmly as if I were already there."

"After that revelation, do you believe yourself incapable of committing mortal sins?"

"I know nothing about that, but in everything I defer to God."

"That is a very weighty response."

"And I hold it also a great treasure."

The interrogation closed on that statement; it may well have influenced Jean de La Fontaine's decision to leave Rouen after trying to counsel Joan.

During her imprisonment, Joan said she counted almost daily on the assistance of her voices "and indeed I had great need of it." Again: "I would be dead were it not for the voice that comforts me every day." Her faith was unshakable. In the session of Wednesday, March 28, she reports without apparent embarrassment a prayer that also reflects this quality. The recorder and transcribers never converted it into indirect discourse or translated it into Latin; they simply left it in French, just as Joan said it:

> Very sweet God, in honor of Your Holy Passion, I beg You, if You love me, that You reveal to me how I should answer these men of the church. I know well, regarding my clothes, the command that I received, but I do not know anything about the manner in which I should drop it. On that, may it please You to instruct me.

On March 12 toward the end of the morning session, Joan made this surprising confidence about angels: "They often come unseen among Christian people; often I have seen them among Christian people." Little was made of this admission during the "ordinary trial." Whatever skepticism her judges, mostly university intellectuals, may have had about such spirits, as a tribunal of the Inquisition they could hardly accuse someone of heresy because of a belief in angels. However, Cauchon was doubtless certain that he had ensnared Joan when the question of the Church Militant arose. On March 15 Jean de La Fontaine had opened the interrogation by asking:

> "If it should happen that you have done something against the Faith, would you defer to the determination of our holy mother the church, to whom you should indeed defer in such matters?"
>
> "Let my answers be seen and examined by clerics and let them tell me afterward if there is anything that is against the Christian faith. . . . If there is anything evil against the Christian faith that God has ordered, I would not wish to maintain it and would be very upset to come out as opposed to [the church]."

Either La Fontaine or one of the two members of the university then present, Nicolas Midy and Gérard Feuillet, undertook to explain to the accused the difference between the Church Triumphant and the Church Militant. Put simply, the Church Militant was the Catholic church on earth; the Church Triumphant was the church in heaven; the Church Suffering was those of its members in purgatory. Joan, who was not familiar with these abstract categories, answered simply: "I shall not answer you anything else for the present." Having now understood by her reluctance that this was a key question, the judges would return to it indefatigably. This question of Joan's submission to the church was raised more than twenty times thereafter. On March 17, Joan had an answer that should have removed any hesitation on the part of judges: "It is my sense that it is all one, God's and the church's, and that there should be no difficulty about it. Why do you make difficulties about its being one and the same thing?" When asked if she felt required to tell the whole truth to the pope, she replied: "Bring me before our lord the pope, and I shall answer him on everything that I should answer."

When the "ordinary" process began on March 26, Cauchon knew that he finally had grounds for a valid accusation: inadequate submission to the Church Militant. By then, Jean de La Fontaine, as we have seen, had ceased to interrogate Joan. He was still present, however, on Tuesday, March 27, when, "in the room next to the great hall of the castle of Rouen," a new public session took place, in the course of which Pierre Cauchon made an appeal to the assessors for their advice on the brief drawn up by the *promotor*. The first of the assessors to express himself on this point was Nicolas de Venderès (II, 69), a canon of Rouen, licensed in canon law; he was punctual at the following sessions, in which he played an active role. It was necessary in his eyes for the accused to swear another oath. If she refused, she should be excommunicated. La Fontaine agreed with this advice; the majority of the other assessors demanded that Joan be read the articles drawn up by the *promotor* before being declared excommunicate. Some of them, such as the Benedictine Pierre Miget, prior of Longueville (II, 66), who eventually would vote that she be handed over to the secular arm of justice, declared that, regarding the articles to which Joan was unable to respond, one could not require that she answer yes or no as was customary.

The seventy articles of the brief from the verbose and sometimes vulgar pen of Jean d'Estivet were read to Joan on March 27 and 28. The brief expanded on most of the questions asked Joan but was barely connected to the answers she had given during the hearings. Article 7, for example, says: "Joan often had the habit of carrying a mandrake in her bosom, hoping through this talisman to have a prosperous fortune in wealth and temporal things, affirming that a mandrake of that type had force and effect." The transcript contained Joan's energetic reply: "That article about the mandrake she denied entirely." The same level of distortion appears in a subsequent article dealing with the young man who took Joan to court at Toul on a complaint of marriage refusal: "In prosecuting that suit, she went frequently to Toul, and exposed on that occasion, as it were, everything she had."

The brief is marked by such twisting of evidence. In Article 13, Joan is reproached for having worn male attire (a "short, reduced, and dissolute" man's suit); Joan's categorical reply, which appears in the French minutes of the trial, was omitted from the Latin transcript. In the brief, men's clothes were accorded a place of increasing importance. The costume that Joan had considered entirely reasonable—as had the inhabitants of Vaucouleurs, her companions on the first journey, the king, even the bishops of the investigation of Poitiers—became a point of obsession for these judges. On March 15, they had gone as far as to try a form of blackmail. Since Holy Week was approaching, they offered Joan the chance to hear mass if she agreed to put away men's clothes. She offered a counterproposal: "Have a long dress touching the ground, without a train, made for me and give it to me for going to mass." Or then: "Give me a dress of the sort that a bourgeois girl would wear—a long skirt with something like a woman's hood—and I will take them to go to mass in." This offer produced no result.

Several of the articles fraudulently contradicted Joan's explicit declarations. For example, Article 56: "Joan frequently bragged of having two counselors, whom she called 'Counselors of the Fountain,' who came to her after she was captured." The judges were also determined to associate Joan with Catherine de La Rochelle. That connection somehow led them to the conclusion that "Joan would escape from prison with the aid of the Devil if she were not well guarded." The transcript of her response to the brief does concede that "to this article Joan responded that she would hold to what she had already said, and as for the 'Counselors of the Fountain,' she did not know what that was." Again, always in the same line of thought, she was charged with having ordered melted wax to be poured on the heads of little children in order to practice "divinations by this charm." Unperturbed, she denied these alleged acts of divination and returned to her previous answers. To the text of the brief, though it was fraudulent on many points, the responses Joan made on April 18 were later added. The last of these articles insisted on her submission to the Church Militant:

> "So long as she [the church] does not command something impossible to do— and what I call impossible is that I revoke the deeds I have done and the words I have said in this trial concerning the visions and revelations that were given to me from God, for I will not revoke them for anything; what Our Lord has made me do and has commanded and may yet command, I shall not fail to do for the sake of any man alive, and should the church wish that I do something against the commandment that was given me by God, I would not do it for anything."

"If the Church Militant tells you that your revelations are illusions or somehow diabolic, would you defer to the church?"

"In that case, I would defer as always to God, whose command I have always obeyed, and I know well that what is contained in this trial comes through God's command, and what I have affirmed in this process that I have done by God's command. It would be impossible for me to do the contrary. And should the Church Militant command me to do otherwise, I would not defer to any man of the world, other than our Lord, whose good command I have always done."

"Do you believe that you are subject to the church of God that is on earth, that is to say, to our lord the pope, to the cardinals, archbishops, bishops, and other prelates of the church?"

"Yes, so long as Our Lord is first served."

"Have you received the command from your voices not to submit to the Church Militant, which is on earth, nor to her judgment?"

"I shall not answer anything that comes into my head, but what I do answer is at the command of my voices; they do not command me not to obey the church, God being first served."

On March 31, Joan was interrogated once more behind closed doors in the hall where she was held prisoner; this interrogation bore more sharply than usual on obedience to the church. Joan must have spent that Easter Day in prison without being able to hear mass. New Year at that period began on April 1, on which Easter also fell that year; thereafter, the acts of the trial are dated 1431. The following days, from April 2 to April 7, were devoted to drawing up twelve articles extracted from the seventy previous ones; according to inquisitorial procedure, these were to be sent to the doctors and prelates called in for consultation. It was necessary to submit both the charges and the résumé of the hearings to doctors uninvolved in the process so that they could pronounce the degree of the accused's guilt. The group included a certain number of assessors, among whom were delegates of the University of Paris, as well as two English prelates: William Haiton (II, 54), one of the two negotiators of the marriage of Henry V to Catherine of France in 1419, and Richard Prati, who would later become bishop of Chichester. Also present was Friar Isambart de La Pierre, a Dominican who had appeared frequently in the interrogation sessions behind closed doors since March 10.

The next interrogation session took place on Wednesday, April 18, in Joan's cell. She was sick, and Cauchon thought it appropriate to assure her "that the doctors and masters would come to see her in a friendly and charitable manner to visit her in her illness, so as to console and to comfort her." Two of the doctors who visited that day testified later during the nullification trial. Jean Tiphaine, the duchess of Bedford's own physician, who served as an assessor in Joan's trial, recalled:

When Joan was ill, the judges ordered me to visit her, and I was brought to her by one named d'Estivet. In his presence, and that of Master Guillaume de La Chambre [II, 56], a master of medicine, and several others, I took her pulse in order to discern the cause of her illness, and I asked her what she felt and where she hurt. She told me that a carp had been sent her by the bishop of Beauvais, that she had eaten some of it, and that she thought it caused her illness. Then Estivet reproached her, saying that what she said was false; he called her a slut, saying: "It's you, slut, who ate a shad and other things that have made you sick"; she answered that that was not so, and they exchanged lots of insulting words. Afterward, wishing to learn more about Joan's illness, I heard it said by the men who were there that she had vomited a great deal.

The carp to which Joan attributed her illness raises questions about whether she might have been accidentally or deliberately poisoned. Up to this point, there is no indication that Joan, whose constitution was exceptionally robust, had ever fallen ill, despite wounds, injuries, fatigue and the often stressful conditions of her expeditions, campaigns, and imprisonment. Estivet's fury at her implication that she was poisoned seems excessive. Is it possible that Pierre Cauchon had found a more expeditious way of terminating this disappointing trial? The other doctor summoned to examine Joan, Guillaume de La Chambre, testified in the nullification trial to the powerful English reaction:

As to her illness, the cardinal of England [II, 8] and the earl of Warwick [II, 43] sent me to find out about it. I appeared before them, with Master Guillaume Desjardins [II, 14], a master in medicine, and other doctors, and the earl of Warwick told us that Joan was sick, according to what had been reported to him, and that he had had us summoned to take care of her, because more than anything in the world the king did not wish her to die a natural death. The king considered her very precious and had bought her dearly, and he did not wish her to die except at the hands of justice and he wished that she should be burned. We did so much, visiting her with care, that she got well. I went to see her along with Master Guillaume Desjardins again and the others. We palpated her on the right side and found her feverish, and thus we decided to bleed her; when the matter was reported to the earl of Warwick, he said, "Be careful with the bleeding, because she is wily and might kill herself." She was bled nevertheless, which relieved her immediately; once she was so cured, a certain Master Jean d'Estivet arrived. He exchanged insulting words with Joan and called her a whore and a slut; Joan was very irritated, so much so that she took fever again and fell sick once more.

Discordant voices were making themselves heard. Fortunately for Cauchon, the University of Paris, which had been consulted on April 12, agreed entirely with his conclusions and adopted all the articles drawn up by Estivet. A large group of the assessors—Zanon de Castiglione, bishop of Lisieux; Philibert de Montjeu, bishop of Coutances; and Gilles de Duremort, abbot of Fécamp, and his chaplain, Jean de Bouesgue, all of whom appear in the account books of the king of England—also approved this inquest without reservation. However, the abbots of Jumièges and Cormeilles, Nicolas Le Roux and Guillaume Bonnel, demanded that the trial be conducted in the presence of the University of Paris, so that Joan might be better instructed and that the articles be read to her in French, explaining clearly the danger that she incurred. Eleven lawyers of the jurisdiction of Rouen also expressed reservations, and three of the assessors— Pierre Minier, Jean Pigache, and Richard du Grouchet—protested that Joan's revelations should not be interpreted in so negative a fashion. Yet another, Raoul Le Sauvage, thought that the question should be submitted to the Holy See.

News sometimes traveled so slowly in medieval Europe that the people of Rouen were not yet aware that Pope Martin V had died on February 20. Worse news for their party was the accession on March 3 of Eugenius IV, who had been opposed for many years to the guiding spirits of the Council of Basel, especially to Thomas de Courcelles (II, 50), a political ally of many of the assessors at Joan's trial.

Then there was the scarcely veiled hostility of the cathedral chapter of Rouen; after an early meeting on April 13, the canons had taken refuge in the pretext that they were not numerous enough to undertake valid deliberations: In modern terms, they claimed they lacked a quorum. On the following day they reached agreement that the twelve articles should be read to Joan in French and that she should be better informed on everything concerning submission to the Church Militant. It may be significant that neither this letter nor the letter from the bishop of Avranches, Jean de Saint-Avit, who formally opposed the trial in its entirety, was preserved in the trial transcript. Several other clerics of Rouen, such as Jean Lohier and Master Nicolas de Houppeville (who was thrown in prison for his position), vehemently opposed the trial.

Unanimity had not been achieved in the case of Joan the Maid. What was left in the way of a charge? First, Joan was charged with lack of submission to the Church Militant, but she had just been advised by Jean de La Fontaine and two religious—one of them Isambart de La Pierre—to modify her attitude on that subject. Second, Joan was charged with the wearing of men's clothes, but this seemed a thin basis for condemnation. Nevertheless, the wish of the English partisans was clear: Joan must be formally condemned in a way that would entail both dishonor and discredit for Charles VII (II, 1). Cauchon would fail in his task if he did not find a way to comply with these instructions.

The meeting of April 18 was devoted to what was called "charitable warning" in the vocabulary of the Inquisition. There also may have been hope that in her weakened state, Joan could be led to make some compromising statement, but this did not occur. Joan thanked the bishop for what he had said "for her salvation" and added: "It seems to me, in view of the sickness that I have, that I am in great danger of death; and if such is God's pleasure for me, I ask to make confession and receive the sacrament of the Eucharist and be buried in consecrated ground."

Taking advantage of her request, the bishop proceeded:

> "Since you ask that the church give you the sacrament of the Eucharist, do you wish to submit yourself to the Church Militant? In that case, we promise to give you that sacrament."
>
> "Whatever happens, I will not do or say anything other than what I have said before. I am a good Christian, and well baptized, and I shall die as a good Christian. . . . As to God, I love Him, I serve Him, I am a good Christian, and I would wish to aid and support the church with all my power."
>
> "Do you want us to plan a fine and worthy procession to bring you back to good health if you are not in that state?"
>
> "I hope that the church and Catholic people will pray for me."

Joan seems to have regained her strength when the second "charitable warning" was issued on Wednesday, May 2. In that session Master Jean de Châtillon, a bachelor in theology at the University of Paris and a friend of Cauchon and Beaupère, led the interrogation. Regarding the Church Militant, Joan answered their questions unequivocally: "I believe fully in the church here below. I believe that the Church Militant cannot err or fail; but as far as what I have said and what I have done, I rely entirely on God, who has made me do what I have done." And when they spoke to her of the pope, she answered: "Bring me to him and I will answer to him."

Eight days later Jean Massieu went once again to find Joan. He led her not into the hall of judgment but into the great tower of the castle. Joan found herself face to face with Cauchon and some assessors whom she had already seen several times: Jean de Châtillon, Guillaume Érard (II, 51), André Marguerie, Nicolas de Venderès, the Englishman William Haiton, Nicolas Loiseleur, Aubert Morel (an advocate at the court of Rouen), and the Benedictine monk Jean Dacier, abbot of Saint-Corneille at Compiègne. There were also two men Joan did not know, Maugier Leparmentier, the executioner, and his assistant. She was threatened with torture: Joan declared, "Truly, if you pull my members apart and make the soul leave the body, I will not tell you anything else, and if I should tell you something, afterward I shall always say that you made me say it by force."

They were clearly not ready for that response. Cauchon decided to suspend the proceedings and get approval for this latest initiative from a larger group. On the following Saturday, he assembled in his house a dozen assessors, of whom only three declared that it seemed to them "expedient" to put Joan to the torture, so as to "know the truth about her lies": They were Aubert Morel, Thomas de Courcelles, and Nicolas Loiseleur. It seems that Cauchon finally perceived the wisdom of Raoul Roussel's suggestion (II, 68): The first of the assessors to be asked for advice, he declared that he was opposed to torture "so that a process as well conducted as this one not run the risk of calumny."

The major local event of the following day is not mentioned in the official transcripts; Joan was not directly involved. On Sunday, May 13, Richard Beauchamp, earl of Warwick, gave a banquet to which he invited many of the principal characters in Joan's story. His account book dedicates two pages to the purchases made for that feast rather than the single page that was usually sufficient. At the end of that sumptuous repast, the guests decided to visit the place where Joan was being held prisoner. She saw entering her cell John of Luxembourg (II, 28); his brother, Louis (II, 29), bishop of Thérouanne; Humphrey, earl of Stafford; the intimates of the castle; and the earl of Warwick himself, accompanied by a Burgundian knight whom she knew from a previous encounter, Aimond de Macy. The account book also expressly mentions among the guests Pierre Cauchon, bishop of Beauvais, and Jean de Mailly, bishop of Noyon (II, 61). Those two judged it inopportune to visit the prisoner. In the nullification trial, Aimond de Macy reported the scene:

> [John of Luxembourg] addressed Joan, saying to her, "Joan, I have come to pay a ransom for you provided that you are willing to promise that you will never take up arms against us again." She answered, "In God's name, you are mocking me, for I know well that you have neither the power nor the will to do this." And she repeated that several times, because the count persisted in saying so; and she said then, "I know well that these English will have me dead, because they think after my death they will win the kingdom of France. But were there a hundred thousand *Godons* more than there are at present, they will not have the kingdom." [*Godon* was a current slang term for the English, who to French ears seemed constantly to repeat the expletive *Goddamn*.] At these words, the earl of Stafford was enraged, and pulled his dirk halfway out of its scabbard to strike her with it, but the earl of Warwick prevented him.

Aimond de Macy himself reports that he first saw Joan when she was in prison in the castle of Beaurevoir, and that he had conversed with her several times there. He admits: "I tried several times, playing with her, to touch her breasts, trying to place my hands on her chest, which Joan would not suffer, but pushed me away with all her strength. Joan was indeed an honest woman, as much in her words as in her deeds." Aimond saw her once again at the castle of Le Crotoy, and he reported that the chancellor of the church of Amiens, Nicolas de Queuville, had come several times to celebrate mass in the prison, and: "He said much good of Joan." The Burgundian knight prolonged his stay at Rouen; he was present a little later, during the "abjuration of Saint-Ouen."

During the dinner of May 13, Warwick told the bishop of Beauvais that the trial had gone on too long. Cauchon received another important communication on the following day, when the rector of the University of Paris sent him a letter to announce that after numerous consultations and serious deliberations provoked by the visit of Jean Beaupère, Nicolas Midy, and Jacques de Touraine, who had communicated to them the twelve articles drawn up on the brief of Estivet, they had finally reached "unanimous consensus" that it was time to act so that "the unjust and scandalous demoralization of the people" provoked by "a woman by the name of Joan who is called the Maid" would cease. This statement was followed by commentary on the twelve articles, which clearly declared her an apostate, a liar, a schismatic, and a heretic. Pierre Cauchon hastened on Saturday, May 19, to convoke the assessors once again in order to consider the conclusions of these venerable masters of the faculties of theology and canon law of "our Mother, the University of Paris." Once again, on the following Wednesday, Joan was given the formal admonition of the Inquisition and answered in her own fashion:

> I wish to maintain the manner in which I have always spoken and behaved in this trial. If I were already judged and saw the fire lit, and the bundles of sticks ready and the executioners ready to light the fire, and even if I were within the fire, I would nevertheless not say anything other. I would maintain unto death what I have said in this trial.

She made this response to Pierre Maurice (II, 64), a young master fresh out of school with a license in theology, one of the brightest lights of his generation, who reported it twenty-seven years later. This rejoinder made an impression on him. He went to Joan's prison when she had just learned what death she was to die. When she cried out, "Master Pierre, where will I be this evening?" he responded: "Have you not good hope in God?"

On Thursday, May 24, after the feast of Pentecost, Cauchon organized a spectacle designed to impress the prisoner. In the cemetery of the abbey of Saint-Ouen, several platforms were set up, one for Joan and the others for the assessors who were present under the presidency of Cardinal Henry Beaufort, bishop of Winchester. Louis of Luxembourg; Jean de Mailly, bishop of Noyon; and William Alnwick, bishop of Norwich, private secretary and keeper of the privy seal to Henry V and Henry VI, were there as well, along with the abbots of Fécamp, Cormeilles, Jumièges, Saint-Ouen, Le Bec-Hellouin, Mortemer, and Préaux. Guillaume Érard, canon of Rouen and a master of the University of Paris whom the king of England would charge to represent the royal interests four years later at the negotiations of Arras, preached a solemn sermon at Joan. Several witnesses later interrogated in the nullification trial, in particular Friar Isambart and Martin Ladvenu (II, 57), another Dominican at the convent of Rouen, recollected certain passages. Ladvenu reported that the preacher had cried out: "O Royal House of France! You have never known a monster until now! But now behold yourself dishonored in placing your trust in this woman, this magician, heretical and superstitious." At this Joan interrupted him, crying out: "Do not speak of my king, he is a good Christian." Jean Massieu, the usher, who was at Joan's side on the same platform and so was well situated to report the scene, reported that the preacher gave him a sign meaning "Make her be silent." His sermon completed, Guillaume Érard addressed Joan directly:

> "Look at my lords the judges, who many times have summoned you to submit all your words and deeds to our holy mother the church, explaining to you and remonstrating that in your words and deeds there were many things that, as it seemed to the clergy, were not good to say and to support."
>
> "I shall answer you. Regarding the matter of submission to the church, I have answered you on that point: of all the works that I have done, let a report be sent to Rome to our holy father, the sovereign pontiff, to whom, and to God first of all, I appeal. As to my words and deeds, I have done them on God's orders and charge no one else with them, neither my king nor any other. If there is any fault, it is mine and no one else's."

To a further question, she persisted in replying: "I appeal to God and to our holy father the pope." There are many instances of inquisitorial trials in which the appeal to the pope was enough to interrupt the process, but that did not happen here.

Three times Guillaume Érard repeated his exhortation, while Jean Massieu handed Joan a cedula, a slip of parchment designed to be attached to a legal document. Someone had written a letter of abjuration on this slip; Massieu urged her to sign it. At that moment, as Massieu reported a quarter-century later, "a great murmur arose among those who were present; at one point, I heard [Bishop Cauchon] say: 'You will have to pay for that.' At that time, I warned Joan of the peril that was threatening her, and I instructed her about signing this cedula and I saw clearly that she did not understand this document."

To Joan's appeal to the pope, no other response was given than "It is impossible to go find our lord the pope at such a distance." Her request to have the cedula explained to her met with the same reaction. According to the testimony of Massieu, Joan demanded that the document be inspected by the clerks and that they should give her counsel; Guillaume Érard answered: "Do it now,"—presumably he meant for her to sign it—"otherwise you will end your days by fire."

Aimond de Macy, who was present, asserted however that it was the secretary of the king of England, Laurence Calot, often among Warwick's guests at the castle, who pulled from his sleeve a little cedula and handed it to Joan to sign. She first drew a circle; Laurence Calot held her hand and made her draw a cross on the document.

What was on that slip of parchment? The cedula was said to contain a promise that Joan would no longer wear men's clothes. According to the testimony of Guillaume Manchon, who in his capacity as notary should have been aware of the meaning of this scene, Joan laughed. We may ask if the cross that she had just drawn in place of a signature (we have seen that she signed her name on several letters, from the end of 1429) might not have been a reference to the cross that she had sometimes put on military messages, as a previously agreed signal indicating that whoever received that letter should consider it null and void.

All of this occurred in a strange confusion: The bishop of Beauvais was reproached by the Englishmen present for not having condemned Joan, while Jean Massieu read her the letter of abjuration. That letter, according to the later report of eyewitnesses, was six or eight lines long, whereas in the trial transcript the cedula of abjuration consists of forty-seven printed lines in the French translation (forty-four in the Latin text). As Jean Massieu declared in the nullification trial:

> It was given to me to read to her, and I read it to Joan, and I remember well that in that letter it was noted that in future she would neither carry arms, nor wear men's clothes, nor would she cut her hair short, and many other things that I do not remember anymore; and I know well that cedula contained about eight lines and no more, and I know absolutely that it was not registered in the transcript of the trial, because what I read her was different from that which was inserted in the record, and that [the one he read her] is the one Joan signed.

This scene surprised everybody. "The English were indignant with the bishop of Beauvais, the doctors, and the assessors of the trial because Joan had not been convicted and condemned and handed over to execution." Their attitude was threatening: "The king has spent his money very badly on you." Specific punishments meted out to reformed heretics seem to have varied, but the normal period of imprisonment was three years; if punished as a reformed heretic, Joan might well have expected to be freed eventually and to return to Domrémy. An eyewitness, Jean Favé, master of royal appeals, said:

> I heard men say that after that sermon, when the earl of Warwick complained
> to the bishop and to the doctors, saying that it would go badly for the king
> because Joan would escape them, one among them answered: "My Lord, do not
> worry; we will catch her again."

The conclusion of this episode is tellingly related by the notary Guillaume
Manchon:

> As we were leaving the preaching at Saint-Ouen, after the abjuration of the Maid,
> Loiseleur said to her, "Joan, you have spent the day well and, please God, you
> have saved your soul." She asked, "Well, as to that, some of you men of the
> church, [arrange to] take me into your prison so that I be no longer in the hands
> of these Englishmen." To which my lord of Beauvais answered, "Take her back
> to where you found her." Which is why she was brought back to the castle she
> had left.

Only those who had relapsed—that is, those who having once abjured their
errors returned to them—could be condemned to death by a tribunal of the
Inquisition and delivered for death "to the secular arm." Despite his earlier loss
of hope that he would find a proper charge, Cauchon had succeeded only in
making men's clothes the symbol of Joan's refusal to submit to the church. The
cedula containing a promise no longer to wear men's clothes became the
instrument of a game to make Joan relapse.

What were the exact circumstances that constrained Joan to relapse? By
the following Sunday, three days later, Joan once more wore male attire: She
reclaimed male garments when she was returned to the secular prison and
exposed to further abuse by her English guards. Martin Ladvenu affirms that
"someone approached her secretly at night; I have heard from Joan's own mouth
that an English lord entered her cell and tried to take her by force." Jean Massieu
gives a slightly different version: Having returned to women's clothes on the
Thursday after Pentecost, at the moment when she woke up in the morning of
the following Sunday, Trinity Sunday, she could not find her women's clothes
because the English guards had taken these away from her after throwing her a
sack in which were exclusively men's clothes; and so "she dressed herself in the
men's clothes which they had thrown her." For whatever reason, Cauchon
learned on Sunday, May 27, that Joan had resumed wearing men's clothes.
Wasting no time, he arrived the following morning at the prison, accompanied
by the vice-inquisitor, Jean Lemaître, and several assessors.

> Joan was dressed in men's clothes, that is, a tunic, a cape, and a short robe and
> other men's clothes, a costume that on our orders she had previously put aside,

and had taken on women's clothes. And so we interrogated her, to learn when and for what reason she had once more assumed men's clothes: "I did it on my own will," Joan declared; "I took it again because it was more lawful and convenient than to have women's clothes because I am with men; I began to wear them again because what was promised me was not observed, to wit that I should go to mass and receive the body of Christ and be freed from these irons. . . . I would rather die than stay in these irons; but if it is permitted for me to go to mass, and if I could be freed of these irons, and if I could be put in a decent prison and if I could have a woman to help me [her expression, *avoir femme,* is written on the minutes but not on the official transcript of the trial], I would be good and do what the church wishes."

"Since Thursday, have you heard the voices of St. Catherine and St. Margaret?" [Cauchon asked.]

"Yes."

"What have they told you?"

"God has expressed through St. Catherine and St. Margaret His great sorrow at the strong treason to which I consented in abjuring and making a revocation to save my life, and said that I was damning myself to save my life."

In the margin, the recorder noted: "A deadly reply."

After saying explicitly that her voices had told her what was to happen at the cemetery at Saint-Ouen that Thursday, she added: "I did not say or intend to deny my apparitions, that is, that they were St. Catherine and St. Margaret." "That being understood," adds the 1431 transcript, "we removed ourselves from her, to proceed according to right and reason."

Two witnesses later attested that on leaving this encounter, Cauchon spoke cheerfully to several Englishmen, including Warwick himself, who waited in the court of the castle: "Farewell, make good cheer. It is done."

On Wednesday, May 30, early in the morning, two Dominicans, Martin Ladvenu, whom she had already seen sitting as an assessor in the trial, and his assistant, Jean Toutmouillé, went to Joan's cell. In the transcript Toutmouillé has left us a moving report:

The day that Joan was abandoned to secular judgment and delivered to be burned, I found myself in the morning in the prison with Friar Martin Ladvenu, whom the bishop of Beauvais had sent to tell her of her coming death and to induce her to true contrition and penance, and also to hear her confession, which Ladvenu did very carefully and charitably. And when he announced to the poor woman the death that she was to die that day, which her judges had ordered, and when she had understood and heard the hard and cruel death that was coming, she began to cry out sorrowfully and pitiably to tear and pull her hair. "Alas! that they treat me so horribly and cruelly that my body, clean and whole, which was never corrupted, should be today consumed and reduced to ashes! Ah! I would prefer to be beheaded seven times than to be burned like that! Alas! If I had been in an ecclesiastical prison to which I submitted myself, and if I had been guarded by men of the church, not by my enemies and adversaries, it would not have turned out for me as miserably as it has. Ah! I protest before God, the Great Judge, the great wrongs and grievances that they have done me." She then made marvelous complaint in that place of the oppression and violences that had been done to her in prison by the jailers and by the others they had made enter against her.

After these complaints, the bishop arrived, to whom she said immediately: "Bishop, I die because of you." He began to remonstrate with her, saying: "Ah, Joan, take it patiently, you will die because you have not held to what you promised us and because you return to your first witchcraft." And the poor Maid answered him: "Alas! If you had put me in the prison of a church court and handed me over to the hands of competent and agreeable ecclesiastical caretakers, this would not have happened to me. That is why I complain of you before God." That being done, I went outside and heard no more.

The usher Jean Massieu, who had also been sent by the bishop of Beauvais, told how Martin Ladvenu heard Joan's confession, after which she asked to receive the Eucharist. The Dominican was perplexed: Should he give communion to an excommunicate? He sent someone to ask the bishop of Beauvais, who made this surprising response: "Let them give her the sacrament of the Eucharist and anything she asks." Massieu himself went to find a stole and a candle, so that the sacrament could be given her with dignity. As Robert Wirth (on the WWW discussion group, joanofarc@seas.smu.edu on June 22, 1999), "to hear the confession of, and to give communion to a relapsed heretic, was absolutely unthinkable . . . That one incident alone" proves to him that "the trial was judicial murder, even if there were no other evidence."

Joan was then led to the Old Marketplace, where, as for the spectacle at the Saint-Ouen cemetery, several platforms had been set up, for she had to endure a final oration, this one delivered by Nicolas Midy.

The investigation of her relapse had been managed with dispatch. Beauchamp, having established on Monday the twenty-eighth that Joan had resumed men's clothes, quickly convoked the assessors for the next day, May 29, to bring them up to date on this sign of insubordination to the Church Militant and to deliberate what should be done. He was able to convene forty-two assessors, to whom he posed the question of what to do with Joan, given the manner in which she had returned to her errors. In the course of this final session, thirty-nine of the assessors declared that the cedula should be read to her anew and should be explained to her. Only three of the assessors were of the opinion that she should be abandoned to secular justice without further effort: Denis Gastinel, Nicolas de Venderès, and a certain Jean Pinchon, who had been awarded posts as canon at the cathedrals of Paris and Rouen while still archdeacon at Jouy-en-Josas. This was perhaps an unexpected, but merely formal obstacle, since the assessors had only a consultative voice, whereas Cauchon was the judge along with the vice-inquisitor, Jean Lemaître, whose name does not appear in the records for this final session. Cauchon moved ahead and made preparations for the resolution of this overlong trial.

In haste, Cauchon flouted the procedural rules of an inquisitorial trial. Laurent, the bailiff of Rouen, later recalled that in a similar case, a malefactor condemned by ecclesiastical justice had been brought to what he called "the mob"—that is, to the hall in which the bailiff heard cases—so that a regular secular sentence could be pronounced. Cauchon did not obtain the sentence of a secular court. This was a serious irregularity. Cauchon simply delivered Joan directly to be burned at the stake prepared in the Old Marketplace:

> The sentence was pronounced as though Joan had been abandoned to secular justice. Immediately after that sentence, she was put in the hands of the bailiff, and before the bailiff or I, to whom it belonged to pronounce such a sentence, had the chance to pronounce one, the executioner seized Joan without further ado and led her to the place where the wood had been prepared and she was burned.

All of this took place in the presence of a large number of armed men: 800, according to Jean Massieu. Massieu was not always exact in his estimates, and this number may be exaggerated, but it is not improbably large since, besides the regular garrison of the castle, a considerable number of men-at-arms must have been assembled for a planned attack on Louviers. Guesdon captures an atmosphere of haste among a mass of soldiery supervising the scene and surrounding the scaffold, ready to contain the crowd:

> While Joan was making her devotions and pious lamentations, I was strongly pressed by the English, and indeed, by one of their captains, to leave her in their hands so as to make her die more quickly; they said to me, whose office was to comfort her on the scaffold: "Priest, are you going to let us get done in time for dinner?" And impatiently, without any form or indication of judgment, they sent her to the fire, saying to the master of the work: "Do your job." And so she was brought and attached to the stake, continuing to praise God and the saints while lamenting devoutly; the last word she cried in a high voice as she died was: "Jesus!"

This haste, this crush of the crowd, these hundreds of English men-at-arms, this executioner—his name was Geoffroy Thérage—all for one young girl who in a high voice lamented and invoked God. One gesture of sympathy is mentioned:

"With great devotion, Joan asked to have the cross, and hearing that, an Englishman who was present there made her a little one in wood from the end of a stick, which he handed her, and she took it devoutly and kissed it, making a pious lamentation to God, our redeemer, who had suffered on the cross, of which cross she had the sign and representation, and she put that cross in her bosom, between her flesh and her garments."

Hearing that request, Friar Isambart de La Pierre went to find in the nearby church of Saint-Laurent a cross "to hold elevated right above her eyes up to the moment of death, so that the cross on which God hung during His life could be continually before her sight." And he attested that Joan, "being already surrounded by the flame, never ceased up to the end to proclaim and to profess in a high voice the holy name of Jesus, imploring and invoking without cease the aid of the saints of paradise, and again, which is more, while surrendering her spirit and letting her head fall, she uttered the name of Jesus as a sign that she was fervent in the faith of God."

These cries in the Old Marketplace, which she uttered in a high and strong voice, according to those who were there, above the crackling flame amid the noise of crowd, moved many who were present, including some of the English. Several witnesses in the retrial of 1456 remembered the tears of Louis of Luxembourg, bishop of Thérouanne, who was entirely devoted to the English cause. The executioner who had been called to torture her in the dungeon in Rouen, Maugier Leparmentier, said: "Once in the fire, she cried out more than six times, 'Jesus!' and especially in her last breath, she cried with a strong voice, 'Jesus!' so that everyone present could hear it; almost all wept with pity." Isambart reported an event that marked Joan's fellowship with the martyrs according to the sensibility of medieval Christianity:

> One of the Englishmen, a soldier who detested her exceptionally and had sworn that with his own hand he would bring a bundle of sticks to Joan's stake, at the moment he did it and heard Joan crying the name of Jesus in her last moment, stood struck with stupor as though in an ecstasy and had to be led to a tavern near the Old Marketplace, so that with the help of some drink he could regain his strength. And having had a meal with a friar of the order of Friars Preachers, this Englishman confessed through the mouth of that friar who was also English that he had sinned gravely and that he repented what he had done against Joan, whom he now took to be a holy woman; for as it seemed to him, this Englishman had himself seen, at the moment that Joan gave up her spirit, a white dove emerge from her and take flight toward France. And the executioner, after lunch on that same day, came to a convent of Friars Preachers and told me as well as Friar Martin Ladvenu that he was damned because he had burned a holy woman.

Pierre Cusquel, who had seen her several times because he did masonry work at the castle, had not been present "because my heart could not have stood it and would have suffered from pity for Joan," but he recounted: "I have heard it said that Master Jean Tressart, secretary to the king of England, coming back from Joan's execution, lamentably afflicted and moaning over what he had seen in that place, said: 'We are all lost, for it is a good and holy person that was burned,' and that he thought 'that her soul was in the hands of God, and that, when she was in the midst of the flames, she had continuously called upon the name of the Lord Jesus.'"

One of the assessors, Jean Alespée (II, 45), a canon of Rouen who was one of the agents of the king of England when that city had surrendered to the English in 1419, wept abundantly, according to the witnesses, and said: "I wish that my soul were where I believe this woman's soul is."

Warwick ordered her ashes to be collected and thrown into the Seine so that no relics could be claimed later. Even so, rumors began to spread, as Jean Massieu (II, 63) tells us: "I heard it said by Jean Fleury, a clerk of the bailiff and the recorder, that the executioner told him that although her body had been burned in the fire and reduced to ashes, her heart remained intact and full of blood, and he was told to gather the ashes and everything that remained of her and to throw them in the Seine, which he did." According to Friar Isambart, the executioner affirmed that: "despite the oil, the sulfur, and the carbon that he had applied to the entrails and the heart of Joan, he still could not make them burn in any way, nor could he reduce her entrails and her heart to ashes, at which he was as astonished as if by a confirmed miracle."

CHAPTER EIGHT

THE VERDICT OF ROUEN NULLIFIED

Joan's condemnation and death at Rouen seemed for about a year to strengthen the English cause in France. A number of military victories led to the coronation of the boy-King Henry VI (see Part II, Section 2) at Paris. But after the spring of 1432, French forces (often commanded by Joan's former companions-in-arms) won as often as they lost. By December 1435, when the Treaty of Arras put an end to the long estrangement between Charles VII (II, 1) and Philip of Burgundy (II, 3), the French definitely reclaimed the initiative in both warfare and diplomacy. Paris fell to the French in 1436; in 1438, Charles VII reclaimed control of the church in France. In 1449, he called for the pope to authorize a new trial for Joan. It opened at Paris in November 1455 under the presidency of Guillaume d'Estouteville, the papal legate who was also a cousin of King Charles. Moving in December to Rouen, it concluded its deliberations on July 7, 1456, after lengthy interrogation of 115 witnesses, many of whom had been involved in the trial that condemned Joan in 1431. That former trial was declared to have been procedurally flawed from its inception and was therefore nullified.

IN THE DAYS THAT FOLLOWED THE BURNING OF JOAN AT THE STAKE in Rouen, the attitude of Pierre Cauchon suggests anxiety. Heated discussions had taken place in the city at the convent of Saint-Jacques (home of Friar Isambart de La Pierre and Friar Martin Ladvenu [II, 57]), provoked by Friar Pierre Bosquier, who insisted that those who had judged Joan had done ill. In retribution, Cauchon sentenced him to ten months in prison on bread and water, until Easter of the following year. On June 7, 1431 the bishop convoked several of the assessors, his faithful intimates: Nicolas de Venderès (II, 69), who had drawn up the abjuration cedula; Nicolas Loiseleur (II, 60), who had tried to extract confidences from Joan by passing himself off as a fellow countryman and then had attended a session of the trial in the course of which he had voted for her undergoing torture; Pierre Maurice (II, 64), the young and brilliant university graduate; Thomas de Courcelles (II, 50), to whom would be entrusted the task of translating and putting in order the notarial minutes kept daily during the trial (see III, 13) so as to compose an authentic record of it (he would take advantage of that position to remove his name from the list of those who had voted for torture); a graduate of the university named Jacques Le Camus, a canon of Reims, who had left that city swiftly when it welcomed Charles VII (II, 1) and was later compensated for his losses by the king of England (II, 2), who granted him the benefice of the church of La Trinité at Falaise (Cauchon had summoned him for the hearing on Joan's relapse, and he had been in her company at the prison on the morning of the execution); and the friars Martin Ladvenu and Jean Toutmouillé. Cauchon also summoned the notary of the trial, Guillaume Manchon (II, 62), but he refused to come: Since the trial was terminated, so was his task, he said; anything he could add would have no legal standing. According to the confidences he later revealed, Guillaume Manchon had been powerfully moved by Joan's execution: "I never weep for much of anything that comes my way, but for a month thereafter I was not able to find any peace. With part of the money I was paid for my work during the trial, I bought a little missal, which I still have, so that I could pray for Joan."

Cauchon wished the assessors to agree that Joan had formally denied her voices. All of them declared that she had done so:

> She understood and knew that she had been tricked by them. . . . The voices and apparitions coming to her of which she had made mention in the trial had deceived her, for if these voices had promised that she would be delivered and released from prison, she clearly learned the contrary. It was true that she had been deceived. Since they had deceived her so, she believed that they were no longer good voices or good things. "I do not wish to add any further faith to these voices."

Nicolas Loiseleur went so far as to say that she had begged "with the greatest contrition of heart the indulgence of the English and the Burgundians because as she herself avowed, she had caused them to be killed and put to flight, and caused them so much loss."

It was evidently not coincidental that this information was recorded on June 7, for on the following day the king of England addressed a letter about

Joan, a masterpiece of its kind, to the emperor as well as to the kings, dukes, and other princes of all Christendom. After having "seduced the populace," Joan was finally brought "into our hands and our power by an act of divine clemency. We had nevertheless no manner of intention to avenge the wrongs we had suffered or to deliver that woman immediately to secular justice so that she might be thereby punished." Handed over to the ecclesiastical authority in response to a request of the prelate in whose diocese she had been taken prisoner, she was judged guilty of numerous crimes against the faith and of "not recognizing any judge upon earth." Finally she abjured her errors, but "the fire of her pride flared up again in pestilential flames; so that she was finally abandoned to the secular power." At that moment, she "confessed without any ambiguity that the spirits who she affirmed had many times appeared to her were evidently wicked and deceptive. . . . She confessed herself to have been tricked and deceived by them."

Cauchon's drama of the previous evening was thus necessary. Without delay, he had "letters of guarantee" given to him on June 12 by Henry VI, and received the same for Louis of Luxembourg (II, 29) and Jean de Mailly, the bishop of Noyon (II, 61): "On the king's word of honor, if it should happen that anyone of the persons who were engaged in the trial should be sued on account of this trial or its consequences, we shall aid and defend them and we shall see that these persons are aided and defended in any legal action at our own cost and expenses."

Three weeks after his first circular letter, the king of England issued on June 28 another letter in more or less the same terms "to the prelates, dukes, counts, and other nobles and to the cities of his kingdom of France," inviting them to make known to the public "through preaching and public sermons and otherwise" the "truth" of the story of Joan the Maid, and how she had finally recognized that her "voices" had mocked her. Finally, the University of Paris wrote in similar language to the pope and the College of Cardinals.

In all the occupied parts of the kingdom, sermons and processions ordered in the name of King Henry VI took place, notably at Paris, where Jean Graverent, the Inquisitor of France (II, 53), arranged a solemn sermon and public procession at Saint-Martin-des-Champs on July 4. The *Journal of a Bourgeois of Paris,* composed by a pro-Burgundian clerk of the university, summarizes that sermon, which depicted Joan's life as "full of fire and blood [causing] the murder of Christians, until she herself was burned." Elsewhere, the Bourgeois of Paris described the stake at Rouen without disguising the differing reactions it had aroused: "Many people said here and there that she was a martyr and that she had been sacrificed for her true prince. Others said that she was not and that he who had protected her for so long had done ill. So said the people, but, whether she did well or ill, she was burned on that day!"

Clément de Fauquembergue, conscientious registrar of Parlement, inevitably mentions in its register that: "On the 30th day of May 1431, Joan who called herself the Maid, who had been taken as she made a sortie from the city of Compiègne by the men of my lord John of Luxembourg, was thoroughly burned in the city of Rouen. My lord Pierre Cauchon, the bishop of Beauvais, pronounced the sentence in an ecclesiastical trial."

The trial transcript would be translated and edited in the following months under the direction of Thomas de Courcelles. Pierre Cauchon waited with some nervousness for his nomination to the archbishopric of Rouen; his disappointment must have been keen when he received, in the month of January 1432, an offer of the bishopric of Lisieux instead. Louis of Luxembourg finally attained the coveted Norman archbishopric in 1436 while he hurriedly prepared to leave France for refuge in England, where he received the bishopric of Ely. There he would die in 1443.

The military offensive resumed soon after Joan's death, a fact that some people regarded as more than a coincidence. "Since the English are generally a superstitious lot," the prior of the Benedictine priory of Saint-Michel near Rouen, Thomas Marie, declared later, "they believed that there was something magical about Joan [and] . . . impatient after her burning, they went to lay siege to Louviers, being of the opinion that so long as she lived they would never achieve glory nor success in acts of war." An English campaign to besiege Louviers began immediately after Joan's death. The earl of Warwick (II, 43) ordered necessary food supplies when he went there in the first days of June 1432, and soon after June 2 Henry VI's secretary Laurence Calot (who had taken from his sleeve the cedula of abjuration that he had forced Joan to sign by holding her hand), ordered the treasurer to transfer the sums necessary to underwrite the siege. A French campaign had already been launched in Normandy in December 1429, under the command of La Hire (II, 22), who had been named captain general of that province. The Bastard of Orléans (II, 16) had gone to join him precisely at the moment of Joan's trial in March 1431. In spite of that constellation of military power, the French effort was inadequate, and on October 28, 1431, Louviers surrendered. In the meantime, on June 30, fresh English troops debarked at Calais and entered service in Normandy.

King Charles VII suffered another setback. On July 2 his brother-in-law, King René of Anjou, whom he had hoped to see receive the inheritance of Duke Charles of Lorraine (who had asked Joan to visit him and who died in January 1431; [II, 26]), was vanquished and taken prisoner during the bloody Battle of Bulgnéville. Yet another royal defeat occurred between Beauvais and Savignies in Champagne. For this battle, Regnault of Chartres (II, 13) mobilized his famous Shepherd of the Gévaudan, Guillaume, who he claimed "would do neither more nor less than Joan the Maid," but Warwick easily took the shepherd-boy prisoner. The French troops scattered in the shock of that defeat. Far worse, Poton de Xaintrailles (II, 44) was also captured in the rout, which was called with some derision 'The Battle of the Shepherd.' By the end of July 1431, the king of France might well have concluded that the fortunes of war had turned against him.

The English felt fortune surge on their side once more, and they chose a dramatic symbol to reassert their prestige in France. If Joan's execution was considered to discredit Charles's anointing at Reims, then the time seemed propitious to oppose him with another duly consecrated king of France. Henry VI, therefore, was brought to France; his anointing was the occasion for a great ceremony, at once royal and popular, at Notre Dame of Paris. A stately procession of the earl of Warwick and his household brought the nine-year-old king up the Seine toward the capital. This procession, which began between the Saint-Denis Gate and the suburb of La Chapelle, surely included the ecclesiastical peers assigned to carry out this coronation: Louis of Luxembourg, Pierre Cauchon, Jean de Mailly, the "cardinal of England" Henry Beaufort (II, 8), William Alnwick, bishop of Norwich (II, 46), and also the bishops of Paris and of Évreux. Also in attendance were the regent of France and his wife, Anne of Burgundy, as well as some of the numerous English lords who had established themselves in France, such as Humphrey, earl of Stafford. The procession, organized according to the established traditions, was preceded by minstrels, by heralds and pursuivants-of-arms, and by squires bearing the insignia of royal majesty: an ermine mantle and the sword of justice. It included also, surrounded by archers, the unfortunate little shepherd Guillaume, who had been captured six months previously and who would soon be stitched into a sack of leather and thrown in the Seine.

At the entry to the suburb of La Chapelle, the town counselors and the Provost of the Merchants took up a canopy of blue cloth embroidered with golden fleurs-de-lys to carry above the little king's head for the length of the solemn entry, which brought Henry, riding his white hackney, across the city past the walls of the Châtelet overlooking the Seine and the palace of the Ile-de-la-Cité up to the palace of the Tournelles, residence of the duke of Bedford (II, 9), who lodged Henry there during his stay. According to custom, the Parisian guilds assembled in formal array, each of which—master drapers, master grocers, master moneychangers, goldsmiths, merchants of hides and furs, and master butchers—prepared to carry the canopy part of the way. At intervals along the route, mimes amused the entourage by enacting short scenes from the mystery plays, as the traditional staging of royal entries required. At the cemetery of the Innocents, a hunting tableau had been mounted, while at the Châtelet a pageant presented a child the age of Henry VI seated on a throne, with two crowns cleverly balanced above his head. The procession passed the palace of Saint-Pôl, home to the dowager queen, Isabeau of Bavaria (II, 23). The *Journal of a Bourgeois of Paris* notes that "when the young Henry . . . passed the place where she lived, he raised his hat and saluted her and she bowed toward him humbly, then turned away weeping." He was her grandson, the child of her daughter Catherine.

Henry's coronation took place at Notre Dame of Paris on Sunday, December 16, 1431. The traditional coronation regalia had been brought there by the English on their earlier withdrawal from Reims—with one exception. Missing was the Holy Vial of Reims and its sacred coronation ointment; some therefore considered this coronation a travesty, although traditional ritual was otherwise scrupulously observed. The feast that followed, at the "marble table" of the palace—the great hall surviving beneath the floor in what is still called the Palace of the Ile-de-la-Cité—contributed little to the new king's popularity. Even though the Bourgeois of Paris was profoundly committed to the English cause, his lack of pleasure in English cuisine marks a persistent cultural divide: "Nobody found anything to praise in the meal; the greater part of the meats, especially those destined for the common people, had been cooked on the previous Thursday, which seemed strange to the French." Even the sick in the Hôtel Dieu, for whom part of every feast was reserved, found it inedible. As if in revenge, cutpurses and other pickpockets sought profit at the feast, stealing with ease from any number of firmly fastened belt clasps. The joust the following morning also proved disappointing, so poorly staged that the Bourgeois of Paris remarked that any inhabitant of the city would have spent more to marry his daughter than the English had spent to crown their king. More successful was the coronation music; the Bourgeois judged that it was played "quite melodiously." The theme came from the Psalms: "I have sent mine angel." The English effort to construct the coronation as a prestigious symbol was therefore not entirely successful. Henry soon returned toward Rouen down the valley of the Seine under the protection of his mentor, the earl of Warwick, who hastened with his entire household to Calais and crossed over to England.

The following year, 1432, brought reversals for both the English and the French causes. Around February 3, in a daring coup, a French mercenary named Ricarville with a mere hundred companions seized the castle of Rouen itself— the castle of Bouvreuil that one year earlier had been home to Joan of Arc, Bedford, and the earl of Warwick. The English reinforced the garrison to repel the coup, but only a few of the English troops, commanded by the earl of Arundel, succeeded in finding refuge in a strong chamber in one of the towers that overlooked the town. From that tower, on the following morning, Arundel harangued the confused crowd; an arrow carelessly shot by one of Ricarville's partisans killed an infant in the crowd, at which point the massed populace in front of the fortress rallied to the English. The earl of Arundel had himself lowered in a basket into the moat. Gathering all his available forces, he turned to besiege the castle, directing against it the fire of a bombard. Ricarville surrendered after several days, and he and all his men were beheaded in the Old Marketplace.

On February 20, however, the Bastard of Orléans (II, 16) retook Chartres, thanks to an Orléans fish merchant who pretended he was delivering salt and shad to the townspeople, and who then succeeded in blocking the drawbridge with his wagons while French partisans killed the Englishmen mounting guard at the other gates of the city. The bishop Jean de Fétigny, the populace, and a part of the garrison then proceeded to the cathedral to hear the sermon of the Jacobin friar who had engineered the plot, and that evening Chartres returned to French rule.

Six months later, the duke of Bedford was constrained to raise the siege of Lagny, an important fortress that could block convoys between Paris and Champagne. Bedford returned to the capital for the feast day of August 15, "so as to confess himself." Three months later, on November 14, 1432, his wife died. His most precious ally and the sister of Philip the Good (II, 3), she had often succeeded in smoothing difficulties troubling the Anglo-Burgundian alliance. Although Bedford expressed profound grief, he wasted no time in remarrying. In early 1434, he chose the seventeen-year-old daughter of the count of Saint-Pôl, Jacqueline of Luxembourg, as his bride.

In the meantime, the French court witnessed a palace revolt. Three young men—Jean de Bueil, Prigent de Coëtivy, and Pierre de Brézé—conspired with Yolanda of Sicily and her daughter Marie of Anjou, queen of France, against Georges de La Trémoïlle (II, 25). An attack on him took place at Chinon in the castle of Couldray (where Joan had been received four years earlier), yet the sword thrust into La Trémoïlle's fat belly did not kill but caused only a superficial wound. He was briefly imprisoned before being expelled from the court just at the moment that Arthur de Richemont (II, 36) recovered favor with the king. La Trémoïlle's displacement signaled a new active phase in Charles's conduct of the kingdom's affairs.

His new involvement came just in time. One year later a strong English offensive would be directed against Mont-Saint-Michel. Sir Thomas Scales (II, 39), with impressive artillery under his command, lacked the sustained military drive to reach the monastery proper but was able to breach the town walls. He managed to plant his banner of lilies quartered with leopards on one of the ramparts, but Louis d'Estouteville, the defender of the Mount, ripped it off with his own hands and cast it into a ditch. Eight days later Scales mounted a new assault, so violent that the townspeople took refuge in the abbey itself. The monks then aroused the townsmen to resist the attackers, who soon fled in disorder. The two bombards the English had to abandon can still be seen at Mont-Saint-Michel. Mont-Saint-Michel had proven impregnable. For a short time the English went to fortify the islet of Tombelaine and held on there until d'Estouteville dislodged them and also took Granville up the coast.

In that same year, 1434, the Norman Bessin (the region around Bayeux) revolted against the demands of Bedford, who levied 344,000 livres in taxes upon the Estates of Normandy. That province had been increasingly exploited by mercenary troops, who have left to the French and English languages the word "brigand," from the *brigandine,* the type of helmet they wore. The rowdy troops, inadequately controlled by poorly supervised captains, turned into shameless pillagers and extortioners. The chronicler Thomas Basin provides a terrifying description of this period of insecurity in Normandy. Here and there peasants got together, striving to escape either from the English or from the brigands. The duke of Alençon (II, 4), with the aid of Jean de Bueil, undertook the siege of Avranches but was forced to abandon that effort after a few days. An expedition of the earl of Arundel in the region of the Caux was stopped by La Hire and Poton de Xaintrailles and cut to pieces near Gerberoy; Arundel, badly wounded, subsequently died in captivity at Beauvais.

The city of Orléans chose that moment in 1435 to stage a mystery play featuring the story of Joan's military exploits there. All the bourgeoisie were mobilized, and stages were set up at every gate of the city. A magnificent performance of *The Mystery of the Siege of Orléans* ensued, the manuscript of which survives (III, 14). The town account books record that one of Joan's companions, Gilles de Rais (II, 34), took part in this huge theatrical production.

All this while, diplomatic offensives continued. René of Anjou (II, 5), a prisoner at Dijon, was well placed to pursue reconciliation with Philip the Good, to which policy his mother, Yolanda, was strongly committed. For his part, the duke of Burgundy felt little personal sympathy for the regent Bedford; as his chronicler Olivier de La Marche wrote, "French blood boiled in his stomach and around his heart." On January 16, 1435, peace negotiations began at Nevers. The French and Burgundian delegates separated after three weeks, promising to rejoin at Arras.

On August 5, 1435, in the abbey of Saint-Vaast at Arras, a solemn session brought together French, Burgundian, and English delegates, but to their later cost, English envoys quickly abandoned the conference. Word arrived of the death on September 12 of the duke of Bedford in the castle of Rouen, which had been Joan's prison. The death of Isabeau of Bavaria followed on the twenty-fourth. In the meantime, on September 21, the Treaty of Arras between France and Burgundy was concluded. The ambassador of Charles VII, Master Jean Tudert, made public and formal restitution as dictated by contemporary codes of honor: He bent his knee before the duke of Burgundy in his king's name. From his side, the duke forswore revenge for the murder of his father at Montereau. The treaty was definitively sealed on October 28 and ratified at Tours by Charles VII on December 10. Civil war thus ceremonially ended, and the fissure that had divided France closed. Armagnacs and Burgundians had come together in the "good, solid peace that lasts a long time" that Joan of Arc had so desired.

One more year, and "the English would forfeit more than they ever had in France," again fulfilling one of Joan's predictions. On April 17, 1436, Constable Richemont (II, 36) entered Paris. His campaign had begun with the taking of Meulan, then of Pontoise, in February 1436. Thereafter, the French enjoyed control over the principal water routes from Meulan on the Seine to Lagny on the Marne. Caught between those two strategic points, Paris experienced a steadily worsening famine, and Louis of Luxembourg, the governor chosen by Bedford before his death, alienated himself from the populace with his pride and insensitivity. Two thousand English troops sent as reinforcements were cut to pieces on the plain of Saint-Denis on April 6. With the help of the Bastard of Orléans and the Burgundian captain Villiers de l'Isle-Adam, Arthur de Richemont undertook the siege, which this time was helped by resistance within the city. The regular troops entered the city by the Gate of Saint-Jacques on the Left Bank.

While the English cried treason, it was recorded that the bourgeoisie of Paris threw furniture, chests, and footstools at the English troops who passed within range. In the name of the king, the constable promised amnesty to "renegade" Frenchman. The English took refuge in the fortress of Saint-Antoine, but soon, pressed by hunger, they requested a parley and were authorized safe-conduct from the city. Boats on the Seine took them to Rouen. As they passed, the crowd shouted, "After the fox!" and "By the tail!" The king, however, did not enter the reconquered capital city until a year later, on November 12, 1437. Even then, to the disappointment of Parisians, Charles VII stayed there only three weeks.

Yet another epilogue to Joan's story was the return of Charles of Orléans in 1440 (II, 31), after twenty-five years spent in English prisons. "I should have taken enough Englishmen to have him back," Joan had said at her trial, for she considered the return of this duke part of her mission. It is probably no coincidence that, in July of that same 1440, Joan's mother, Isabelle Romée, arrived at Orléans. After the death of her husband and her eldest son, she found herself in financial difficulty. The bourgeoisie of Orléans were moved by that news and invited her to come live with them. We find notices in the town account books thereafter of the 48 sous per month she received. The town also assumed the expenses of the doctor who visited her when she was ill. She took up residence near the collegiate church (now restored) of Saint-Pierre-le-Puellier, which became her parish. Isabelle was joined in Orléans by her son Pierre, once held as a prisoner with Joan. He brought his wife and his son Jean. Under the date 1443, we find a record of the gift to him by the duke of Orléans of the island in the Loire known today as Ile-aux-Boeufs.

A year earlier, some of the people of Orléans had been deceived by an adventuress named Claude (III, 12), who pretended that she was Joan escaped from English prisons. As the *Chronicle* of the dean of Saint-Thiébault of Metz reported, she dissembled so well "that many were deceived." She appeared first in the region of the Meuse and was received by Elizabeth of Görlitz, a member of the family of Luxembourg. It seems that Joan's third brother—the one called Jean or Petit-Jean—managed to convince the city of Orléans to forward him 12 francs under the pretext that he wished "to come see his sister." This false Joan married a lord Robert des Armoises and arranged to be received at Orléans itself, where on July 28, 1439, the town account books mention the reception staged for her. The Bourgeois of Paris relates in his *Journal* how the impostor was publicly unmasked at the city's palace. There are records of two other adventuresses who, in these troubled times, knew how to exploit public credulity and present themselves as Joan, since so many did not wish to believe that the English had imprisoned and executed her.

In 1449 the most decisive epilogue to Joan of Arc's military story was played out: the recovery of Normandy. The episode began with the capture of the castle of Fougères by François de Surienne, an Aragonese mercenary in the service of the English. This action violated the truce concluded between France and England five years earlier, when on May 28, 1444, King Henry VI was betrothed to the French princess Margaret of Anjou, daughter of René of Anjou and niece of Queen Marie. That marriage, hailed across Europe as a first step toward a final peace between the two kingdoms, took place at Nancy in February of the following year, and the coronation of the young queen took place at Westminster on May 28, 1445, exactly a year after the betrothal. The coup at Fougères threatened that peace. Charles VII had at hand a reorganized army equipped with powerful artillery, whereas the king of England now commanded unruly vassals. On July 17, 1449, the Normandy offensive began. The French had already entered Pont de l'Arche using a ruse. A French mercenary, Robert de Flocques (II, 17), was on the way to capture Conches when, thanks to the connivance of a resident of Verneuil whose mill was built against the rampart, he took that town as well.

Beginning in August, Charles VII established his headquarters in Louviers and directed the military response in person. When he learned that the townspeople of Rouen were in revolt against the English, he marched toward the Norman capital and made his solemn entry on November 10, 1449. The English governor, Somerset, arranged his own safe departure upon delivery of hostages and of several fortified towns, including Caudebec and Honfleur. Retreating toward Caen, Somerset tried to rally the English forces, but they then controlled no more than a few islands of territory in Normandy.

The arrival of the new English army assembled by Henry VI in a supreme effort (he had pawned his crown jewels to meet its expenses) provoked a new

French offensive. The English force debarked in Cherbourg under the command of Thomas Kyriel, who promptly drove the French counteroffensive, commanded by the count of Clermont, into retreat. French fortunes revived when Arthur de Richemont appeared with 1,500 men-at-arms. The result was a decisive victory for the French at Formigny on April 15, 1450.

All the while, Joan's story continued to unfold. Shortly after his entry into Rouen, Charles VII decided to show his gratitude. He must have heard people from Rouen recall Joan's execution, and he undoubtedly had brought to him the trial records kept in the archbishop's palace. On February 15, 1450, he dictated to his counselor Guillaume Bouillé a letter destined to open a new chapter for our understanding of Joan of Arc:

> As heretofore Joan the Maid was taken and seized by our ancient enemies and adversaries the English and brought to the city of Rouen, against whom they caused to take place a certain trial by certain persons who had been chosen and given this task by them, in the process of which they made and committed many falsifications and abuses, so much so that, by means of this trial and the great hatred that our enemies have against her, they caused her death iniquitously and against reason, very cruelly indeed; for this reason we wish to know the truth of the aforesaid trial, and the manner according to which it was conducted and carried out. We command you, instruct you, and expressly enjoin you to inquire and inform yourself well and diligently on what was said; and that you bring before us and the men of our council the information that you will have gathered on this event under a closed seal . . . for we give you power, commission, and special instruction by these presents to carry this out. Given at Rouen, the 15th day of February, the Year of Grace 1449 [New Style, 1450].

Guillaume Bouillé went to work rapidly, launching an inquest that revealed "the truth of the aforesaid process" carried on nineteen years earlier. The testimony of the notary of the trial of condemnation, Guillaume Manchon, was heard all day on March 4, and then that of six other witnesses. Four Dominican friars of the convent of Saint-Jacques testified, two of whom—Isambart de La Pierre and Martin Ladvenu—had accompanied Joan to the stake and two of whom—Guillaume Duval and Jean Toutmouillé—had played at best accessory roles in that event. The usher Jean Massieu (II, 63) gave testimony as well, and by a stroke of improbable luck Master Jean Beaupère (II, 47), who had often been Cauchon's aide during Joan's interrogations, arrived in town as the investigation began. He frequently visited Rouen to collect the revenues of his canonry, although he lived most of the time in retirement at Besançon. The primary revelation of this first inquest was a judgment that Joan's trial had been arbitrary in nature, for she was a prisoner of war initially treated as a political prisoner who had then been charged with heresy and condemned to death.

Nevertheless, since she had been condemned by a tribunal of the Inquisition, Joan could be cleared of the crime of heresy only by the church itself. To appreciate this juridical paradox fully, one must understand what had happened in Christian law in the two decades between the time when the ideology constructed by the masters of the University of Paris had inspired the political trial at Rouen and the time of that ideology's collapse. By 1450, it was clear to the Christian world that the University of Paris no longer held "the keys to Christendom." Having experienced serious internal divisions through most of the fourteenth century when the popes resided in Avignon, the church had been deeply shaken by the Great Schism. (See "Prelude.") Between 1378 and 1417, when Pope Martin V was elected, two and sometimes three popes claimed the triple-tiered papal tiara at once. Some of them resided at Rome, while their rivals at Avignon were supported by the professors of the University of Paris, who tended to consider final church authority the prerogative of periodic councils—a kind of parliamentary government substituted for the single person of the pope, the successor of Peter. These doctrinal and institutional disputes mingled with problems of a financial nature, such as the collation of benefices. Clerical vacancies attributed to the war and the Black Death caused benefices to accumulate, several examples of which occurred among the judges at Joan's trial.

A number of these judges came together again at the Council of Basel after July 1431, and they soon won from Pope Eugenius IV decrees abolishing the pope's role in the collation of benefices and annulling some of the stipends on which the Roman Curia depended for revenue. Faced with the demands of that assembly regarding papal prerogatives, Eugenius IV decided to transfer the council to Ferrara, then to Florence, where in 1439 a delegation from the Byzantine emperor came to proclaim the union of the Greek and Roman churches—a union no more popular in the East than the union declared in 1274 at the Second Council of Lyons had been. As a consequence, the fathers of the council who stayed behind at Basel deposed Eugenius IV in open rebellion and elected in his place a layman, Amadeus VIII, duke of Savoy. Choosing the name of Felix V, he would be the last of the antipopes. Thomas de Courcelles, an active promoter of this election, acquired for himself a cardinal's hat.

Antipope Felix had to abdicate ten years later, in 1449; and among the negotiators who persuaded him to do so was a featured player in Joan's history— John, count of Dunois (II, 16). Meanwhile, King Charles VII had unilaterally adopted a series of measures voted by the assembly of the clergy of France, which he had convoked at Bourges in 1438. This tentative establishment of a significantly independent French national church is generally known as the

Pragmatic Sanction of Bourges. Among other reforms, it abolished taxes the pope levied on the parishes and dioceses. It also withdrew collations of benefices from the pope, and it affirmed as superior to the pope's authority the authority of a council instructed to meet every ten years. The papacy never accepted the Pragmatic Sanction, and Louis XI had to abolish it upon his succession to the throne in 1461.

Despite disorder and resentment of the papal claim of control over the spiritual life of the Christian people, the papacy manifested its force with surprising vigor during the Jubilee of 1450, when crowds of pilgrims descended upon Rome, their piety presenting a striking contrast to the assemblies of prelates and university professors convoked at Basel or elsewhere. At that point, Pope Nicholas V, who had decided to rebuild the ancient church of St. Peter, sent to France his legate Guillaume d'Estouteville, one of the chief supporters of Pope Eugenius IV during his stormy pontificate. Guillaume was the brother of Louis d'Estouteville, the energetic defender of Mont-Saint-Michel; he was also a close relative of King Charles VII—his maternal grandmother had been the sister of the "Wise King," Charles V. Once accredited as papal legate by the king at Tours in February 1452, Guillaume d'Estouteville went to Rouen two months later. Normandy was by then fully liberated and the campaign of Guyenne was well under way, commanded by the man no longer called Bastard of Orléans but rather count of Dunois, supported by the artillery reorganized by the brothers Jean and Gaspard Bureau. The Inquisitor of France was then a Norman, Jean Bréhal, prior of the convent of Saint-Jacques at Paris. Guillaume d'Estouteville fully understood that even after the exhausting series of wars and the factional division the French people had suffered—the people to whom he was sent as the representative of papal authority—one question still needed to be settled: the trial of Joan. That trial was now a symbol of complex cultural fissures in search of closure: of the internal fractures of a riven France, of national splits enervated by English invasion, and of religious and civil power struggles sustained by the University of Paris.

The first session of the investigation into Joan's trial was opened officially by Guillaume d'Estouteville and Jean Bréhal in the city of Rouen, whose population, according to the register of the parishes, had dropped from 14,992 to 5,976 under English occupation. After studying the transcript of the condemnation trial, Estouteville and Bréhal—assisted by two Italian prelates expert in canon law, Paul Pontanus and Theodore de Leliis, both members of the legate's staff—drew up a model of interrogation. The first interrogatory consisted of twelve articles corresponding to the twelve articles on which Joan had been condemned. Five witnesses appeared on May 2 and 3: Guillaume Manchon, the notary; Martin Ladvenu; Isambart de La Pierre; Pierre Miget (II, 66), one of the judges of the first trial; and a bourgeois of Rouen, Pierre Cusquel, a master of masonry. Their testimony quickly made it clear that the twelve questions inadequately represented the conditions under which Joan's trial had developed. The interrogatory was expanded on May 4 into twenty-seven articles, which thereafter served as the basis for the whole process of interrogation. Witnesses were asked to confirm or deny the truth of each of these articles.

THE TWENTY-SEVEN ARTICLES

1. That because she had come with the aid of the most Christian King of France and fought with the army against the English, Joan was pursued by a mortal hatred and was hated by the English, and that they sought her death by every means. And so it was and that is the truth.

2. As Joan had inflicted numerous defeats on the said English in the war, they greatly feared her, and therefore sought by every way possible to deliver her to death and to put an end to her days so that she could harm them no longer. And so it was and that is the truth.

3. That in order to give this an appearance of virtue, they brought her to this city of Rouen, then held in the tyrannical power of the English; and that they imprisoned her in the castle and caused to be brought against her a false prosecution for heresy, and this under fear and pressure. And so it was and that is the truth.

4. That neither judges, confessors, or consultants, nor the promoter and others intervening in the trial, dared to exercise free judgment because of the severe threats made against them by the terrorizing English; but that they were forced to suit their actions to their fear and to the pressure of the English if they wished to avoid grave perils and even the peril of death. And so it was and that is the truth.

5. That the notaries recording this trial, because the English caused them the same fear and directed threats against them, could not report the truth or faithfully set down the true version of Joan's replies when writing and editing their account. And so it was and that is the truth.

6. That the notaries, prevented by fear, were expressly forbidden to insert in their account words pronounced by Joan which seemed in her favor. Instead, that they were constrained to omit favorable remarks and insert statements held against her that she never said. And so it was and that is the truth.

7. That because of these same fears and terrors nobody could be found to advise Joan, or conduct her case for her, or instruct her, or direct her, or protect her.

Moreover those who sometimes put in some positive words for her suffered very great danger to their lives, for the English sought to throw them in the river as rebels, or to deliver them to some other form of death. And so it was and that is the truth.

8. That they kept Joan in a secular prison, her feet fettered with irons and chains; and that they forbade anyone to speak to her so that she might not be able to defend herself in any way, and that they even placed English guards over her. And so it was and that is the truth.

9. That Joan was a girl of nineteen or so, simple and ignorant of the law and of judicial procedure; that alone, without direction or advice, she was not capable or clever enough to defend herself in such a difficult case. And so it was and that is the truth.

10. That the English, desiring her death, went by night to her prison. Pretending to be inspired by some revelations, they exhorted her not to submit to the judgment of the Church if she wished to escape death. And so it was and that is the truth.

11. That in order to trap her in her own words, the examiners plied her with difficult, insidious interrogations and questions, and that for the greater part of the time they interrogated her about things that she did not in the least understand. And so it was and that is the truth.

12. That they wore her out with their long interrogations and examinations, so that when she was finally exhausted they could seize on some unfortunate word in her replies. And so it was and that is the truth.

13. That often, in court and elsewhere, Joan affirmed that she submitted herself and all her acts to the judgment the Church and of our Holy Father the Pope; and that if anything in her words or deeds diverged from that faith she herself wished to retract it and to obey the judgment of the clerics. And so it was and that it is the truth.

14. That also, in court and elsewhere, Joan often affirmed that she submitted herself and all her acts to the judgment of the Church and of our Holy Father the Pope; and so it was and that is the truth; and that she would have been sorry if there had been anything in her that was in opposition to the Catholic faith. And so it was and that is the truth.

15. That although her words of submission to the Church were often repeated to her both in the court and elsewhere, the English and those who favored their cause did not permit but rather forbade them to be inserted or written in the acts or in the record of the so-called trial. And that they caused them to be written

down in another form, although this was a perversion of the truth. And so it was and that is the truth.

16. That if Joan ever affirmed that she would not submit to the judgment of our Holy Mother the Church, even the Church Militant, it was not proved by the previous article. And so it was and that is the truth.

17. In any case in which it might appear that Joan said something implying her nonsubmission to the Church, the promoter says that she did not understand what the Church was, and that she did not understand by this term the community of the faithful, but believed and understood the Church of which her interrogators spoke to consist of those ecclesiastics there present, who had embraced the English cause. And so it was and that is the truth.

18. That the alleged report, originally written in French, was translated into Latin with no great accuracy, many things having been suppressed that told in Joan's favor and even more having been added, in defiance of truth, that prejudiced her case, and therefore that the said record disagrees with its original in numerous and substantial points. And so it was and that is the truth.

19. That, the preceding truths having been recognized, the said trial and sentence does not deserve the name of a judgment and sentence, since there can be no real judgment where the judges, consultants, and assessors are too fearful to exercise judgment. And so it was and that is the truth.

20. That, for the preceding reasons, the alleged record is in many parts untrue, vitiated, corrupt, and neither perfectly nor faithfully written; that it is also so defective that no faith can be put in it. And so it was and that is the truth.

21. That the preceding and other points being weighed, the case and the sentence are both null and most unjust, since they were conducted and passed without due observance of legal formalities by judges who were not the rightful ones and who had no jurisdiction in such a case or over such a person. And so it was and that is the truth.

22. That moreover, the said trial and sentence are both null and tainted with manifest injustice for the additional reason that on so grave a charge Joan was given no facilities for defending herself. Furthermore, that defense itself, which exists as a natural right, was totally denied her by manifold and insidious means. And so it was and that is the truth.

23. That although it was abundantly apparent to the judges that Joan had submitted to the judgment and decisions of Our Holy Mother the Church, and that she was so faithful a Catholic that she was allowed to receive the body of Our Lord, nevertheless, out of their excessive zeal for the English, or not wishing

to extricate themselves out of fear and pressure, they most unjustly condemned her as a heretic to the pains of the fire. And so it was and that is the truth.

24. That without any further sentences from the secular judge, the English, inspired by rage against her, immediately led her to the stake under a large escort of armed men. And so it was and that is the truth.

25. That Joan continuously, and notably at the moment of her death, behaved in a saintly and Catholic manner, recommending her soul to God and invoking Jesus aloud even with her last breath in such a manner as to draw from all those present, and even from her English enemies, effusions of tears. And so it was and that is the truth.

26. That the English perpetrated and caused to be perpetrated against Joan each and all the preceding acts, in deed and against the law, by means of pressure, because they had a lively fear of Joan, who supported the party of the most Christian king of France. They hated her and pursued her with a mighty hatred so that the most Christian king might be discredited for having availed himself of the aid of a woman so utterly damned. And so it was and that is the truth.

27. That each and all the preceding facts were and are of public fame and popular report, and that they are commonly said and known in the diocese of Rouen and throughout the kingdom of France. And so it was and that is the truth.

The twenty-seven articles addressed the bias of the former trial; the hatred that the English had declared toward the accused; the judges' and notaries' lack of freedom to act; Joan's lack of an advocate, in violation of well-established custom of inquisitorial trials; the conditions of Joan's imprisonment; her real sentiments, notably concerning submission to the pope and to the church; and the discrepancies between the Latin and French texts (the notary Guillaume Manchon brought forward the minutes in French that he himself had written). The questionnaire presented to various witnesses also addressed the degree of the judges' competence, the circumstances of Joan's execution along with its irregularities, Joan's attitude in her last moments, and finally the root cause of the whole affair, the English desire to discredit Charles VII and the French cause.

The inquest resumed on May 8, the anniversary of the deliverance of Orléans. Most of the witnesses were judges in the first trial, but the principal protagonists had died: Cauchon had died suddenly on December 14, 1442, while being bled by his barber-surgeon. Nicolas Midy (II, 65), who had delivered the sermon at the Old Marketplace on the morning of Joan's death, died as a leper at about the same time, long after he delivered a sermon before the young King Henry VI during his entry into Paris in December 1431. The body of Jean d'Estivet (II, 52), the *promotor,* had been found in a sewer on October 20, 1438. As to the vice-inquisitor, Jean Lemaître (II, 59), who had played only a small role in the trial, it remains unclear whether he was still alive, but he fails to appear in any known text after 1452. After the inquest was complete, Jean Bréhal drew up a *Summarium,* or digest of the affair, which, according to customary procedure, had to be presented to ecclesiastical tribunals and to specialists— jurists, doctors in canon law, and theologians—who would have to pass judgment on the case. This was ordinary procedure, and one to which Cauchon himself had adhered, although the text he submitted deviates in major instances from Joan's actual testimony. About the *Summarium,* the questions were simple: Ought the same conclusions be drawn from Joan's answers as were drawn by the Rouen judges? Most simply, was Joan of Arc a heretic? Finally, how did anyone manage to make her look like a heretic? A long series of consultations ensued both inside France and outside. The *Summarium* was even sent to a theologian at the University of Vienna, Leonhard of Brixenthal.

Guillaume d'Estouteville was named archbishop of Rouen in 1453. Jean Bréhal resumed the task of the nullification trial. Only the pope could make the decision. After traveling to Rome, Jean Bréhal obtained from Pope Calixtus III (who had succeeded Nicholas V on April 8, 1455) a rescript authorizing the new trial with the close family of Joan acting as plaintiffs. Three commissioners, all of whom had been partisans of Charles VII, were appointed to keep track of the affair in the pope's name: Jean Juvénal des Ursins, archbishop of Reims; Guillaume Chartier, bishop of Paris; and Richard Olivier, bishop of Coutances.

On November 7, 1455, a moving ceremony took place at Notre Dame of Paris: An old woman—Joan's mother, Isabelle Romée—surrounded by a group of the inhabitants of Orléans who accompanied her, advanced toward the three prelates appointed by the Holy See. She spoke "with pitiable plaints and mournful supplications" echoed by the crowd:

> I had a daughter, born in legitimate marriage, whom I fortified worthily with the sacraments of baptism and confirmation and raised in the fear of God and respect for the tradition of the church, as much as her age and the simplicity of her condition permitted, so well that, having grown up in the middle of the fields and of the pastures, she went frequently to church and every month, after due confession, received the sacrament of the Eucharist despite her young age and gave herself to fasting and to prayer with great devotion and fervor, on account of the necessities then so grave in which the people found themselves and with which she sympathized with all her heart; nevertheless . . . certain enemies . . . betrayed her in a trial concerning the Faith, and . . . without any aid given to her innocence in a perfidious, violent, and iniquitous trial, without shadow of right

> . . . they condemned her in a damnable and criminal fashion and made her die
> most cruelly by fire.

Joan's next trial was about to begin.

Under the direction of the papal delegates, witnesses in the previous inquests as well as others summoned for this occasion—115 were interrogated in all—gave depositions, their liberty to do so being guaranteed by "letters of abolition" (that is, amnesty guaranteed by the king). They testified to the parts they had played in the condemnation trial and in the events that accompanied it. Sessions were public. The tribunal moved from Paris, where the first sessions took place on November 17, to Rouen, where they were heard between December 12 and 20 in the Great Hall of the archbishop's palace. On December 15, 1455, in the archbishop's palace, Simon Chapitault, licentiate in canon law, was appointed prosecutor, and Guillaume Manchon, who had been clerk of the court during the condemnation trial, was identified among the spectators and required to submit all documents regarding that first trial to the court. The results were shocking if not unexpected, since Manchon testified that many attempts were made (especially by Nicolas Loiseleur and Guillaume Colles) to alter the accurate record of Joan's statements. Then an inquest took place in Joan's home country, starting on January 28, 1456. Finally, at an inquest at Orléans, between February 22 and March 16, an enthusiastic crowd came forward to testify. Joan's family was represented by its advocate, Pierre Maugier, and by various procurators of whom the principal was Guillaume Prévosteau. Two clerks appointed to record the oral testimony, Denis Lecomte and François Ferrebouc, put their signatures, as was customary, to each page of the authentic transcript, which was drawn up in three copies, all of which have been preserved. As Pierre Duparc's 1988 Latin and French critical edition demonstrates, the nullification trial as a whole contains a treasure trove of information for the cultural historian, for beyond its eyewitness testimony about Joan's life, it contains the reflections of bishops, clerics, and lawyers who delve into knotty issues about fifteenth-century customary, secular, and canon law as well as into secular and ecclesiastical attitudes and reactions to a multitude of such complex questions as: "How can we judge a claim of mystical experience?" and "Can truth be discovered through torture and fear?"

A different image of Joan emerges from this group of testimonials, rich in nuance, each with its local accent. Alongside the judges of the condemnation trial—frequently struck by a degree of amnesia—we see marching past Joan's old companions-in-arms or companions of youth, princes of royal blood like Dunois or the duke of Alençon, and the simple bourgeois of Orléans. They create a vivid portrait of the Maid that matches the image that emerges from Joan's verbal responses to her judges.

On July 7, 1456, the nullity of the first trial was solemnly declared in the Great Hall of the archiepiscopal palace of Rouen; its annulment was symbolized by tearing a copy of the transcript before the crowd. Many ceremonies followed, first in the Old Marketplace, then in many cities of France, Orléans among them. Orléans celebrated its festival on July 27 in the presence of Guillaume Bouillé, who had launched the initial inquest, and Jean Bréhal, who had managed the affair from beginning to end, finally drawing up the *Recollectio* that refuted the accusations point by point according to the depositions of witnesses.

Isabelle Romée was present in the crowd at Orléans; she died two years later, on November 28, 1458, probably in the little village of Sandillon.

CHAPTER NINE

JOAN AS MEMORY

It is only in the detailed testimony of the nullification trial of 1455–56 that we can recover Joan's childhood and youth. Especially valuable for this inquiry is the testimony gathered at Domrémy in January and February 1456. The peasants among whom Joan had grown up before she left on her mission twenty-seven years previously gave a striking picture of her and (unconsciously) of themselves and of the culture that formed them. Most surprising is Joan's apparent ordinariness before she answered her call to save France: she was "just like everyone else," except that she was more charitable and more "willing" than the norm. The character of the popular religion that produced her and her neighbors is significant for the study of the history and sociology of religion as well as of politics.

THE TRANSCRIPT OF THE NULLIFICATION TRIAL makes the early years of Joan the Maid accessible for us across the span of more than five centuries.

On the morning of January 28, 1456, in the priest's residence of the church of Domrémy, four officials established temporary residence while the inhabitants gathered in a crowd in the village square. On the previous Sunday the priest invited all who had known Joan the Maid to come before the tribunal of the church to give depositions and recount their memories. The officials responsible for the inquest included Master Simon Chapitault, *promotor* of the cause of revision of the inquisitorial process, who had come for that purpose from Paris; Master Réginald Chichery, dean of the church of Notre-Dame at Vaucouleurs; a canon of the cathedral at Toul named Wautrin Thierry; and a young scribe of the same cathedral, Dominique Dominici.

Joan had left Domrémy twenty-seven years before. Had she lived, she would have been around forty-four. Many of the witnesses about to be interrogated were that old or "thereabouts," as they said in those days. They had reached an age when people begin to value childhood memories. Having seen her live through sixteen or seventeen years in their midst, Joan's neighbors felt that they could trust their memories.

Jean Moreau, a plowman who resided in the hamlet of Greux, aged about seventy, provided one of the most detailed depositions. He saw "Jeannette" born and grow up; he was present as godfather when she was baptized in the church dedicated to St. Rémi, and he listed the godmothers: the wife of Étienne Royer, Béatrice; the widow Estellin (they both lived at Domrémy); and Jeannette, widow of Tiercelin of Viteau, who lived at Neufchâteau. He knew her father, Jacques Darc, and her mother, "Isabellette," well; both of them farmers like himself, but at Domrémy. They were faithful Catholics, and farmers of good reputation. Jeannette—almost all the inhabitants of Domrémy loved her. Yes, she was well and fittingly raised in the faith and had good morals. She knew her belief as well as little girls of her age could. She was "of honest conversation," corresponding to what one could hope for in a girl-child of her estate, her parents being "not too rich." She used to be seen going to help the plow team and sometimes watching the animals in the fields, and she also did "women's work, spinning and all the rest."

What struck Jean Moreau about Joan was her piety: "She went willingly and often to church"; when she heard the bell ringing, if she was in the fields, she would go all the way to "the village and to the church" to hear mass. Jean Moreau spoke of the hermitage of Notre-Dame-de-Bermont, where Jeannette went willingly, almost every Saturday afternoon. (Colin, son of Jean Colin, of Greux, added this last detail; he was one of Jeannette's companions and with his comrades often teased her about her piety.) Another comrade, then a cultivator at Burey, Michel Lebuin, often accompanied her: "Many times when I was young, I went with her on pilgrimages to the hermitage of Notre-Dame-de-Bermont. She went almost every Saturday to that hermitage and there lit candles."

At the age of forty-four, as old as Joan would have been at the time of this interrogation, Colin declared with a touch of pride, "I was her companion." She went to confession during the Easter season and other solemn feast days to the parish priest, Messire Guillaume Front. He had died, but one of his colleagues, the parish priest of Roncessey, near Neufchâteau, Étienne de Sionne, attested that Front had often said to him: "'Jeannette, called the Maid, was a good and simple girl, pious, well raised, fearing God, such as had no equal in the village; she confessed her sins often,' and he said that if Joan had any money of her own, she would give some to her parish priest to have masses said. This priest said that every day when he celebrated mass, she was there."

Jean Colin concurred. He had often heard Messire Front say of Joan that "he had no better parishioner."

From the confidences of her closest friends, Mengette and Hauviette, we hear the same echo: She led a simple life, marked only by the piety that astonished, even disconcerted, her group. Hauviette, who had become the wife of a peasant of Domrémy, Gérard de Syonne, was happy to evoke the memory of her friend: "From my youth I knew Joan the Maid, who was born at Domrémy of Jacques Darc and Isabellette, spouses, honest farmers and true Catholics of good reputation. I know it because often I was in Joan's company, and being her friend, I went to the house of her father."

She adds that Joan was a little older than she: "three or four years, according to what they said." There is a contradiction here, because she had declared to the clerk that she herself was "forty-five years old or thereabout."

Because of the grandeur of her life and deeds, even today some hold a ludicrous hypothesis that Joan must have had noble blood, that she was a "Bastard of Orléans." Hauviette's testimony is cited as evidence that Joan could have been born earlier than is usually asserted (see III, 3), and proponents of the royal-Joan hypothesis propose a birthdate before 1407, the date of the death of Louis of Orléans. He is the father they provide for Joan, ignoring the beginning of Hauviette's deposition, which established, like all the others, Joan's parentage. Hauviette's memories are perfectly simple: "Joan was a good, humble, and sweet girl; she went often and willingly to church and to holy places, and often she was ashamed of what men said when she went so devotedly to church. She kept herself busy like other young girls, she did housework and spun, and sometimes—I saw her—she watched over her father's flocks."

"Like the others." From one deposition to the other, this phrase recurs, almost irritating in its monotony: She was just like everybody, she did everything like everybody else, and, except for her notable piety, she rarely distinguished herself from her group. For example, she loved to hear the church bells sound. "When I did not ring Compline, Joan caught up with me and chided me, saying that I had not done well." These are the words of Perrin Drappier, the churchwarden of Domrémy—he was then about sixty—who recalled Joan's annoyance when he forgot to ring the bells. She promised him little gifts to be more faithful. Her neighbors also noted her charity. "She gave lots of alms," the same Drappier reported. Mengette also recalled Joan's charity. Her house was almost next door to the house of Joan's father, and she often spun in her company or did other housework with her. Michel Lebuin reported the same: "She willingly gave for the love of God everything she could have." Isabellette, the wife of Gérard of Epinal, went even farther: "She willingly gave alms and welcomed the poor; she wanted to sleep under the chimney shelf so that the poor could sleep in her bed." A plowman who was forty-four when he gave his deposition, Simonin Musnier, had suffered ill health in childhood: "She took care of the sick and gave alms to the poor; I saw that myself, for when I was a child, I was sick myself, and Joan came to comfort me."

In these testimonies, Joan is also associated with the term "willingly":

> She went often and *willingly* to church and to holy places. . . . She went often and *willingly* to church. . . . She *willingly* took care of the animals of her father's house. . . . She confessed herself *willingly*. . . . She worked *willingly* and took care of many responsibilities, spun, did housework, went to help with the harvests, and when it was time, sometimes, she watched over the animals while spinning.

No word recurs more frequently in these depositions, which reinforce one another and produce a portrait of a young girl taking joy in daily labor. That this girl who bore such a destiny could be so accessible to others, and remain like them to the point where no one suspected her secret calling, is perhaps the most astonishing aspect of the testimony from the people of Domrémy.

"Popular religion" in the fifteenth century is often imagined as a tissue of superstitions, little ritual stupidities, and small devilries practiced by the wretched, ignorant peasants in their naïveté. That view is thoroughly challenged by this testimony from Domrémy. Although it would be impossible to extract from this testimony an abstract definition of the Church Militant (any more than could be done from Joan herself), these peasants are precise in their manner of expressing themselves, of judging and of remembering her. The essential elements of their "belief"—prayer, the Eucharist and other sacraments, and particularly frequent confession—were the essential components of their Christian life. The depositions reflect how natural and consistent with authentic piety they found love and respect for others, a willingness to welcome and help strangers, and a joyously active daily life.

The questionnaire prepared for the interrogation at Domrémy touched points that are still capable of startling historians: the Fairy Tree, for example, or those dances "near the fountain." Joan had recalled those moments when the youth of the countryside met under the tree to sing and dance. It is striking to see more or less the same description from each of these peasants who reported without embarrassment the legends of the Fairy Tree and the merrymaking carried on year after year by the young people of the country. They formed from such ancient folklore a culture very much their own and transmitted it from one generation to the next. Joan's godfather reported with pleasure what he had heard about this Fairy Tree:

> I heard tell often that women and the enchantresses who are called fairies used to go dance there beneath that tree, but, according to what they say, ever since

the Gospel of St. John was read in these parts, they do not go there anymore. In our time, on the Sunday when at the Introit of the mass *Laetare Jerusalem* is sung, the young girls and young men of Domrémy go out to that tree and often they eat there and when they come back they go to the fountain at Rains and while walking about and singing they drink the water of this fountain and play roundabout and pick flowers.

Joan's godmother Béatrice added, "It's a very beautiful tree." Another witness, Gérardin of Epinal, said, "That tree in the spring is as beautiful as lilies and its branches are spread very wide; its leaves and its branches touch the ground." There is no hint of devil worship or sorcery in their testimony.

What had her companions been able to learn of Joan's amazing secret? A plowman of her age or a little older than she, Jean Waterin, reported that "I often saw Jeannette the Maid, and in my youth I drove her father's plow with her, and with her and the other girls I was in the field and in the meadow. Often when we were playing together, Joan would go away from us a little and often spoke with God, it seemed to me."

But he added: "I and the others, we made fun of her." She began to share a little confidence about her mission with another companion, Michel Lebuin, and he kept a vivid recollection of those conversations. He had often accompanied her to Notre-Dame-de-Bermont and had often seen her go to confession:

> Once, Joan herself told me, on the eve of Saint John the Baptist, that there was a maid, between Coussey and Vaucouleurs, who before a year was out would have the king of France anointed, and in the year that came the king was crowned at Reims. And I don't know anything else.

This confidence, given on St. John's Eve, no doubt thanks to the excitement of the bonfires of that midsummer celebration, had remained fixed in his memory. There was also the "Burgundian" of Domrémy, Gérardin of Epinal, of whom Joan said, "I would have been delighted if he had had his head cut off!" But she quickly added, "If that had pleased God!" She had said to him one day, "Compère, if you weren't for the Burgundians, I would tell you something." "I thought," Gérardin reported, "that it concerned some friend she wanted to marry." Pro-Burgundian though he was, he nevertheless joined others, including Michel Lebuin, to meet Joan and the royal entourage for the coronation; the four peasants had joined her at Châlons.

The dominant impression one absorbs from these interrogations from Domrémy and Greux is one of clear transparency, the same transparency found in the recorded words, the actions, and the person of "Jeannette." Among all these limpid creatures, she had a particular limpidity, a clear reflection of that invisible world with which she felt herself in touch. Prophets of the Old Testament thought themselves the mere bearers of God's word, transmitting what had been dictated to them. Joan became a heroine of this biblical type, and from the existing record we can sense that her prophetic character came from her belief that she transmitted the message of her voices without adding or deleting. "I tell you nothing that I take in my head," she kept saying to her judges. Throughout her trial, she indicates that she feared above all to exceed what her voices had dictated, to be an insufficiently faithful instrument. This fidelity was in her view also reflected in her dedicated chastity, a vehicle that the Spirit might use to transmit what came to her from elsewhere. ("I asked that they send me back to God, whence I came," she had said.) Her holiness is best refracted by the judgment of her intimates and fellow townspeople: They matched the median level of human virtue, their spirit was upright, and they knew how to appreciate uprightness: "There was nothing but good in her."

Of what did this popular religion consist? The importance that the inhabitants of Domrémy accorded to baptism is striking. For them, it was more than simply a ritual—witness the importance of the godfathers or godmothers. One of the witnesses says of Joan, "She was my *commère*," referring to the fact that they were both godmothers of a boy named Nicolas. "I am a good Christian and well baptized," Joan herself protested. The only deed of her active year that was then or later regarded as miraculous was the episode at Lagny, where it was said that she restored to life a child everyone thought was dead, in order to get him baptized. To be baptized was to become a "member of the church," part of the community of beings who acknowledged themselves as redeemed by the blood of Christ. Good Christians were those who remained faithful to their baptism. Their sense of the demands of baptism inspired their behavior, their respect for their neighbors, their daily ethics, their recourse to the sacraments of the church—without neglecting the joys that their daily lives offered. Thus, in the hardest of times, they would dance around the Fairy Tree because the tree was beautiful, because it had inspired legends, and because it was part of their natural setting.

This same mood inspired them to pay homage to Joan, that girl who had been among them just like everyone else and did everything *willingly* until she presented the most striking proof of her faith, crying out "Jesus!" in the flames before the dumbstruck crowd in the Old Marketplace of Rouen.

A pen and ink sketch by Clément de Fauquembergue, the secretary of the Parlement of Paris (10 May 1429).

Charles VII and his Council; Joan appears below at right. A miniature from *Chroniques de Charles VII* by Jean Chartier (fifteenth century), Rouen B.N. MS 112.

Joan and the standard. A miniature of the late fifteenth century, Paris Archives Nationales.

Joan of Arc. An engraving by Couché the Younger after Vauzelles, itself derived from the Portrait of the Échevins. Detail from the work of Lebrun des Charmettes.

Within the painting: IEANNE · DARC · DICTE · LA · PVCE
DORLEANS ·

A unique and little-known Joan of Arc from the seventeenth century. A painting of the French School. Portrait Gallery, Beauregard-en-Blesois.

attrib: Photo Éditions Combier.

(Facing page) The Maid. An eighteenth-century engraving from *La Galerie des femmes fortes* [The Gallery of Strong Women] by Le Moyne.

Joan of Arc: an engraving by Chaussard (1806) after the stature by Gois.

Joan of Arc at Sully. A lithograph by Albert Ligier from the end of the nineteenth century.

Joan of Arc, The Maid of Orléans. The statue by Marie d'Orléans (early nineteenth century).

Sur la Route de la Victoire.

Pinx S Solomko.

Si je n'y suis, que Dieu m'y mette,
Et si j'y suis, que Dieu m'y tienne

Reproduction interdite.
2252
I. M. L.

"On the road to victory." A patriotic postcard (1916).

Joan of Arc: an engraving by Albert Decaris (twentieth century).

A letter of Joan of Arc to the inhabitants of Riom (9 November 1429) signed in her own hand.

THE CAST OF PRINCIPAL CHARACTERS

(IN THREE ALPHABETICAL LISTS)

THE PERSONS PROFILED HERE are presented either because their encounter with the Maid played a significant role in the drama that was her life or because their own story enriches her context. The "principals" in Joan's drama are arranged in three alphabetical lists: the three noble princes whose factions divided her France (Charles VII, Henry VI, Philip the Good), their subjects, and the most prominent of Joan's judges at the Rouen condemnation trial.

Dunois, the Bastard of Orléans—son of Prince Louis—was the first major figure to appear in her drama. Joan never met his half brother, the poet-prince Charles of Orléans, but she saved his duchy; once captured, she regretted that she had not been able to force his return from imprisonment in England. Joan's devoted companion La Hire—Étienne de Vignolles—came to her side next; then the cast expands to include Salisbury, though Joan never met him; he began the siege of Orléans that she would raise. At Joan's side along with La Hire was Poton de Xaintrailles.

Robert de Baudricourt arranged Joan's risky departure from Domrémy and Vaucouleurs and became widely known for that involvement once she reached her goal—after which he became of interest to the historical record. She had a complicated interaction with Raoul de Gaucourt, who had been serving as captain of the city of Orléans before Joan arrived. A happier, warmer association bloomed with her "fair duke," John of Alençon, a prince of the blood royal. About the same time, her judge, Pierre Cauchon, became involved with

Joan's story; in III, 13, we discuss the most recent discoveries regarding the preparation of the transcript of the trial of condemnation. Joan's most resolute enemy at the French court was Georges de La Trémoïlle, leader of a powerful faction. Regnault of Chartres, archbishop of Reims and one of Charles VII's favorite advisors, was sometimes her friend and sometimes a foe.

Three dashing Bretons championed the French cause in the Hundred Years War, when their home province almost went the other way. Bertrand Du Guesclin, who had rescued the France of King Charles V, was one of Joan's heroes; although unlike Joan a noble, he too rose to public adulation from relatively humble, provincial origins. Arthur de Richemont, who died as duke of Brittany, was Joan's ally and La Trémoïlle's rival. The third Breton, Gilles de Rais, who was at first Joan's ardent companion, died in some ways like her after a sensational trial involving the issue of witchcraft—but otherwise led a life as different from the Maid's as possible.

Joan's English opponents are represented here by John Talbot (who surrendered his sword to the Maid after her victory at Patay), Sir Thomas de Scales, and the earls of Suffolk and Warwick as well as their fellow commander, the earl of Salisbury. And then, to complete the pentad, their supreme commander in France was Duke John of Bedford, uncle of the boy-king Henry VI. Jacques Gélu and Jean Gerson represent the sector of the intellectual elite that admired Joan and credited her improbable claim to a divine mission rather than scorning her, as did the majority of the Parisian intelligentsia. Christine de Pisan, historian and moralist as well as a major poet and a vocal Valois partisan in difficult times, gives incomparable voice to Joan's impact on patriotic idealists and intellectuals. Here also appear Isabeau of Bavaria, the oft-maligned queen of France who is credited by some with the disinheritance of her son, the future Charles VII; and Isabelle of Portugal, who, it is said, was a vocal advocate, on Joan's behalf, with her husband Philip the Good.

John of Luxembourg merits attention as well; he kept Joan as a prisoner for four months and then delivered her into the hands of the English. Perrinet Gressart, a typical self-made nobleman of the French fifteenth century, defeated Joan and was a crucial link in the Anglo-Burgundian alliance. A multitude of figures with smaller roles completes the cast. Also, included as a supplement, is Robert de Flocques, one of fifteenth-century France's infamous freebooters. This translation has relied on information from the work of Pierre Champion to construct thumbnail sketches of the careers of the judges who condemned Joan and thus offer some insight into what manner of men they were.

THE THREE NOBLE PRINCES

1. CHARLES VII, KING OF FRANCE

Historians often judge Charles VII (1403–1461) harshly. His weakness during the first years of his reign, his "cowardly abandonment" of Joan of Arc, his later ingratitude toward Jacques Cœur, the devoted merchant who had been one of his most generous financial supporters during the rebellion of 1440, and his final years dedicated to pleasure rather than to the duties of his station make him a less than sympathetic figure, but his contributions to the restoration of the French kingdom should also be noted.

Georges Chastellain, the Burgundian chronicler, describes France at the beginning of the fifteenth century: "turned upside down, a footstool for mankind, the winepress of the English, bootwipe for brigands." Drastically different was the legacy that Charles VII, dying after a thirty-nine-year reign, would leave his son, Louis XI, in 1461: "At his death, he left his kingdom in better peace, justice, and tranquillity than it had known since Clovis, the first Christian king" (*Chronique abrégée jusqu'à Louis XII*, B.N. fr. 4954).

At the coronation at Reims, made possible by Joan of Arc, the man whom enemies tried to dismiss as a bastard child of Queen Isabeau became "king of France by the grace of God" and acquired a ratified legitimacy. Charles VII then turned his efforts toward the reconquest of the kingdom, facilitated by the reconciliation between Armagnacs and Burgundians in 1435 at the Peace of Arras. The king released bands of extortionist mercenaries so they could fight elsewhere, in Switzerland and Germany. Above all, with the Ordinance of Orléans in 1439, he established the foundation of a permanent army and created the Free Archers, who would become the gendarmes of modern France.

His military reforms were at first misunderstood and disliked because the regional quartering of the army and the naming of its commanders by the king went against the traditions of medieval feudalism. Those reforms provoked a revolt of the great feudal lords in the Praguerie of 1440. Charles VII also reformed the judiciary, as shown by the Great Ordinances he granted at Montils-lès-Tours in 1436. In 1454 he commissioned edited records of regional customs and reestablished the three traditional Chambers of Parlement: the Great Chamber, the Chamber of Inquests, and the Chamber of Petitions. In the Pragmatic Sanction of Bourges of 1438, he regulated relationships between the church of France and the papacy by drastically reducing the powers of the latter, retaining as sovereign the right to name the bishops and the superiors of monasteries. Finally, he undertook the nullification trial of Joan of Arc from 1450 to 1456 as a work of personal justice and of reconciliation among the French people.

This king, whom his contemporaries called "the Victorious," was judged by the residents of Châlons in 1429 to be "sweet-tempered, gracious, full of pity and mercy, a fine person, of fine carriage and high understanding" (Letter to the inhabitants of Reims, in Quicherat IV, p. 298). His biographers often emphasize his piety and mercy toward his subjects. Joan of Arc herself said, in the course of her trial, "Speak not of my king, he is a good Christian." With his favorites, his generosity often became a weakness. Georges de La Trémoïlle was only one of many who found it easy to gratify themselves with grants of royal power and pensions.

Jean Juvénal des Ursins, one of the great humanist bishops of the age, also left a portrait of the king: "His life and his government are fair, honest, and pleasing to God." Charles VII was a cultivated man. Fluent in Latin, he excelled in history and the sacred sciences; he could be charming and his voice had a pleasant timbre; he loved the arts, often played the harp, but had little interest in hunting.

The king suffered fits of terror when he recalled certain events of his childhood and youth. An abnormally large number of his brothers and sisters died before him. He was the eleventh child of Charles VI and Isabeau of Bavaria. Their eldest, Charles, was born on September 25, 1386, and lived just over three months, dying on December 28. Then came Isabelle, born on November 9, 1389. She only lived until the age of twenty, dying on September 13, 1409, as duchess of Orléans after having been queen of England: At age seven she had been married to the ill-fated Richard II, later deposed then murdered to the advantage of the first Lancastrian king, Henry IV, father of Charles VII's most deadly enemy, Henry V. Jeanne (January 24, 1391–November 20, 1433) lived to the comparatively old age of forty-one, dying as countess of Montfort and duchess of Brittany.

The second Charles, the fifth child of this brood, lived for eight years (February 6, 1392–January 13, 1401), long enough to be designated dauphin. Next in line was Marie (August 22, 1393–August 19, 1438), who died at forty-five as a nun at the royal convent of Poissy (where she may have known Christine de Pisan), outliving her elder sister the duchess of Brittany by five years. Michelle (January 12, 1395–July 8, 1422) died at twenty-seven as duchess of Burgundy, the second wife of Duke Philip the Good, her brother's rival. Louis (January 22, 1397–December 18, 1415), the eighth child and second dauphin of the royal couple, died at eighteen (when the future Charles VII was twelve) as duke of Guyenne, a title successfully contested by Henry V of England, who had defeated him at the catastrophic Battle of Agincourt less than two months previously. John, Charles and Isabeau's ninth child, was born on August 31, 1398, and died in April 1417, when his brother the future king was fourteen. Catherine (October 27, 1401–June 3, 1438), queen and then queen mother of England from 1420 to 1438, married Henry V as a condition of the Treaty of Troyes, which disinherited her younger brother Charles; their son, Henry VI, was both Charles's nephew and his rival. She died at thirty-seven, when her brother's military successes were destroying her young son's reign and life. Charles, Joan of Arc's dauphin and then king of France, was his parents' eleventh child and fifth son. He was born on February 22, 1403, and died on July 22, 1461, at fifty-eight, outliving all ten of his siblings. The dauphin Charles was an insecure twenty-six when he first met Joan at Chinon. His parents' twelfth and last child, Philip, was born and died on November 10, 1407, when Charles was three. Rife as infant mortality was in medieval families of every class, the French royal family seems to have been exceptionally unfortunate in that generation.

After a nearly mortal accident at La Rochelle in October of 1422 when a wooden floor collapsed beneath him while he was holding court, Charles retained a morbid fear of wooden structures, nor would he ride across wooden bridges. Some speculate that this obsession intensified after the murder of John the Fearless on the bridge at Montereau. Charles could be disconcerted by the sight of strangers; it is reported that if he noticed a strange man while dining, he would stare at him during the entire meal and forget to eat.

Charles was physically unprepossessing: "He was skinny and of meager corpulence, he had a weak constitution and walked strangely without balance," according to Chastellain. He was of medium height and his limbs were poorly proportioned. Since short robes revealed how knock-kneed he was, he wore his robes long; so attired, he could appear majestic.

Surviving portraits show him with a sad and anxious air. They aptly illustrate the judgments of his contemporaries: "He was a solitary person; it was enough for him to spend his time living." Yet he was the first of the kings of France to have an official mistress acknowledged by title, the loyal and adroit Agnès Sorel (d. 1450).

Throughout his life, Charles VII understood how to be well served, and even his enemies knew how to appreciate his qualities. The earl of Suffolk said, "I have seen so much great honor and good in the king of France that I wish everyone to know that I would serve him against all, saving the person of my master." This sentence, uttered in 1445, when efforts were under way to achieve reconciliation both in France and in England, is flattering but demonstrates the positive opinion his contemporaries, adversaries or not, had of "Charles the Well-Served."

2. HENRY VI, KING OF ENGLAND (AND OF FRANCE?)

King Henry VI of England, and for a while Henry II of France, was the only son of Henry V, the deadly campaigner and victor of Agincourt, and of his queen, Catherine, the ninth child and fifth daughter of Charles VI and Queen Isabeau; Henry V won her as his wife in the Treaty of Troyes (1420). Their son was born at Windsor Castle on December 6, 1421: That was the feast of the popular St. Nicholas, and thus it was seen as a happy omen for the reign of this child destined to be king of two great kingdoms. Unfortunately, young Henry's luck quickly took a turn for the worse: First of all, his father died on August 22, 1422, leaving him king of England at the age of nine months. His grandfather Charles VI died less than two months later; thus all who observed the terms of the Treaty of Troyes hailed this eleven-month-old child as king of France. When he was six years old he was dubbed a knight by his godfather and uncle, Duke John of Bedford; in the same Pentecost ceremony he dubbed several other knights (most of them adolescents) himself. By then, Henry already had appeared in state before Parliament, at ceremonies in St. Paul's Cathedral, and in splendid processions winding through the streets of London; in the winter of 1428, several months before his knighting, the six-year-old king had formally opened a session of Parliament. His godfathers, his uncle John of Bedford and his great-uncle Henry Beaufort, the cardinal of Winchester, persuaded the other regents to have this child play the king on many occasions. They also took considerable care in arranging what they considered an appropriate royal education, including instructions to his governess (Dame Alice Butler) to "chastise [him] reasonably from time to time." The nurse appointed to take care of his material needs a few months after his second birthday (a month before Dame Alice's appointment) was paid as much as a member of the privy council.

The second blow to Henry's precocious hopes was Joan's raising of the siege of Orléans on May 8, 1429, when he was only seven and a half. The third, two months later, was the crowning of Charles VII at Reims. Bedford and Beaufort tried to counter that double calamity by having Henry crowned at Westminster on November 6, 1429, and at Paris on December 16, 1431. Before settling on a coronation by Cardinal Beaufort in Notre Dame of Paris, Bedford tried to retake Reims. Most of the traditional coronation regalia of the French monarchy was in Plantagenet control, but the Holy Vial containing the sacred anointing oil was still at Reims, which had for centuries been the site of the anointing and coronation of most French kings. Joan's success in reversing Burgundian control of Champagne pushed Reims out of reach. However, the Paris coronation was not the public relations success it was intended to be, and the ten-year-old king, a far grander dual monarch than Europe had seen for centuries, returned to England only six weeks later.

In 1434 Bedford left England to resume the direct management of his regency in France, never to return. The twelve-year-old monarch involved himself directly in the peace process but lacked both his uncle's innate political skill and his experience as a judge of character. Although Henry VI returned to Rouen during Joan's trial and occasionally sat in on interrogation sessions, Bedford carefully minimized the presence of the boy-king.

In 1435 double blows of misfortune fell on Henry once again. Bedford died in France, and Philip of Burgundy abandoned his alliance with England by signing the Peace of Arras. The latter desertion deeply upset the fourteen-year-old Henry: He is said to have wept openly at the news. Two years later his mother Catherine died; she had been removed from court by Henry's regents for some time.

The rebellion of French nobles against Charles VII in the Praguerie of 1439–1440 encouraged Henry to view his future prospects more hopefully, but no durable benefits ensued. In 1444 Henry married Margaret of Anjou, daughter of King René, who had been a loyal partisan of Charles VII. Margaret was to outlive him, and was a strong emotional support for her husband during the remaining 24 years of his increasingly unhappy life. She was not, however, politically astute, and her ill-advised coalitions exacerbated the intrigues of the English court, finally dooming Henry's chances of remaining in control of his kingdom.

Henry became gravely ill in July 1453, losing the capacity to stand or walk as well as his rational powers and his memory. The causes have been variously described; a stroke combined with an onset of grave depression now seem most likely. Contemporaries suggested that the "madness" of his grandfather, Charles VI of France, had struck him. Some six months later Henry regained "sanity" but never recovered whatever political judgment or firmness of purpose he had possessed. The loss of Normandy and Aquitaine to the armies of Charles VII reduced his prestige drastically, a weakness successfully exploited by his cousin Richard, duke of York.

York defeated the forces of Henry, Queen Margaret, and her favorite, the duke of Somerset, at St. Albans on May 22, 1455. To cut a long and painful story short, Duke Richard's son Edward overthrew Henry and his partisans in many engagements, and proclaimed himself King Edward IV in March, 1482. For the next ten years Henry hid in the back country of northern England, was at length captured and confined in the Tower of London, was trotted out from time to time as a figurehead to bless this or that Yorkist policy, and was finally murdered on May 21, 1471, very likely by Richard, duke of Gloucester, the future King Richard III.

After the Lancastrian party gained vengeance in Henry Tudor's defeat of Richard III at Bosworth Field, the new king, Henry VII, attempted to have Henry VI declared a saint. Henry VI seems to have been a sweet person, distressed by violence and brutality, who loved books and learning, felt concern for the poor, and was overly pious.

Henry's most durable and memorable achievements were the foundation of King's College at the University of Cambridge and of Eton College near Windsor Castle, which was to prepare poor scholars for the former. He founded both in the late 1440s, one of the happiest, most tranquil periods in his life. On July 26, 1446, he laid the cornerstone of the magnificent King's College chapel—finished in the sixteenth century by Henry VIII. He had already laid the cornerstone for the first new building at Eton. He visited both schools as frequently as he could. Queen Margaret also founded a college (Queen's College) at Cambridge and encouraged her husband's cultural benefactions.

We do not know Henry's reaction to Joan's success at Orléans or to the trial at Rouen.

3. PHILIP THE GOOD, DUKE OF BURGUNDY

Four dukes descended in the direct male line from the royal house of France ruled the princely duchy of Burgundy between 1363 and 1477. The first of these Valois dukes, Philip the Bold (1342–1404; reigned from 1363 to 1404), was the fourth son of King John II, the chivalrous king who spent five of the fourteen years of his reign as a prisoner in England after his capture at the disastrous Battle of Poitiers (1356). A loyal supporter of his eldest brother, King Charles V the Wise, and his nephew Charles VI, Philip did not neglect his own interests. His marriage to Margaret, heiress of Flanders and four other rich counties in the Lowlands, laid the foundation for the territorial expansion that would make his heirs the richest princes in Christendom.

Philip the Bold's son John the Fearless (1371–1419; reigned 1404 to 1419) loved conflict more than diplomacy and was avid for combat and conquest. At twenty-five, he was one of the leaders of the unsuccessful crusade that ended in defeat by the Turks at Nicopolis (1396). He resented the restraints imposed by his first cousin Louis of Orléans, brother of Charles VI, and arranged for his assassination in 1407. This act was justified as preemptive tyrannicide by the Paris intellectual Jean Petit. (Duke Louis was supposedly planning to murder his brother the king and usurp the crown of France.) In revenge, the Orléans faction, led by Count Bernard of Armagnac, arranged Duke John's assassination during a parley (that is, under truce) at Montereau on September 10, 1419. The dauphin Charles, also implicated, was obsessed with guilt for this action for the next sixteen years (until the Treaty of Arras in 1435).

Duke John's son Philip the Good (1396–1467; reigned from 1419) came to the ducal throne of Burgundy and one of the richest legacies in Europe at age twenty-three. Eldest son of his father's marriage to Margaret of Bavaria, he would rule his diverse states in eastern France and the Lowlands (now Belgium, The Netherlands, and much of northern France) for nearly fifty years. In the course of that long and successful reign, he greatly expanded his territory and came close to converting it into an independent state, the "kingdom of Lorraine"; he amassed and spent a huge treasury and became Europe's most lavish and astute patron of the arts. He acquired his contemporary epithet, "the Good," for his frequently asserted and apparently sincere intention to go on crusade against the Ottoman Turks. Each of his four marriages was dynastically brilliant; he also maintained in handsome fashion the households of numerous mistresses and bastards.

Duke Philip's first territorial expansion was handed him by the Treaty of Troyes (1420). He moved quickly to take military command of the provinces north of Paris awarded him by that treaty; in one of his finest victories, at Mons-en-Vimeu, he defeated the skilled mercenary captains La Hire and Poton de Xaintrailles.

Philip, however, had little love for his allies the Plantagenets of England. Determined to dominate France himself, he finally used his diplomatic skills to make peace with Charles VII in the Treaty of Arras sixteen years after the murder of his father, John the Fearless, at Montereau. His erstwhile English allies had good reason to be wary of him. Philip's sister Anne, wife of the English regent for France, Duke John of Bedford, was an important link in the Anglo-Burgundian alliance; by the time of her death in September 1432, Philip had squeezed what he wanted from the English. Control of Champagne and Lorraine was essential to connecting his lands in Burgundy with those in the Lowlands; Philip's claims were recognized by Bedford and secured by Burgundian troops at the Battle of Bulgnéville (1431). From Charles VII as well as Bedford he received a string of strategic cities along the river Somme in Picardy, connecting Champagne with the English Channel. He tried to take Calais from the English in 1436, the year following the Peace of Arras.

In 1440 Duke Philip secured the release from imprisonment of his Valois cousin Charles of Orléans, through whom he hoped to control Charles VII and thus France. He had just dabbled in the noble revolt called the "Praguerie," encouraging the king's disaffected eldest son, the future Louis XI, to participate in it. Charles riposted by encouraging Philip's eldest son and heir, Count Charles of Charolais, to filial disobedience. When Charles VII died and Louis XI became king in 1461, Philip soon discerned that his son Charles, the future Duke Charles the Bold (or Rash), was no match for Charles VII's son Louis, the proto-Machiavellian monarch known for good reason as "the Spider King."

Scholars disagree as to whether Philip the Good hoped to establish an independent Kingdom of Lotharingia (Lorraine), or whether he even had a conscious plan to connect Burgundy territorially with his lands in the Low Countries. (Perroy doubted the independence scheme, Vaughan assumes the desire to establish at least a secure connecting corridor through Champagne and Lorraine.) Yet whatever Philip's true aims, people like Joan and the other villagers of Domrémy—born on the frontier between Champagne and Lorraine and living near one of the highways linking Burgundy and the Low Countries—would have had rational grounds for fearing such a "Grand Design." After all, Domrémy had remained faithful to the French rather than the Burgundian party, and when Joan left that beleaguered pocket of French resistance to raise the siege of Orléans, Philip may have manipulated English reactions to the consequences of that event in an attempt to gain support for an eventual complete takeover of Champagne and Lorraine. Joan's insistence on crowning the dauphin in Reims then threatened what was already Philip's indirect control of Champagne, and her subsequent determination late in the summer of 1429 to retake Compiègne and other cities in the northern Ile-de-France close to Burgundian Picardy must have annoyed Duke Philip still further. Thus, in the spring of 1430 when she returned to that theater of operations, thereby abandoning a deflection southward earlier engineered by Georges de La Trémoïlle, one of Philip's sympathizers at the French court, it must have been more than the adroit duke could accept or ignore.

Did Philip have something to do with Joan's surprise capture at Compiègne, which was a target of particular strategic importance for him? We do not know what he said to her just afterward. He delayed many months before letting his protégé John of Luxembourg sell her to the English. Was he perhaps relieved to let his foreign allies take responsibility for her elimination? Although he was expert at intrigue, Philip the Good's specialty was the grand public gesture, which sometimes served serious policy. He seems to have understood exactly what Joan the Maid's dramatic deeds and statements could do to the policies he had so carefully crafted.

One of Philip's grandest gestures was the Banquet of the Vow of the Pheasant in 1454, at the climax of which the "Grand Duke of the West" vowed to go on crusade to rescue Constantinople from the Turks, who had finally taken it the year before. Fifty-eight years earlier, his grandfather, John the Fearless, had made the same attempt, meeting inglorious defeat at Nicopolis. Among other things, the dynasty's honor needed aveng-

ing. To make the expedition possible, Philip called on Charles VII to protect his holdings, but Charles was too canny to fall for that ploy, so Philip never went on crusade. More effective was Philip's creation in 1430 of the Order of the Golden Fleece, a chivalric order modeled on the English Order of the Garter founded by Edward III and on the literary tradition of King Arthur's Round Table. Philip, the new Arthur and the new Jason, invited twenty-five noblemen, supposedly outstanding for their chivalry but equally key players of the political game in the scattered and diverse territories he ruled, to join this brotherhood. The order had its own chapel at Dijon, an associated chapter of clergymen, and a chancellor, treasurer, registrar, and king-of-arms (chief herald). The Companions were to meet every year to feast and plan noble exploits (that is, Burgundian policy). These assemblies did not long succeed in meeting annually, and the number of Companions rose to thirty, but until its dissolution in 1559 (by which time the Austrian Habsburgs had inherited the Burgundian legacy) Philip's romantic institution did much to keep together the disparate states his dynasty had assembled by marriage and conquest.

Philip's extravagance involved lavish support for the arts. Jan van Eyck (1385?–1441), the Flemish painter, was one of Philip's emissaries to the court of Portugal during negotiations for his marriage to the Portuguese princess Isabelle (1428); Philip rewarded him handsomely for his portraits of the princess and of himself and for much other work. Jean Fouquet (1420?–1481), who blended elements of Italian Renaissance style with the northern traditions that had reached their peak in van Eyck, carried out important commissions for Duke Philip as well as for Kings Charles VII and Louis XI. Philip commissioned the official history of his reign and duchy by Georges Chastellain (1415–1475), a Flemish intellectual who was eventually made a Knight of the Golden Fleece after composing dramas and verse epistles on political and moral topics as well as his great *Chronicle of the Dukes of Burgundy*. The *Cent nouvelles nouvelles*, an important collection of tales in several genres on a wide range of subject matter (and of taste and morality), began as entertainment at Duke Philip's banquets. It is interesting that the first voice in Joan's favor after her condemnation is heard in a manuscript dedicated to Philip in 1440—Martin Le Franc's *Champion des Dames*, a debate not unsympathetic to her side.

THEIR SUBJECTS

4. JOHN, DUKE OF ALENÇON

Duke John I of Alençon perished on the battlefield of Agincourt in 1415. Pierre, his son by Mary of Brittany, succeeded him but died in 1425, whereupon his brother, John II (born in 1407 at Argentan), became duke. On the death of her husband, the duchess of Alençon fled the duchy—which Henry V of England had given to his brother the duke of Bedford—and entrusted her son John to the dauphin Charles. In 1420, the dauphin would name him, at age thirteen, lieutenant general for the duchy of Alençon—a riposte to Henry V's grant of that duchy to Bedford (Letter of Charles VII, June 23, 1420: Archives de la Manche, H. 15344, in *Chroniques du Mont-Saint-Michel*). He served as godfather to Charles's young son, the future Louis XI. Appointed to the royal council in 1423, he bore arms for the first time in the Battle of Broussinière; at Verneuil, on August 6, 1424, he was found among the wounded and taken prisoner.

Having fallen into the hands of the duke of Clarence, John of Alençon was set an exorbitant ransom of 80,000 gold saluts, which would not be settled until February 21, 1429. John's wife, Joan, daughter of the duke of Orléans (himself a prisoner), pawned her jewels; John had to yield the barony of Fougères to his uncle the duke of Brittany as well as his lordship of Saint-Christophe in Touraine to Ardouin du Bueil, bishop of Angers. He was, however, freed of his oath to surrender them in May 1429, after the Battle of Orléans (A quittance of Bedford for May 15, 1429, B.N. fr. 18945; cited in Pierre Gourdin, "Monseigneur d'Alençon, le Beau Duc de Jeanne en Touraine," *Bulletin de la Société Archéologique de Touraine* [1980]).

In the nullification trial of 1456, John of Alençon recalled his first interview with Joan: "When Joan arrived near the king, the king was at Chinon and I at Saint-Florent; since I was hunting quails, one of my beaters came to find me and told me that a maid had arrived at the king's court, asserting that she had been sent by God to chase the English away and raise the siege they had laid to Orléans" (deposition of the duke of Alençon, in Oursel, p. 329). The duke rushed to Chinon, where he saw Joan on the following day. He remembered that she had been intrigued when she saw him and that she asked the dauphin Charles who he was. Joan's exclamation when she learned

his identity remains famous: "You are very welcome; the more the blood of France is gathered together, the better it shall be." She seemed joyous to find in the dauphin's company the man whom she would always call thereafter "my fair duke."

Joan and the duke of Alençon practiced jousting together; the duke, surprised and charmed by the ease with which Joan handled arms, offered her a horse. John was present also when Joan calmed the dauphin, assured him that he would recover his kingdom, and instructed him to "make a gift of his kingdom to the King of Heaven." In addition, he commanded the royal army during the Loire campaign, up to the taking of Jargeau. At Patay he and Joan shared the victory. We also know that the Maid met his mother and his wife, Joan, during several days between May 22 and June 2 at Saint-Laurent, near Saumur (Pierre Gourdin, "Le commandement de Jean II d'Alençon et la date du voyage de Jeanne d'Arc en Anjou," *Actes du 5e Congrès National des Sociétés Savantes*). The Maid promised Joan of Alençon that she would send her husband back safe and sound, in "better shape than he is now!"

John of Alençon recalled during the nullification trial a scene between Joan and himself at Jargeau:

> The heralds cried, "To the assault!" And Joan herself said to me, "Forward, gentle duke, to the assault!" To me, this was premature. Joan answered, "Have no fear, this is the hour that pleases God, and when God wills it, that is the moment to take action. Help yourself, and heaven will help you!" And she added, "Gentle duke, are you afraid? Do you not remember that I promised your wife to bring you back safe and sound?"

This companion of Joan also remembered that she had saved his life. He had walked onto a place that she advised him to leave quickly, which he did. He added, "'If not,' she said, showing me a war-machine set up in the city, 'that engine will kill you.'" Seconds later, Monseigneur du Lude was killed in that very place. The "Fair Duke" remarked, "In retrospect, I had great hope in her, and I marveled greatly at Joan's statements."

John of Alençon dashed to the king's coronation and was knighted by Charles VII on that day, July 17, 1429, at Reims. He wanted to continue fighting the English as much as Joan did, and the two of them laid siege to Paris at the Saint-Honoré Gate. But an order arrived from Charles VII to abandon the combat and return to positions at Gien, where the army was disbanded on September 21.

The duke continued to wage war in Maine, Anjou, and Normandy. His relations with Charles VII grew strained. Joan wanted to travel with him to the aid of Mont-Saint-Michel when it was under siege, but the king preferred that she proceed instead up the Loire valley, to attack La Charité.

For more than twenty years, up to 1444, John of Alençon continued to fight; he joined those opposing Charles VII in the plot known as the Praguerie. Finally, in 1449, he reentered his city acclaimed by its people, but by then he was a ruined man. For some time he had wished to marry his daughter Catherine to the eldest son of the duke of York. Catherine was his child by Marie d'Armagnac, whom he had married after the death of Joan of Orléans in 1435. The match did not, however, appeal to Charles VII, who went so far as to have John of Alençon arrested during Joan's nullification trial. Charged with this mission, Dunois apologized to Alençon: "My lord, it distresses me sorely to have a commission that the king has given me against your person, but it is necessary that I make you his prisoner and therefore I lay my hands on you for him." Dunois conducted John of Alençon to the king, who imprisoned him in the fortress of Aigues-Mortes (Chastellain, *Chroniques*, vol. 3., p. 100).

In 1458 his peers, assembled in Parlement at Vendôme, finally judged Alençon guilty of treason, and he was conducted to Loches, under guard of Guillaume de Ricarville, who received these instructions: "[John of Alençon] should never remain alone, should never speak to anyone other than his guardians, and should not receive any letter; he may, however, at any time, read and play chess with his guards, but should never have money with him."

Upon the death of Charles VII in 1461, Louis XI freed his godfather, restoring all his rights, but required Alençon to give him three of his fortresses as well as the wardship of his children René and Catherine until the king should marry them off. These terms were unacceptable to the duke. He was arrested once more and conducted first to the castle of Rochecorbon, then to Loches, and finally to Paris. A new trial before the Parlement of Paris saw him condemned to death on July 18, 1474. Still, he was not executed. Kept a prisoner in the Louvre, he died there in 1476. Louis XI lost no time in reuniting the duchy of Alençon to the crown, making his solemn entry

into the city of Alençon and expelling from it Marie d'Armagnac, who took refuge in Mortagne. She predeceased John of Alençon by three years.

5. RENÉ THE GOOD, DUKE OF ANJOU

René of Anjou was born at Angers in 1408. The son-in-law of Charles II (sometimes counted as Charles I) of Lorraine, he was the second son of Louis II, duke of Anjou, count of Provence—who also claimed the kingdoms of Sicily, Naples, and Jerusalem—and Yolanda of Aragon. He was brought up together with the dauphin Charles. A young man of taste, his passion for the arts won the affection of his maternal great-uncle, Louis, who was a cardinal, duke of Bar, and brother to the queen of Aragon. It was through this doting uncle's influence that René came to be engaged (in 1420) to Isabelle the daughter of Duke Charles of Lorraine.

René would encounter numerous difficulties. For example, obliged to swear his loyalty to Henry VI for that part of his duchy subject to the crown of France, he often was required to fulfill his obligations as a vassal. His repeated refusal to do so put him in open revolt against Louis, duke of Bar, his great-uncle and an English partisan, and against Duke Charles, his father-in-law, a partisan of the duke of Burgundy. Some ten years after his marriage, Cardinal Louis died, bequeathing the domains of Bar to René, who was by then count of Guise. Charles I of Lorraine died a short time later, and so at the tender age of twenty-two René found himself the master of vast domains.

After his county of Anjou passed into the possession of John, duke of Bedford, René had to endure the loss of his county of Guise to John of Luxembourg (1424). He participated in the siege of Vaudémont and the campaign against Metz.

Some scholars have postulated that he was in secret sympathy with Joan. However, on April 13, 1429, he was still paying homage to the king of England's lieutenant; René swore an oath to the English regent Bedford on April 29 with his uncle the cardinal as intermediary, but he withdrew from that obligation shortly after the coronation of Charles VII. On May 5 of the same year, Duke Charles of Lorraine swore fidelity to Bedford in René's name. On August 3, he swiftly disavowed the homage he had sworn to the boy-king Henry. Although he was not present at the anointing of Charles VII, he is nonetheless to be found among the royal army from that time on, often demanding to follow the Maid in leading the van. René was taken prisoner at the Battle of Bulgnéville on June 30, 1431. He was imprisoned at Dijon until Philip the Good freed him in 1437. Unsuccessful in his efforts to regain authority over the kingdom of Naples, King René lived in Anjou and Provence until his death. He was a lover of books, poetry, and women, a composer of pastorals, and, in the style of the Flemish artists, a painter. He died at Aix-en-Provence in 1480.

6. JOHN IV, COUNT OF ARMAGNAC

John IV (1395–1450), count of Armagnac (1418–1450) was the son of Count Bernard VII of Armagnac, constable of France, a victim of the Cabochian uprising in Paris. Count John, who had married Isabelle of Navarre and had sworn fidelity to the king of England in 1421, espoused a circuitous diplomatic policy of which he was later the victim.

He initially supported the Avignon popes Benedict XIII and then Clement VIII in the Great Schism. Martin V (Otto Colonna) was elected pope in 1417. He was recognized by nearly the entire kingdom. But John IV continued to have negotiations with the antipope, Benedict XIII, who retired to the rock of Peñiscola (on October 27, 1418), and who had accorded the count and his family a series of spiritual favors. In 1420 the rupture was complete. Upon the death of Benedict XIII in 1424, John IV of Armagnac supported Gilles Muñoz, who took the title of Clement VIII. Rebellious and submissive in turn, John IV was declared, on March 4, 1429, a schismatic and an apostate, and was placed under interdict. After renouncing Clement VIII, John was pardoned by Martin V. On March 4, 1430, he was relieved of the interdict and given back his possessions. At that point he wrote to Joan requesting her judgement on which of these popes was valid. What motive did he have for consulting Joan on such a tangled and technical question? Did he wish to color his change of attitude with a pious pretext?

Count John was an ambitious man who let nothing stand in the way of increasing his possessions: He made an alliance with the English, he looted crown lands, he failed to recall the services that his ancestors had so proudly rendered the king of France, and he openly harbored André de Ribes (a mercenary captain who devastated Guienne), thus acquiring the epithet "Bastard of Armagnac."

The houses of Foix and of Armagnac had long disputed the succession of the county of Comminges; Charles VII decided to transmit the heritage to the old Countess Marguerite, the last descendant of the counts of Comminges. Shortly thereafter, Charles forbade the count of Armagnac to style himself "count by the grace of God." John IV appealed to the Parlement and to the pope, and finally he rebelled by invading the territories of the king. He was unsuccessful and imprisoned by the dauphin in 1444. It was not long before Charles VII gave him his liberty and his domains with the exception of Rouergue, which he gave to the dauphin Louis. John IV died in 1450.

7. ROBERT DE BAUDRICOURT

Robert de Baudricourt, a loyal supporter of the dauphin Charles, was the first nobleman and member of the dauphin's circle to accept at least the possibility of Joan's mission. His letter, which she brought to Charles, was critical to her winning an audience with the dauphin at Chinon.

Robert de Baudricourt was the son of Liébaud, a gentleman of Lorraine and chamberlain to the duke of Bar, and Marguerite d'Aunoy, a lady of Champagne. In 1415, he succeeded his uncle Guillaume, the Bastard of Poitiers, as bailiff of Chaumont, as well as Jean Daunois as captain of Vaucouleurs. He also served as counselor and chamberlain to King René of Anjou. First squire, then knight, he was made lord of Baudricourt in eastern Lorraine.

Robert de Baudricourt and the young René of Anjou were close friends, and it may be safely assumed that when Joan went to Nancy to visit Duke Charles, René of Anjou, duke of Bar arranged her voyage. We know that on January 29 René sent a message to Robert de Baudricourt; their exchange of letters may have arisen from a desire to test Joan before sending her on to the dauphin (Luce, *Jeanne d'Arc à Domrémy*).

Baudricourt remained attached to the duke of Bar and was at his side on July 2, 1431, during the disastrous Battle of Bulgnéville. All the duke's partisans were eager to fight, but their leader, the duke, did not command. The youngest and most fiery of the captains, Guilhem de Barbazan, judged in a flash how difficult it would be to win the assault but wished to fight anyway, saying "He who has a fear of leaves should not go into the woods." Barbazan was killed and Robert de Baudricourt saved himself only by flight. He may not, however, deserve the cowardly epithet "Fugitive of Bulgnéville," that frequently has been attached to him (Bataille, 51: 140–142; 52: 184–188). Jean, Robert's son, was the first son of

Lorraine to bear the baton of a marshal of France and he was still alive in 1450.

Baudricourt was one of the first to believe in Joan, although he showed understandable reluctance to accede immediately to her first request that he give her an escort to Chinon; he took the precaution of collecting authorized advice and, above all, of sending a messenger to Chinon to ascertain whether she would be received there.

8. HENRY BEAUFORT, BISHOP OF WINCHESTER

The bishop of Winchester was grand chancellor to both Henry V and Henry VI and a man of powerful ambitions. He performed the coronation of Henry VI at Paris on December 16, 1431.

Henry Beaufort, bishop of Winchester and cardinal, was the second illegitimate son of John of Gaunt (brother of King Edward III) by Catherine, the widow of Sir Hugh Swynford. His parents were married in 1396, and a year later, King Richard II declared their children legitimate. He, with his brothers John, earl of Somerset, and Thomas, duke of Exeter, took his name from Beaufort Castle in Anjou, the place of his birth.

Although he is often said to have studied at Oxford, he spent the larger portion of his youth at Aachen, where he studied law, both civil and canon. He was appointed as prebendary of Thame (1389) and of Sutton (1391), both of which were in the diocese of Lincoln. He was dean of Wells (1397) and, having been appointed to the bishopric of Lincoln under papal provision, was consecrated in that position July 14, 1398. The following year he became chancellor of the University of Oxford.

He gained prominence when his half brother Henry of Lancaster ascended the throne as Henry IV. Together they upheld the Lancastrian dynasty while simultaneously opposing the policies of Archbishop Arundel. Beaufort was made chancellor and a member of the king's "great and continual council" in the same year (1403). When William of Wykeham, bishop of Winchester, died in 1404, Beaufort was translated by papal provision to the see of Winchester in the spring of 1405. Upon his translation to Winchester, he resigned the chancellorship.

It is often said that he was the tutor of the prince of Wales (later King Henry V). Whether or not that claim is accurate, Beaufort exercised considerable influence over him. Henry IV had made peace with Arundel and given him a powerful voice in the royal councils, but the prince aligned himself with the younger and more popular party led by Beaufort.

After the death of Henry IV, Henry V immediately took the chancellorship of England back from Arundel and gave it to Beaufort (1413). Opening Parliament on November 4, 1415, Beaufort lauded the noble exploits of the king in the war with France and made an appeal to the gratitude of the people, an appeal that was answered with a sizable grant. The war, however, placed the king in a constant money crunch; Beaufort always found a willing and ready leader in the person of his great-uncle. Beaufort did not inherit any great estates, and the income of his bishopric, while considerable, was not large enough to supply him with either the vast sums he lent the crown or the means to support his extravagant lifestyle; it is therefore probable that his unfailing ability to find ready money was the result of an extraordinary financial talent. He knew how to use money, and to use it with boldness. Beaufort was careful to maintain his credit and unafraid to put that credit into service—he became immensely wealthy. While these habits have earned him the reputation of a miser, he never hesitated to lend his wealth in support of the crown. For instance, in 1416 he lent 14,000 pounds to the king, with customs dues as collateral, and received a gold crown (the first of many) in compensation; in 1421 he lent a further 14,000 pounds. By then, the king owed him 22,306 pounds, 18 shillings, 8 pence. Beaufort was, in every sense, deeply invested in the Lancastrian conquest of France.

Beaufort was nominated cardinal-priest of St. Eusebius on May 24, 1426. The new cardinal lost no time in obeying the papal call for help in the Hussite war. Having received the full approval of the emperor, he accepted the office of legate in Germany, Hungary, and Bohemia. After he entered Bohemia, three armies of the crusaders made a combined attack upon the Hussites at Mies. The attack failed, and Beaufort met the retreating German army in full flight at Tachau. He exhorted them to turn upon their pursuers and, planting a cross in their path, succeeded for a moment in his attempt to rally the panic-stricken army. When they saw the advancing Bohemian army, the crusaders again turned and fled; Beaufort tried in vain to check the tide of retreat, and in his indignation, he tore the flag of the empire and threw it down at the feet of the German princes. He was forced, in the end, to flee with the German army.

Beaufort was a persistent enemy of the duke of Gloucester, Bedford's brother. Gloucester, alarmed at Beaufort's increasing power, persuaded him to go to France in April 1430; he was constantly involved in the king's affairs until his return to England in May 1432. A holder of one of the keys to Joan's cell and present for the duration of the trial, Beaufort was the highest-ranking English clergyman in attendance. Between November 1430 and his death on April 11, 1447, he lent the crown roughly another 37,000 marks, 14,800 pounds, and 15 or so shillings, earning for him the epithet "banker of the state." His niece, Isabelle, married Duke Philip the Good of Burgundy.

For a man of such commitments and resources, the peasant Maid of Orléans must have been an insufferable nuisance. How appropriate that today a statue of "St. Joan of Arc" stands opposite Beaufort's tomb statue in Winchester Cathedral; her image is fully armed and holds a drawn sword, menacing the recumbent "Cardinal of England."

9. JOHN OF LANCASTER, DUKE OF BEDFORD

John of Lancaster, duke of Bedford, earl of Kendall and of Richmond, was a younger brother of Henry V. Born in 1389, he was knighted when he was ten, received in the Order of Garter at eleven, and made constable of England by his father, King Henry IV, at age fourteen. In 1415 he was appointed lieutenant (in effect, military regent) of England by his brother Henry V when the latter launched the French campaign that culminated in the smashing victory of Agincourt. He held that post again between late July of 1417 and late December, 1419; his chief challenge then, as earlier in his active adult life, was trouble on the Scottish border. For the last fourteen months of his royal brother's life (June 1421 to August 31, 1422), he was lord lieutenant once more. As he lay dying, Henry V appointed Bedford guardian of England and of the infant Henry VI, and instructed him to persuade Philip of Burgundy to accept the regency of France for the child-king.

The duke of Burgundy refused that loaded honor, so Bedford became regent of France as well as the ranking member of the regency council for England. He juggled these responsibilities quite effectively and remained regent of France until September 1429, when the disarray of the English army after Joan's victory at Orléans four months earlier led the Parlement and the University of Paris to suggest that Philip the Good assume that office. Nevertheless, Bedford was acknowledged as Plantagenet regent for France from 1430 almost until his death on September 14, 1435, and he acted accordingly. He died at Rouen, which he had made the capital of Plantagenet France after Paris, once a hotbed of pro-Plantagenet sentiment, began to feel exposed to French advances in all directions and hence unsafe.

Bedford won many victories in the field and at the bargaining table. The English lost France despite his talents and his unflagging energy. His peak period of military success climaxed in the summer and autumn of 1424; his victory at Verneuil on August 17 was almost as a destructive to the French nobility's military leadership as Agincourt had been nine years earlier. He relied heavily on a triumvirate of skilled commanders, the earls of Salisbury, Suffolk, and Warwick. Always a cautious believer in consolidated positions, he was hesitant to order the siege of Orléans, Salisbury's pet project. The impact of Joan's raising that seven-month siege proved Bedford's strategic instincts right in the long run. For the two months after that reversal, followed by defeats in the field at Meung, Jargeau, and Patay, Bedford managed the English defense with inspired tenacity. He nearly restored English military and diplomatic dominance.

Bedford's wife, the kindly and persuasively influential Anne of Burgundy, Duke Philip's sister, died at Paris on November 13, 1432. After that loss, Bedford's increasingly strained relationship with Philip the Good unraveled quickly. Its fraying was hastened by Bedford's swift remarriage (on April 20, 1433) to Jacqueline of St. Pôl, the daughter of a vassal of Philip's—the Grand Duke of the West did not favor any spread of English influence in his own domains. The English still held Paris when Bedford died at Rouen in 1435, a week after the English envoys to the peace conference at Arras withdrew, since the reconciliation between the Valois and Burgundian factions was clearly unpreventable.

John of Bedford's loyalty to the causes of his brother Henry V and his nephew Henry VI never wavered. Although his brother Duke Humphrey of Gloucester often made Bedford's life difficult, he handled his responsibilities with exceptional (and widely respected) competence. Always severe toward his enemies and to anyone suspected of heresy or other forms of deviant behavior, he was the architect of Joan's trial. Frequently merciful to prisoners, thanks often to the intervention of his duchess Anne, he showed Joan no mercy, although it was always within his power to spare her life or moderate the relentless harshness and duplicity of Pierre Cauchon.

10. JACQUES BOUCHER

Jacques Boucher, Joan's host while in Orléans, was the loyal treasurer and later receiver of finances for Charles, duke of Orléans. His house was near the Renard Gate. On February 10, 1416, Jacques Boucher appears as clerk of the duke's bailiffs; he was granted 14 livres for having attended the duke and his council at Calais in November 1415. He succeeded Pierre Renier as treasurer of the duchy between February and September 1422. On December 18 of that year, he obtained a safe-conduct so as to negotiate the count of Angoulême's ransom. In June 1439, Boucher delivered 40 gold écus to Duke Charles at Calais. He died shortly before January 3, 1444, when he was succeeded in his fiscal responsibilities by Jean Chardon, the duke's secretary. It is not unlikely that Jacques Boucher visited Charles of Orléans during his lord's captivity in England.

11. CHARLES I, DUKE OF BOURBON

Charles I (1401–1456), fifth duke of Bourbon, was count of Clermont during Joan's lifetime. He was the son of John I, fourth duke of Bourbon; his father was captured at the Battle of Agincourt and died as a prisoner in England (1433). Charles was espoused to Catherine of France until John the Fearless, who imprisoned him in Paris (1408), gave him his freedom on the condition that he would marry John's daughter Agnès (still an infant at the time). After the assassination of John the Fearless on the bridge at Montereau, Charles joined the Armagnac party and, believing himself freed from his obligation toward Duke John, gave Agnès back to her brother Duke Philip the Good.

Charles proved himself as valorous as his ancestors, but at the same time he displayed a severity that bordered on cruelty toward the garrisons of numerous places he conquered, especially Aigues-Morte and Béziers. After pacifying that stretch of coastal Languedoc, he was named governor of the Bourbonnais, the Nivernais, the Lyonnais, the Beaujolais, the Mâconnais, and of Forez. He later received charge of the government of Languedoc and Guyenne as lieutenant general, and then of the Dauphiné. He was made lieutenant general of the king in the Bourbonnais, Auvergne, and Forez.

In 1425 his sister, Bonne d'Artois, married Philip the Good, thus easing the tensions between Charles and Philip.

He vehemently attacked Georges de La Trémoïlle and physically assaulted his chancellor,

Gouge de Champaigne, then for a short time reconciled himself with the duke of Burgundy and asked for his fiancée back again. Handsome, enterprising, and very much the adventurer although he remained at Blois during the siege of Orléans, he sent an army to Charles VII for the relief of that city. He fought and was wounded at the Battle of the Herrings, and was present at the siege of Troyes and at the coronation of Charles VII, where he fulfilled the function of a peer and conferred knighthood. He was present at the battle of Montépilloy, communicated with Joan at Senlis, took part in the attack on Paris, and witnessed with great dissatisfaction the rapid retreat of Charles VII. He was created lieutenant general of the Ile-de-France, but later renounced this last honor and lost the château of Gournay-sur-Aronde. Later, jealous of the influence his brother in-law Charles du Maine had in the government, he took part in the Praguerie revolt of 1439-1440 and was reconciled with the Burgundians. When the Praguerie failed, Charles was compelled to surrender at Cusset in Auvergne and to beg on his hands and knees for the king's mercy. For his part in this intrigue, he lost the castles of Vincennes, Loches, and Corbeil, and, even more distressing to him on a personal level, he was forced to watch as his brother, Alexandre, was tortured to death. After more than a year passed, his son was married to Joan of France, daughter of Charles VII. A little later, he retired to his domains and died shortly thereafter.

12. JEAN DE BROSSE

Jean de Brosse, de La Brosse, or (in common current usage) Debrosse, was a brilliant military leader and commander of the king's special bodyguard of one hundred men. He was several times a companion-in-arms of the Maid.

Debrosse, often styled marshal of Boussac or marshal of Sainte-Sévère from the names of his fiefs, was born in 1375. At the instigation of the constable of Richemont, he killed Camus of Beaulieu, a favorite of the dauphin's. Afterward he distinguished himself by more honorable exploits: at the siege of Orléans and at Saint-Pierre-le-Moûtier, at the battle of Patay (1429), at the liberation of Compiègne (October 25, 1430), at Lagny, and at La Charité-sur-Loire.

He was one of the four guardians of the Holy Chrism at the coronation of Charles VII at Reims and was appointed the king's lieutenant beyond the Seine, Marne, and Somme.

On June 5, 1430, Charles VII announced to the people of Reims that he was going to liberate

Compiègne. That bold initiative owed everything to Debrosse's arrival. He commanded a column of wagons that followed the army of Xaintrailles and Vendôme and participated in two decisive assaults on October 24. Later, he was among those who encountered Burgundian troops at Montidier in November. On February 3, 1432, a troop of 600 Frenchmen under his command approached Rouen, hoping to scale the walls at night. A flower of chivalry, Jean Debrosse died in 1433, laden with military honors.

13. REGNAULT OF CHARTRES, ARCHBISHOP OF REIMS

First a friend and then an adversary of Joan, Regnault of Chartres (1380–1444) was the archbishop of Reims. His father was Hector of Chartres, lord of the Norman fief of Onz-en-Bray and grand master of forests and waters in Normandy and Picardy. Hector died at Paris during the Cabochian uprising of 1418, a casualty of the Burgundian capture of the city; Regnault was merely imprisoned. Three of his brothers had died already at Agincourt.

Regnault rose through the ecclesiastical ranks very rapidly; he was dean of the cathedral of Beauvais before 1410 and master of the Cholets schools. On September 17, 1412, he appears in the documents as chamberlain of Avignon (that is, of the Avignon pope John XXIII), one of the referendaries and constant dinner companions of the pope; he was soon elected bishop of Beauvais and was thus a predecessor of Pierre Cauchon. In 1414 the pope named him archbishop of Reims despite resistance from the city government and the cathedral chapter. He attempted to explain the pope's flight to the Council of Constance; in August 1414, he urged Emperor Sigismund to move the Council from Constance. John XXIII sent him as ambassador to Louis II of Anjou and to Charles VI. These missions enhanced Regnault's standing in French diplomacy, and from 1414 he addressed himself unsuccessfully to the task of reconciling the houses of Orléans and Burgundy. Appointed to the dauphin's council in 1417, he was present in 1418 at the conference at Montereau, representing the dauphin and the count of Armagnac. In 1417 he was sent to England and in 1418 to Languedoc, where he recruited soldiers, and to Savoy. In 1420 he went to Scotland seeking support for the dauphin, and in 1422 he traveled to Spain on the same mission. In 1425 he was at Rome. After the dauphin appointed him chancellor of France on May 8,

1424, his house in Paris was confiscated. About that time, Charles granted him 4,000 gold écus to arrange the marriage of one of his nieces to the Sire de Vauvert.

Prudent to excess, Regnault the instinctive diplomat labored to end the Hundred Years War by undermining the Anglo-Burgundian alliance. He witnessed the decisive meeting between Joan and the dauphin and served on the board examining her at Poitiers. The historian Charles T. Wood suspects that he purposely lost the transcript of that first "trial" of hers. (See the introduction to III.) Charles sent him to Blois to direct the relief of Orléans. From Troyes he wrote to the inhabitants of Reims, encouraging them to receive their king with great honor. He consecrated the dauphin king and in the process recovered his cathedral. His behavior toward Joan after the coronation shows him already at odds with her; from then on Regnault returned to his former grand design for peace through a rapprochement with Burgundy. The letter he addressed to the people of Reims on the day after Joan was captured reveals his political instincts. Joan had become a hindrance rather than an asset. Guillaume de Flavy, Regnault's half brother, has been seen as a traitor for shutting the Maid out of Compiègne. (See III, 10.) After Reims, Regnault always supported the cause of peace in the king's council against Joan and those who preferred action to words, such as the duke of Alençon. Unfortunately, he did not know of the memorandum of the Burgundian Hugues de Lannoy, which advocated strengthening the Anglo-Burgundian alliance. Regnault de Chartres died laden with honors in late Lent 1445, at Tours, still negotiating for peace between France and England. His major policy triumph was the peace of Arras.

14. GUILLAUME DESJARDINS

Guillaume Desjardins or Desgardins, a doctor of medicine, was born about 1370 at Caudebec in the Caux (northeastern Normandy). By 1403 he was a priest in the diocese of Rouen, master of arts studying medicine. In 1408 he ranked first in the examinations for the licentiate in medicine at the University of Paris and was soon appointed a master regent of that faculty. Desjardins did not teach at Paris between November 1412 and November 1413, but resumed his course load again in 1414. On December 6, 1418, the faculty considered him for a regency although he was absent in Rouen because of illness. Desjardins never returned to Paris. In 1421 he was appointed canon of the two Norman cathedrals of Bayeux and Rouen (where his brother Robert died in August 1438), which strongly suggests his partisan sympathy for the English.

A rich man, holding a rich fief at Sahurs, Desjardins owned handsome books. Practicing medicine at Rouen as well as exercising his clerical offices, he moderated his prosperity with liberal donations. A benefactor of the Norman Nation at the University of Paris, he contributed toward the purchase of a study hall for their use. He is also listed among the benefactors of a hospital at Rouen, the Hôtel-Dieu-de-la-Madeleine.

At Warwick's command he visited Joan in prison when it appeared she might die of natural causes. When he arrived, he found that she had a high fever and, with his colleague Guillaume de La Chambre, prescribed that she be bled. At her trial his opinion echoed that of Gilles de Duremort, abbot of Fécamp.

15. BERTRAND DU GUESCLIN

The Breton knight Bertrand Du Guesclin (1320?–1380), Joan's precursor in the effort to save France, was one of her heroes. His appointment as constable of France by Charles V in 1370 climaxed twenty years of remarkable service to the French crown. In the 1360s King Henry I of Castile named him constable of Castile, duke of Molina, and king of Granada (in the hope that he would conquer that kingdom from the Moors). His skeleton was interred among members of the French royal family at the royal abbey of Saint-Denis, an honor almost without parallel in the Middle Ages. His heart was buried at Dinan, the fortress city that served as capital of the region of Brittany from which he came and the hometown of his beloved wife, Tiphaine Raguenel. Two other sites claimed other parts of his body; in an age when kings traditionally divided their mortal remains among three honored shrines, this tribute to the memory of a rude knight sprung from the lesser nobility of a backward province was an extraordinary recognition of his patriotic heroism, marked by tireless devotion to the Valois cause, first in his native Brittany, then throughout the kingdom and south of the Pyrenees in Spain, as well as by his extraordinary list of military victories.

Celebrated in the generation of Joan of Arc as a paragon of chivalry as well as a resolute warrior, Bertrand Du Guesclin was in fact better at guerrilla warfare and at surviving defeat than at battlefield combat. Eldest of the ten children of Robert, lord of the minor castle of La Motte-Broons in northeastern Brittany, Bertrand was so small and so ugly that it was said that his parents preferred not to see him. They so neglected his education that he was said in later life to have trouble signing his name. According to tradition, he grew up among the kitchen staff of his old but impecunious family and learned how to fight with the peasant boys of the neighborhood; his later career revealed his deep understanding of how ordinary people felt about the cost of warfare and diplomatic gamesmanship.

Although he was not dubbed a knight until 1354, around age thirty-four, Bertrand's career as a warrior began when he was still in his teens. It was said that he arrived at a brilliantly attended tournament about 1337 at Rennes, the provincial capital, riding a plowhorse and so ill-armed that he was denied entry. A kindly kinsman contacted in secret equipped him in more knightly fashion, and Bertrand proceeded to sweep the lists. As he raised his helmet's visor before the judges' stand, his father, thunderstruck, called him "fair son" and promised to treat him right thereafter.

In 1357, when Bertrand was already a local champion of the pro-French side of a Breton civil war, he achieved another feat of arms that won him a wife. He was commanding the defense of Dinan against a besieging English army commanded by the duke of Lancaster when his brother Olivier was captured in violation of a truce. A large ransom was demanded. Bertrand challenged the English knight who had captured Olivier, defeated him, and was awarded the ransom as his prize. This exploit so impressed a learned and highly cultivated young noblewoman of Dinan, Tiphaine Raguenel, that she began negotiations to marry him, which occurred four years later. In 1374, when he was a widower, Du Guesclin married Jeanne-Anne de Laval, the lady of Tinteniac. This union with one of the oldest and wealthiest of Breton noble lineages allowed Joan of Arc's friend Gilles de Rais, a member of the house of Laval, to boast that he was the "nephew" of Du Guesclin. Gilles's two young cousins Guy and André de Laval came to join Joan's army shortly after she raised the siege of Orléans in May 1429, and Joan sent their grandmother, Du Guesclin's widow, the present of a gold ring as an act of homage. Her husband the constable had died nearly fifty years before.

In 1359 Du Guesclin was called to fight in the Ile-de-France. After the humiliating Peace of Brétigny (1360), which acknowledged that Edward III of England had won the first phase of the Hundred Years War, Du Guesclin defended the territories of the dukes of Orléans and Anjou and the count of Alençon against further encroachment by the victorious English and their allies. The year 1364 may have been his finest: Honored by appointment as the king's chamberlain in April, Du Guesclin defeated the Plantagenet party's best field commander at the Battle of Cocherel in Normandy on May 16. He was rewarded with the county of Longueville and the post of royal lieutenant for Normandy.

Charles V, known as Charles the Wise, then sent Du Guesclin south to help his brother Duke Louis of Anjou restore order in the province of Languedoc. Campaigns beyond the borders of the French kingdom, in Provence and then in Spain, followed. The armies that Du Guesclin commanded in Spain first won, then lost (he was captured and held for a huge ransom, swiftly paid by Charles the Wise), then won again; in 1369 Du Guesclin installed Henry of Trastamara as king of Castile, whereupon he was showered with honors.

In 1370 Charles V called Du Guesclin home and made him constable of France. Du Guesclin reconquered lost territory and defeated new English incursions, mostly by avoiding pitched battles. In 1378 the constable faced his most severe political test. Charles V decided to absorb Brittany, ending its five-century-old autonomy within the French kingdom. Du Guesclin was unable to execute the military side of that policy. The pro-English claimant to the Breton ducal throne, John IV, father of Arthur de Richemont, returned and swept through the duchy. Du Guesclin then spoke of going to Castile. His enemies at court, always numerous, were delighted; Charles the Wise sent him to Auvergne, the mountainous center of France, to subdue bands of unemployed mercenaries who were terrorizing that province. While carrying out that assignment, Bertrand Du Guesclin died at Châteauneuf-de-Randon on July 14, 1380. He was buried with the highest honors. His finely carved tomb statue, showing how small this giant was, is still on view at Saint-Denis. It is hard to imagine that Joan did not pause by it at some point between August 26 and September 9 in 1429.

16. JOHN, COUNT OF DUNOIS, BASTARD OF ORLÉANS

Dunois's name is indissolubly linked to the story of Joan and more generally to the reign of Charles VII. Born the year before the king (November 23, 1402, at Paris), he was the natural son of Louis of Orléans and Mariette of Enghien (called "the lady of Cani"). His governess, Jeanne du Mesnil, guided his early steps at the castle of Beauté-sur-Marne. Until the age of ten, he was raised with the dauphin Charles, and their comradeship lasted through the long years of war. During the "reconstruction of the kingdom of France," Charles VII expressed his appreciation in these words:

> Out of consideration for the services that our dear and beloved cousin John, the Bastard of Orléans, count of Dunois and great chamberlain of France, has done us all his life, both in our presence, where for a long time he was raised, and in the midst of our wars, in the encounter with our ancient enemies and adversaries in many armies and battles, in which from his early age, and indeed as soon as he could arm himself and carry harness, he has always greatly and with great care, concern, and diligence, made use of everything in his capacity to recover our lordship. . . .

Dunois was around fifteen when he took up arms for the kingdom. The Bastard had been trained early to make decisions and to survive in an atmosphere of violence. (His father had been killed in 1407 by the bodyguard of the duke of Burgundy.) Valentine Visconti (of Milan), the duchess of Orléans and wife of his father, took charge of his education; she found him a precocious boy who might one day avenge his father—according to the chronicler Enquerrand de Monstrelet, she wrote with pain: "none of the other children is able to revenge the death of his father." She died, unexpectedly, one year after her husband. In 1415, John's half brother the young Duke Charles of Orléans became an English prisoner, and so Dunois was charged with raising the money for the duke's ransom. He took up arms on September 21, 1417 (at around the age of fifteen) against the forces of John the Fearless, duke of Burgundy.

The Bastard was taken prisoner by the Burgundians and remained two years under close surveillance. During that time the Cabochian Revolt drenched Paris in fire and blood, as the city fell under the domination of the duke of Burgundy. John was finally freed from the castle of Saint-Germain and rejoined his family at Blois, but his joy was short-lived: His half-brother Philippe de Vertus died, leaving him the active head of the House of Orléans. When hostilities resumed with Henry V, the Bastard took part in his first pitched battle at Baugé and performed well. On that occasion, having already reached the requisite age of twenty-one, he was knighted;

thereafter, he had the right to command a company and wear his sword attached to the knightly girdle. As a knight, he was entitled to double damages at law. (But if he lost, he had to pay twofold.) He had the right to wear a tabard emblazoned with his own coat of arms over his armor. After Baugé, he continued to fight in the armies of the dauphin Charles, who in 1422 took refuge at Bourges, where John married the daughter of Louvet, the president of the Parlement.

Dunois once again took up arms against the English in defending Mont-Saint-Michel (1425); he succeeded in crushing, with a handful of men, the enemy troops on the moors of Montargis, and compelled them to raise the siege (1427).

The Bastard of Orléans struggled with great financial problems. The ransom of Charles of Orléans came high, the devastated countryside produced paltry crops, and the captains' payments drained the budget. And, in a sudden change of fortune, the Bastard was exiled to Provence in 1426 on the order of the future Charles VII. The heir to the throne had quarreled with President Louvet, and the family fell into disgrace. The king was then under the influence of other counselors, such as the lord of Giac. But soon a new English offensive called John back to action; his exile had lasted about a year.

In 1427, the English moved on the duchy of Orléans and besieged Montargis. The Bastard of Orléans, an accomplished knight and courageous captain at age twenty-five, took charge of defending the city against the English. On September 5, Montargis and its castle were liberated. Then the English besieged Orléans. We know the famous episode of Joan's arrival at Chécy and her argument with Dunois (see I, 3), who, during the nullification trial, would eloquently describe Joan's exploits at Orléans, expressing his admiration for her.

After Joan's death, the Bastard continued the battle for the recovery of the kingdom. As a reward for his exploits, Charles VII named him grand chamberlain—that is, first officer of the king's chamber, replacing Georges de La Trémoïlle. John, "one of the finest French speakers there is of the language of France," as Jean Chartier called him, prepared the Treaty of Arras among France, England, and Burgundy. Charles VII also gave him the task of ending the Great Schism by demanding that Amadeus VIII of Savoy, the antipope Felix V, abdicate and acknowledge in his stead Nicholas V on October 11, 1447.

After the death of his first wife, the Bastard of Orléans married Marie d'Harcourt, countess of Tancarville, in 1440 in the cathedral of Orléans.

The couple resided at Beaugency, rather than in the crude fortress of Châteaudun. Marie received into her household Dunois's natural son by Isabelle of Dreux. She herself had a daughter, also named Marie, in November 1440.

When preparations began to receive Charles of Orléans, freed at last by the English, the Bastard contributed actively from his base at Blois. Dunois went on to serve as intermediary between the dauphin Louis, whose mentor he was, and King Charles VII. He took part in Louis's first expedition against Dieppe, freeing the city on August 11, 1443. This victory led to the reduction of all of Normandy and, in 1449, to the capture of Rouen. Dunois was by then the father of a legitimate son, who would not, however, live to reach his majority.

Dunois was made count of Longueville and involved himself in the rebuilding of his capital, Châteaudun. He had wanted to make that castle his residence, but the restoration proved too costly. Now older than fifty, the Bastard was nevertheless obliged once more to take up his sword and march toward Guyenne.

Following the death of Charles VII on July 22, 1461, Dunois quarreled with the new king, Louis XI, who dismissed him from court. Dunois's wife fell ill while he was in Brittany settling disputes among John of Angoulême, Charles of Orléans, and King Louis. He returned quickly, for Marie lay dying; she was interred at Cléry. Dunois died on November 23, 1468, finally reconciled with Louis XI, who in fulfillment of his vow definitively ensured the position of the House of Orléans-Longueville. Dunois is buried in the family vault installed in the collegial church of Notre-Dame-de-Cléry.

17. ROBERT DE FLOCQUES

He signed himself "Floquet," used "Robinet" as his popular name, and also styled himself Robert de Flocques. He was one of the most famous of "the Flayers," highwaymen who terrorized fifteenth-century France. The name derived from the fact that "all who ran into them, whether on one side of the conflict or the other, were divested of their garments and left with nothing but their shirts" (de Bueil, vol. 2, p. 80). These men-at-arms made the years 1435 to 1444 one of the blackest periods of French history. The bands of Flayers were composed of different sorts of people: descendants of the great families of France (such as the Chabannes), minor nobles driven off their fiefs (like Robert de Flocques), peasants impelled by poverty, defrocked priests, loose women. These small armies took prisoners for ransom, raped, killed, and pillaged in Hainaut, Touraine, the Auxois, Champagne, and elsewhere. They practiced what today we would call racketeering, extorting from a village, a city, or an individual payments in return for protection from pillaging. If the funds flowed slowly, they simply took what they could.

But Robert de Flocques—like his counterparts La Hire, Chabannes, and Xaintrailles—remained faithful to Charles VII, apparently feeling that pillaging and holding to ransom were not so treasonous since the profits from those activities allowed them to remain actively committed to their king's cause (Plaise, 1984).

Little is known of Robert de Flocques's early career. Was he at Orléans? Did he participate in the campaign of the Loire at Joan's side? Was he at Compiègne? None of these questions has been answered. The first time his name appears in documents, in 1432, he was in the Beauvaisis, where he ransomed a Burgundian poet scheduled to be executed on the orders of Charles VII. To complete the bargain favorably and collect 1,000 gold saluts for the ransom, he kept La Hire and Xaintrailles with him.

He appears again in 1437 at Tancarville, fighting the English. He would in fact wage war on the occupier all his life. To find resources, he was obliged to scour the duke of Burgundy's territory. The duke complained to Charles VII that the commitments made at the Treaty of Arras (1435) were not being kept, and the king's reaction was swift. He disavowed the captains whom he required in a formal letter to stop the pillage: Poton de Xaintrailles, Gauthier de Brussac, the Bastard of Bourbon, Antoine de Chabannes, Robert de Flocques, and others.

The Estates of Burgundy spent more than 6,000 gold saluts to convince the Flayers to leave. The brigands then turned toward Lorraine and Alsace, where they achieved the limits of atrocity. Unable to attack the well-defended cities of Strasbourg and Basel, they took vengeance on the open country, burning more than a hundred villages before returning to Burgundy. Charles VII reacted with the ordinance of November 2, 1439: "Captains and men-at-arms will be stationed in garrisons in places along the frontiers." Thereafter, there would be no captains other than those chosen and named by the king, who paid them directly. In this ordinance we see the beginning of the standing army, although this revolutionary idea was widely resisted, since war had always been the prerogative of the nobles and princes. To restrain the Flayers, Charles VII made

an example of Alexandre de Bourbon, formerly a canon and companion of another Flayer, Rodrigo de Villandrando. Alexandre was arrested in 1441 and then, at the end of a summary trial, was sewn in a sack and thrown from the bridge of Bar-sur-Aube. Eight of his companions were hanged, and twelve had their heads cut off. The impact of these convictions was great but short-lived: The Flayers soon resumed their life of random pillage.

The victory of Charles VII over the Praguerie was attributable partly to the Flayers who had rallied to his side, following the example of Rodrigo de Villandrando. Xaintrailles, Pierre de Brézé, and Robert de Flocques were also active in the earlier campaigns of this rebellion and then pursued the rebels deep into Auvergne. But troubles arose during the twenty-two months (from June 1, 1444, to April 1, 1446) of truce negotiations. What was to be done with the Flayers? Charles VII made the most of the chance to send them far away, using as a pretext the difficulties of Ferdinand III of Austria with the Swiss cantons and of René of Anjou with the people of Metz. Sending them as help to these allies, and putting the dauphin Louis at the head of this force, Charles mightily irritated the duke of Burgundy by intervening thus in the affairs of Burgundy's eastern neighbors.

Notorious massacres followed, and the Flayers' return to France was just as bloody. After Alsace, they sacked and put to ransom much of Burgundy, which had been spared most of the ravages of the Hundred Years War. But in achieving the recovery of Normandy, a royal army was finally established, and the king succeeded in convincing it to remain in garrison quarters. Amply paid, the troops had no need to provide for themselves by pillaging.

Robert de Flocques built a reputation for retaking towns either "by treason," from the English viewpoint, or "with subtlety," from the French perspective. He and his friends found spies and others on whom they could rely in most towns. Flocques was well rewarded by Charles VII, receiving among other prizes the mansion that Talbot possessed at Honfleur. He did not participate in the royal entry to Rouen, because he had just broken his leg: To allay his suffering, the canons of the cathedral sent choirboys to serenade him with canticles.

Toward the end of his life, Robert held on to his command and cut a figure among the great captains of Charles VII. He had then one hundred men-at-arms and two hundred archers and appeared with this retinue in the shows of force organized regularly every three years.

18. RAOUL DE GAUCOURT

Raoul de Gaucourt, governor of Orléans when Joan arrived there, entered the service of Charles VI as a keen young squire, first seeing combat in 1396. Named chamberlain of the duke of Orléans, he took part in the siege of Harfleur, where he was taken prisoner; he remained in England six years. His father, the bailiff of Rouen, was assassinated by the inhabitants of the city in a revolt. Ruined by the ransom he had to pay Henry V, Raoul de Gaucourt retained only the properties of his wife, Jehanne de Preuilly, in Touraine and in Berry.

After his release in 1404, Gaucourt often participated in combat. He was at the side of La Hire at the taking of Montargis, which cost him dearly—his battle preparations obliged him to pawn a gold crown mounted with precious stones that he liked to wear atop his helmet in tournaments. The king compensated him with the captaincy of Chinon and in 1428 named him bailiff of Orléans. He would later become governor of the Dauphiné, assisted by his lieutenant Jean Juvénal des Ursins, the future archbishop of Reims. In 1449, as a member of the royal council, he was in the company of Charles VII when the king entered Rouen. Charles VII later sent Raoul de Gaucourt to Pope Calixtus III in order to arrange a review of the original trial of Joan of Arc. He was eighty at the time of the nullification trial; his deposition at that trial is unusually complete.

19. JACQUES GÉLU

Like Gerson, Jacques Gélu (?–1432) wrote a treatise on the Maid. The archbishop of Embrun, Gélu enjoyed a reputation for tranquility and humanist wisdom. Jean Girard, president of the Parlement of Grenoble, and Pierre Lhermite, an intimate counselor of Charles VII, had written to ask Gélu's advice on Joan's "marvelous" arrival at Chinon. They explained that the doctors of the church had already examined her at Poitiers. Gélu warned the dauphin to take care lest he be tricked by an intriguer, and he made the following points: "One should not lightly alter any policy because of conversation with a girl, a peasant, raised in solitude, of a fragile sex, so susceptible to illusions; one should not make oneself ridiculous in the sight of foreign nations; the French are already sufficiently infamous for their natural susceptibility to being fooled." With Lhermite acting as intermediary, Gélu recommended that the king follow some pious exercises so as to be spiritually enlightened, and he asked that they interrogate the girl carefully. He added that three factors rendered her suspect: She came from Lorraine, the frontier of the hostile territories of Burgundy and Lorraine; she was a shepherdess, the sort who were "easily seduced"; and she was a girl, so "it may appear to her a slight matter to wield arms, to lead captains as well as to preach, to render justice, and to serve as an advocate." He recommended nonetheless that she be welcomed and treated with consideration.

A cultured man, whose opinion was valued by his contemporaries, Gélu was born in the duchy of Luxembourg, completed his studies at Paris, and prepared for a legal career. He was befriended by the duke of Orléans. Upon the death of his brother, Charles VI named Gélu president of the province of the Dauphiné. But Gélu had now decided on a religious vocation and asked the king for an appointment as a canon at Embrun. Charles VI acquiesced, even arranging his election as archbishop of Tours (in 1414). The king called Gélu back to court frequently, however, and gave him responsibility for the royal finances before sending him to the Council of Constance with the delicate (and finally unsuccessful) task of persuading Benedict XIII to reconsider his decision to maintain the papal schism. He then attended the pope at Perpignan and worked on an alliance between the kings of France and Castile. Returning to Constance during the election of a new pope, he himself received some votes before Martin V was elected. Having returned to Paris, Gélu opposed the Treaty of Troyes with all his energy, writing to the king of England and to the Breton lords who had taken up the English cause. But, seeing that his efforts had failed, he traveled to Rome and there was named archbishop of Embrun in 1427. Much of this story is known from Gélu's autobiography, a project he unfortunately abandoned in 1421.

Once he had determined that the Maid had "achieved a marvel," Gélu adopted a sympathetic stance and composed a treatise for Charles VII that summarized the current arguments about Joan of Arc. It began: "The marvels that have just been accomplished for the eternal glory of Your Highness and of the House of France echo in all ears, and a very young woman is the instrument." The archbishop discerned in Joan's deeds the hand of God. He detailed the terror the English had inflicted on France, dividing the kingdom and reducing the king to such a profound distress. This wretchedness, Gélu concluded, impelled God to send this young girl in "virile costume" (for he accepted the clothes Joan had adopted). He insisted on the legitimacy of Charles VII, saying that it would offend natural, divine, and human law for his parents to remove him from the throne. He evoked as well the glorious merits of the king's predecessors. Despite the upheavals brought on by the war, he wrote, the people had never despaired of God's goodness and mercy. Gélu raised, in order to refute them, the rumors that pictured Joan as an envoy of Satan. As a conclusion to his treatise, Gélu urged the king to call upon Joan every time he had a problem to resolve, because she was the envoy of God. He also recommended that, without neglecting human efforts, the king "do every day some deed particularly agreeable to God and confer about it with the Maid."

Jacques Gélu died on September 7, 1432.

20. JEAN LE CHARLIER DE GERSON

Familiarly known as "Gerson" from his birthplace, Jean Le Charlier was one of the greatest theologians of his century. Jean Gerson, as he called himself, was born on December 14, 1363, in the Ardennes and died at Lyons on July 12, 1429, shortly after Joan's initial victory.

Identified while young by the priest of his village as a gifted and studious child, he did brilliantly in formal study even though he came from modest origins. Having entered the famous College of Navarre at Paris, he became a doctor of theology in 1388 and finally the college's chancellor at the age of thirty-two.

Gerson wrote treatises castigating idolatry, magic, astrology, and superstition in general. Supporting reform in popular education, he composed several studies on this issue in French, so that his work could circulate more widely. He played his greatest role at the Council of Constance as one of those who ended the papal schism. He wrote an essay arguing that even a regularly elected pope could be subject to the judgment of a council. Thanks to his intervention, John XXIII, successor of Alexander V, was deposed on May 29, 1415; Gregory XII abdicated; and Benedict XIII was deposed in July of 1417. The council-approved electors chose Martin V and so ended the schism, which had lasted since 1378.

At Constance, Gerson also succeeded in securing the condemnation of the doctrine of Jean Petit, apologist for the murder of the duke of Orléans. Petit, whom Gerson had opposed consistently, had the support of the duke of Burgundy. That success led to Gerson's persecution during the Cabochian uprising in Paris; he escaped the mob only by hiding in the towers of Notre Dame.

Without waiting for the council's final conclusions on Petit, he thought it wise, fearing the duke of Burgundy, to move to Lyons.

To students of Joan of Arc, Gerson's most interesting work is the apologia he wrote for her. At Lyons, he received a request for his opinion about her activities. Among those who had examined her at the "trial of Poitiers" was Gérard Machet, the king's confessor and Gerson's friend and disciple. Gerson's short treatise on Joan must have been widely read in France and even in Italy, because the merchant Morosini sent a copy of it to his family and to the doge in Venice. It was entitled *De mirabili victoria cuiusdam puellae de postfoetantes receptae in ducem belli exercitus regis Francorum contra Anglicos* [Concerning the Admirable Triumph of a Certain Maid, Who Went from Guarding Her Sheep to Becoming the Head of the Armies of the King of France at War with the English (B.N. lat. 14904 [Vict. 516]: 14905 [Vict. 699], followed by Dupin; lat. 5970, followed by Quicherat)]. Gerson argued that the Maid did not use prohibited magic, superstition, or fraudulent cunning and that she pursued no personal interest. On the contrary, she was exposing herself to danger as a proof of her faith. One could support her, he concluded, in all safety and piety. He insisted as well that the reader consider the position in which the kingdom of France found itself: It had become absolutely necessary to drive out the English (Monnoyeur, 1930). The theologian concluded with three principles justifying "the wearing of masculine clothes." It is interesting to observe that early in her public life, the idea that Joan "should not wear garments other than those of her female condition" had gained wide acceptance. It was permissible to wear such clothes, Gerson argued, because Joan was exposing herself to danger as a female warrior and thus like a man-at-arms; she had in fact done well to cut her hair short in order to wear her warrior's helmet.

In her 1988 Harvard doctoral thesis, "Palingenesis of Joan of Arc," Gertrude M. H. Merkle contended that Gerson's actual position was more ambivalent than the foregoing summary suggests. According to Merkle, Gerson's authentic teaching on female cross-dressing can be found in an analysis of his language in Martin Lefranc's *Champion des dames*. According to that account, composed less than twenty years after Joan's and Gerson's deaths, Gerson was thought to be referring to ancient judicial law, that of the Old Testament, which would be rendered obsolete by the New Dispensation of Christian law "unless superior authorities had established and confirmed it anew." Thus Gerson, a master of casuistry, might well have granted Joan's judges at Rouen the right to refer to the strictures of Deuteronomy against cross-dressing if it seemed appropriate. As theologians and her judges, were they not the Maid's superiors? Martin Lefranc characterized Gerson's treatise on Joan as "more subtle than we thought."

Merkle finds in Gerson's *De mirabili victoria* "a certain ambivalence in these ecclesiastical semantics, a refusal to declare himself absolutely in favor of Joan's providential mission, and an overall prejudice against women." This reticence, Merkle maintains, would not have escaped the notice of the Venetian merchant who as early as November 20, 1429, sent a copy of Gerson's treatise to Venice and noted that the University of Paris had begun plotting against Joan; thus, the message of Gerson's treatise was that believing in Joan's mission was not sinful, but neither was it a sin against faith to doubt the validity of her mission. While not wishing to appear opposed to Joan's activity, Merkle argues, Gerson wanted to dampen her effect on the credulous public. Since Merkle's ingenious argument requires a rejection of the plain meaning of Gerson's text, preferring instead a retrospective interpretation by a later writer close to the duke of Burgundy, her thesis has not won universal agreement. A more succinct and easily obtainable statement of her hypothesis may be found in her essay: "Martin Le Franc's Commentary on Jean Gerson's Treatise on Joan of Arc."

Gerson dated his treatise precisely in its closing sentence: "at Lyons, 1429, on the 14th of May, the eve of Pentecost, after the victory of Orléans and the end of its siege by the English, this little work was written by Chancellor Gerson." At his death barely two months later, on July 12, a cry went up in the streets of Lyons: "The Saint is dead!"

21. PERRINET GRESSART

Perrinet Gressart was an adventurer in the pay of Burgundy and of England; his was the representative life of a fifteenth-century mercenary. Whether they hired themselves out to the king of France, the king of England, or the duke of Burgundy, or whether they passed from one to the other or even acted on their own account, men like Gressart, La Hire, François de Surienne, and Robert de Flocques all headed for the same destination: a battlefield. They thrived on war, with its pillaging, its prisoners taken for ransom, and its extortions from the populace. From time to time, one or another of these captains might

espouse a loftier ideal, but they fixed their attention mainly on adventure and the craft of arms.

Perrinet Gressart was captain of La Charité-sur-Loire when Joan of Arc first caught sight of that fortified town. At the end of September 1429, Joan began preparations for a new campaign. She found the autumn season convenient because the Loire, swollen by rain, then allowed the best possible conditions for the transport of the royal army's matériel and the provisioning of the troops. One of the bombards (artillery pieces) that had served at the siege of Orléans, "the Shepherdess," was put aboard ship at that point. The Shepherdess had traveled by road from Orléans to Jargeau, where it had brought down three large towers of the city wall, and was intended for future service with the army of Joan and of d'Albret, but Gressart captured it and handed it over to the duke of Burgundy. Although bombards like the Shepherdess could be dismantled into two major pieces, the volley and the chamber, the volley required twenty-nine horses led by twelve wagonmasters to move, and the chamber required the draft of seven horses. It was also necessary to strengthen bridges and repair roads before and after its passage—one indicator of the immense effort involved in besieging a city.

At the siege of La Charité, command of the army was awarded to Charles d'Albret, half-brother of Georges de La Trémoïlle, who had been named lieutenant general by the king. At d'Albret's side were Joan and Louis de Bourbon, count of Montpensier. At the end of October, the Maid arrived to conduct the siege of Saint-Pierre-le-Moûtier. Their failure encouraged them to proceed immediately to La Charité, demanding reinforcements from the duchy of Bourbon while they were at Moulins on the way to La Charité. The army marched northward and was joined by men under Marshal de Boussac. The siege, begun a little before November 24, 1429, turned into a defeat, apparently due to the rigors of the weather and the lack of troops. As Perceval de Cagny observed, "The siege did not succeed because the king sent neither food nor money." La Trémoïlle was also accused of having kept for himself some of the money destined for the army. In any case, Gressart defended the city well. While receiving pay from the English, he acknowledged a certain dependency on the duke of Burgundy. Since a truce had been signed between France and Burgundy covering any activity in the Nivernais, Gressart received more support than Joan and Charles d'Albret had received.

Perrinet Gressart's origins are shadowy. (See Bossuat, 1936.) Sprung from the common people, he declared himself a nobleman in 1417 and signed his acts with a seal bearing his arms—a fess with three cinquefoils. He had thus become "noble through arms," since as the old maxim has it, "Arms ennoble any man whatever" (de Bueil, vol. 2, p. 80). Little by little, the mercenary raised himself socially. In 1426 he bought a small fortress, La Motte-Josserand, and called himself "lord of La Motte-Josserand." He was able to impose discipline and command the respect of the brigands who surrounded him. If he was hard on those he led, he also knew how to protect them and provisioned them with letters of pardon when they were obliged to leave a region where they had been active. He was also concerned with establishing a family. He married a certain Huguette de Corvol, who seems to have had some property, and his best man, François de Surienne, married one of his nieces. In 1426, Gressart set up headquarters at La Charité-sur-Loire to defend the people of that city and to assure himself a refuge while he conducted raids elsewhere in the Nivernais. La Charité had a natural strategic importance: It was then one of the few places where the Loire could be crossed when the river was swollen.

Gressart's career began in Picardy. He was encouraged by the lax command of the duke of Burgundy, John the Fearless, who allowed his Burgundian adventurers to spread out on their own during his campaigns around Sancerre. Gressart became the head of a band of soldiers, hiring them out to whoever could afford them, holding men and women for ransom, and amassing his fortune to the detriment of the peasants. He campaigned this way in the Nivernais as well, where he specialized in ransoms. But he remained loyal to the duke of Burgundy, whose interests he consistently served. In 1420, when the attacks of the Armagnacs against the duchy became increasingly serious, Gressart blocked them, setting himself up at Paray-le-Monial at the head of a company paid for by the duke. With another of his companions, he defended the Charolais.

The adventurer Perrinet Gressart made himself a lord thanks to his profitable dependency on the duke of Burgundy; he did business exclusively with the duke or his chancellor, Nicolas Rollin. Since payment came from the duke of Burgundy irregularly, however, Gressart chafed in his role as keeper of the pantry to Philip the Good and became an agent of John, duke of Bedford, the English regent for France. Bedford enjoyed using him as a pawn in the game with Burgundy. It was in Burgundy's interest for Gressart to guard La Charité in the duke's name; the duke did not wish the English to be too powerful so close to home,

so he signed agreements with Gressart and made an effort to pay him what he owed—that is, 2,400 livres a month to support the garrison.

Gressart also had dealings with the Armagnacs—first with Richemont, the instigator of treaties, and then with La Trémoïlle. A local truce survives from 1427, signed by Gressart before two notaries and sealed with his seal, committing him to abstain from holding the region to ransom. For him that agreement was little more than a scrap of paper. Complaints soon arose from all directions. He had pillaged Berry, the inhabitants of the Nivernais were not spared, and he went so far as to sequester La Trémoïlle, then the head of an Armagnac delegation to the duke of Burgundy, when he was passing through La Charité, even though La Trémoïlle had a safe-conduct and was accompanied by the marshal of Burgundy and other officers of the ducal house. On the day of his capture, December 30, 1425, Gressart and François de Surienne made La Trémoïlle sign an agreement to pay a ransom of 14,000 écus "of good weight." La Trémoïlle signed because he wished to be freed as soon as possible, fearing that he might be delivered directly to the English. From La Charité, he wrote to his brother, to Jean de Vecel, and to the marshal of France begging them to hasten his deliverance and to comply with Gressart's letter. Once free, La Trémoïlle expressed his gratitude for the fashion in which he had been treated and lavished gifts upon Perrinet's wife, Huguette de Corvol. In arresting La Trémoïlle, Perrinet Gressart knew perfectly well that he was not pleasing the duke of Burgundy and demanded that La Trémoïlle sign letters in person pardoning Gressart.

Gressart continued to lead the bandit's life, marching one day in the direction English-occupied territory and the next day toward Burgundy. Just when La Hire had to relax his grip on the English before Montargis and the French regrouped at Gien, Bedford promised Gressart a reinforcement of "Englishmen from England" (Departmental Archives of the Côte-d'Or, B 11916). But Gressart declined to accept these reinforcements, fearing he would alienate the duke of Burgundy. That fear did not, however, prevent him from accepting goods offered by the English. The bandit thus found himself linked to Henry VI of England by feudal bond; Gressart rendered him the homage of a vassal.

At the time of the siege of Orléans, Perrinet Gressart occupied a part of the Nivernais on behalf of the English; they held Saint-Pierre-le-Moûtier and numerous castles, including Rosemont, the principal point of passage over the Loire between Decize and Nevers; Passy, on the route between La Charité and Versy; Dompierre-sur-Nièvre; and La Motte-Josserand in the valley of the Nohain, from which Gressart could threaten Gien.

This deployment changed when the French armies achieved their first victories. But for the king to profit from these victories against the English, Burgundy had to remain neutral. The counselors of Charles VII busily began to sign truces. Auxerre, engaged in truce negotiations, thus escaped attack during the march toward Reims. The Burgundians adopted a comparable position; more conciliatory than they had been previously, they posed no obstacle to the royal troops making their way to the coronation. On the following day, truces that were supposed to last until Christmas were signed. This agreement with the newly validated king of France in no way implied a rupture of the good relations between Burgundy and England. The Burgundians were anxious; they had seen the royal armies marching about the frontier of their duchy, taking strategically important locations on the line of the Oise—that is, Compiègne and Creil—that commanded Picardy. Clearly, Paris might change sides; not even Normandy was a secure fortress for the English any longer.

Gressart feared losing La Charité when Joan of Arc laid siege to it. He knew the reason for that maneuver: "This city was besieged at the request of my lord de La Trémoïlle" (Gressart, *Lettres*, in the Departmental Archives of the Côte-d'Or, B 11918). Evidently, the latter had not forgiven his capture and ransom. More important, the king had to protect Berry, constantly threatened by the incursions of the mercenary and his troops. The Bourbonnais, a territory of the count of Clermont, was menaced as well. La Trémoïlle and Clermont had a common interest in Gressart's disappearance. Finally, La Charité happened to be a strategic site along the Loire, and the commerce of that river valley remained active despite occasional disruptions by mercenary attacks.

In view of the inspiration Joan of Arc had given the Armagnacs to reconquer territory, the Burgundian position would be gravely weakened once Charles VII exploited his victories by abandoning his policy of truce-making. Peace between Gressart and Charles VII was concluded on November 22, 1435; the king granted Gressart the places he held and named him captain of La Charité for life, with a payment of 400 livres per year to be levied on the revenues of La Charité and Cosne. The further sum of 2,000 golden saluts would be paid him within three months; 8,000 saluts would be paid by Burgundy, whose duke paid him an additional 1,000 saluts, due him from the king of England. Still, Gressart protected himself against delays in payment by Burgundy or the Armagnacs and placed a guard on the convoys of wine vats and kegs of silver coins headed his way (Departmental Archives of the Côte-d'Or, B 1660).

Thereafter, Gressart dealt no more with the duke of Burgundy but directly with the king of France. He was made an officer of the count of Nevers and began to rid the country of pillagers, although he himself had been one, and he called upon Charles VII for help in this altruistic endeavor. The last documentary mention of Gressart appears in September 1438; he probably died about then.

Perrinet Gressart's talent was evident in his ability to resist by turns the English, the Burgundians, and the Armagnacs for twelve years. Neither the French nor the Burgundians managed to profit from his military skill and cunning. Jean de Wavrin, the Burgundian chronicler, draws a flattering portrait of him: "As long as he lived, Perrinet Gressart waged strong war against King Charles more than any other of his estate; for he was wise, prudent, and a man of great enterprises, knowing how to conduct himself in every situation. I myself, author of this present work, was with him on many campaigns and honorable enterprises" (Wavrin, vol. 1, p. 264).

22. "LA HIRE," ÉTIENNE DE VIGNOLLES

Étienne de Vignolles was one of Joan's most reliable military supporters. Better known as "La Hire," his image survives as the Jack-of-Hearts in the traditional French pack of playing cards. His epithet appears to reflect a character trait: *Hire* means "anger." We know that he was violent and easily inflamed; the English, in mockery, called him "Holy Ire of God" or "Gracious Ire of God"—but only at a safe distance.

Born at Préchaq-les-Bains in Gascony and a man whose childhood was disrupted by the Hundred Years War, he developed a need for independence and a taste for arms. He seemed little concerned with the intellectual, spiritual, or emotional sides of life (F. Rousseau, 1968). He completed his first military service under the constable Armagnac. We do not know if he was at the Battle of Agincourt in 1415. From 1418, with his faithful companion Poton de Xaintrailles, he rallied to the dauphin Charles. His first exploit was retaking the castle of Coucy, after which he adopted as his motto, "I am neither a prince, nor a duke, nor even a count: I am the lord of Coucy"

[Roi ne suis ni prince, ni duc, ni comte aussi; je suis sire du Coucy]. The following year, a chambermaid betrayed him by freeing some of his Burgundian prisoners, who promptly became masters of the castle once more. But this loss did not lessen his prestige, and Charles VII employed his "valiant captain" in other expeditions.

La Hire and Poton went on to wage war in the Vermandois and the Laonnois, then in Lorraine, where they fought in the pay of the cardinal of Bar. Étienne de Vignolles appears in the records again at Baugé in 1421. In that year, his leg was broken while he was asleep at an inn. (The fireplace had collapsed on him.) Crippled in that leg for the rest of his life, he nevertheless continued his career as an adventurer and a mercenary.

On Monday, October 25, 1428, "there arrived in Orléans, to support, aid, and assist it, many noble lords, knights, captains—and Étienne de Vignolles, known as La Hire, of great renown, and valiant men of war in his company" (*Journal du siège d'Orléans*). His movements in the years 1428 and 1429 can be followed thanks to the *Journal of the Siege of Orléans*. This captain of the Vermandois had earlier assumed the burden of announcing to the king the loss of the fort of the Tourelles and then of requesting reinforcements and war subsidies. The pay instructions of Pierre de Fontenil, the treasurer of Chinon, attest to his importance in the eyes of Charles VII: "To Étienne de Vignolles, 100 écus of gold and 825 livres tournois, which according to the command and order of the king were given and delivered at various times and in various places. To Xaintrailles and Étienne de Vignolles, called La Hire, as much on their estates as on the payment of fifty-nine pages to the sum of 512 livres tournois" (Chambre des Comptes fr. 2342, fol.42, cited by Vallet de Viriville).

At Orléans, La Hire remained active. On February 3, with Jacques de Chabannes, he pursued the English back to the rampart of Saint-Laurent. But after the "Day of the Herrings," Saturday, February 12 (see I, 3), La Hire was "in profound grief." He resented the orders of the count of Clermont, which required him to wait for the count's arrival before attacking. This strategy gave the English time to regroup and to organize their defense, so that Poton and La Hire were able only to protect the French retreat.

La Hire continued to travel back and forth between Orléans and Chinon to procure funds from the king. He may have been at Chinon when Joan arrived. In any case, he was among the first who "achieved the faith to believe in her" and became one of Joan's most faithful companions.

She exerted some moral influence over him: "at her instigation and her request, La Hire went to confession, and so did many others of his company" (Nullification trial, deposition of master Pierre Compaign). It was also thanks to his contact with Joan that he changed his famously vulgar language and thereafter cursed only "on his baton." This valiant captain participated in all operations to free Orléans and the Loire valley. Charles VII made him captain general of Normandy. When Joan of Arc perished at the stake, La Hire was a prisoner at Dourdan. Charles VII took responsibility for part of the payment of his ransom to the Burgundians, which permitted him to resume life as a mercenary in the king's pay.

Having survived cold, epidemics, and many wounds, La Hire fell ill at Montauban during the reconquest of the southwest and died on January 11, 1442. The favorite prayer of this bloody mercenary is still remembered: "May you do for La Hire what you would like La Hire to do for you, if you were La Hire and La Hire were God."

23. ISABEAU OF BAVARIA, QUEEN OF FRANCE

Isabeau of Bavaria (ca. 1370–1435) was a dynamic figure who strove to impose herself upon the public consciousness and quite often succeeded. She was the wife of Charles VI and mother of his children, including Charles VII; in her capacity as mother she became the nexus of many convergent interests.

Isabeau was the daughter of Stephen II, duke of Bavaria, and Taddea Visconti. At fourteen she met and, quite soon after, married the young king Charles VI (July 17, 1385). Charles had been smitten at their first meeting and gave magnificent feasts in honor of her arrival in Paris. She so affected Charles VI that he married her without benefit of a marriage contract or dowry.

From the beginning their marriage was troubled by Charles's mental unrest (recently diagnosed by R. C. Famiglietti as schizophrenic in nature). Isabeau was well acquainted with political intrigue. On July 1, 1402, Charles granted her power, along with whatever counselors she might choose, to conduct the business of government in his absence. She chose Louis, duke of Orléans, as lieutenant general of the realm, an appointment that not only deeply infuriated John the Fearless, duke of Burgundy (who had until that time held the reins of government), but that also later returned to haunt the monarchy and Isabeau herself. Although she had been quite acceptable as regent the first time Charles VI became incapacitated (1403), the intensely partisan nature of her politics made Isabeau unacceptable thereafter. At the same time, various tensions and encounters among the princes of the blood made them equally undesirable choices as regent. To solve this apparent impasse, a set of royal ordinances were issued in April, 1403, which consigned the actual business of government to "the advice, deliberation and counsel" of the queen, the princes, other members of the royal family, the constable, and the chancellor. This system was reissued as a perpetual edict on December 26, 1407, a month after a bodyguard of John the Fearless assassinated Louis of Orléans.

Isabeau seems to have given only cursory support to Louis of Orléans until late 1404 or 1405, and she stood firmly against the duke of Burgundy until he rescued her from the exile imposed on her by the Armagnacs (the Orléanist party) in 1417. She did everything in her power from 1409 until that time to see that her eldest surviving son would replace the king when he was under the effects of his malady and thus retain power within the nuclear royal family.

In January 1418, assuming the king and dauphin to be prisoners of the Armagnacs in Paris, she and John the Fearless formed a rival government in Troyes. She played an integral role in the negotiations that led to the Treaty of Troyes (1420), which disenfranchised her son, the future Charles VII. In 1435, when Philip the Good changed his allegiance (effectively dissolving the Treaty of Troyes), the followers of Henry VI found it necessary to create a new precedent upon which to deny the legitimacy of Charles's kingship. They found rich fodder for such redirected frustrations in the political career of Isabeau of Bavaria—most especially as they touched on Louis of Orléans. Thus, in the antidauphin Paris of 1422–1429, a probably groundless charge of adultery by Isabeau became a weapon for English partisans. In effect, the Treaty of Troyes was said to have disinherited Charles VII not for his involvement in the murder of John the Fearless but rather for the "fact" that he was not the son of his royal father. Instead he was rumored to have been the product of an affair between Isabeau and Louis of Orléans. The English party succeeded in using these rumors to undercut the legitimacy of Charles VII; until very recently most scholars shared the opinion of Isabeau's grandson, Louis XI, who called her "a great whore" (Lewis, p. 114).

Isabeau of Bavaria died alone (1435), isolated in the Hôtel Saint-Pôl in Paris where she stayed from the time of Charles VI's death in 1422.

24. ISABELLE OF PORTUGAL, DUCHESS OF BURGUNDY

Scholars have speculated, supportably, that Isabelle of Portugal attempted to persuade her husband, Philip the Good, not to hand Joan of Arc over to the English—or, at any rate, tried to ameliorate the conditions of her captivity.

Isabelle of Portugal, the third wife of Duke Philip the Good of Burgundy and mother of his heir Duke Charles the Bold, was the daughter of the intellectual and daring King John of Portugal (1385–1433: he began the systematic exploration of the West African coast, organized by his brother Prince Henry the Navigator) and his queen, Philippa of Lancaster (daughter of King Edward III and Queen Philippa of England). Isabelle was born at Évora in Portugal on February 21, 1397.

A marriage to Henry V of England had been projected for Isabelle, but after Henry chose Catherine of France (daughter of Charles VI and sister of Charles VII) instead, negotiations for her marriage to Philip the Good began. The Flemish painter Jan van Eyck was one of Philip's envoys on that mission, in the course of which he painted a famous portrait of Isabelle, now unfortunately lost. Philip and Isabelle were married on January 10, 1430, at Bruges, the capital of Flanders, amid splendid ceremonial celebration. It was on this occasion that Philip founded the Order of the Golden Fleece. Isabelle bore three sons, two of whom died shortly after birth, but the surviving child, Charles, would live to be the dashing last duke of Burgundy (dying at Nancy in 1477). Described as "beautiful, grave, adroit, and prudent," Isabelle was, like her husband, a great patron of intellectual and artistic activity at the Burgundian court. She seems to have dictated to Eleanor of Poitiers, a member of her entourage, the first known book of etiquette, *Les honneurs de la cour.*

Isabelle's diplomatic efforts were extremely successful. She had a hand in the Peace of Arras (1435) and four years later negotiated a treaty between England and Burgundy. She achieved the liberation of Charles of Orléans and arranged his marriage to Marie of Clèves (whose family she had assisted in marriage negotiations with the Holy Roman Emperor and other rulers). While duchess of Burgundy she continued to encourage the scientific explorations of her uncle Prince Henry. She made great efforts to assist her husband's crusade plans; one favorite project of hers was the collaboration of the Portuguese fleet with the Burgundian land army. Besides these foreign projects, Philip enlisted Isabelle's political talents in domestic administration. In 1434, for instance, he left Burgundy in her hands when he went to Flanders for an extended stay in the northern territories.

Isabelle died at the ripe old age of seventy-four at the Flemish castle of Aire on September 17, 1471. She had retired to that part of Flanders in the winter of 1456-1465/7, ten years before the death of her husband, perhaps partly because her son Charles the Bold resented her influence at the court but certainly because of her pious desire for the contemplative life. Philip consented to her withdrawal despite the great assistance she had rendered him in matters political, diplomatic, and courtly during the previous quarter century of their marriage.

Isabelle was buried at the Carthusian monastery at Dijon, the Burgundian capital.

25. GEORGES DE LA TRÉMOÏLLE

When Joan arrived at Chinon to meet the dauphin, Georges de La Trémoïlle had for two years been grand chamberlain of France and the dauphin's lieutenant general for Burgundy (that is, manager of the dauphin's household and his primary representative in negotiations involving Burgundy). Whether or not La Trémoïlle took an instant dislike to her, he soon became her most resolute enemy at court. He set out to restrain Joan's aggressive impulses and to manipulate her in ways that would serve his interests. The clearest instance was his control of her activity in the winter of 1429–1430, when she was sent to avenge his honor against Perrinet Gressart and then spent two months at his castle of Sully-sur-Loire. It is generally supposed that La Trémoïlle must have influenced Charles VII's startling refusal to assist or rescue Joan once she was captured by Burgundian forces.

Georges de La Trémoïlle retained his influence at the French court for two years after Joan's death, until an attempted assassination in June 1433 by three young gentlemen inspired by Queen Marie and her mother, Yolanda of Sicily (always in conflict with La Trémoïlle), made King Charles realize that La Trémoïlle's growing unpopularity had finally rendered him more of a liability than an asset. Briefly held prisoner at Chinon by his enemies, La Trémoïlle paid them a ransom of 6,000 gold écus and then was banished from court in 1453, making way for his longtime rival, Arthur de Richemont. He died thirteen years

later (1466), still out of favor. In an attempt to recoup his influence, La Trémoïlle joined the unsuccessful aristocratic revolt called the Praguerie in 1440. Charles did not punish him for that involvement, perhaps as repayment for the large sums La Trémoïlle had lent him before 1433.

Born in 1385 to Guy VI de La Trémoïlle and Marie de Sully (heiress to the important fief of Craon as well as to the strategic castle of Sully on the Loire), Georges was the thirteenth of that noble lineage to bear the name of the fief of Trémoïlle in Poitou. Direct descendants of Count William III of Poitou (who was also duke of Aquitaine) and thus distant kinsmen of the Plantagenet and Valois descendants of Eleanor of Aquitaine, the La Trémoïlles had risen high in the world. Georges's father Guy and his uncle Guillaume were both chamberlains of Duke Philip the Bold of Burgundy, the first of the Valois dukes of that mighty principality. Always close to the royal court, they were loyal also to King Charles VI. Both died on the crusade to Nicopolis (1396).

As a young man, Georges served Duke John the Fearless of Burgundy as chamberlain. Appointed master of waterways and forests of France by Charles VI in 1413, Georges was captured by the English at Agincourt in October 1415 but soon regained his freedom. In 1416 he married Joan, countess of Boulogne and of Auvergne, a great lady in her own right, widow of Duke John II of Berry, King Charles's uncle. A major patron of the arts, John of Berry left no male heirs when he died in the summer of 1416; by marrying his widow shortly thereafter, Georges de La Trémoïlle improved his own status. Their sons, Louis de La Trémoïlle and Georges de Craon, both served as hereditary chamberlains of Burgundy but retained the family tradition of maintaining loyalty to the French king (by then, Charles's son Louis XI). Louis II de La Trémoïlle (1460–1525), Georges's grandson, was one of the leading commanders of the armies of Kings Louis XII, Charles VIII, and Francis I. He became one of the prime movers of the Valois attempt to master Italy, recruiting men and raising funds for that imperial enterprise.

Nothing could have been further from the instincts of his grandfather Georges. As cautious as he was corpulent, Georges's strategy for saving Charles VII was to make peace with Philip the Good of Burgundy and then hire foreign mercenaries to fight the English. Joan of Arc thus struck at the heart of his policy and his personal ambition, as did the dashing Constable Arthur de Richemont.

26. CHARLES II (OR I) THE BOLD, DUKE OF LORRAINE

Charles II (some scholars refer to him as Charles I—this usage excludes the tenth-century duke of the same name) had Joan brought to Nancy but did not receive her as Robert de Baudricourt did. He later gave her a sum of four francs to pay for her trip (Durand Laxart's deposition) and a black horse (Jean Morel's deposition) on which she returned from Nancy to Vaucouleurs at the end of February 1429. (Both of these depositions are to be found in the nullification proceedings.)

Charles was born in 1365 and died in 1431; his reign was little more than one long-drawn-out war. After taking part in an expedition against Tunis, he helped drive the Turks back in Hungary. This prince, who had checked the attempts of Louis of Orléans to establish himself on the Rhine, was a feudal vassal of the Anglo-Burgundian power.

Lorraine was a duchy of the Holy Roman Empire and Charles therefore owed his allegiance primarily to the Emperor. However, he also held some domains from the Crown of France. Annoyed at his failure to be consistently loyal to the Plantagenet cause in those domains, the high court of Parlement at Paris banished Charles, declaring his lordship of that city forfeit. Philip the Good intervened on his behalf. In 1416, Charles followed the Burgundian armies into Paris and replaced Bernard of Armagnac as constable of that city. Consequently Charles VII stripped him of his honors and consigned him to Nancy. He married Margaret of Bavaria, who bore him only daughters.

Joan's remonstrance to him was most likely aimed at his passion for his mistress, Alison May of Nancy, whose mother sold vegetables in a shop near the ducal palace and whose father was a precentor of the collegiate church of Saint Georges. On January 2, 1425, he granted Alison the house she was living in, together with its furnishings and plate (both gold and silver). At his death, Alison was dragged into a public square and murdered by the mob.

In 1420 Charles's daughter Isabelle of Lorraine married René of Anjou, titular king of Sicily, who succeeded him as duke of Lorraine in 1431.

The dubious *Chronique de Lorraine* states that—most improbably—Joan was armed by Charles II and that she engaged in a tournament on the castle grounds at Nancy.

27. JOAN OF LUXEMBOURG

It is generally believed that Joan of Luxembourg, together with her niece-in-law, Joan of Béthune, did nearly everything in their power to prevent John of Luxembourg from handing the Maid over to the Plantagenet party.

Joan of Luxembourg was the sister of Count Waleran. The chronicler Monstrelet described her as "very ancient" in 1430. That year she was at Beaurevoir "where Messire John of Luxembourg, her nephew, governed." She had just inherited the lordships of her brother as the nearest heir of Philip of Brabant and hence was countess of Ligny and of St. Pôl. "And because she loved her nephew [John] so dearly" she willed him the bulk of her estate, which aggravated his older brother the lord of Enghien. Joan was the sister of Saint Peter of Luxembourg and godmother of Charles VII. She died at Boulogne-sur-Mer on October 13, 1430.

28. JOHN OF LUXEMBOURG

Joan of Arc was captured at Compiègne by the bastard of Wandomme, a vassal of John of Luxembourg, to whom she was surrendered. (See chapter 5, p. 88). Luxembourg then abandoned the siege of Compiègne, well defended by Guillaume de Flavy. On October 26, badly wounded, he abandoned his artillery to retreat with his troops. It is important to remember that Luxembourg had the option of selling Joan to the English or delivering her to Charles VII for a ransom.

John of Luxembourg, lord of Beaurevoir and count of Ligny, was devoted to the duke of Burgundy (as count of Ligny, he took part in a tournament of the Knights of the Golden Fleece in 1431) and also in the pay of the king of England, receiving the sum of 500 pounds a year as counselor to Henry VI. Moreover, his older brother Louis, a cardinal in the English church, was chancellor of England and thus sat on the king's council. Governor of Arras in 1414, John of Luxembourg vigorously attacked the partisans of the Valois. He won Senlis in 1418; was wounded at Mons-en-Vimeu (1421); made many expeditions into Picardy and Hainault; was put in charge of the siege of Guise by Bedford in 1424; led an Anglo-Burgundian expedition against the French forts of the Argonne; and ravaged the district of Beauvais. In August 1419, at the head of an embassy, he went to Compiègne, bringing Charles VI false promises of peace.

The very evening the Maid was captured, John wrote to inform his elder brother, who received the letter on May 25 at Paris, of Joan's capture. Joan remained his prisoner for four months. John of Luxembourg surely informed the king of England, and we can only wonder why he failed to deliver his prisoner to the Anglo-Burgundians immediately.

At Beaurevoir Joan was well received by the count's aunt, Joan of Luxembourg, and by his wife, Joan of Béthune. It may be that Joan of Luxembourg, godmother of Charles VII, implored her nephew not to sell Joan to the English. Luxembourg delivered Joan to them as soon as his aunt left for Avignon, where she died on September 18, 1430. The sum of money Luxembourg took for Joan was a simple payment, not a "ransom," which is a price paid to liberate rather than trade a prisoner. John of Luxembourg hesitated for four months before handing over Joan.

Pierre Cauchon, bishop of Beauvais, lost no time. On May 26, 1430 a letter from the University of Paris demanding that Joan be handed over to the Inquisition arrived at Beaurevoir; Cauchon probably instigated that letter. On July 14 the university sent a new demand for the prisoner's delivery. On August 4 the Estates of Normandy voted a tax of 120,000 livres tournois for continuing the war, and 10,000 of that amount was earmarked for Joan's "ransom." Cauchon went twice to see the prisoner and tried to convince John of Luxembourg to deliver the Maid for judgment by the university on religious charges. Luxembourg eventually acquiesced; thus, the English paid for Joan with funds from conquered Normandy.

The paid protector of the towns of Picardy, John of Luxembourg tried to shield them from the pillaging of de Flavy and the French captains. He refused to sign the Treaty of Arras in 1435 and, in reprisal, continued to ravage the country about Soissons and Laon. (In 1436, La Hire took possession of Soissons.) In 1437 he reached an agreement with Charles of Orléans. This battle-hardened Burgundian partisan died at the château of Guise in 1440.

29. LOUIS OF LUXEMBOURG

Louis of Luxembourg was a high churchman of the Anglo-Burgundian party whom admirers of Joan tend to see as less unsympathetic than Pierre Cauchon, although he was at least complicit in the Maid's downfall. The following entry is an adaptation of Pierre Champions's biographical notice available in W. P. Barrett's translated edition, *The Trial of Jeanne D'Arc.*

Louis of Luxembourg, bishop of Thérouanne and chancellor of Henry VI, was the brother of John of Luxembourg, who sold the Maid to the bishop of Beauvais.

Luxembourg was elected dean of the church of Beauvais on May 31, 1414, and resided at Rouen at times before 1430, living in the archbishop's palace. He espoused the interests of the English entirely and responded to the call that Bedford issued to the nobility of Picardy. He was in charge of preparing the defenses of Paris when Bedford retired to Normandy. Present at the coronation of Henry VI at Notre Dame, he was the executor of the will of Isabeau of Bavaria.

On April 7, 1432, King Henry ordered his treasurer general in Normandy, John Stanlawe, to pay to Louis of Luxembourg, his chancellor in France, 1,000 livres "to help him support the great expenses which in the cause of our service he has had, and has, to pay." In 1422 he was head of the embassy that went from France to London to aid the young Henry VI's accession to the throne. He was favorably looked upon by the chapter of Notre Dame of Rouen, which, on the news that the bishop of Thérouanne had been named archbishop by the pope, decided on January 13, 1430, to take steps to urge him to accept the nomination.

Louis of Luxembourg was strongly allied with Bedford; he was, in fact, the executor of Bedford's will, and after the death of Bedford's duchess Anne, Louis arranged the marriage of his niece, Jacqueline de Saint Pôl, then seventeen, to Bedford. Their union irritated Philip the Good, contributing not a little to the alienation between the duke of Burgundy and England. During the Parisian insurrection against the English in 1436, Louis of Luxembourg took refuge in the Bastille, where he was besieged by Richemont. He had to abandon his property to the conquerors and was transported to Rouen down the Seine. On January 15, 1437, as he journeyed to England, the chapter of Rouen had a mass said for his voyage and reminded him of Bedford's legacies to the churches of Rouen. He was named archbishop of Rouen on October 24, 1426, and was later made cardinal by Eugene IV (1440). When he finally went to England he became bishop of Ely but kept all his prerogatives as archbishop of Rouen. Raoul Roussel, who replaced him, was one of his intimates. Louis of Luxembourg did not lack the means of indemnifying himself for his losses. Henry VI gave him a pension of 1,000 marks from the Exchequer and 1,000 livres. Louis of Luxembourg rarely resided in his see, which he administered through a procurer. He lived splendidly in his manors, moving with a great train of baggage and horses. He was appointed an ambassador to Charles VII by Henry VI in December, 1442. Louis died on September 18, 1443, in his castle of Hatfield. Pasquier de Vaux was the executor of his will. His heart was sent to Rouen and his body was buried in a magnificent tomb in Ely Cathedral.

While charged with the defense of Paris, Louis of Luxembourg, then bishop of Thérouanne—who, the *Journal d'un Bourgeois de Paris* assures us, was a "full-blooded man"—had brought from Saint Denis the Maid's armor and negotiated her sale to the English. He was present at her trial and her abjuration. According to the testimony of André Marguerie, he wept for Joan: something of a surprise, since he was one of those whom Perceval de Cagny denounced as authors of Joan's death.

30. JEAN DE METZ

Jean de Metz was one of the Maid's earliest companions. He was also known as Jean de Nouillonpont, after a village located on the right bank of the Othain, in the arrondissement of Montmédy in Lorraine.

Upon the Maid's arrival in France on April 21, 1429 Jean de Metz received from Guillaume Charrier, receiver-general of the king, 100 livres for his expenses and the Maid's while in Chinon. That grant was followed by another 200 livres for "the Maid's expenses" and 125 livres to buy himself armor. He was quartered with the rest of the Maid's retinue at the house of Jacques Boucher, the treasurer of Orléans. In March 1444, Charles VII ennobled him "in consideration of the laudable and very welcome services which he rendered us in our wars and elsewhere." Gobert Thibault (by then the king's equerry as well as judge of the city of Blois), testifying at the nullification trial, said that Jean was one of his friends. Jean himself gave testimony at that trial; the transcript describes him as a nobleman about sixty-seven years old residing at Vaucouleurs.

31. CHARLES, DUKE OF ORLÉANS

While Joan was raising the siege of Orléans, its duke, Charles, was a prisoner in England where he had been since he was left for dead at the Battle of Agincourt (October 25, 1415). He was then twenty-four. He had fought courageously, with the energy of despair, in the vanguard of the French army. For twenty-five years he remained a prisoner of that day's victors.

Charles is an important figure in the history of French literature, traditionally given the epithet "Prince of Poets." This Valois prince began composing moral verse when he was a boy of ten, added love poetry in his youth, and continued writing both types of lyric verse during and after his quarter century of captivity. Formerly considered an author of obsolescent charm, the last of the courtly love poets, he is now seen as a sophisticated forerunner of writers such as Baudelaire. Although he and Joan never met, the mere fact of his existence as the legitimate lord of his strategically crucial duchy remained a factor of prime diplomatic and political importance both during and long after her mission.

Henry V, king of England, fully appreciated the importance of this captive, and a clause in his will specified that "in no case should the legitimate chief of the Armagnac party be given his liberty." In England, Charles of Orléans joined his brother John, count of Angoulême, already a prisoner; the youngest of the family, the count of Vertus, would die a little later. Their half brother, the future count of Dunois, John, the Bastard of Orléans, became head of the family in France.

Charles was first held prisoner in Windsor Castle. In 1421 he was transferred from Pontefract to the castle of Fotheringay in Northampton, and in May 1422 he was at Bolingbroke. In 1430 he was finally transferred to London.

By letter patent of May 27, 1422, his guards were paid 20 shillings a day. The English government found this expense too heavy for public funds and put his guard up for auction. William de la Pole, fourth earl and first duke of Suffolk—the man defeated by Joan and the royal army at Orléans and at Patay—won the bidding and paid 15 shillings, 4 pence per day for the guard of that prisoner. The duke paid his own expenses, including the guard fee, which was what made the assignment so attractive. Charles of Orléans ended his captivity with a stay at the castle of Wingfield between 1435 and 1440.

The duke continued to direct his affairs from prison. He had his jewels sold to pay the ransom of many of his companions in misfortune. He managed his own revenues in order to prepare for his eventual release and recommended to his appointed officers an exact regimen of procedures and economy measures. For these tasks, he relied principally upon his chancellor and his treasurer general, who were placed under the direction of the Bastard. The chancellor, Raoul de Gaucourt, and the treasurer general, Jacques Boucher, traveled occasionally to England, but regular contact between the poet-prince and his city was maintained through a squire.

From the beginning of his captivity, and therefore from the beginning of the resumption of hostilities between France and England, the duke of Orléans attempted to reduce the damage that the movement of armies inflicted on the population. Since all troops lived off the land, he instructed that provisions be purchased. He strove also to reduce combat for the sake of the cities of his duchy and especially of its capital, Orléans. Orléans should have been spared by the English, since its lord was their prisoner, but by then the chivalric rules of previous centuries had fallen into disuse. From 1424 to 1426 the city accounts make frequent mention of the issuance of truces. For example:

> Further receipts of a loan made by the aforesaid city for its own business. One of them to establish Pierre Framberge, previously procurator of the city by the hands of Guillaume Garbot, as tutor of the infants of Oudin du Loich, for the sum of 100 écus of old gold . . . to borrow from him to deliver to my lord de La Trémoïlle certain sums granted to him by the inhabitants of the aforesaid city of Orléans, and of the counties of Blois and of Dunois to guarantee the cessation of war against the duke of Burgundy within the aforesaid counties.

Numerous other loans are mentioned: "For my lords the deans and chapters of the church of Sainte-Croix . . . from Jacques Boucher . . . also because of cessation of hostilities toward the duke of Burgundy or toward the king of England." An early treaty between Charles and Burgundy was signed on July 17, 1427, at London, but it was not ratified by Duke John of Bedford, so hostilities resumed and Orléans was forced to defend itself. Once again, Charles oversaw the preparations closely. He had inventories taken in his castles, fortresses, and cities to keep exact account of arbalests, shafts, powder, and cannon. Watches were reorganized, fortifications consolidated, and suburbs leveled. The enemy could then attack: The city was ready to defend itself, which it would be required to do for seven months.

It is unclear whether Charles of Orléans knew until long after the event of the immense favor the Maid did him in delivering the capital of his duchy. It is also uncertain whether he had any simultaneous knowledge of her trial at Rouen. We do know that shortly after Joan's capture at Compiègne, Antonio Astesano, a Pavian scholar, did send Charles a Latin poem about Joan, based on a letter of Percival de Boulainvilliers to the duke of Milan, but it is not certain that the poem ever reached Charles in England.

Charles of Orléans, habitually prolix, rarely speaks of Joan of Arc, at least in the manuscripts we possess. However, when Joan returned to Orléans on June 20, 1429—after the victories of Jargeau, Meung, Beaugency, and Patay—the duke had a gift of garments in the colors of Orléans prepared to thank the Maid for her services. It was common usage in the Middle Ages to offer gifts of clothing with one's own arms, sometimes called one's livery, as thanks. The accounts of the city of Orléans record the payment: "To Jaquet Compaing, for half an ell of two green textiles purchased to make the nettles for the Maid's dresses, 36 sous of Paris." This instruction for this expenditure is dated June 16, 1429. For the date of September 30, 1429, we read:

> Charles, duke of Orléans and of Valois, count of Blois and of Beaumont and lord of Coucy, to our friends and faithful ones, the men of our accounts, greetings and affection. We commend you for paying 13 écus of old gold of the weight of 64 to the mark, which by our beloved and faithful treasurer general Jacques Boucher was paid and delivered in the month of June of the previous year to Jean Lhuillier, merchant, and Jean Bourgeois, the tailor residing at Orléans, for a robe and a tabard that the men of our council had made to be delivered to Joan the Maid when she shall be in our aforesaid city of Orléans; having consideration for the good and laudable and pleasant services that the Maid has done us in confronting the English, the ancient enemies of my lord the king and of ourself.

This document is explicit: The duke of Orléans has had a robe and a man's tabard made to thank Joan for the liberation of the city. Its end provides further details:

> To wit, to the aforesaid Jean Lhuillier, for two ells of fine vermeil Brussels cloth of which the aforesaid robe was made at the price of 4 écus of gold per ell, 8 écus of gold; for the lining of the same, 2 écus of gold; and for an ell of deep-green cloth to make the aforesaid tabard, 2 écus of gold; and to the aforesaid Jean Bourgeois for the fashioning of the aforesaid robe and tabard and for white satin, scarlet, and other materials, 1 écu of gold.

These instructions were issued at Orléans on the last day of September 1429. The fine Brussels cloth is a handsome fabric made in the city of the same name, and the scarlet cloth (called "sandal") was made of silk. These were expensive garments, reconstructed in 1929 by the French scholar Adrian Harmand in a fully documented treatise that suggested possible masters for the tailoring of Joan's robe and tabard. In those days male vestments stopped at the knee. The tabard was worn so as to be recognized by soldiers of one's own company and to weaken the sun's blinding reflections. Harmand concluded, after a detailed study of her costume, coiffure, shoes, and military equipment, that "Joan of Arc, of well-proportioned limbs, strong, beautiful, and well-formed, must have reached a height of approximately 1.58 meters [5 feet, 2 inches] because the length of her robe in fine Brussels cloth measured 80 centimeters [2 feet, 7 7/16 inches]."

The account books offer interesting information. For example, the nettle leaf was, during those years, one of the emblems of the family of Orléans; as for the deep-green color, some argue that the Orléans family had at the time adopted dark-green or verdigris livery to express their grief over the imprisonment of their legitimate chief. One detail in the reconstruction of these garments for Joan of Arc is missing: the source of the fur that must have bordered both the tabard and the robe.

The duke of Orléans also showed himself generous to his half brother, the Bastard, the king's lieutenant general for the war in the Orléanais, who was paid an annual pension. In 1439 he received command of Romorantin and of Blois for services rendered, and received as a gift the county of Dunois, with the right to carry the title of count. The Bastard exercised full ducal authority in the estates of Orléans and of Tours as well as at the diplomatic conferences at Arras, Calais, and Gravelines.

In 1435 hope for the captive was revived. Twenty years after Charles's capture at the Battle of Agincourt, the English began to feel the effects of the defeat of Orléans and of their progressive expulsion from France. The Treaty of Arras between the king of France and the duke of Burgundy; the death of Bedford, the regent; the marriage of the count of Charolais, son of Philip the Good, to the daughter of Charles VII; the siege of Calais, personally undertaken by Duke Philip of Burgundy—all these changed the conditions of the conflict and presaged the end of the Hundred Years War. Although still a prisoner, Charles of Orléans became the mediator between France and England. He accompanied the English delegation

to the Arras conference, but his request for liberation—upon payment, to be sure, of a heavy ransom—was rejected yet once more, and he had to return to his prison at Wingfield in May 1436. But the duchess of Burgundy, Isabelle of Portugal, became sympathetic to the duke's plight. Abetted by the cardinal of Winchester, one of the most influential members of the royal council at London, she made the poet's liberation her personal project.

Five years passed before she realized her goal. During that period much changed: The constable Richemont put his sword to work in the service of the victorious Charles VII; the Bastard, Xaintrailles, and Gaucourt continued the work begun by Joan; and little by little, cities and fortresses were restored to the royal domain. Paris was liberated in 1437; the Estates General convened in 1439 at Orléans. On this occasion, definitive peace between the two kingdoms was demanded, and at the end of 1439 diplomatic conferences began to arrange it. The much-desired truce, however, was not concluded until several months later.

Negotiations resumed at Gravelines in February 1440; this time the duke's liberation was guaranteed. The ransom, established at 120,000 écus of gold—an immense sum—was then paid. Remarkably enough, several years previously the duke of Burgundy had offered to pay a fourth of it from his personal revenue; the then-dauphin, Charles, and other lords offered themselves as guarantors of the rest. The prince was then set free on his word of honor that the balance would be paid, and after twenty-five years Charles of Orléans returned to France. The duke and duchess of Burgundy received him at Gravelines. Eight months later, on November 16, 1440, he married their daughter, Marie de Clèves. On January 24, 1441, accompanied by his wife, Charles made his solemn entry into the capital of his duchy.

When the happy news arrived at Orléans that the duke had disembarked at Calais, public prayers were recited in all the parish churches of the city. Yet again an appeal to the population of Orléans requested "2,000 écus of gold to equip my lord the treasurer, with the prayer to go in person and without delay to carry them to the duke at Calais" (Morchoasne: for December 30, 1429). The procurators organized processions to beg God "that He might wish to accord peace and give good deliverance to my lord of Orléans." The people of Orléans celebrated the return of their duke with enthusiasm. The king of France authorized the city council to levy a tax of 2,000 livres, and then another of 4,000 écus, to pay for the celebration (Morchoasne: letter of Charles VII,

December 21, 1440). The populace staged several mystery plays, the principal one being *David and Goliath*, then much in fashion, and another entitled *The Moral Virtues*. Two trestles loaded with food were set up at the crossroads, and two fountains ran with claret and milk. Lute players and fiddlers appeared in the streets. A dais covered in cloth-of-gold augmented by six ells of sandal and fringed with silk was prepared to receive the duke and the duchess; church bells rang; and relics of St. Aignan and St. Euverte, the patron saints of the city, were borne in a thanksgiving procession throughout the city. The city offered Charles of Orléans a bowl containing 4,000 écus of gold as well as a silver table service (more valuable than 211 marks in weight) when he left Orléans for Blois. The silver service had been engraved with his arms and with those of the duchess on the order of the treasurer general Jacques Boucher.

The duke of Orléans was finally free, but it immediately became necessary to find the money for the balance of his ransom. Once more the treasurer general, assisted by Étienne Le Fuselier, a counselor of the duke, set about satisfying his master's debt. Charles had already pawned part of the duchy while a prisoner, by letters of April 2, 1437. Philip the Good had offered to pay part of the ransom, and Charles VII, in his turn, had made considerable gifts from the royal revenues. According to letters patent preserved at Orléans and dated April 20, 1440, the king took into consideration:

the great expenses and charges of his beloved cousin Duke Charles of Orléans because of the war on account of which he and the count of Angoulême, his brother, were for long prisoners in England. Wishing because of that to come to his aid, [the king] gives and provides to him for one year, beginning on October 1, 1440, and finishing on the last day of September 1441, all the profits and dues from the salt tax and the salt warehouses established in the duchies of Orléans and of Valois, the counties of Blois and of Dunois and other lands and lordships belonging to himself and to his brother throughout the kingdom.

Orders went out to the granary keepers of the duchies, counties, and lordships of Charles of Orléans's domains to hand over to Boucher the money coming from the salt tax. Charles VII authorized the city of Orléans to tax itself 3,000 livres so as to pay part of the ransom. These letters were recorded in the city account books in 1438

and in 1440. On August 24, 1440, the procurators called for a voice vote to authorize the loan of 6,000 livres to "subvene the ransom of my lord the duke." Finally, by a letter given at Saumur dated December 6, 1441, the king acknowledged the sacrifices of the people of Orléans and authorized them to tax themselves 4,000 livres, to aid their duke "as much in the matter of his ransom as to sustain his estate." This sum was also delivered to Jacques Boucher.

Charles of Orléans spent the last part of his life at Blois, where he had succeeded in reconciling Charles VII with Philip the Good. He had also served as intermediary between the duke of Burgundy and Charles of Bourbon and between Charles VII and his son the dauphin Louis.

After sixteen years of marriage, the duchess Marie gave birth to a daughter, named Marie. Then there was a son, Louis, destined to mount the throne of France as Louis XII; his godfather was King Louis XI. A third child, Anne, became abbess of Fontevraud.

After his release, Charles did not speak of Joan, while the good city of Orléans never ceased honoring her memory in the annual celebration of May 8. (After 1435 the city paid the expense of the celebration.) The indifference of Charles of Orléans may be surprising to the twentieth-century mind. In this regard, we cannot ignore his giving to Pierre d'Arc hereditary title to the Ile-aux-Boeufs on July 29, 1443, which was done "in favor and contemplation of his sister, Joan the Maid."

Charles of Orléans died at Amboise while returning from the Assembly of Tours during the night of January 4 and 5, 1465, at the advanced age of sixty-nine. His body, carried to Blois, was buried in the Church of the Holy Savior. Pierre de Bourbon, the fiancé of little Marie and the famed lord of Beaujeu, led the funeral cortege. After him came the household of the dead prince—forty-three gentlemen, five priests, thirteen choristers, and the organist—then the chancellor general of finances, accompanied by the treasurers, minters, valets, apothecaries, and barbers.

Marie of Clèves, Charles's widow, wore a long robe of fine black cloth-of-gold and a hood and long mantle furred with lynx and black lamb bordered by otter and a piping of white ermine. Nurses accompanied the children of the household; the little Marie, aged seven, was dressed in a mantle and robe of black Rouen cloth; Louis de Valois, aged two and a half, accompanied by two pages, was dressed in black cloth lined in black lamb. Finally, in her nurse's arms, came little Anne, only a few months old. The household of the duchess, her ladies-in-waiting, washerwomen, and chambermaids followed. Marie of Clèves established at Orléans an annual mass in memory of her husband and made diverse gifts in his name. Louis XII showed Charles's mother respect and upon her death had her reburied with her husband at the convent of the Celestines at Paris.

32. CHRISTINE DE PISAN

Joan of Arc was not the only woman in France to challenge the increasingly rigid gender roles that shaped women's lives in late-medieval European society. Christine de Pisan lived at the French court for the greater part of six decades, although she was neither French in origin nor a child of the international European nobility with access to those high circles. Her father, a Bolognese doctor-astrologer named Tommaso de Pizzano (suggesting remote ancestors from Pisa), came to France at the invitation of King Charles the Wise as resident expert in astrology a few years after Christine's birth in or about 1364. A studious daughter, encouraged in her intellectual tastes by her parents, Christine grew up in the court. At sixteen, she married a young French notary named Étienne du Castel, who won a good post at court thanks to that marriage. To Christine's enduring grief, he died ten years later, leaving her with three children and her mother, by then a widow, to support. Christine de Pisan never remarried, an uncommonly independent decision at that time.

Around the age of thirty, Christine began to write poems on love, courtly and exploitive, true and false. By her mid-thirties (around 1399), her love poems, often lengthy and complex in their allegorical structure, began to address political issues as well. Like Dante nearly a century before, she proposed a world monarchy to solve the internal problems of a Christendom that seemed determined to destroy itself by internecine wars. She also composed a long didactic poem expounding the ideals of chivalry. Much of her work in this period was sponsored by Duke Louis of Orléans.

In 1404, the duke refused to appoint her son Jean du Castel to a post he was seeking, so Christine de Pisan looked for patronage elsewhere. The aged duke Philip the Bold of Burgundy commissioned her to write a biography of his late father, Charles the Wise. This ambitious undertaking, Christine de Pisan's first prose work, appeared within the year and was a huge success. About that time, she finished two of her most strikingly original works: the *Cité des dames* (The City of Ladies), a utopian sketch of a world for women, based on classical and biblical as well as later historical exemplars; and the *Livre des trois vertus* (Book of the Three Virtues), which offered women advice on how to cope with the world in which they lived.

In 1405 Louis of Orléans and young John the Fearless of Burgundy became overt foes; John had Louis assassinated in 1407. For Christine de Pisan, the situation seemed more than tragic. Personally and through her writings, she lobbied Queen Isabeau, Duke John of Berry, and the young dauphin, Louis of Guyenne, to end the conflict in order to maintain the integrity of the French kingdom. Her remarkably prolific pen produced major theoretical works on politics and morality over the next seven years, including the *Livre des faits d'armes et de la chevalerie* (Book of Feats of Arms and of Chivalry), which became one of the foremost manuals on the subject. As Christine pointed out, the practice or abuse of chivalry affected everyone—a basic social and moral assumption with which Joan the Maid would have agreed entirely.

The death or capture of so many of the men of her circle at Agincourt in October 1415, and the premature death of Dauphin Louis in December of that year, brought Christine and others close to despair. Some time thereafter, she retired to a convent (Poissy, northwest of Paris, where her daughter had long been a nun, is the most likely site), where she wrote a book of contemplation on Christian life and death, perhaps after her son's death in 1425.

Christine greeted the news of Joan's incredible victory at Orléans with joy. That seeming miracle inspired her last poem, one of her greatest, the *Ditié de Jehanne d'Arc*, which it is generally assumed she wrote immediately after the coronation of Charles VII at Reims in 1429. It used to be asserted that she died within the year; however, Charity Cannon Willard, an authority on Christine de Pisan's life and work, prefers the estimated death date of 1430. It is interesting to note that Joan's other prime intellectual partisan, Jean Gerson, had been a supporter of Christine at court.

33. BERTRAND DE POULENGY

Bertrand de Poulengy, a friend of Gobert Thibault, the king's judge at Blois, was the squire who escorted Joan to Chinon. The dauphin paid for his armor, and in Orléans he was quartered with the rest of Joan's party at the house of Jacques Boucher.

He testified at Toul during the nullification process in 1455. The transcript described him as noble, a royal equerry, sixty-eight years old or thereabouts. In his testimony he stated that as a young man he had known Joan's parents, who were "good workers"; he had visited their house. Bertrand described Joan as a good, devout young woman, "as good as a saint," and affirmed that she tended her father's cattle and horses.

Poulengy encountered Joan at Vaucouleurs and with Jean de Metz got her some arms and armor. Then they were off to find the dauphin, in the company of Bertrand's servant Julien, Jean de Metz and his servant Jean de Honnecourt, Richard the archer, and Colet de Vienne the royal courier.

34. GILLES DE LAVAL, BARON DE RAIS

It is an improbable fact that Gilles de Rais seems to have been a sincere and ardent supporter—"follower" would seem the more accurate word—of Joan of Arc during her brief period of military command and a champion of her memory thereafter. It would be difficult to find two personalities more disparate in any period. The transcripts of Joan's trials make her a figure of unique documentary significance; the transcript of Gilles's own trial at Nantes, the capital of Brittany, in 1440 on charges of witchcraft and related perversions is sensational in its own right. Gilles sexually abused and then murdered perhaps as many as 150 children at his castle of Tiffauges in southeastern Brittany. French folklore has associated him with Bluebeard, the wife killer.

Born in 1404 and executed at Nantes in 1440 by burning after strangulation (a favor not accorded to the peasant Joan of Arc), Gilles de Rais (or de Retz) was one of the richest men in Europe. He was the son of Gilles de Laval (who died when the boy was eleven) and of Marie de Craon. At sixteen he married Catherine de Thouars, adding to his great inherited wealth her important Poitevin dowry. In 1427 he declared himself a partisan of the dauphin Charles, as befitted a great-nephew of Bertrand Du Guesclin; he adhered to the military advice of Joan of Arc with an ardor and consistency uncommon in the entourage of Georges de La Trémoïlle (his cousin and early patron at court); in July 1429 Gilles accompanied Joan and Charles to Reims. At the coronation, he was made marshal of France by Charles VII. He was then twenty-five years old.

After Joan's execution, he fought the English in the west of France as much as La Trémoïlle's policy allowed, but gradually grew tired of military life. By 1435, at age thirty-two, he withdrew to his Breton estates and began to squander one of Europe's largest fortunes. Avid for pleasure, he sought the company of alchemists, magicians, necromancers, and mountebanks as well as of more standard courtiers, on whom he spent at least 200,000 écus in less than eight years. His bodyguard seems to have been a chilling gang of cutthroats. He was passionate about the theater and made his rural castles the scene of endless dramatic performances. His relatives finally obtained a royal decree blocking further expenditure, and rumors of his perverse behavior brought him before an inquisitorial court presided over by the bishop of Nantes and other dignitaries. He was executed outside the city on October 26, 1440.

35. FRIAR RICHARD

Friar Richard was a Franciscan *illuminatus* distrusted by respectable theologians, who certainly contributed to Joan's discredit. Driven from Paris at the end of April 1429 for preaching that the Antichrist was about to be revealed and that the world would end in the following year (1430), he surfaces in the record in July 1429 at Troyes. There he preached that Joan was privy to the secrets of God and the saints, and could penetrate any city's defenses. Monstrelet asserts that Friar Richard was later expelled from Troyes as a partisan of Charles VII. In March 1431—two months before Joan's execution—Friar Richard was sequestered in the Franciscan convent of Poitiers, deprived of permission to preach by agents of the local bishop, the Inquisitor of France, and the Parlement. All factions seem to have agreed that the good friar was as heretical as he was unstable.

36. ARTHUR DE RICHEMONT

After Joan of Arc, no one contributed more to saving France at the end of the Hundred Years War than the Breton prince who died in 1458 as Duke Arthur III of Brittany. He was most widely known throughout his long and active life as Arthur de Richemont: His eldest brother, Duke John V, had awarded him the county of Richmond in England, an ancestral legacy, when he was seven or eight years old. Arthur derived little benefit from that territory, of which he lost control when he left the Plantagenet party to become a Valois partisan in 1424.

Born at the ducal castle of Succinio on the south coast of Brittany on August 24, 1393, Arthur was the third son of Duke John IV of Brittany and Joan, daughter of King Charles the Bad of Navarre and later queen of England. (Widowed, she married King Henry IV in 1403.) Short but vigorous, endowed with facial features that made him look eternally sullen (Charles VII called him "Old Lip" since he seemed always to be curling his lip in a pout), Arthur was a born scrapper. He fought for both the Valois and the Plantagenet sides, beginning as an ardent Armagnac partisan in 1410, when he was seventeen. Raised to military maturity by his great-uncles Duke Philip the Bold of Burgundy and Duke John II of Berry, he became the close friend and companion-in-arms of the dauphin Louis of Guyenne, heir of King Charles VI and elder brother of Charles VII.

Since his mother had married King Henry IV of England, it is not surprising that Arthur joined the Plantagenet party after being captured at Agincourt (October 25, 1415). But Arthur made the change slowly: He remained a prisoner in England for nearly five years after Agincourt; it was only during the negotiations for the Treaty of Troyes (October 1420) that he appeared on the side of Henry V. After the deaths of Henry V of England and Charles VI of France in August and October 1422, respectively, Richemont stayed loyal to the Plantagenet party partly because of his marriage in 1423 to Margaret of Burgundy, widow of the former dauphin Louis. She was the sister both of Duke Philip the Good and of Anne of Burgundy, wife of Duke John of Bedford, regent of France for the infant Henry VI. Despite those connections, Richemont switched to the Valois side after his brother-in-law Bedford refused him a much-desired command (June 1424). Queen Yolanda, the dauphin Charles's mother-in-law, had him appointed constable (chief military commander) of France in March 1425.

Eager to galvanize all available forces to attack the English, the new constable was endlessly frustrated by factionalism at Charles's court. From September 1427 to June 1433 Richemont was in effect denied access to the king because of Georges de La Trémoïlle, whose rise to power Richemont had assisted. Charles VII, who never liked Richemont personally, exiled him from court in 1428. In July 1429 Charles excluded him from the coronation at Reims, where his office entitled him to carry the sword of state in front of the king (see p. 67). Guillaume Gruel, a loyal follower who composed the fulsome *Chronicle of Arthur III, Duke of Brittany* after Richemont's death, reported that Joan was displeased at Richemont's exclusion from "her king's" coronation; he had fought enthusiastically and effectively at her side at the battles of Meung, Beaugency, and Patay in June 1429.

After the fall of La Trémoïlle in 1433, Arthur de Richemont worked tirelessly for the expulsion of the English and the reform of the French army. He had a hand in the Treaty of Arras between Charles VII and Philip the Good of Burgundy (September 1435). On April 13, 1436, he entered Paris and formally reestablished there the main institutions of the royal government: a Parlement favorable to Charles, the Chambre des Comptes, and a royal council. To Richemont's and the Parisians' distress, Charles visited the ancient but recently disloyal capital a year later for only three weeks; like most of the Valois kings thereafter, he preferred the châteaux of the Loire.

By the autumn of 1441, Richemont had cleared the Ile-de-France of English partisans. Nine years later Normandy was reclaimed as well. Richemont was present at the decisive Battle of Formigny in April 1450 and at the surrender of Caen and of Cherbourg in June and August. Some of his most effective campaigning in Normandy was undertaken in collaboration with his nephew Duke Francis I of Brittany. In September 1457, after the death of a second childless nephew, Duke Peter II, Arthur became duke, but he reigned briefly, dying the day after Christmas, 1458.

Duke Arthur III of Brittany's most durable achievement was his collaboration with Charles VII in the redesign of the French army. For centuries a loose, poorly disciplined rallying of feudal levies commanded by their hereditary lords and of mercenary bands commanded by self-serving freebooters, the army was rapidly turned into a standing force of paid professional soldiers living in regular garrisons and commanded by officers chosen directly by the king or his constable. This new model threatened the interests and offended the sensibilities of many; Richemont seems to have enjoyed punishing rebellion against these innovations. In 1439–1440, he put down the Praguerie, an uprising of noblemen including men as diverse as his nephew John of Alençon, Joan's ally, and their mutual enemy Georges de La Trémoïlle. With even greater gusto, he led the new *compagnies d'ordonnance* in rounding up and executing "the Flayers" and other bands of mercenaries, many of whom had long fought alongside the constable's newly disciplined troops.

Lucky in war, Arthur de Richemont was less fortunate in marriage. His long marriage to Margaret of Burgundy, widow of his closest youthful friend, Louis of Guyenne, ended without surviving children in February 1442. In August of that year he married Jeanne d'Albret, daughter of his later companion-in-arms Charles d'Albret, but she died just over two years later, again without issue. His third wife, who survived him, was Catherine of Luxembourg, daughter of Peter of Luxembourg, count of Saint-Pôl and sister of the second wife of John of Bedford, who thus became for the second time Richemont's brother-in-law: The conjugal network of the fifteenth-century European ruling class was tightly woven. The only surviving child of Duke Arthur III of Brittany was his natural daughter, Jacqueline, who was legitimized in 1443 and married to one of her father's squires.

37. CATHERINE DE LA ROCHELLE

Catherine de La Rochelle, like her sometime companion Friar Richard, was a member of the vagabond lunatic fringe who did Joan no good. Catherine claimed to have access to "the high secrets of Our Lord God" when the Eucharist was celebrated at mass. After a few conversations, Joan decided that Catherine was talking nonsense and should go home to attend to her family. Catherine later reciprocated by testifying to the ecclesiastical court at Paris that "Joan would have left her prison by the aid of the devil if she had not been well guarded." The record indicates that Catherine also denounced the city of Tours and its inhabitants—which worried the city council enough that they paid an Augustinian friar familiar with the royal council to convey letters defending that city's reputation.

38. THOMAS DE MONTACUTE, EARL OF SALISBURY

The earl of Salisbury began the siege of Orléans that Joan would raise. The Burgundian chronicler Enguerrand de Monstrelet reported Salisbury's death as the earl surveyed the city of Orléans on October 27, 1428, from the height of the fort of the Tourelles: "He studied the land around that fort carefully to imagine how he could take that city. While he was at the window, the stone of a cannon from the aforesaid city struck the window where the earl was, at the noise of which blow he pulled back; nevertheless, he was wounded most grievously and mortally and had a large part of his face carried away by it." Salisbury's death came soon after the beginning of the siege the English laid to Orléans, whose lord, Charles of Orléans, was a prisoner across the Channel. Many viewed Salisbury's death as the judgment of God, feeling that the earl should have spared a city deprived of its legitimate chief and defender. The *Chronicle of Normandy* reports that when in 1428 Salisbury had assembled his troops at Chartres and informed them of his intention to lay siege to Orléans, "a magician," Master Jean de Meung, warned him to "watch his head."

Thomas de Montacute, fourth earl of Salisbury, and elder son of John de Montacute, third earl, by his wife Maud, was born in 1388. After his father's lands had been forfeited for his treason, the king returned a portion of them to Thomas, who extended them by marrying Eleanor, fourth daughter of Thomas Holland, earl of Kent. He was restored to the remaining dignities held by his father in 1421 and was generally considered the "most subtle and expert and fortunate of all the captains in England." He took part early in the third phase of the Hundred Years War. Made a knight of the Order of the Garter in 1414, in the following year he fought in France with Henry V at Agincourt, then at the sieges of Caen (1417), Rouen (August 1–September 1, 1418), and Harfleur (January 4–March 12, 1419). In Normandy, in April 1419, he was named lieutenant general of the king, and with this promotion came such possessions as Neubourg, Perche, and Longwy. In the name of Henry VI, John of Bedford, Henry's regent in France, later gave him all of the possessions of Duke John V of Brittany situated outside John's duchy.

Henry V, and following him the duke of Bedford acting for Henry VI, distributed to the English captains the lands of the Armagnacs in this fashion. In Normandy, many lands were awarded by Henry V himself: He gave to his "dear cousin" William de la Pole, earl of Suffolk, the domains of Bricquebec and Hambye, which had belonged to the deceased Foulques Paynel, and thus deprived Foulques's widow, Jeanne, of them. Another companion of Henry V, Lancelot de L'Isle, received the lordship of Nohant; Henry FitzHugh received from the king the castle of L'Aigle and the donjon of Chambois. The duchy of Alençon became the apanage of Bedford. Many other fiefs were distributed in Normandy, Picardy, and the Beauce as well as in Paris, where the mansions of the Marais were parceled out among Bedford, Warwick, Stafford, and others.

Salisbury helped implement the Treaty of Troyes; he was at the siege of Melun (ended November 6, 1419) and at Paris on December 1, 1420; and then at the battlefield of Baugé (March 21, 1421), where he took the place of the duke of Clarence, who had been killed there. Thereafter, he became governor of Champagne and of Brie, won the Battle of Cravant, and in the following year took part under Bedford's command in the Battle of Verneuil. He returned to England to seek reinforcements "in many great festivals, ornamented with great riches." It is said that he had some part in a plot with Gloucester and Bedford against Philip the Good, who had been paying court to Gloucester's wife, the beautiful Eleanor Cobham. Although busy expanding his possessions on the continent, Salisbury did not forget his English domains or his own wife, who had considerable wealth.

In 1428 Salisbury again crossed the Channel at the head of an army, having signed an indenture on March 24, 1428 at Westminster, before members of the royal council. When he returned to France, he organized his army for a six-month campaign starting from June 30, 1428.

The indenture was a peculiarity of the English army—in a sense, a military service contract, the name of which came from a document not unlike the two sides of a zipper: The text was written twice on a piece of parchment, the two pieces of which were then separated following a zigzag line, each of which was to be handed to each of the contracting parties. The authenticity of each piece could be established by bringing the two halves of the parchment together, each contracting party having signed the half that was handed to his counterpart.

These documents were detailed, indicating the number of fighting men, the soldiers' equipment, and the payment due men-at-war; they established the number and type of combatants, the destination of their service, the pay, and various obligations. They also established the compensations soldiers could claim and, finally, the term of their enlistment. Enlistments could last forty days, sometimes a third of a year, sometimes two years, or "as it shall please the king." Wage deposits were paid in advance, most often for a trimester. The English indenture corresponded loosely to the French "letter of retinue," a document much less precise and not fully a contract, in that it did not set the length of service.

With this new army, Salisbury took Rambouillet, Meung, Beaugency, and Jargeau and on October 12 laid siege to Orléans. The *Journal of the Siege* reports that, on October 27, "the count Salebris [Salisbury] passed away at night in the city of Meung de Loire; at his death, the English maintaining the siege were powerfully amazed and doleful." Mortally wounded, the English captain had been transported to the city of Meung, where he died November 3. The body was returned to England and buried in his priory of Bisham at his father's side. His first wife, Eleanor, bore a daughter, Alice, who married Robert Neville. His second wife (her second marriage) was Alice, the daughter of Thomas Chaucer and granddaughter of Geoffrey, by whom he had no issue. He also left a natural son named John (Dugdale, *Baronage*, vol. 1, p. 652). He had no male descendants, so his son-in-law assumed the title earl of Salisbury. A portrait of Salisbury appears in Harley MS 4826.

39. THOMAS DE SCALES

Thomas de Scales, the seventh Lord Scales, was one of Bedford's lieutenants and, from November 1428, of equal authority with Suffolk and Talbot.

Born about the year 1399 (he was twenty-one in 1420), Thomas was the younger son of Robert, fifth Lord Scales, by either Joan (his first wife), daughter of William, lord Bardolf; or Elizabeth (his second wife). Succeeding his older brother Robert to the lordship of Scales (1420), he also took up his brother's active part in the war. In 1422 Thomas crossed to Normandy with a company of men-at-arms and served under John, duke of Bedford. He was captain of Vermeuil with a salary of 2,461 livres (1423). He campaigned with Fastolf and others in retaking the fortresses of Maine (1424–1425); he was subsequently made Knight of the Garter (1425).

While captain of St. Jacques of Beuvron, Thomas performed with great credit in the siege of Pontorson (1427) and defeated an attack made on him by the baron de Coulonce at Bas-Courtils, between Pontorson and Avranches, as he was covering the siege and bringing supplies to Warwick (April 17, 1427). In her letter of March 22, 1429, Joan refers to Thomas as one of Bedford's lieutenants; after being promoted to the rank of Suffolk and Talbot (November), he was the king's lieutenant in the Orléanais (December 16, 1428). In this position, he received 3,000 livres to lead an army against Orléans.

He was taken prisoner while attempting to give aid at Orléans and quickly ransomed; he was again defeated in the unsuccessful attempt to relieve Beaugency in June 1429 and taken prisoner again at Patay (June 18). Thomas was a captain with men-at-arms at Louviers (order of September 1430). Subsequently he was one of the commanders sent by Bedford to aid John V, duke of Brittany, against the duke of Alençon (1431). In 1433 he was captain of Danfort and of Saint-Lô (1435). He was made seneschal of Normandy in 1434 and, two years later, captain of Rouen. In 1435, Arundel and he were besieged in Avranches; later that year he assisted in the sieges of both Mont-Saint-Michel and Saint-Denis. Early in 1436 he defeated La Hire near Rouen and continued to fight with Talbot in defense of Normandy after Paris had again fallen into French hands.

Scales probably remained in France until the English possessions were lost. Afterward he returned to the family seat at Scales Hall, Middleton, Norfolk. As a prominent citizen of Norfolk, he had frequent contact with the Paston family. Thomas de Scales was murdered while being transported down the Thames after his surrender of London, which he had been defending in the name of Lancaster (July 18, 1460). By his wife Emma, daughter of Sir Simon Whalesburgh (probably of Cornwall), he had two children, a son (who died a minor) and a daughter, Elizabeth (his heiress). Elizabeth married first Henry Bourchier and second Anthony Woodville, who through her inheritance was called Lord Scales and afterward became the Earl Rivers (his sister was married to Edward IV) immortalized in Shakespeare's *Richard III*.

40. JOHN TALBOT, EARL OF SHREWSBURY

John Talbot, earl of Shrewsbury, was one of the high commanders of the English army. Born in 1373 at Blechmore, the second son of Richard Talbot of Goodrich Castle in the Welsh Marches, fourth Baron Talbot, John Talbot served his king for more than sixty years, dying with weapons in hand at the age of eighty. His family, originally from the Caux district in Normandy, went to England with the William the Conqueror. John Talbot acquired financial security through his marriage to Maud Neville, his first wife, who bore him three children, including two sons who would perish in 1450 at the Battle of Northampton during the Wars of the Roses. By his second wife, Margaret Beauchamp (eldest daughter of Richard Beauchamp, earl of Warwick), he had two daughters and three sons, of whom the eldest, John, was killed at his side at Castillon in 1453.

John Talbot began his warrior's career early; he received from Henry IV the command to fight the Welsh between 1404 and 1407. When Henry V succeeded his father, Talbot was imprisoned in the Tower of London, but he soon left it to serve as the king's lieutenant in Ireland, where at that time the crown faced endless difficulties. Henry V called him "cousin." Talbot later followed his master to France, took part in the sieges of Caen and Rouen, briefly returned to England, then appeared back on the continent under Henry VI. He took part in the Battle of Verneuil, which won for him the Order of the Garter. He then became lieutenant of the king in Ireland for a second term. But Bedford sent him back to France, and during this period of service he achieved his greatest renown.

He took part in the Battle of Montargis lost by Warwick, then in the capture of Laval, the retaking of Le Mans in 1428, the siege of Orléans, and the Battle of Patay, where he was taken prisoner. When he was freed in 1433, Bedford covered him with honors, appointing him lieutenant general of the king and of the regent for military affairs in the Ile-de-France and in the regions between the Seine, the Oise, and the Somme. He received the county of Clermont-en-Beauvaisis and was named captain of Saint-Germain-en-Laye and of Poissy; the regent awarded him a revenue of 300 gold saluts. But Bedford died on September 14, 1435, and the Treaty of Arras was concluded between Charles VII and Philip the Good.

Talbot delayed England's defeat. He defended Normandy and helped the earl of Willoughby take Ivry and Pontoise although he failed to stop the advance of the French armies. He tried in vain to save Meaux and made himself master of Harfleur, but Pontoise was lost the following year, 1441. After suffering another reversal in the siege of Dieppe, he withdrew to Ireland, where he served as governor. He again crossed the Channel upon the capitulation of Rouen in 1449, only to be taken hostage by Charles VII, who restored his liberty the following year. Lieutenant general of Henry VI in Guyenne, Talbot promptly reduced that province to his control, but his military career reached its end at the battle of Castillon, where the aged warrior died with his son John.

Venerated by the English, Talbot earned respect from the French side as well "because he made war honorably." His name is cited repeatedly in the documents from the siege of Orléans. He brought reinforcements on December 1; on the thirtieth, he set up his headquarters at the *bastide* of Saint-Laurent and later reorganized the *bastide* of Saint-Loup. His letter of retinue for the siege of Orléans, signed on January 28, 1429, authorized him to recruit forty-eight men-at-arms and a hundred archers. After the siege he defended Meung and Beaugency. At Patay, he would have preferred to confront the French rather than to obey Fastolf, who commanded retreat.

Although Talbot owned extensive lands in France as well as England, he strove his whole life to enhance his inheritances in England, particularly those of his wife's family, the Berkeleys, whose male heirs he despoiled. His desire to rise into the upper ranks of the barony was evident: The Talbots sought always to extend their influence through their friendship with the king.

This model of honor and chivalry, Talbot, "watchdog of England," is portrayed in a miniature in the Shrewsbury Book, one of the most well-known illuminated manuscripts of the 15th century.

41. WILLIAM DE LA POLE, EARL OF SUFFOLK (AND HIS BROTHER JOHN)

William de la Pole, fourth earl and first duke of Suffolk, formed for a time, along with John Talbot and Thomas de Scales, the English military triumvirate in France. De la Pole would go on to play a major role both in the peace that ended the Hundred Year's War and in the broader field of English politics.

William, the second son of Michael de la Pole, second earl of Suffolk (who died before the siege of Harfleur), was born on October 16, 1396, at Cotton in Suffolk. He entered the campaigns of Henry V as a very young man. He served in the French campaign of 1415, from which he was sent home to recuperate the wounds he received during the siege of Harfleur. His elder brother, the third earl, was slain at Agincourt, and thus William became earl of Suffolk when only nineteen. Suffolk served in the expedition of 1417 with thirty men-at-arms and ninety archers, and in 1418 was employed in the recovery of Contentin. He was granted the lordships of Hambye and Briquebec on March 12, 1418, and that same summer served under Humphrey of Gloucester (Bedford's brother) at the siege of Cherbourg. When Cherbourg fell in October, he went to join the king as he besieged Rouen. He was appointed admiral of Normandy on May 19, 1419, captain of Pontorson in June, and captain of Mantes and Avranches in August.

Suffolk began his diplomatic career as guarantor of the truce with France (June 27, 1420) and served at the siege of Melun that autumn. He was one of the commanders left in charge of Normandy when Henry V took Catherine to England (February 1421) and was appointed one of the conservators of the truce with Brittany (February 10). He was captured and imprisoned at Baugé on April 3, 1421, and received the Order of the Garter (May 3) as successor to Thomas, duke of Clarence.

After the death of Henry V, Bedford appointed Suffolk guardian of the Contentin, the castle of Saint-Lô, and the town of Coutances (October 10, 1422). Two years later (September 26, 1424) he was made governor of Chartres and in October captured Senonches, Nogent-le-Rotrou, and Rochefort. A month later he was in Paris, attending the festivities held by Philip the Good. From Paris, Bedford sent him to attempt a reconciliation between Gloucester and the duke of Brabant.

In 1425 he was appointed lieutenant general of Caen, the Contentin, and Lower Normandy, and constable of Salisbury's army. In May of the same year, he was detached from his post as constable to oversee the siege of Mont-Saint-Michel by land and sea. In early 1426 Suffolk was making raiding forays into Brittany as far as Rennes. Almost immediately afterward he resigned his command in Normandy to the earl of Warwick. Around this time he was created earl of Dreux.

Suffolk was quite active in the following year's warfare. He laid siege to Vendôme (May 26) and joined Warwick before Montargis (July 1). The latter siege was raised by the French after only two months. In the summer of 1428 Suffolk served under Salisbury in the campaign that led to the siege of Orléans; in September of the same year, he was commissioned captain general of Saint-Lô.

After Salisbury's sudden death, Suffolk replaced him as commander of the English troops in France (November 1428). Under his supervision and direction the siege of Orléans progressed quite satisfactorily, so well in fact that in February 1429 Orléans and the French cause seemed doomed. Then Joan of Arc made her entrance on the stage.

The siege was raised in May, and Suffolk fell back to Jargeau. He was besieged in that town by Joan and the duke of Alençon and was forced to surrender on June 12—a fatal day for his family; his brother, Sir John de la Pole, was taken prisoner with him and a third brother, Alexander, was slain. Suffolk was the prisoner of the count of Dunois; to obtain his freedom, he was forced to sell his lordship of Briquebec to raise money for his ransom of 20,000 livres, and to give his brother Thomas as a hostage.

Suffolk was reappointed to the command of Caen and the Contentin (March 15, 1430). In July he laid siege to the castle of Aumâle and captured it, and afterward took part in the siege of Compiègne. These engagements mark the end of Suffolk's active participation in the war; although he remained captain of Avranches (from 1432) and was captain of the islet of Tombelaine (appointed 1436 for a two-year term) and of Regnéville (mentioned as such for November 10, 1436 and in 1438), he exercised his authority through lieutenants.

Suffolk's later life was occupied with the politics of England. He sat in on the meeting of the royal council on both November 10 and 28, 1431; at the end of that month he was formally admitted as a council member, taking his oath on November 30. It was about this time that he married the widowed countess of Salisbury (Alice, daughter of Thomas Chaucer). This marriage may have inclined him toward connections with the Beauforts. His long association with war in France seems to have moved him, in later life at least, toward peace. Suffolk was a cultivated man who wrote verse in French for his own pleasure. His inclination toward peace may have been strengthened through his friendship with the captive Charles of Orléans. (He had purchased, at auction, the right to guard Charles on July 21, 1432.)

In 1432, Suffolk was created steward of the royal household, a position of considerable influence, and was striving actively for peace when Hugues de Lannoy came to England as Philip the Good's ambassador. Charles of Orléans and Suffolk met with Lannoy and his colleagues at Suffolk's London house, and it is apparent that Suffolk made use of Charles of Orléans to accelerate the peace process. The negotiations had progressed so far by 1435 that a general congress was arranged, and Suffolk was appointed one of the chief English representatives after Cardinal Beaufort. Suffolk and the majority of the English delegation arrived at Arras for the congress on July 25. (Beaufort arrived later.) At length, it became apparent that the English were not prepared to yield to the demands of the French; they withdrew from the talks on September 6. Hot on the heels of their withdrawal came both the reconciliation of Philip the Good, duke of Burgundy, to the French crown and the death of the regent, John of Lancaster, duke of Bedford.

At one fell swoop the face of English politics was entirely reconstructed. For a time Humphrey of Gloucester and the pro-war party enjoyed a revived power base. Suffolk quickly took up the lead in opposing Gloucester, and thus the remainder of his life revolved around his rivalry with the king's uncle. For a time war spirit threatened to sweep away the English, and Suffolk was appointed to return to France in December 1435. Richard, duke of York, was to have the chief command, but he and Suffolk did not cross to France until May 1436. Suffolk, York, and Richard Neville, earl of Salisbury, were commissioned to negotiate for peace; these negotiations had no practical result.

In 1442 it was planned that Henry VI should marry a daughter of the count of Armagnac, but Suffolk managed to thwart this match (which was Gloucester's pet project). Instead, Suffolk proposed Margaret of Anjou as a candidate for Henry VI's hand. (It is not known whether Charles of Orléans, who had been released in 1440, had any influence on this selection.) It would, however, seem that Orléans suggested Suffolk should be the chief ambassador in negotiating this match. But Suffolk, who was regarded widely as the most responsible of Henry's advisors after Cardinal Beaufort, could see only the dangers to himself and to his policies of such a position.

Under Suffolk's influence negotiations for peace continued through 1446, with little tangible result. The government, nevertheless, passed wholesale into Suffolk's hands. The king was completely alienated from his uncle Gloucester, who made Suffolk the object of repeated open attacks. To Suffolk and the queen, the complete overthrow of Humphrey's power seemed of paramount importance. On December 14, a parliament was summoned to meet at the pro-Suffolkian abbey of Bury St. Edmunds. Gloucester arrived on February eighteenth (eight days after the parliament's convocation) and was immediately arrested. He died five days later, presumably from natural causes accelerated by the shock of imprisonment.

Suffolk's fortunes would soon change. After peace had been achieved, he was embroiled in scandal. Those who opposed him said that he had sold England to the French. In just four years, after traversing a maze of treason accusations and imprisonment, a compromise between the two parties was reached and Suffolk was banished for a term of five years. On his way across the Channel, he was accosted by a ship called *Nicho-*

las of the Tower. On May 2, 1450, Suffolk was taken out in a little boat, and a knave of Ireland, "one of the lewdest men on board," took a rusty sword and cut off his head with half a dozen strokes. His body was taken to land and thrown upon the beach near Dover. Henry VI ordered his body removed and buried at Wingfield. He was succeeded by his son John de la Pole.

42. LIONEL, BASTARD OF WANDOMME

The Bastard of Wandomme, the man who captured Joan at Compiègne, was a follower of John of Luxembourg. That coup was his most memorable deed. He appears in the historical record some seven years earlier in a tournament, where he fought on foot with a battle-ax against a mounted French knight. In April 1428 the Bastard served Luxembourg as a squire at the siege of Beaumont-en-Argonne. When he captured Joan, he commanded a contingent of six men-at-arms and sixty-two yeomen; on the following day (May 24, 1430) he was awarded 277 livres for this signal service. The Bastard appears to have been a courageous fighter who finally had to abandon his military career after a splintered lance left him with a crippled arm.

43. RICHARD BEAUCHAMP, EARL OF WARWICK

Among the English lords Joan of Arc encountered, one of the most important was her jailer, Richard Beauchamp, earl of Warwick. On December 23, 1430, when Joan was delivered to Rouen as prisoner of the captain of the castle and of the city, she found herself lodged in the castle of Bouvreuil, the imposing fortress built by Philip II Augustus. The city had surrendered to Henry V in 1419, after a siege in which a third of its population perished. Besides an enormous indemnity, the conqueror demanded the construction of a new castle to serve as his "new palace." Work was begun immediately, but the construction lasted several years; Henry V was never to see it completed. It was in this extension of Bouvreuil Castle that Joan would be imprisoned; the tower called today the Tower of Joan of Arc is the donjon of the older castle. Warwick had held its captaincy since 1427. Sir Thomas Malory, later author of the *Morte Darthur,* reputedly served under Warwick.

Descended from an old Anglo-Norman family, Richard Beauchamp built his military career in the company of Henry V; he served as a counselor in the king's efforts to assert his claim to France and became one of the king's best friends. The dying Henry V named Warwick his son's mentor and protector.

Richard Beauchamp was born at Salwarp, Worcestershire in 1382 (January 25 or 28), the son of Thomas de Beauchamp (who died in 1401) and Margaret, daughter of William, Lord Ferrers of Groby. At eighteen Richard was made a knight of the Order of the Bath; he received the Order of the Garter in about 1416. He had conducted a pilgrimage to the Holy Land in 1408. Passing through Paris, he was received by Charles VI, who gave a banquet in his honor in November of that year. Beauchamp embarked at Venice for Jaffa, equipped with a fifteen-day pass to complete his pilgrimage to Jerusalem. England had a new king, Henry V, by the time he returned to London. Their destinies soon became linked. Warwick placed his sword and his talents in Henry's service and helped arrange the marriage of his sovereign to Catherine of France, daughter of Charles VI. Efficient at managing his master's affairs, he could also manage his own. He married one of the richest heiresses of England, Elizabeth Berkeley, with whom he had three daughters. One of them, Margaret, married the famous warrior John Talbot. After Elizabeth's death, Warwick married another heiress, Isabel Despenser, with whom he had a son and a daughter.

In France Richard Beauchamp prosecuted the war for the young Henry VI. In 1427, he commanded the army at Montargis, a city that long preserved a "banner of Warwick." During these years he frequently traveled between England and the continent to seek funds, make war preparations, and settle his family's succession problems.

The relationship between the Maid and her jailer remains poorly understood, but Joan was certainly a prisoner at Bouvreuil, where she underwent interrogation, and thus was under Warwick's ultimate authority. Bedford paid the judges of Rouen, but Warwick did so as well. He intervened when Joan was attacked in her cell by the soldiers guarding her, and he also intervened when she fell ill, lest she die of a disease before she could be condemned.

We know from the account book of his household, *The Beauchamp Household Book,* that Joan never appeared at Warwick's table, whereas her judges, including Pierre Cauchon, were invited. On May 13, 1431, the protector of Henry VI presided over a great banquet, to which he invited Cauchon, the bishop of Thérouanne, the Burgundian knight Aimond de Macy, and

Stafford, the chancellor of England. This document also records that two months after Joan's death, Poton de Xaintrailles was a guest at the castle as a prisoner of Warwick. This fact emphasizes the class difference between the lowly shepherdess and the noble captain of war—Xaintrailles took his place at that lordly table, as Joan never did.

Richard Beauchamp died at Rouen in 1439. His remains were carried to England and buried in the castle chapel in his city of Warwick. His son-in-law Richard Neville, who took the name Warwick upon the death of Beauchamp's last direct male heir, is known in English history as "the Kingmaker."

44. POTON DE XAINTRAILLES

Another of the adventurers who made their living from the craft of warfare, Poton de Xaintrailles (or Saintrailles) was made captain by Charles VII along with La Hire "because of their valor," according to Martial d'Auvergne.

In 1424, Poton took part in the struggle in Hainaut against the English, under the banner of Burgundy. We find him later on the Armagnac side, fighting alongside Joan of Arc against the enemies of the kingdom. Eventually, he would become a prisoner of the English: He was brought, like Joan, to Rouen upon his capture at the Battle of the Shepherd on August 11, 1431. A list made the following day places him among those who took their meals at the table of Richard Beauchamp, earl of Warwick, in the castle of Bouvreuil: "Poton prisoner cum 1 scutifero": Poton the prisoner with one esquire (M.-V. Clin-Meyer, *Le registre des comptes de Richard Beauchamp, comte de Warwick, 14 mars 1431–1415 mars 1432* [thesis, École des Hautes Études en Sciences Sociales, 1981]). Xantraille's imprisonment forms a stark contrast to that of Joan: He was received like John of Luxembourg, with the nobility of England and young King Henry VI, in the great dining hall of the castle under the direction of Talbot's wife, Warwick's daughter Margaret.

On November 14 Poton was taken to Dieppe; several days later Richard Beauchamp's family left for Paris to take part in the coronation of Henry VI, but Poton was still at Dieppe when they returned on January 14. For that date, the account books list four extra horses acquired for Poton, his squire, and two valets, so that the entire company could rendezvous at Abbeville, where they arrived on the evening of January 17. On January 21 Warwick and his entourage were at Montreuil, and they arrived at Calais on January 23. The embarkation took place on February 9. We lose track of Poton in the account books from that date, but it is reasonable to suppose that he was brought over to England.

He appears again in 1435 at the head of a band of mercenaries suppressing the peasants who had revolted in the course of what is now called the Insurrection of Normandy. Charles VII then made him bailiff of Bourges. The new position, however, did not keep him from holding men for ransom, just like his friends Robert de Flocques, La Hire, or Pierre de Brézé. That was how, according to Jean Chartier, he acquired a "great abundance of beasts, both beasts with horns and those with wool, with a great quantity of prisoners of diverse station." The king cited Poton de Xaintrailles specifically when he commanded the mercenary bands to cease their misdeeds.

The dauphin, the future Louis XI, recognized in Xaintrailles a congenial companion and a man able both to command and to serve. Louis made him an esquire and brought him on his 1444 German campaign. Despite that elevation Poton continued to rape, pillage, and steal, and he was among the troops who surrounded Metz. (Louis was aiding the German emperor against the rebellion of the Swiss cantons and then turned against him in Alsace and Lorraine.) After that expedition, Poton changed his manner of life. He was active in the recovery of Normandy and was at the king's side during the solemn royal entry into Rouen on November 10, 1449, carrying the great sword.

HER JUDGES AT ROUEN

With the exception of William of Alnwick and Pierre Cauchon—numbers 46 and 49—the following entries are adaptations of Pierre Champion's biographical sketches presented in W. P. Barrett's translated edition *The Trial of Jeanne D'Arc*.

45. JEAN ALESPÉE

Jean Alespée, born in 1357, the son of Pierre Alespée, was licentiate in civil law and bachelor of canon law at Paris and canon of Rouen cathedral from 1412. He was treasurer of the diocese of Rouen under Archbishop Louis d'Harcourt (1412–1413) and later Louis's vicar-general along with his close friend Nicolas de Venderès (1415–1422), who made an inventory of his possessions. Thanks to the nomination of Henry V, he was concurrently canon of the cathedrals of Evreux and Bayeux and of the collegiate church of Andelys as well as pastor of a rural church. He died at Rouen at the home of Jean Marcel on August 16, 1434, reportedly in his seventy-seventh year, after having been ill for some time at the home of Pierre Miget, prior of Longueville. Jean Alespée was a rich man and a lover of books. In 1424, his colleagues placed him in charge of the construction of the cathedral's library. Alespée was related to the distinguished families of Estouteville and Mallet de Graville, and hence kinsman to Guillaume d'Estouteville, the papal legate who initiated the nullification trial.

Jean Alespée appears to have been an especially timid, intellectually insecure man, tending to follow the opinions of his theological mentors; he was, not surprisingly for an ambitious man in his situation, an English partisan. However, Jean Riquier, a witness at the nullification trial, reported that Alespée wept freely at the burning of Joan of Arc and said publicly: "I wish that my soul were where I believe this woman's soul is."

46. WILLIAM OF ALNWICK

One of the ecclesiastical peers assigned to carry out the coronation at Paris of Henry VI, and one of the assessors present, under the presidency of Cardinal Henry Beaufort, at Pierre Cauchon's rhetorical spectacle in the cemetery of the abbey of Saint-Ouen, William Alnwick (d. 1449) was an important ecclesiastical figure in the England of both Henry V and Henry VI.

William was bishop of Norwich (1426–1436) and later of Lincoln (1436–1449). He studied at Cambridge, where he earned a doctorate in law. William was later a monk of St. Albans and became a confidant of Henry V; he speedily obtained a reputation for erudition and piety. He was consecrated bishop of Norwich on August 18, 1426, at Canterbury and was installed on December 22 of the same year. At that time he was appointed keeper of the privy seal.

While bishop of Norwich, he was appointed confessor to the young King Henry VI. In 1425, Henry recommended William to the Holy See for the bishopric of Ely. In Norwich he was a relentless persecutor of the Lollards; at least 120 were forced to abjure Lollardy and sentenced to various punishments, some even to death.

After his translation to Lincoln, William influenced the academic foundations of Henry VI and contributed to the architectural restoration of Lincoln Cathedral. He died on December 5, 1449, and was interred near the west door of Lincoln Cathedral.

47. JEAN BEAUPÈRE

Jean Beaupère was born in the diocese of Nevers. Master of Arts c. 1397, he completed the lengthy university course in theology by 1419 and received his *licentia* in theology at the end of that year. A man of considerable importance, he was rector of the University of Paris in both 1412 and 1413 and served as chancellor in Gerson's absence. In 1415 Pierre Cauchon and he were among the Burgundian envoys at Constance.

On July 30, 1420, Jean Beaupère received a papal appointment as canon of Notre Dame of Paris in place of Jean Charreton; at first, his colleagues protested this intrusion. On June 27, 1420, he took possession of the canonicate of Eustache de Laitre at Beauvais; in 1419 he was sent to Troyes with Pierre Cauchon to advise Charles VI. In 1422 he went on an embassy to the queen of England and the duke of Gloucester to obtain confirmation of the university's privileges. In 1423, en route between Paris and Beauvais, he was attacked by brigands who robbed him and left him for dead. He lost the use of his right hand in this attack and thus could not occupy his benefices, since he was no longer able to consecrate the eucharistic Host and therefore could not function as a priest. Nevertheless, Martin V granted him confirmation of the post he held as canon of the cathedrals of Besançon, Sens, Paris, and Beauvais, as well as for the archdiaconate of Salins (March 1424). Nominated canon of Rouen cathedral on September 6, 1430, by Henry VI, he received, on April 2, 1431, an honorarium of 30 livres from the English crown. In 1432 he was cellarer at Sens, canon of Besançon, Paris, Laon, and Rouen, and chaplain of the Brie. He also sought to become a canon of Autun cathedral, pastor of Saint-Jean-en-Grève and sacristan of Saint-Merry at Paris, and canon of Lisieux cathedral, among other offices. He was, in short, an outrageous pluralist.

He left Rouen on May 28, 1431, for the Council of Basel, where he arrived on November 2, 1431. At Basel he played an important role, having been commissioned to convince the pope that the papal presence was necessary there, a commission that he undertook with determination and zeal. The council sent him as ambassador to Philip the Good in 1432. Strongly pro-conciliar and antipapal, he was disavowed by the chapter of Rouen in 1438 and had to prove his orthodoxy to retain his canonicate there. When the city returned to French domination he took pains to present himself as a loyal Frenchman. Beaupère resided most often at Besançon in the Empire. He died there in either 1462 or 1463.

Beaupère was very active in the condemnation trial; his voice was at once authoritative and tractable. He was sent to Paris to discover the opinion of the university. He testified in 1452 at the time of the preliminary nullification investigations and stood firm in his opinion that Joan's voices had "natural causes" arising from the malice inherent in the nature of women.

48. BOISGUILLAUME

Guillaume Colles, known more commonly as Boisguillaume, a member of the Colles de Bois-guillaume family, was a notary of the ecclesiastical court of Rouen and a recorder at the condemnation trial.

In 1421 he is cited as pastor of Notre-Dame-de-La-Ronde (a benefice at the disposition of the king of England). The name Guillaume Colles appears as a signature on a writ of excommunication in 1424. He was the notary at the inquisitorial trial of Jean Seguent, which was conducted by Jean Graverent between July and November 1430, and signed the act by which the clergy of Rouen assembled in the archbishop's chapel declared vacant the benefices of their brothers who lived in territory still loyal to the dauphin. He also appears in records pertaining to an inventory of the king's property that was requested from the court of Rouen, at least ostensibly, by Henry VI. He was later pastor of Notre Dame near Bernay, "under sentence of excommunication, aggravated and further aggravated . . . obstinate and a bad example to our mother the church." His property was ordered sold so that the money might be used for the benefit of his absolution.

Guillaume Colles lived at Rouen in the parish of Saint-Nicolas. He was a witness at the nullification trial and, on December 18, 1456, gave a description of the notarial procedures in the earlier trial, testifying that it had been conducted with English financial support, recognizing the documents that were presented to him, and setting forth at least some of the questionable methods of Nicolas Loiseleur and Jean d'Estivet.

49. PIERRE CAUCHON

Pierre Cauchon, bishop of Beauvais and Joan of Arc's tireless persecutor, was born about 1371 near Reims. Was he from a family of vineyard owners, as Jean Juvénal des Ursins says, or had he descended from a noble family that settled in Reims after the affair of the Templars in the early fourteenth century? The question cannot be answered with certitude. We can nevertheless find relatives linking Pierre Cauchon to Jean de Rinel, the future secretary of Henry VI. Husband of Cauchon's niece Guillemette Bidault, Rinel was his nephew-in-law, and all their lives these two men worked together for the glory of the king of England. Cauchon studied at the University of Paris, where he was licentiate in law (1398) and one the students who voted to ignore the orders of Pope Benedict XIII; he was a sixth-year student in theology in 1403. Cauchon became rector of the University of Paris after a brilliant academic career. As rector he craved a benefice from the chapter of Reims, even though he already had a canonicate and a prebendary in Châlons, and pastoral duties in the parish church of Égriselles located within the diocese of Sens. In 1406 he took the matter of refusing obedience to Benedict XIII before the Parlement of Paris. The following year, thanks to his juridical and rhetorical skills, he was part of the large embassy to Italy (charged with ending the Great Schism) that called upon Benedict XIII to renounce the papacy. In compensation for his service in this matter he was granted the major chaplaincy of Saint Étienne at Toulouse in 1408. He was later named canon at Reims and then the bishop's deputy (in the same diocese) in 1410, and canon at Beauvais (*Register of the Cathedral Chapter*: June 28, 1410), although technically he should not have been allowed to combine these two functions. (The piling up of ecclesiastical benefices was one of the running sores of the church at that time. The manpower gaps left by the devastation of the Black Death caused many vacancies in benefices; skillful clerics maneuvered themselves into these assignments and then did not exercise the concomitant responsibilities and functions.) In 1412 he was one of the reformers charged with overseverity in regard to the excesses of the Armagnacs.

Vidame (temporal lord) of the church at Reims, Pierre Cauchon attached himself to the duke of Burgundy, Philip the Good. At Paris, where he was among the intimates of the ducal court, he became a plotter of the Cabochian revolt (1413). Cauchon helped persuade the Parisian mob to attack the Bastille, wreck the Hôtels of Guyenne and of Artois, break into the chambers of the dauphin, and seize his officers. Shortly thereafter opinion shifted, and the hall of the Paris butchers' guild was leveled. On September 27, 1413, the count of Armagnac made his entry into the capital and banished Cauchon. The duke of Burgundy then sent this prelate with radical revolutionary sentiments to the Council of Constance (1415), where he defended the theses of Jean Petit, the Burgundian who made himself the champion of tyrannicide in order to justify the assassination of Louis of Orléans.

Named master of requests for the government of Henry V (1418), he petitioned for the provostship of Lille (vacant at the death of Jean de Montreuil). On this occasion the university asked the pope to grant Cauchon the right to unite several incompatible benefices, arguing that his courage and his works for the greater good of the church were worthy of such high reward. He then became archdeacon of Reims, canon of Chartres and Châlons (later archdeacon), and chaplain of the duke of Burgundy at Dijon. He also held, in the diocese of Bayeux, the benefice of St. Clair: All of which (when added to his other canonicates, prebendaries, and benefices) gave him approximately 2,000 livres a year. In 1419 he was a referendary of Pope Martin V, for whom he had campaigned, and then conservator of the privileges of the University of Paris. In this capacity, he was with his niece's husband Jean de Rinel at Troyes, where he prepared the text of the treaty disinheriting the dauphin Charles. Thanks to that treaty and the growing discord between the Armagnacs and the Burgundians, Henry V took an interest in French politics. The Burgundians reclaimed Paris; there was no way to avoid the ensuing massacre. (Tanguy du Châtel saved the dauphin then by taking him to Vincennes in the dead of night.) On August 21, 1420, Pierre Cauchon was named bishop and count of Beauvais under the protection of the duke of Burgundy, whom he would serve faithfully. He received his bishopric on the recommendation of the University of Paris. It was through the favor of Philip the Good—who himself came to attend Cauchon's investiture—that he was made an ecclesiastical peer of the kingdom. Now fully in the service of the English party, he followed Henry V to Paris, where he fought with the cathedral chapter and with Bishop Courtecuisse. At the instigation of John, duke of Bedford, he arranged for the bishop to be removed to Geneva, even though he had been appointed by the pope. Cauchon was equally successful in gaining the regent's confidence. Fully supported by the University of Paris, Cauchon represented it at the court of Pope Martin V while also acting as envoy of the king of England. He was bishop of Beauvais for nine years. In Bedford's confidence, an executor of the will of Charles VI, and counselor of King Henry VI of England, the bishop received an annual pension of 100 livres tournois (Paris, B.N. fr. 20882, fol. 61: the accounts of Pierre Surreau); he was also guardian of the privy seal in the absence of the chancellor.

In 1429 after the liberation of Orléans, Joan of Arc led the dauphin to Reims. Several weeks before the anointing, Cauchon visited Reims, where he reconciled the chapter and the bishop on the subject of the cardinalate and carried the Blessed Sacrament during the Corpus Christi procession on May 26. Leaving the city for his diocese of Beauvais, he had to seek refuge at Rouen when the people of Beauvais expelled the English and the Burgundians (August 1429). The English indemnified him for the loss of his revenues and placed him in charge of special missions in England, Paris, and elsewhere. The trial of Joan of Arc was one such mission. Bedford then tried to have Cauchon named archbishop of Rouen, which he had administered in matters spiritual and temporal, but Cauchon had to be content with the bishopric of Lisieux (1432). The clergy of Rouen were opposed to him, and Bedford, wishing to manipulate both parties, abandoned the effort. Cauchon lived for the most part at Rouen, near the grand hall of the council, of which he was a member.

In the name of Henry VI, Cauchon undertook to purchase Joan and have her judged by a tribunal of the Inquisition in Rouen, a sympathetic city in pro-English France, invoking thereby his rights as bishop of Beauvais, the territory in which Joan had been captured. He went to Compiègne and then to the castle of Beaurevoir to deal with John of Luxembourg, who held Joan prisoner. After several months of effort, he succeeded in launching her trial.

After Joan's death, Cauchon took part in the coronation of Henry VI at Paris on December 16, 1431, as the chronicler Enguerrand de Monstrelet confirms:

> There was with him from the nation of England [Henry's] uncle, the cardinal of Winchester, and the cardinal of York, the duke of Bedford, and the rich duke of York, the earls of Warwick, Salisbury, and Suffolk,

as well as noble knights and squires of the House of France, and there were the bishop of Thérouanne named my lord Louis of Luxembourg; of Beauvais, Master Pierre Cauchon; of Noyon, Master Jean de Mailly (Monstrelet, vol. 1, chap. 109).

Bedford had arranged for the peers of France favorable to his king to take part in the anointing, and the bishop was at the solemn banquet that followed the mass and the ceremony: "And on the side of the chamber of Parlement at that table, the aforesaid cardinal of Winchester and Master Pierre Cauchon, bishop of Beauvais, and Master Jean de Mailly, bishop of Noyon, were in attendance as peers of France" (Monstrelet, vol. 1, chap. 109).

As bishop of Lisieux, Cauchon took possession of the manor of the Hôtel Saint-Claude or Hôtel de Lisieux at Rouen, which displeased the Rouen clergy. He continued to serve as a general envoy of Henry VI, going to Calais in 1433 at the time of the negotiations for the liberation of the duke of Orléans. Serving as the queen of England's chancellor in France, Cauchon attended the Council of Basel as a deputy of England in 1435; there he joined Thomas de Courcelles, Jean Beaupère, and Nicolas Loiseleur, his associates in Joan's trial. That same year he was present at the Council of Arras, where he sustained the exclusive right of Henry VI to the crown of France. Upon Bedford's death (September 14, 1435), which was followed swiftly by the death of the archbishop of Rouen, Louis of Luxembourg was named the ecclesiastical head of Normandy, in which post he was supported by Cauchon. The two associates appear again at Paris in 1436, when the troops of Charles VII took the city. Cauchon was nearly captured in the Bastille Saint Antoine, and both men were forced to flee, Luxembourg to England and Cauchon to Rouen.

In that same year Cauchon was charged with calling together at Caen the Three Estates of Normandy and with informing them of the king of England's intention to found a university at Caen. In his last years he fulfilled numerous diplomatic missions relative to the English peace (including the conferences of Calais and Gravelines, to name but two). On July 29, 1437, he gave a receipt to the treasurer-general of Normandy for 770 livres, the balance of a sum of 2,177 livres for a trip from Paris to Rouen in the king of England's service (B.N. fr. 26,063). In 1439 and 1440 Cauchon was commissioned to undertake several trips to Calais and to England to treat for peace between the two kingdoms and to seek the liberation of the duke of Orléans.

Cauchon died suddenly, while he was being shaved, at his residence in Rouen, on December 18, 1442, at the height of his honors, before the final collapse of the English cause. Cauchon's body was carried in state to Lisieux, accompanied by his friend and executor, Nicolas Caval, canon of Rouen. He was interred near the altar in the magnificent Chapel of the Virgin, which he had rebuilt and decorated at his own expense. It is remarkable to note that the Frenchman who succeeded him as bishop of Beauvais, Jean Jouvenel des Ursins, made only a brief allusion to his predecessor and did not mention Joan's trial in this connection: "And although they held your adversary for lord, that was because the lord bishop was in this foolish error; but always they were your servants at heart. . . . "

During Joan's nullification trial, Cauchon's family had to answer for his acts. He left as heirs his nephew, Jean Bidault, canon of Reims and Lisieux, and Jeanne Bidault, wife of Jean de Rinel, secretary of Henry VI, whose name appears at the end of the Treaty of Troyes. His great-grandnephews, while negotiating their inheritance, wished to avoid polemics and wrote to the judges of the nullification trial, through the intermediary of the procurator, Jean de Gouvis, to disclaim any responsibility: "We have heard it said that Joan the Maid, despite her Christian, pure, and flawless life, was the victim of the hatred of the English, who did not forgive her for having caused them great damage in war and for having served well the king of France." The heirs made it clear they wished to live tranquilly in their large house on the rue de la Cayne. The trial was none of their concern, they insisted, "for we were all little children or not yet born at that time." Thus, Cauchon's own family, hard-pressed to remain in the good graces of the new government, rejected him absolutely.

In the 1990s some French scholars have taken a more sympathetic look at Cauchon, seeing him as a sincere and educated cleric with high if somewhat rigid professional standards, for whom Joan the Maid and her supporters embodied everything from which he wished to save his country. How far this effort at rehabilitation will go is difficult to foresee at this juncture (May 1998).

50. THOMAS DE COURCELLES

Thomas de Courcelles was born at Amiens in 1393. A zealous university man and rector of the faculty of law in 1426, he taught theology at Paris for many years; he died on October 23, 1469, as dean of the chapter of Notre Dame of Paris.

Rector of the university in 1430, he went in this capacity to the court of Rome. In 1435 he was sent to Arras, where he spoke for peace and "proposed so many fine and solemn words that it seemed as if an angel of God were speaking, and of those present many were moved to tears." At the Council of Basel from 1433 to 1438, Thomas de Courcelles shone as one of the lights of the French church. He remained at his post in 1433, despite the plague that ravaged Basel. Courcelles was involved in several papal elections, usually unsuccessfully. He was delegated by the council to vote in the next papal election and was among those who declared Pope Eugenius IV (1431–1447) an apostate in July 1439. He was sent by the fathers of Basel to the Diet of Mainz for the election of a new pope and in December made an address before the antipope Felix V that eventually resulted in the promotion of many to the rank of cardinal. In 1440 he discoursed eloquently before Charles VII at Bourges on the Gallican constitution of the French church. On July 18, 1442, at Saint-Magloire, he preached before the people a solemn sermon that put an end to the troubles of the university, announcing that the king "had liberally reconfirmed and given anew to our mother the University all her privileges." On July 17, 1447, he returned to the chapter of Notre Dame of Paris where he was received as canon on September 11. That chapter already counted in its ranks Guillaume de Courcelles, named chancellor in 1425 in place of Jean Gerson, and Jean de Courcelles, referred to as doctor of law and archdeacon of Josas through the king's favor, who had been canon since July 23, 1446; the latter was a brother of Thomas. Thomas de Courcelles was at Lyons in August 1447, among the ambassadors who were negotiating for Amadeus, duke of Savoy's renunciation of the papal office. In a letter of April 8, 1448, the confessor of Charles VII states that Thomas de Courcelles was entrusted with the pope's verbal commissions. Courcelles journeyed to Rome to be near Nicolas V (1447–1455) and took the title of papal archdeacon. In 1458 he was named dean of Notre Dame of Paris. In 1450 he spoke against the founding of a university at Caen. By that time he had accumulated many benefices.

The role that he enjoyed in the trial, where he came out in favor of torturing Joan, is well known. This young prelate with a promising future, this cleric "very solemn and excellent," enjoyed the full confidence of Pierre Cauchon, who later put him in charge of translating the minutes of the trial into Latin. Questioned in 1456

at the nullification proceedings, this doctor whose eloquence was praised by his contemporaries and remarked on his tombstone failed to recall key information. Thomas de Courcelles was doubtless embarrassed later in life by his participation in the first trial, and afterward, during the definitive editing of that trial's documents, he suppressed his name wherever it figured in the French minutes. He tried to give the impression that he had taken little part in the trial; its transcript shows him less fiercely hostile to Joan than Cauchon or Guillaume Érard. (See below.)

51. GUILLAUME ÉRARD

Guillaume Érard, a native of the diocese of Langres, was a master of arts, a bachelor and doctor of theology, and became rector of the university on February 26, 1421. He was procurator of the French Nation in the University of Paris in 1426 and was in communication with Jean Graverent, the Inquisitor, on the subject of heretics who had appealed to the pope. He received his degree as licentiate and then as master of theology in 1428. Érard taught at Paris from September, 1428, at the same time as Pierre Dyerée, Pierre Le Mire, Jean Gravestain, and Guillaume Adelie.

In an interesting document from December 1430, Érard was engaged in a suit against Geoffroy le Normant before the Parlement of Paris. Érard testified that he had been ordained "master of grammarians of the College of Navarre." In 1429 Érard had been sent to Champagne by the king of England, along with Pierre Cauchon; Geoffroy le Normant protested that it was Érard's duty, not his, to teach children "and he ought to employ himself in preaching"—rather than to serve as Érard's substitute. This document indicates that Érard then had an income of more than 30 livres, and that he was a canon of Laon cathedral and canon and sacristan of Langres cathedral. Érard also alluded to a journey he had made to Basel. He was at Paris in September 1431 among the regent masters, and on January 25, 1432, he presided at Paris over the examination for the licentiate, when Thomas de Courcelles received first rank. Nicolas Loiseleur was Érard's pupil at Paris in 1431–1432. Guillaume Bonnel, abbot of Cormeilles, dean of the faculty of law, took action against him for "at the last licentiate examination (1432) he opened the list of licentiates which the master had given him." In 1433 Érard is called the vice-chancellor of Notre Dame. In August he lodged a complaint with the Parlement of Paris in the name of the university, protesting a royal ordinance on the repurchase of the rental income of the churches and colleges in Paris. Guillaume Érard is mentioned for the last time among the regent masters in September 1433; he then moved for a while to Normandy.

Érard entered the chapter of Rouen on July 17, 1432. Later he visited Paris to "further the liberties of the Church." Named archdeacon of Grand Caux in 1433, he fulfilled in turn the posts of chancellor, precentor, and vicar-general of Rouen cathedral. On February 7, 1434, he was named professor of theology at the University of Paris and made canon at Notre Dame cathedral on the recommendation of the bishop of Paris, Jacques de Chatelier, a worldly prelate who was elevated to that rank through the favor of the duke of Bedford and Philip the Good of Burgundy. Érard was the executor of the will of Hugues des Orges, archbishop of Rouen in 1434. He was opposed to the promotion of the wealthy Jean Alespée to a canonicate at Notre Dame, and finally succeeded in alienating him from the chapter. This conflict went so far as to produce appeals to the pope.

A friend of Louis of Luxembourg, Guillaume Érard went to England to swear fealty to Henry VI in Louis's name as bishop of Ely. Henry charged Érard to go to Arras with Raoul Roussel and Jean de Rinel in 1435 to treat for peace; while there Érard responded very dryly to the much applauded discourse of Thomas de Courcelles. On November 12, 1436, Érard presided at an assembly of prelates "for a certain need touching public affairs and the coming of certain English lords" to Normandy. In 1437 he was named chaplain to King Henry VI and received an annual income of 20 pounds sterling for services rendered to the crown. From then on Érard lived in England; the canons of Rouen commissioned him to reconfirm or reclaim the legacies made to their church by Henry V and Bedford. Named dean of the cathedral in place of the late Gilles Deschamps, Érard did not succeed in taking possession of this dignity, which he had gladly accepted and which shows how much hope the canons reposed in his supposed influence with the English court. He died in England in 1439, leaving great sums to the cathedral of Rouen and to the college of the community, and an enameled silver chalice to the chapter. He bequeathed likewise a legacy of 40 livres to the University of Paris. The executor of his will was the rigorous Pasquier de Vaux, bishop of Evreux.

As pro-English as his patron Louis of Luxembourg, forceful and unscrupulous in all his dealings, Érard appears in the transcript of the condemnation trial as one of the most impassioned judges of Joan of Arc, whom he condemned violently on the day of her abjuration.

52. JEAN D'ESTIVET

Jean d'Estivet, called Benedicité, promoter-general of the diocese of Beauvais, was canon of Beauvais and Bayeux cathedrals, being named canon of the latter church on January 16, 1430. He obtained a canonical prebend at Rouen on April 25, 1437. Pierre Cauchon exempted him from the tithes that clerical students of law paid at the University of Paris.

Intimately connected with Cauchon, he was one of Joan's most rancorous judges. He insulted her in prison, talking to her as if she were a prostitute. Entirely devoted to the English, Jean d'Estivet entered Joan's cell, like Loiseleur, pretending to be another prisoner. According to Guillaume Manchon, he sent the Twelve Articles to Paris without seeing that they were completely corrected. He is the author of the list of charges read at the session of March 27, and it was he who ordered Joan to be taken back to the castle of Rouen after her abjuration. The recorders, whom he paid for their work, detested his overbearing manner. Boisguillaume placed a great deal of responsibility on him in his testimony at Joan's nullification proceedings: "And he believed that God, at the end of his life, punished him, for he ended miserably: he was found dead in a certain sewer outside the Rouen gate"—a favorite topos for the end of the wicked in Christian hagiography. In Estivet's case, however, this unattractive accident seems actually to have happened—on October 20, 1438, in fact; it was long interpreted by the populace as divine retribution for Estivet's conduct during Joan's trial.

53. JEAN GRAVERENT

Jean Graverent, a Dominican and the Grand Inquisitor of France, was referred to in 1413 as master of theology of Paris and was present at a council held there, where he gave an opinion in favor of appealing to the pope the question of Jean Petit's defense of tyrannicide. He succeeded Jacques Suzay as Inquisitor in 1425. On August 16, 1429, as prior of the Jacobin convent in Paris, Jean Graverent took the oath of loyalty to the English government before the Parlement of Paris. He directed the trial of Jean Le Couvreur, a burgess of Saint Lô, which was still under way on March 4, 1431; thus this Dominican, who seems to have been an adherent of the Burgundian party, could not take part in the trial of Joan of Arc. On July 4, 1431, Jean Graverent preached a sermon in Paris, accusing Friar Richard of being "beau père," that is, the mentor, of four suspect female visionaries: Joan, Catherine de La Rochelle, the Breton Perrinaik, and her maidservant.

54. WILLIAM HAITON

William Haiton was an Englishman and a bachelor of theology as well as secretary of requests to the English king. He was ambassador to the court of France in 1419 to arrange the marriage of Henry V with the princess Catherine. He was a member of the English council in 1431; however, he lost his position as secretary on March 1, 1433. In 1445 he appears in volume IV of Henry VI's *Calendar of Patent Rolls*. William Haiton and Gilles de Duremort, abbot of Fécamp and his colleague in the king's council, voiced the same opinions during Joan's trial and execution.

55. ROBERT JOLIVET

Robert Jolivet of Montpichon was a Norman Benedictine, a bachelor of law in 1416, who became abbot of Mont-Saint-Michel in 1411. He fled his abbey, which remained faithful to Charles VII, and took refuge with the English about 1419. He went on various missions for Bedford and became his chancellor and keeper of his privy seal in 1423. On May 27, 1428, Jolivet was Bedford's representative at the foundation of the Carmelite convent in Rouen.

Extremely devoted to the government of Henry VI, this monk played an important role in diplomacy and even in military matters, inspecting troops and visiting fortresses. He was a member of all of the important councils. He was commissioned by the king of England in 1425 to recover the abbey, which he had fortified admirably before his departure. Between April and June 1428 Robert Jolivet was at Paris awaiting the coming of Salisbury and the English army "to advise and conclude where he would be sent." In November he went to Mantes to see Bedford about the siege of Orléans. On September 12, 1430, Jolivet is cited as chancellor with the considerable salary of 800 livres a year. Not surprisingly, he resided at Rouen in order to serve his king better. On November 16, 1431, King Henry ordered the payment of the wages of the ten lancers and thirty mounted archers who had escorted Jolivet (along with the abbot of Fécamp) to Paris where he had been summoned. On July

23, 1436, King Henry VI ordered him, the bishop of Lisieux, and the earl of Suffolk to call together the Three Norman Estates at Caen and to take part in the project of establishing a university there.

Jolivet was buried at Rouen in the church of Saint Michel in July 1444.

56. GUILLAUME DE LA CHAMBRE

Guillaume de La Chambre the younger was born about 1403, the son of Guillaume de La Chambre the elder, physician to Queen Isabeau, who at one point testified that the dauphin Charles was not the son of King Charles VI. Guillaume the younger was awarded his licentiate in medicine from the University of Paris on March 6, 1430. Immediately thereafter he began teaching as a member of that faculty and was still a regent master in November 1452. In 1430, the year he earned his license, Guillaume sold to the Norman Nation of the University of Paris a house on the rue Galande that he owned in common with his brother Jean.

An assiduous judge at the condemnation trial, Guillaume de La Chambre visited Joan as a physician and was present at her execution. He testified at the nullification trial that his vote was forced upon him by the bishop of Beauvais. His testimony was entirely favorable to the Maid.

57. MARTIN LADVENU

Martin Ladvenu, a Dominican from the Jacobin convent at Rouen, was among those who sought to enlighten Joan, since he was her confessor and spiritual advisor during her imprisonment at Rouen.

Very little is known about Ladvenu. He was in Paris at the time of the trial of Gilles Deschamps, one of Joan's judges. The following year at Neufchâtel he lectured a sorceress, Jeanne Vancril, suspect in matters of faith. He was described in 1452, in the transcript of the preliminary sessions of the nullification trial, as a friar of the convent of the Jacobins at Rouen, "special confessor and advisor to Joan the Maid in her last days."

58. JEAN DE LA FONTAINE

Jean de La Fontaine, a clerk of the diocese of Bayeux described in 1403 as master of arts and student in law, was promoter of the University of Paris in 1421 and was sent to the duke of

Bedford and King Henry VI in 1422 to have the university's privileges confirmed; he won his licentiate in law in 1424. In 1427, with Guillaume Colles, Guillaume Manchon, and Robert Guerould, he edited Cauchon's carefully prepared transaction between the archbishop and the chapter of Rouen. It was Jean de La Fontaine who proclaimed Charles VII's confirmation of the university's privileges in 1436.

Commissioned as an assistant counselor at the trial and given by Pierre Cauchon the responsibility of questioning Joan, La Fontaine advised her to submit to the Church Militant. According to the testimony of Manchon and Jean Massieu, he had to flee Rouen when he was being threatened by Cauchon, who evidently thought him too helpful to the accused. He was also a friend of Nicolas de Houppeville, to whom he passed a letter while the latter was in prison. There is also a Guillaume de La Fontaine cited as lieutenant general of Jean Salvain, the bailiff of Rouen in 1432, as well as a Jacques de La Fontaine, bachelor of law, secretary, and intimate friend of the pope, who was on March 27, 1429, occupied in exchanging his canonicate of Beauvais.

59. JEAN LEMAÎTRE

Jean Lemaître (Lemaistre or Le Maistre), a Dominican and a bachelor of theology from some university other than Paris, was vicar of the Inquisitor of France in the diocese of Rouen from 1424. In 1431 he is listed as prior of the Dominican convent at Rouen, where he was a noted preacher. He was still living at the time of the first investigations made at Rouen for Joan's nullification trial. He preached a sermon in January 1452. It is probable that he was dead by 1455. At any rate, he was not consulted or cited in the course of the nullification trial.

He has been represented by later historians as acting under threat from Pierre Cauchon and even as speaking out about the irregularities of the first trial. In fact, he was less zealous than Jean Graverent, the Grand Inquisitor of France, at that time detained at Coutances by another trial, who ordered Lemaître to join Joan's trial and preached at Paris against Joan's memory. Lemaître reserved his opinion on the matter of torture, but he condemned the monk Pierre Bosquier, who spoke critically of Joan's sentence. On April 24, 1431, Jean Lemaître received from the English government a gratuity of 20 gold saluts "for his pains, labors and diligences in having been present and having assisted at the trial." He seems to have been a timid man, entirely devoted to Cauchon but little convinced of the trial's regularity (at least according to the testimony of Nicolas de Houppeville). Lemaître certainly hesitated to approve the trial's procedures and took the precaution of protecting himself by hiding behind the Inquisitor General. On December 7, 1443, however, he preached to the people on the occasion of the election of Raoul Roussel as archbishop of Rouen—Roussel was one of Joan's most pro-English judges and successor to the like-minded cardinal of Luxembourg.

60. NICOLAS LOISELEUR

Nicolas Loiseleur was born at Chartres in 1390 and was master of arts at Paris in 1403. He did not commence his studies as bachelor of theology until October 1431. Already a canon of Chartres cathedral in 1421, he was made a canon of Rouen, replacing Martin Ravenot, who had remained faithful to the dauphin Charles. Loiseleur undertook many delicate missions for the Rouen chapter, going to Paris, for example, to take part in various trials. On July 8, 1429, he was sent as a delegate by the chapter to negotiate an embassy to Rome. He was, without doubt, very highly regarded by Bedford's government.

A deputy to the Council of Basel with Midy and Beaupère, Nicolas Loiseleur went from Rouen to Paris "for the liberties of the church." He did not attend that council before 1435, when, along with the university and the clergy of Charles VII, he maintained the preeminence of the general council over the pope. This was no longer the opinion of the English government or of the chapter of Rouen, which attempted to recall its ambassador. He was rather badly received in England, where Henry VI secretly supported Eugenius IV. In 1439 the Council of Basel sent him to the Imperial Diet at Mainz; in 1440 he was deprived of his benefice as canon of Rouen by the papal court at Rome. He lived at Rouen, in the rue de la Chaine (the present-day place des Carmes), in a house of which his brother-in-law Pierre Le Marie and his sister Thomasse were the concierges. Pierre Cauchon was a frequent visitor. Loiseleur died at Basel sometime after 1442 and before the nullification proceedings.

An intimate friend of Cauchon's, Nicolas Loiseleur was similarly linked to Nicolas Midy, one of Joan's bitterest opponents; he played a particularly odious role in the trial, that of false confessor—although this was, admittedly, completely in accordance with inquisitorial procedure (Eymeric, *Directorium Inquisitorium*, [Rome, 1585] p. 466, col. 2, *cautela nova*). Boisguillaume assures us, nonetheless, that he wept while witnessing her death. He is mentioned as a Norman by Pius II (*De gestis Basilei concilii*, in the *Opera omnia*, [Basil, 1551]).

61. JEAN DE MAILLY

Jean de Mailly, bishop of Noyon, was one of the principal members of the English king's council and a committed Burgundian.

He was a licentiate in law, a councilor of Parlement (1401), master of petitions at the Hôtel du Roi (1418), and president of the chamber of accounts in 1424. He became dean of Saint-Germain-l'Auxerrois in Paris and was called to Noyon as bishop by Martin V on July 20, 1425. The following year he was asked, along with Louis of Luxembourg, to pacify the dispute concerning heretical witchcraft between the bishop of Paris and Jean Graverent, the Inquisitor. From 1424 on we find him at Rouen, present at the sessions of the Exchequer. He and Pierre Cauchon accompanied the young king to Paris and were present at Notre Dame as ecclesiastical peers at Henry VI's coronation ceremonies.

Jean de Mailly was not very old at the time of the nullification trial. (He was born about 1396.) He alleged, however, that he had been present at only one session of the condemnation trial and declared that he remembered nothing about it. He was, nevertheless, present at the abjuration scene and at the burning of the Maid. In 1443 Mailly welcomed Charles VII to Noyon. In 1435 he took part in the embassy that announced to Charles VII the happy conclusion of the Peace of Arras. He died on February 14, 1472, leaving to his church his Bible, a manuscript on vellum. He was above all else a diplomat and a financier.

62. GUILLAUME MANCHON

Guillaume Manchon, the recorder of Joan's trial and notary of the ecclesiastical court of Rouen, was a canon of Rouen and Evreux cathedrals and pastor of Saint-Martin-de-Vitefleur and later of Saint-Nicolas of Rouen; he was also the almoner of the Confrèrie de la Calende of the deanery of la Chrétienté in the Rouen diocese.

Court promoter from 1437 to 1443, he prosecuted Jean Massieu for bad manners. As court promoter he visited the abbeys and priories

of the diocese in 1440; in 1453 he was in charge of taxes and disbursements. He died on December 9, 1456.

On September 21, 1440, Guillaume de Croiseinare, bailiff of La Madeleine at Rouen, listed some of Manchon's endowments. He is cited as notary of the court of Rouen; pastor of Vitefleur since October 31, 1436; a canon of Evreux; promoter of the ecclesiastical court of Louis of Luxembourg; archbishop of Rouen; and premier chaplain of the notaries by election and appointment of the brothers of that company. A commission of October 1445 indicates that Manchon was authorized to receive the revenues "of curacies situated within the diocese of Rouen, of which the pastors are absent and living outside the jurisdiction of the king." Manchon appears among the witnesses at Joan's condemnation trial. He delivered to the judges of the nullification trial the minutes of the earlier trial and testified before them in 1450, 1452, and 1456. He testified prudently, blaming Cauchon and the English.

63. JEAN MASSIEU

Jean Massieu served as usher during the condemnation trial. On October 11, 1430, the city of Rouen recognized a debt of 7 livres and 10 sous, a sum that he evidently had loaned to the city. He is called the dean of la Chrétienté of Rouen in 1431: according to Quicherat this means that he was syndic of the priests of the diocesan jurisdiction known as the deanery of la Chrétienté. On February 3, 1431, Jean Massieu was fined for receiving money in the cemetery of the cathedral, exempt from the bishop's jurisdiction. Massieu made many trips to Basel on the business of the "liberties of the church"; in 1434 he was sent there to locate a malefactor. At one point Jean Massieu and Thomas Milton, chaplain of the lord of Fauquembergue, were charged with displaying bad manners. Massieu, then priest of the parish of Saint-Maclou, was later prosecuted for misconduct. He is referred to as a canon and pastor of Saint Cande-le-Vieux in a document of Pierre Cauchon's endowing the cult of the Holy Eucharist—perhaps the Corpus Christi celebrations—with 300 livres (1450).

Jean Massieu was a witness at the nullification trial on December 17, 1455. He is described in that transcript as approximately fifty years of age. He denounced the English for their hatred of Joan and accused Pierre Cauchon of extreme docility toward them.

64. PIERRE MAURICE

Pierre Maurice won first place among candidates for the theological license at the University of Paris in January 1429 and was first among those taking the master's degree on May 23 of the same year. On January 2, 1430, a letter of Henry VI named him to a canonicate in the cathedral of Rouen, which an Englishman named Heton had resigned in his favor.

This young theologian was already strongly tied to the English government; he had obtained from Henry VI the benefice of Saint-Sebastien-de-Préaux in the diocese of Lisieux. He was pastor of Yerville and exchanged that benefice for that of the chapel of Saint Pierre in the cathedral of Rouen; he was, in addition, pastor of Paluel and also chaplain of the chapel of Saint Mathurin at the cathedral. On June 5, 1430, he was chosen by the canons to speak in their name at the ceremonies celebrating the entry of Henry VI into the cathedral. He was also elected (on December 3) to plead with Cardinal Beaufort on behalf of Louis of Luxembourg's candidacy for the vacant archbishopric of Rouen. He was further delegated in 1431 to accompany Pasquier de Vaux, ambassador of the English king, to Rome. He went to Basel in 1434 as ambassador of Henry VI and the following year to England at the order of the council of Basil. Named vicar-general on December 5, 1436, he died shortly afterward. The thirty-two precious manuscripts that he owned at his death were willed to the library of the chapter of Rouen; among them were a Terence, a Virgil, a Vegetius, and a beautiful breviary that was purchased by Louis of Luxembourg.

This highly educated theologian was very active in the trial and displayed a great deal of fervor in attempting to enlighten Joan.

65. NICOLAS MIDY

Nicolas Midy, a Paris licentiate in theology in 1424, was named canon of Rouen cathedral by Henry VI on April 21, 1431, and was installed there eleven days before Joan's execution at the stake. On June 11 the canons accorded him remission of the right of annates, as they had in the case of Jean Beaupère, "by special grace, because of the services he had rendered the church." Nicolas Midy greeted King Henry VI upon his entry into Paris in December 1431, as a representative of the University of Paris. He was sent to the Council of Basel in 1432. (Out of regard for the regent, the duke of Bedford, the chapter of Rouen decided on May 12, 1432, that

while he was away at the council, Midy should receive his disbursements as if he were present.) In 1433 Midy became rector of the University of Louvain. Sometime around 1434 he contracted leprosy and had to resign all his commissions and his canonicate, although he retained their revenues. Midy was still living on November 8, 1438.

A convinced partisan of the Anglo-Burgundian cause (in 1416 he had debated with the Norman Nation at the university in favor of the propositions of Jean Petit), Midy was a fanatic supporter of the University of Paris, where he served as rector. His leprosy was interpreted from an early date as a sign of divine punishment for his role in Joan's trial, since he had been the author of the Twelve Articles that formed a summary of Joan's "doctrine" and he was one of Bedford's confidants.

66. PIERRE MIGET

Pierre Miget or Muguet, a Benedictine and doctor of theology, was prior of Longueville-Giffard. He won his licentiate at Paris in 1413 and then became regent master in theology. In 1414 at the Council of Paris he showed himself a zealous partisan of the Burgundian cause, sustaining the propositions of Jean Petit. Henry V restored to him the revenues of his benefice in 1420. He seems to have been strongly linked to Jean Beaupère, who in 1434 entrusted to him the administration of his diocese; the two are also listed together among the masters of the faculty of theology from 1421 on.

Pierre Miget's permanent residence at Rouen was the Hôtel de Longueville, near the gates of the archbishop's palace. Miget was very assiduous and not inclined toward Joan. He testified as a witness at the nullification trial in 1452: In his testimony he claimed to have wept at Joan's execution, of which he had been one of the supporters, and further testified that the sentence rendered against the Maid was unjust. He seriously accused the bishop of Beauvais, whom he had so strongly favored only twenty years earlier, and is thus a prime instance of the dubiety of much of the trial testimony.

67. JEAN DE RINEL

Jean de Rinel was the notary of the Grand Council and secretary to the king of England. His wife was Jeanne Bidault, sister of Jean Bidault, archdeacon of Auge and the cathedral of Lisieux, canon of Rouen and nephew of Pierre Cauchon. Jean de

Rinel was present at a dinner offered by the chapter of Rouen in 1413. He signed two orders of the duke of Bedford, one in 1424 and another in 1428. On May 25, 1437, he received a prebend from Jean d'Estivet, the procurator, as canon of Beauvais cathedral. On September 3, 1434, he was described as the king's secretary and received 4 livres a day as his regular salary in the course of a trip he was about to make from Vire to Savigny to meet Richard Venables and other men-at-arms and yeomen who were at the abbey of Savigny. He also accompanied his uncle-in-law, Pierre Cauchon, in 1439 when he went to England. He had been in the king's service for twenty-four years in 1443 and received ten gold nobles to consecrate to pious work. His great house was situated on the rue de la Chaine at Rouen, the present-day rue des Carmes.

68. RAOUL ROUSSEL

Raoul Roussel, born at Saultchevreuil near Villedieu, licentiate in law in 1416, was dean of the faculty of law at Paris from November 1417 to January 1419 and was elected canon of Rouen cathedral in 1420. A staunch defender of canonical prerogatives, he was elected treasurer the following year and made a deputy to the regent, the duke of Bedford, in order to obtain permission to proceed with the election of an archbishop. In 1424 Raoul Roussel was sent by Bedford on a mission to Bedford's brother Humphrey, duke of Gloucester, to pacify the quarrel between the latter and the duke of Brabant. Roussel even performed military missions at times, since in August, 1428 in the capacity of master of petitions, he gave a receipt to Pierre Surreau, receiver-general of Normandy, for an inspection of fortresses in lower Normandy. On November 7, 1429, his procurator declared to the chapter of Notre Dame of Paris that he would accept the canonicate of the late Jean Gerson, who had remained faithful to the Valois cause.

Canon of Coutances cathedral, vicar-general at Rouen during the archiepiscopal vacancy (1429–1443), counselor, master of petitions of the

English king with a salary of at first 200 and later 300 livres, Roussel was twice ambassador to the French party (1435, 1438). He succeeded the cardinal of Luxembourg as archbishop of Rouen in 1444, but he took the oath of fealty to Charles VII when that monarch entered Rouen. Roussel died December 31, 1452.

Roussel was among the most zealous of the condemnation trial's judges and actively adhered to the opinion of the University of Paris and the theologians. He was most likely present at the preliminary investigations of the nullification process. As a strict legalist, he considered the first trial to have been well conducted; he had advised Cauchon that it was essential not to employ torture, lest it bring the proceedings into bad repute.

69. NICOLAS DE VENDERÈS

Nicolas de Venderès, lord of Beausseré, was born about 1372. Licentiate in law, he swore fidelity to Henry V. He was received as a canon in the cathedral of Rouen in 1422 and was made arch-deacon of Eu. He was one of the first Norman ecclesiastics to adhere to the English government—his name appears in a treaty between the city of Rouen and Henry V (January 13, 1419). The vicar of Archbishop Louis d'Harcourt with a salary of 120 livres (1412–1422) and vicar *sede vacante* (1429–1431), he was nearly elected archbishop of Rouen after the death of Louis d'Harcourt (having received the votes of a majority) and for a while he was treated as such. Nicolas de Venderès was also the pastor of Gisors. He died at Rouen on August 1, 1438. André Marguerie, Nicolas Caval, and Jean Mahommet, priest, also among Joan's judges, were all executors of Nicolas's will (*Archives de la Seine Inférieure G.* 2089). Venderès acquitted himself with zeal at the Maid's trial: He was a friend of Pierre Cauchon, and judged as did his masters in the matter of the Twelve Articles. Like Raoul Roussel at the time of Joan's relapse, he contended that the trial had lasted too long.

ISSUES AND IMAGES

THREE

THE FOLLOWING SKETCHES represent a small but representative selection from the diverse and ample stock of issues and images we have inherited from the life and times of Joan of Arc. Some provide us with factual clarification about matters concerning Joan. Others reveal to us how complex—and incapable of resolution on the basis of our present knowledge—many of the issues associated with Joan remain. There are other, equally knotty issues debated by historians. What, for example, was the content and political consequence of Joan's first trial—the Poitiers trial—and why did the record of that trial disappear? (On this see Wood, "Joan of Arc's Mission and the Lost Record of Her Interrogation at Poitiers.") Was Joan's "mission" to France in any way prompted by a desire to flee marriage? What was the message Joan brought to the dauphin Charles at Chinon on March 5, 1429? How can, and may, we assess the physics of communication represented by Joan's "voices"? Is Joan the last medieval Catholic or the forerunner of Protestantism? Perhaps the most thoroughly analyzed but persistently complicated issue of Joan's ordinary life is the matter of her cross-dressing, for which see Valerie R. Hotchkiss, *Clothes Make the Man: Female Cross Dressing in Medieval Europe* and articles by Susan Schibanoff and Steven Weiskopf in *Fresh Verdicts on Joan of Arc.*

The latter section of this part concerns Joan's afterlife in history, literature, folklore, and art. She is a potent, vibrant, and teasing source of image-making from her own time to ours. Those images have been adoring as well as deprecating, sentimental as well as harsh, and romanticized as well as taut. Most of all, they continue to fascinate.

1. JOAN'S NAME

"In my country, people called me Jeannette, but they called me Jeanne when I came into France," Joan answered during the first session of the condemnation trial when asked to state her name and forename (*nomen et cognomen*).

Joan herself never heard the name "Jeanne d'Arc." As a general rule, in the fifteenth century, people used only forenames, adding a place name (of residence or of origin) and only occasionally surnames. Joan's mother, Isabelle, is called Isabelle Romée in the texts, a surname given her because she had completed a pilgrimage. Joan added that girls in her region were called by the name of their mother. Nevertheless she called herself "Jeanne la Pucelle" (Joan the Maid). La Pucelle was her chosen surname; she gloried in this epithet, declaring chastity the sign of her mission.

In the letter she dictated to the English on March 22, 1429, at Poitiers, this is the way she addressed the regent Bedford and his lieutenants: "Surrender to the Maid, who is sent here by God . . . and believe firmly that the King of Heaven will send the Maid yet more force." On May 5, 1429, in an ultimatum to the English, her scribe wrote as she dictated: "The king of heaven warns and commands you through me, Joan the Maid."

In letters to the inhabitants of Tournai on June 22, 1429, to those of Troyes on July 4 in the same year, and to Philip the Good, duke of Burgundy, on July 17, 1429, she consistently called herself Joan the Maid. The inhabitants of Reims in August 1429 and the count of Armagnac on the twenty-second of that month also knew her by that designation. All three surviving letters signed by Joan's hand are signed "Jehanne." The men of the Armagnac party, the bourgeois of Orléans, and her companions at arms all knew her as Joan the Maid. To her enemies, that was her name. The duke of Bedford called her the Pucelle. To the duke of Burgundy, she was "the one they call the Maid"; to her worst enemy, Cauchon, she was "Jehanne whom they call the Maid"; and to the University of Paris, she was "mulier quae Johannam se nominabat" [the woman who called herself Joan].

Whether they sided with the Armagnacs or the Burgundians, the chroniclers of the time never used "Joan of Arc"—not Jean Chartier, nor William Caxton, nor the anonymous author of the *Journal of the Siege of Orléans*, nor Antonio Morosini, nor Georges Chastellain. To Christine de Pisan and François Villon, she was "the Maid," "Joan the good Lorrainer," "the Maid of France," or "the Maid of God."

Historians encounter the name "Joan of Arc" for the first time in the opening documents of the nullification trial. In 1455 Pope Calixtus III named her brothers "Pierre and Jean Darc, and their sister *quondam* [once known as] Johanna Darc." The archbishop of Reims also mentioned the Darc family, "Isabelle Darc, Pierre and Jean Darc, mother and brothers *defunctae quondam Jeannae Darc, vulgariter dictae la Pucelle* [of the deceased former Joan Darc, popularly called the Maid]." Also in the family's petition one reads, "Ysabellis Darc, mater quondam Johannae vulgariter dictae la Pucelle" [Isabelle Darc, mother of the deceased Joan, popularly called the Maid]. The expression "Maid of Orléans" first made its appearance in the sixteenth century. The first great biography of Joan, that of Edmond Richer, appeared in 1630 with the title *Histoire de Jeanne, la Pucelle d'Orléans*.

The historians Quicherat, Siméon Luce, Ayroles, and Champion wrote the patronymic of Joan's father and brothers as "d'Arc." In his translation of the condemnation trial, Pierre Tisset followed the form "d'Arc." In his translation of the nullification process, Pierre Duparc also used what had become the conventional usage.

The original texts, however, use an extraordinary variety of forms: "Darc" or "d'Arc," but also "Dars," "Day," "Dai," "Darx," "Dare," "Tarc," "Tard," or "Dart." In Joan's time, no standard form seems to have existed. Never in the fifteenth century do we find an apostrophe. "Dalebret," "Dalençon," and "Dolon" were written as unbroken words. Modern spelling introduced *d'* with the connotation of local origin or membership in the nobility. Thus, we find "duc d'Alençon," "duc d'Armagnac," and so on for princely personages, whereas the forms "Jean d'Aulon," "Jean d'Auvergne," "Guillaume d'Estivet," and the like indicate merely local origin.

Scholarship on the family of the Maid takes two directions in which Joan receives either a popular or an aristocratic origin and designation. In chapter 2 of his *Traité sommaire tant du nom et des armes que la naissance et la parenté de la Pucelle d'Orléans et de ses frères, fait en octobre 1612 et revu en 1628* [Summary Treatise as Much on the Name and the Arms as on the Birth and Kinship of the Maid of Orléans and of Her Brothers, Done in October 1612 and Revised in 1628], Charles du Lys wrote that "the very arms of the parents and other descendants of the aforesaid Jacques Darc, carried a bow (*arc* in French) with three arrows . . . ," although we might note that Joan's collateral descendants simply wrote *Darc* without an apostrophe. Bouquet (in

"Faut-il écrire J. Darc ou J. d'Arc?" *Travaux de l'Académie de Rouen*, 1865) pointed out that "[Charles du Lys] an enlightened man, petitioning Louis XIII so as to obtain permission to join the arms of the eldest branch of that family to his own, never neglects in the *Treatise*—composed to justify his request—to separate the particle of his own name *Du Lys*; if he did not one single time put an apostrophe in *Darc* that is because he could not legitimately do so."

Some—such as the Baron de Coston in "Origines éthimologiques et signification des noms propres et des armoiries"—attribute to Joan's father a coat of arms "azure charged with or in fess," which would give her family a noble origin. But why would Charles VII have ennobled the family without giving them arms marked with his own? It was the custom, especially of the Valois kings, to award coats of arms with the fleur-de-lys of the royal house figuring somewhere in the blazoning. Punning arms (a gold "arc" for a family named "Darc") were uncommon before a family was ennobled; they were normally the products of a later imagination.

In *Nouvelles Littéraires* 1198 (1950), Père Doncoeur concluded:

> In our opinion, without any further proof, the form Darc has no reason to be broken down into *d'Arc*. The Latin texts in which this latter word is found constitute firm proof to the contrary. If the patronymic indicated a place of origin, the name of the place in Latin would have been preceded by the particle *de*. Thus, Guillaume Destouteville was written in Latin *de Estoutevilla*, Guillaume Destivet would be written *de Estiveto*, Georges d'Amboise would be written *de Ambasia* or *Ambasianus*. Jacques d'Arc would have been written in Latin *de Arco,* as was the case in 1343 of a Pierre Darc, canon of Troyes, who was listed as *Petrus de Arco*.

As to the apostrophe, which to some conveys an aristocratic connotation, the contrary conclusion of the *Moniteur du soir* in 1866 on the subject of the proper way to spell the name of Joan's father can be cited: "The result of all this research then is that the form *Darc* is preferable to any other, as it conforms most closely to etymological rules and to the popular origin of a young woman who made it famous by her courage and her patriotism!"

One interesting note: In the French transcript of her condemnation trial, preserved at Orléans, Joan's father's name is written *Jacques Tart*, no doubt in an effort to record the harsh plosive dentality of the Lorraine dialect.

2. JOAN'S FAMILY

Described during Joan's nullification trial as "honest husbandmen," "good Catholics," people of "honest demeanor according to their station," Joan's parents belonged to the peasant class and were neither rich nor poor.

From an act of October 7, 1423, when Joan was eleven, we know that Jacques Darc, a native of nearby Ceffonds, had been chosen to serve as doyen of the village of Domrémy. In that capacity, he was required to promulgate decrees of the village council and of higher authorities, to command the watch day and night, to guard prisoners, and to collect taxes, rents, and dues. It was also his responsibility to supervise not only the weights and measures used in the village but also the production of bread and wine. In another act (March 31, 1427) the villagers of Domrémy named him their proctor in a suit they had lodged with Robert de Baudricourt.

Joan's parents had about twenty hectares (roughly fifty acres) of land in the village, of which twelve hectares (nearly thirty acres) were fields—either plowland or meadow—and four were woodland. They owned their house and their furniture, and had some money in reserve. Despite the modesty of their income, they were able to receive and lodge travelers passing through the area. Jacques Darc and his wife, Isabelle, paid the parish priest of Domrémy an annual rent of 2 *gros* for the right to one and a half mowings (of straw, presumably) in other fields of the village belonging to the church; in return, the priest agreed to celebrate two masses every year during the "week of the Fountains" for the intentions of the family.

Isabelle Romée's background is well known. She was the daughter of a modest family of Vouthon, a neighboring village that belonged to the duchy of Bar, a dependency of the crown of France. Isabelle's brother Jean de Vouthon was a roofer; around 1416 he moved to nearby Sermaise. Their sister Aveline had a daughter, Jeanne de Vauseul (Joan's first cousin), who later married Durand Laxart (see I, 3). Another of Isabelle's brothers, Henri de Vouthon, became the parish priest at Sermaise.

Jean Darc, known as Petit-Jean, fled with his sister to Neufchâteau, accompanied her to France, and was lodged at the house of Jacques Boucher at Orléans. He was ennobled in December 1429. Perplexingly, he claimed to recognize his sister in the person of Claude des Armoises at Metz in 1436 and demanded gratuities from the city of Orléans. Later when he was provost of Vaucouleurs, he worked for the nullification of the verdict against his sister, appeared at Rouen and Paris, and formed a commission to get evidence from their native district and to produce witnesses. He was bailiff of the Vermandois and captain of Chartres and was discharged from the provostship of Vaucouleurs in 1468.

Another brother, Pierre, went to seek his sister "in France," fought along with her at Orléans, lived in the same house with her in that city, accompanied her to Reims, and was ennobled with the rest of the family. He was captured with Joan at Compiègne. He declared, as did Jean, that he recognized his sister at Metz (1436); he received many gifts from the king, the city of Orléans, and Duke Charles, among them the Ile-aux-Bouefs in 1443.

Several families have claimed descent from Joan's brothers. Jean du Lys (the ancestor claimed by the Charles du Lys mentioned above) was the son of Joan's brother Pierre, who moved to Orléans. Tradition maintains that Joan's eldest brother Jacquemin died without issue, although some have tried to establish the contrary. In the nineteenth century, the Braux and Bouteiller families attempted to prove their descent from Jacquemin, as did Henri Morel in 1927. The skepticism of Georges Marante, president of the Lorraine Genealogical Society is noteworthy: "For thirty years I worked closely with Colonel Paul de Haldat du Lys on a register of the nobility of Ligny-en-Barrois. At the end of his life, the colonel confided to me that the deeper he went in his research, the more he doubted his kinship to the Maid."

3. JOAN AS ROYAL BASTARD

On a regular and well-publicized basis, authors announce "newly discovered documents" proving either that Joan of Arc was the illegitimate daughter of Isabeau of Bavaria and Louis of Orléans, and consequently the half sister of Charles VII (the "bastardizers"), or that she escaped the stake thanks to a conspiracy of Pierre Cauchon, the duke of Bedford, and the earl of Warwick, who put someone else in her place (the "survivalists").

Such authors repeat one another unimaginatively. Some recite pseudodemonstrations from the seventeenth and eighteenth centuries; others disinter the allegations of Pierre Caze, subprefect of Bergerac, who published in 1805 the first book claiming that Joan of Arc was the illegitimate daughter of Isabeau of Bavaria.

Although firmly refuted, the thesis of Joan's bastardy has enjoyed currency since the nine-

teenth century. According to this theory, Queen Isabeau of Bavaria, wife of Charles VI, was the mistress of Louis of Orléans, her brother-in-law, by whom she had a girl who was hidden from birth at Domrémy with the Darc family. Louis was assassinated on November 23, 1407. At her trial, Joan would therefore had to have been at least twenty-four, not nineteen as she affirmed. Isabeau, however, delivered on November 10, 1407, a son, Philip, who died the same day. Jean would have had to be conceived in the intervening 13 days. Even if physiologically possible, that would certainly have indicated an extreme indecency of haste even for a woman as profligate as Isabeau was accused by her enemies of being.

Those who argue for Joan's royal bastardy by default accuse her of perjury. During the condemnation trial, Joan swore on the gospels, when asked her place of birth and the names of her parents, that she was born at Domrémy and that "her father was named Jacques Darc and her mother Isabelle." At the nullification trial, Isabelle Romée demanded that the Rouen sentence be set aside in favor of her "daughter born in legitimate marriage." All the evidence given in that lengthy trial, including the depositions of godparents and neighbors, testifies that Joan was born at Domrémy of Jacques Darc and Isabelle Romée. Yet amateur historians still insist that all these people—as well as Charles VII, the duke of Alençon, Dunois, Bertrand de Poulengy—carried out an intricate plot to disguise Joan's authentic royal parents. This thesis lacks credible documentation.

4. THE LANGUAGE OF JOAN OF ARC AND HER CONTEMPORARIES

When Seguin Seguin, one of her judges at Poitiers, asked Joan in what language her voice spoke, she answered, "Better than yours!" Seguin explained later that he spoke the Limousin dialect with a pronounced accent, evidently considered inferior to the French of Sts. Catherine, Margaret, and Michael.

Even from the testimony of the nullification trial, we can glean certain characteristic expressions that the Maid employed. Jean Pasquerel, her confessor, reported her response to Glasdale's speech: "Glasidas, rends-ti, rends-ti, au roi du ciel!" [Glasidas, surrender, surrender to the King of Heaven!] We also know from her letter of March 16, 1430, to the people of Reims that she pronounced j or y as ch, because the clerk, having misunderstood her word "joyeux," wrote "choy-eux." Then taking note of Joan's accent, he struck it out and wrote it correctly. The favorite interjection of hers repeated by Aimond de Macy and by Colette, wife of Millet, "en nom Dé," was an expression typical of people from Lorraine. Dunois, a native of the Orléanais, was given to saying "fille Dé,*" that is, "daughter of God."

Joan spoke basic French, but with a strong Lorraine accent that survives to our day. In the dialect of Lorraine, an *i* is often added at the end of words, and *é* is pronounced closed. According to Pierre Marot's *Jeanne la bonne Lorraine à Domrémy*, "Domrémy, that borderland of the upper Meuse, whether in the territory of the French kingdom or the Empire, was French in customs and in language; its Romance speech was marked by influences from Champagne as were its institutions and its art."

From the fourteenth century, according to Philippe Contamine in *La vie quotidienne pendant la guerre de Cent Ans en France et en Angleterre*, the dialect of the Français proper, that is, the inhabitants of Paris and the Ile-de-France, prevailed in the upper strata of society, and that speech soon extended to the entire royal administration. In everyday business, the *langue d'oil* was spoken in the north of France in several dialects (including that of Lorraine and the official dialect of Paris) and the *langue d'oc* was spoken in the south. Certain regions—Brittany, Gascony, and the Basque country—preserved their own distinct languages; Flemish was spoken in Flanders and in the region around Boulogne and Calais. In the south of France, the dialects of *langue d'oc* most widely spoken were the Limousin (*lemosi*) and the Provençal (*prouensal*). They were popular tongues, used only occasionally in formal documents. Latin was an official language, as was the king's language, the Français of Paris. Latin continued to dominate in administrative and juridical documents in the fourteenth and fifteenth centuries.

In England, the dialect of London and the Midlands became the official, unifying language in the fourteenth century. From the Norman Conquest into the fourteenth century, the Anglo-Norman dialect was widely spoken, and that peculiar form of French enjoyed social and cultural preeminence until the English of the capital city finally replaced it by the late fourteenth century. As Philippe Contamine tells us, somewhere between 1300 and 1324, the anonymous author of the *Cursor mundi* proclaimed, "I have drawn up this book so that it could be read in the English language and through love of the English people of England. . . . Let us leave everyone his own language, that would do no one

wrong." Edward III (1327–1377) required that trials be conducted in English and then registered in Latin; in 1363 a parliament opened at Westminster in the English language for the first time. The next king, Richard II, spoke English but also understood French well. The decisive change was completed under the Lancastrian dynasty, whose members spoke only English. The group that took longest to adopt English for their official business were the brewers of London, who began using it in their administrative documents only in 1422.

By then France and England each had its own language, and each wished at least in part to define itself thereby. Henry V ordered that the Treaty of Troyes be translated into English so that it might be known in England; he and Salisbury addressed the burgesses of London in English to announce their victories and to request subsidies. In a letter to Henry VI, Bedford used that language, thoroughly seasoned, however, with French words, to attribute his defeats to the intervention of the Maid:

And Alle thing there prospered for you, til the tyme of the siege of Orleans taken in hand, God knoweth by what advis. At the whiche tyme, after the adventure fallen to the persone of my cousin of Salisbury, whom God assoille [forgive all his sins], there felle, by the hand of God, as it seemeth, a greet strook upon your peuple that was assembled there in grete nombre, caused in grete partie, as y trowe, of lakke of sadde beleve, and of unlevefulle doubte that thei hadde of a disciple and lyme of the Feende, called the Pucelle, that used fals enchauntements and sorcerie. The which strooke and discomfiture nought oonly lessed in grete partie the nombre of youre people.

In such military documents as indentures, formulas varied, depending on whether they were written in England by an English scribe or in France by a French secretary who transcribed as much as he could understand. According to *La langue employée dans les documents anglais de la guerre de France au moment du siège d'Orléans* (Bulletin de la Société Historique et Archéologique de l'Orléanais, 1982), respect for the national language grew, in part, because it facilitated "the relations of the conquerors with the conquered populations whose self-respect it treated carefully. It allowed the use of functionaries and scribes from the country without requiring that they come from beyond the Channel." That is why we find a certain number of French scribes in the English army. While in France, the English tried to adopt French bit by bit in military documents and usually had their names transcribed in a French form. John of Pothe, for example, became Jehan Avothe and then Jean Abote. The descendants of the companions of William the Conqueror also had their names translated, as was the case with William, Alexander, and John Pole, who became La Poule and de la Poule.

Marie-Véronique Clin-Meyer, in *Le registre de comptes de Richard Beauchamp, comte de Warwick, 14 mars 1431–15 mars 1432,* provides other example of the mixture of French, English, and Anglo-Norman as it appears in the language used by the manager of the household of Warwick at Rouen in 1431 and 1432. His daily notations in the account books impart precious information on linguistic coexistence as well as on the people received at the table of Richard Beauchamp. We find such phrases as "Venerunt Madame Talbot cum 1 damicella, 1 scutifero; 2 marchaunts ville" [Madame Talbot came with one female attendant and one esquire; two merchants of the city] and "Item expense: un panyer makerelles, 4 sole empta . . . 50 crevey" [and so there were bought one basket of mackerels and four soles . . . and fifty crawfish].

In addition, Joan's limpid skills as an orator deserve note. She is recorded in the condemnation trial, and her speech is reported in the nullification trial. She is disarming in her straightforwardness: Her speech is direct, her grammar paratactic, her manner unabashed. The effect is that of understated eloquence.

5. JOAN'S ARMOR

After the inquest at Poitiers, Charles VII commissioned a suit of armor for Joan at the same time that he set up a military household for her. The accounts of the treasurer Hémon Reguier refer to the purchase of that suit of armor in April 1429: "100 livres tournois were paid and delivered by the aforesaid treasurer to the master armorer for a complete harness for the aforesaid Maid." With this harness, Joan was then equipped in the same fashion as the men-at-arms of her era. Jean Chartier reported that she was "armed as quickly as possible with a complete harness such as would have suited a knight who was part of the army and was born in the king's court." She was equipped, moreover, like knights of a certain rank: 100 livres tournois was a significant sum. It has been estimated that the purchase of a complete set of military equipment corresponded to two years' wages for a man-at-arms.

A piece of armor that may well have belonged to Joan is the bassinet (shallow helmet) now displayed in the Metropolitan Museum in New York. It comes from the Dino-Talleyrand-Périgord collection and was formerly kept as a votive object in the church of Saint-Pierre-du-Martroi at Orléans. Bassinets at that time were considered "defenses"—that is, protections independent of the rest of a suit of armor. The term "harness" designated the diverse garments of war; to be more precise, one spoke about armor "of the head" or "of the arm." Every piece was independent, as attested in the account books of the armorers, from whom pieces were ordered separately: a leg harness, an arm harness, a gauntlet, and so on. In the inventory of the castle of Amboise, the "head defense" was a mail gorget (collar) with a "gilded border." According to Jean-Pierre Reverseau, director of the Musée de l'Armée in Paris, this description applied to a bassinet: The "gilded border" could correspond either to the decorative trimmings around Joan's bassinet or to the rows of brass rings that made up the border of the mail gorget. The contrast between the color of the brass and the blue of the gorget—for steel items of that sort were generally given a bluish cast—was much admired at the time. The sallet, another head protection, was the most common item of armament. It was fitted with a small movable visor, a slightly accentuated neck cover, and, on the top, a crest that stood out from the rest of the helmet. Joan made use also of a *capeline,* a steel hat equipped with a wide brim, frequently used when scaling fortifications. But her contemporaries remarked that she often went about with her head bare, which was hardly surprising since military commanders of high rank often wore a simple hood or a hat rather than a helmet.

Joan also wore a military garment of Oriental origin, made of rectangular metal plates (usually of steel)—the *jaseran,* which was widely used in the fourteenth century. She also wore a *brigandine,* an armed vest made of a great number of small plates of metal joined by rivets, the heads of which formed a kind of geometric design. The right arm was protected in a lighter fashion than the left, so that a sword or lance could be wielded more freely. The armor of the left arm, by contrast, was folded back to assist in holding the horse's reins. Jean-Pierre. Reverseau, in his *Armement au temps de Jeanne d'Arc* from the Orléans Conference of November 1984, informs us that these pieces of armor were ornamented with "tensely elongated" decorations responding to the aesthetic ideal of the time, which subordinated function to late Gothic style.

In the fifteenth century, the greatest armorers were Milanese, whose work spread from one end of Europe to the other. Christine de Pisan described on several occasions the harness that King Charles V had made for himself in Milan. Many details describing the manufacture of this Milanese armor can be found in the archives of the Datini armory firm.

Infantrymen armed with two-edged swords, archers, and in general most foot soldiers all wore a jacket, a garment of cloth quilted together with leather and laced up in front, or then a brigandine, and protected their limbs by harness and their head by a sallet. They fought with a halberd or a pike, or with a hammer to break up the harnesses of their opponents.

Whether Joan's armor survives remains an unresolved question. Jean-Pierre Reverseau observed in *Les armes et la vie* (Paris, 1982) that "every twenty years, Joan of Arc's suit of armor is rediscovered." A recent rediscovery was announced in the spring of 1996 by Pierre de Souzy, a Paris antiquarian. In the inventory of ancient arms at the castle of Amboise in 1499, we find this entry under *cote* 31: "harness of the Maid, equipped with cloth covering, with a pair of gauntlets, with outfitting for the head including a gorget of mail, gilded on the edge, the inside lined with a double thickness of crimson satin." That this was in fact the armor Joan wore is far from certain, but her equipment could have been so described. The chroniclers and witnesses at the nullification trial agreed on further details. In their depositions, her page Louis de Coutes, the duke of Alençon, and Jean d'Aulon all affirm that "for the safety of her body the aforesaid lord had made for the aforesaid Maid, her own suit of armor fitted to her aforesaid body." The registrar of the city hall of Albi, who saw her, testified that "Joan went armed in white iron, entirely from head to foot." Moreover, Guy and André de Laval saw her on horseback near Romorantin "armed entirely in white, except for the head, a little ax in her hand, seated on a great black courser."

6. JOAN'S SWORD

From the text of Joan's condemnation trial (Tisset, 2.52), we know that Robert de Baudricourt gave her a sword when she left Vaucouleurs: "Also, she confessed that after her departure from the aforesaid town of Vaucouleurs she was in men's clothes, carrying a sword that Robert de Baudricourt had given her, without any other arm, accompanied by a knight, a squire, and four servants." She later sent for a second sword

hidden behind the altar of Sainte-Catherine-de-Fierbois: "She said also that while she was at Tours or at Chinon she sent men to find a sword, which was found in the church of Sainte-Catherine-de-Fierbois behind the altar; and immediately thereafter they found it, all covered with rust."

Joan's inquisitors asked how she knew the sword would be found there and recorded this reply:

> That sword was in the earth, rusted, bearing five engraved crosses; she knew from her voices that this sword was there, and she had never seen the man who went to find the aforesaid sword for her, and she wrote to the men of the church of that place that she hoped it would please them that she should have that sword, and they sent it to her. It was not very deeply buried underground, behind the altar; she did not know if it would be exactly before the altar or behind it. She said again that just after the sword was found the men of the church gave it a good rubbing, and thereupon the rust fell off without effort; it was an armorer of Tours who went to find it; . . . for their part, the men of the church of Sainte-Catherine-de-Fierbois gave her a sheath, as did the people of Tours; she had therefore two sheaths, one of vermeil velvet and the other of cloth-of-gold, and she herself had one made in heavy leather, very strong. . . . When she was captured, it was not that sword that she was wearing but the sword that she had taken from a Burgundian.

"The sword that she had taken from a Burgundian" was the third one Joan possessed. We know also that she had a fourth taken from yet another Burgundian, along with the armor she offered to Saint-Denis. Asked where that fourth sword was, she replied "that she had offered in the abbey of Saint-Denis a sword and some arms." Pressed further, she was reported as explaining that "there is no point in seeking to find out what she did with the sword found at Sainte-Catherine-de-Fierbois and that has nothing to do with the trial and that she will not answer on that point for now." Beyond these, the duke of Burgundy (surprisingly enough) had sent her a dagger after the liberation of Orléans, and "the city of Clermont had made her the gift of two swords and one dagger."

Some witnesses in the nullification trial claimed that one day she broke her sword on the back of a woman at Auxerre or at Saint-Denis, but Louis de Coutes contradicted them explicitly in his deposition: "She did not wish women to be with the army, and once, near Château-Thierry, having noticed a wanton woman, she chased her, with her sword drawn, but she did not hit her, limiting herself to counseling her with gentleness and charity not to be found again in the company of men-at-arms, or she herself, Joan, would take measures against her."

A sword now kept at Dijon, on which are engraved the names of Charles VII and of Vaucouleurs with the arms of France and of Orléans, is often cited as a relic of Joan of Arc, but Doncoeur (1.227 in the Collection of the Centre Jeanne d'Arc) argues that this sword was probably engraved in the sixteenth century by members of the Catholic League—an association of religious fanatics opposed to the danger they perceived in a Protestant king—who had great reverence for Joan. For an analysis of Joan's Fierbois sword and its importance, see Bonnie Wheeler, "Joan of Arc's Sword in the Stone," in *Fresh Verdicts on Joan of Arc*.

7. ORLÉANS AT THE TIME OF THE SIEGE

When English troops caught sight of Orléans on October 12, 1428, they found themselves before one of the most beautiful cities of the kingdom, a strong place surrounded by ramparts reinforced by towers constructed at regular intervals.

Site of the ancient Gallo-Roman city of Cenabum Aurelianense, to which the old suburb of Avenum had been added in the fourteenth century, Orléans in 1345 became the capital of a duchy erected as an apanage by Philip VI of Valois for his second son, Philip. Upon the younger Philip's death in 1375, the duchy was joined again to the royal domain; in 1392 it was made an apanage for the second time, in favor of Louis, brother of King Charles VI. This time, however, the people of Orléans insisted upon their rights and succeeded in obtaining a charter of liberties, by virtue of which they were allowed to elect a twelve-man council in a two-phase election.

Louis of Orléans knew how to make himself popular. In 1393 he gave a brilliant festival in celebration of the birth of his son to which he invited the procurators of his capital city. Flattered magistrates arrived, bearing as a gift from the appreciative populace "several geese and fourteen measures of tripe" all in a great sack, as Lemaire quotes the account book of the city of Orléans in his *Histoire d'Orléans*. It was on that occasion that Louis of Orléans created the Order of the Porcupine, with which he decorated several of the ranking magistrates of the city. The duke's

ceremonial entries into his city were also important festival days for the people of Orléans. They hung carpets and curtains and garlands of flowers from windows; they set up fountains spouting wine, milk, or perfumed water at the crossroads.

Orléans relied on its duke for protection. From the middle of the fourteenth century, its situation had been difficult. In 1358 the English commander Robert Knowles surrounded the city and provoked a panic. In 1367 the troops of the Black Prince had terrorized the populace; the collegial churches and chapels of the suburbs outside the walls had been torn down; and many buildings had suffered from this onslaught, including the church of Saint-Euverte— destroyed by the Vikings in the ninth century, it was reconstructed but destroyed in 1358 and again in 1428, when the English laid siege to the city. The troubles seemed at their worst in 1380, thanks to the campaign of the duke of Buckingham. The people of Orléans turned toward Louis as their natural protector. They attended closely to their defense, as the account books of the fortress and the commune attest.

The ramparts and its five gates underwent regular maintenance: the Gate of Burgundy, through which ran the road to Gien; the Paris Gate, situated close to the Hôtel-Dieu (the central hospital), which would be walled up at the moment of the siege of 1428 and would serve only as a pedestrian passageway; the Bernier Gate, which guarded the route to Paris; the Renard Gate, near which was situated the residence of Jacques Boucher, where Joan would be housed and through which ran the road to Blois; and the St. Catherine Gate on the docks, connecting with the bridgehead. Each gate was flanked by two towers protected by a portcullis and connected through a drawbridge with an open rampart that served as a first line of defense, itself fortified and protected by a parapet of earth and by palisades. To gain access to several of the towers over this circle of ramparts, a wooden staircase situated on the outside of the tower had to be climbed.

The bridge over the Loire was protected on the right (north) bank of the river (the south side of the city) by the tower of the Châtelet and on the left (south) bank by a fortified work, the Tourelles. This consisted of two towers, one with flat sides and the other round, constructed in the river itself. The bridge began at the rue des Hostelleries and the rue de la Porte-Sainte-Catherine; it had nineteen irregular arches and at that time divided an island, the downriver half of which was known as La Motte-aux-Poissonniers; the upriver half was named for the chapel and asylum of Saint-Antoine-du-Pont.

The preoccupation of the citizens of Orléans with their defense is reflected in instructions for expenditures from the fortress account books, which mention payments for work completed for the upkeep of the ramparts and the bridge: "To the aforesaid Gillet for two days' worth of carpentry work spent in restoring two wooden stairways, one for the tower facing the Hégron Field, the other near the St. Flo Tower . . . at the rate of 5 sous, 4 deniers per man per day, amounting to 10 sous, 8 deniers parisis."

The city was equally attentive to the security of its bridge: "a lock for the portcullis of the bridge to which Jean Mahy has the key, 14 sous." The citizens were also anxious about the watch in this troubled time; expense instructions taken from the account book of Jacques Deloynes, (CC 549) for the years 1425–1427 assign "to Bernard Josselin, responsibility for the watch of Saint-Pierre-Empont for the month of April," and: "To Jacquet le Prestre, for expenses undertaken on Friday, the 27th day of April, for inspecting the security of the city, inspecting the grain stocks and the quantities of wheat, or for the persons who followed him: that is to say, eight procurators, eight bourgeois, eight notaries, and eight sergeants."

Thought was given even to lodging for the watchmen: "To Jacquet Champon, the 24th day of May, for the purchase of a bed equipped with a feather blanket, a cushion, and a quilt . . . to provide sleeping for two bourgeois in the New Tower."

Repairs became more frequent as time went on, and during the 1428 siege, the account book of the fortress (CC 550) shows that the maintenance of the ramparts became a daily concern:

> To Jean Boudeau, for 850 pounds of iron requisitioned for the city forge. . . . To Humbert François, mason, for four days of his craft, which he spent in securing the ironwork of the floor of the Bernier Gate. . . . To Jean Chomart, the aforesaid 16th day of April, for silver provided for the purchase of a *toise* [roughly six and a half feet] of wood . . . and nails for the floor of the Tower of the Helmet. . . . To André Godet, locksmith, for a lock . . . placed on the barrier of the rampart of the Bernier Gate. . . . To Jean Coust, carpenter, for two days of his and two other carpenters' work, spent on the rampart of the Paris Gate to make gun carriages for the cannons.

In addition to this defensive armament—maintenance of towers, ramparts, and bridges—the procurators of Orléans busied themselves with offensive armament as well. The account books of the fortress (as in the account book of Jean Hilaire, CC 550) are full of information on the purchase of bombards and cannons and on their positioning, and for lead and gunpowder preparation:

> To Jean Chomart . . . for seventeen days' worth of the work of carpenters who prepared the gun carriages for the cannons, and for having shifted the cannons' positions. . . . To Jean Volant, for silver provided for eleven days of the work of carpenters and four days of masons, who were busy placing the cannon of Montargis in the tower of the vergers of Saint-Sanson. To Jean Savore . . . for having spent eight days in pulverizing cannon powder. . . . To Jacques Boucher, treasurer of my lord of Orléans, for the purchase of 200 pounds of cannon powder bought by him for the needs of the city, each one of them worth 21 *écus* of gold.

The city government also bought crossbow shafts and hired Colin the Lorrainer, a renowned artilleryman, to take charge of the city's defense. Françoise Michaud-Fréjaville, in "Une cité face aux crises: les remparts de la fidélité de Louis d'Orléans à Charles VII d'après les Comptes de forteresse de la ville d'Orléans, 1391–1427" (Orléans Conference, Oct. 1979) analyzed the accounts and concluded that a garrison of about 200 men was regularly stationed at Orléans in those days.

Orléans kept its arsenal with crossbow shafts and gunpowder above the meeting hall of the councillors. All lent their hands to the defense of the city; the guilds strengthened the ditches and the palisades. One problem arose: The members of the University of Orléans, typically enough, declared themselves exempt from these expenses. Charles VII had to send letters patent reminding them that he required all inhabitants without exception to render guard service and pay the costs of fortification.

Moreover, the people of Orléans did not hesitate to destroy the suburbs. On their side of the siege lines, the English began building *bastides* dominating the main highways, naming them London, Rouen, and Paris in honor of their major cities. These *bastides*, connected by palisades and fortified ramparts, effectively isolated the city. The defenders blocked three city gates—the Paris Gate, the Bernier Gate, and the Renard Gate. Only the Burgundy Gate and the St. Catherine Gate on the docks remained open.

The choice of Orléans as a target by the English was justified by its size, position, and trade. It was, at the time of Joan, a beautiful city, the seat of a renowned university specializing in law, and an important commercial center for the grain market of the Beauce. One of the prime ports of the Loire, it was heavily populated for the time, with about 30,000 inhabitants.

8. THE SIEGE OF ORLÉANS

From the time the English first laid siege to Orléans, in October 1428, to Joan of Arc's arrival, on April 29, 1429, any other type of significant military activity appears to have ceased. Several striking events are, however, recorded in the *Journal of the Siege of Orléans*, edited by P. Charpentier and Ch. Cuissard, the published recollections of an Orléans citizen, perhaps a cleric. The account begins with the English arrival and ends when Joan liberates the city. The text provides information on the forces present and the comings and goings of royal heralds or of the lords in charge of the city. It also describes the fortifications, the work done by the inhabitants, and especially the morale of the besieged— according, for example, great importance to the arrival of consignments of swine or sheep in the starving city.

The *Journal of the Siege* is rich in small details that reveal much about late-medieval warfare and truces, such as the Christmas truce, during which minstrels gave a dawn performance and no warlike deed occurred. It shows also how the English and French leaders socialized, exchanged gifts, and so forth. The *Journal* relates the death of the earl of Salisbury on October 27, at the beginning of the siege, and the arrival of his replacement at the head of the English army, John Talbot, on December 1. Talbot was accompanied by more than 300 combatants well equipped with supplies and ammunition. Most important, they brought more bombards, which immediately joined action and achieved their goal. By the end of the month, many houses in the city had been seriously damaged:

They fired against the walls and within Orléans more continuously and fiercely than they had ever done before while the earl of Salisbury was alive, for they fired stones that weighed 824 pounds and did much ill and damage to the city and many houses and fine buildings thereof [nobody was killed, adds the author, to the general surprise, especially since] in the rue aux Petits-Souliers [a stone fell] on the house and on the table of a man who was dining.

During a sortie, one of the defenders of the city, Jacques de Chabannes, was wounded in the foot. On January 2 the English tried to scale the rampart at the level of the Renard Gate, but the alarm was immediately sounded and the English were repulsed and forced to retrace their steps, so that "they succeeded only in getting wet because it was raining very strongly at that hour." On January 6 the author of the *Journal* notes another sortie of the people of Orléans; and five days later Master Jean, a master gunner of Orléans, showed how well he could aim his long cannon when part of the roof of the Tourelles fell in, killing six of the enemy. On January 30 the watch observed from the ramparts the English removing the poles supporting the vines of the vineyards of Saint-Ladre and of Saint-Jean-de-la-Ruelle to warm themselves with the firewood. Finding this desecration of future crops outrageous, the people of Orléans sortied and took several prisoners.

Several days later Jacques de Chabannes and La Hire sortied from the city and took up posts facing the English, but the latter failed to engage them, and each force returned to its defenses. The English troops were soon reinforced by Fastolf, who arrived with 1,200 combatants; the people of Orléans joyfully welcomed the constable of Scotland, John Stuart, at the head of 1,000 men.

The lord of Albret and La Hire also returned with reinforcements, through whom Orléans learned that a convoy of food supplies destined for the English army had left Paris. The convoy was composed of some 300 carts and wagons carrying crossbow shafts, cannons, and cannon balls—but also barrels of herring: The meatless meals of Lent were about to begin. Having left Paris on Saturday, February 12, with "John Fascot" and "Simon Maurier," the provost of Paris, and many English knights and squires, the convoy was escorted by more than 1,500 English, Picard, and Norman troops.

In response, the defenders of Orléans made a sortie under the joint command of the marshal of Sainte-Sévère and the Bastard, while from his sector the count of Clermont led forth 4,000 combatants, but these two groups of the army failed to join up. Clermont went to Rouvray-Saint-Denis, whereas La Hire and Poton de Xaintrailles decided to cut the enemy's route and attack directly. When the English vanguard discerned these movements, the convoy was halted and turned into "a park of wagons in the fashion of barriers"; sharpened spikes were planted all around this formation to prevent the French cavalry from charging. The English waited on horseback, with the archers and crossbowmen prepared to fire. Seeing that formation, the count of Clermont sent message after message forbidding any attack before the arrival of his reinforcements. However, the impatient constable of Scotland, followed by the Bastard of Orléans and William Stuart, lord of Mailhac, with about 400 combatants, charged "most valiantly, but it did them little good, for when the English saw that the large troop, which was fairly far away, came on in a cowardly fashion and did not join up with the constable and the other foot soldiers, they rushed forth hastily from their park [the enclosure made with the wagons] and struck the French, who were mostly on foot, and put them to flight in disarray."

The French had the worst of it, losing 400 men. The English pursued the foot soldiers in the greatest disorder because, as the *Journal* reports, "they were so far one from the other that one could see their standard less than a crossbow shaft's distance from the place where the French had attacked." La Hire and Poton, "who profoundly disliked going away so shamefully," rallied anew with about 60 combatants and pursued what English troops they found separated from the main body and "killed many of them." But even though the two valiant Gascons succeeded in regrouping a number of men, the count of Clermont withdrew.

"Many were the nobles and valiant captains and chiefs of war," recounted the *Journal*,

who died—among others, my lord Guillaume d'Albret; my lord John Stuart, the constable of Scotland; Jean Chabot, the lord of Verduran, etc. Their bodies were brought to Orléans and interred in the Church of the Holy Cross, where a beautiful service was held for them. And there were many wounded men, among whom was the Bastard of Orléans, who had his foot pierced by a crossbow shaft and whom two archers could only with the greatest difficulty pull from the press.

As to the count of Clermont, who was knighted that very day, the people of Orléans viewed his behavior with disdain: "So they took the road back to Orléans," the *Journal* states, "in which they acted not honorably but shamefully."

The English allowed the French to flee, and their own wagons reached to the *bastides*. The return to the city was painful for all the French after the "discomfiture" of the army. La Hire,

Poton, and the Bastard's envoy, Jamet du Tillet, entered the city last of all, for they wished to make sure that "those of the *bastides*" did not attack and cut the French army to pieces.

This "Battle of the Herrings" proved to be the most important clash of arms during the seven months of the siege. The people of Orléans were again disappointed in their defenders on February 18:

The count of Clermont took his leave of Orléans, saying that he wished to visit Chinon to attend the king, who was there then; and he brought with him the lord of La Tour; my lord Louis de Culan, the admiral; my lord Regnault of Chartres, the archbishop of Reims and chancellor of France; my lord Jean de Saint-Michel, the bishop of Orléans, a native of Scotland; La Hire; and many knights and squires of Auvergne, of the Bourbonnais, of Scotland, and two thousand combatants. Those of Orléans, seeing them leave, were not content.

To calm their fears, the inhabitants were told that the departing troops would return with food supplies and more troops. Only the Bastard and the marshal of Sainte-Sévère remained in the city. The anxious inhabitants sent Poton de Xaintrailles to the duke of Burgundy and to John of Luxembourg to request that they take Orléans under their protection, since their own duke, Charles, was a prisoner in England. The regent, Bedford, blocked that solution; in retaliation Philip the Good withdrew his troops from the English army.

One important person who appears to have intervened little during the siege was Orléans's bishop, the Scotsman John of Kirk-Michael (or de Saint-Michel), who fled the city as the English encircled it, taking refuge at Blois. He had been named bishop by the dauphin Charles to honor his allies, the Scots. In 1420 more than 6,000 Scotsmen, commanded by John Stuart, constable of Scotland, and William Stuart, earl of Buchan, had disembarked at Calais. John Stuart was the son of the duke of Albany, regent of the kingdom of Scotland and uncle of King James I (1406–1437), then a prisoner in England. John Stuart owed his appointment as constable to Charles VII (so close had the Franco-Scottish alliance against their common English enemy become). To William Stuart, son of Alexander, duke of Darnley, Charles gave the land of Aubigny in Berry in 1423 and the county of Évreux by letters patent on January 26, 1426. These two lords had always been welcome in Orléans. In 1420 for example, the earl of Buchan received from the councillors two small casks of wine and the constable of Scotland, one. In 1421 John Stuart endowed a mass in the Cathedral of the Holy Cross to be sung daily by the children of the choir. On September 24, 1425, the constable was offered thirty-seven pints of wine and four capons "of high weight." Numerous Scots came to settle in the region; until the nineteenth century there was a Scottish community near Henrichemont in the forest of Saint-Palais. The Scottish troops suffered heavily in their encounters with the English, notably at the Battle of Cravant in 1423 and at Verneuil in 1424, where between 500 and 600 Scotsmen fought among the troops loyal to Charles VII.

Scotsmen accompanied Joan throughout her campaigns. They took part in the convoy of food supplies that left Blois on April 27 and consisted of 100 men-at-arms and 400 Scottish archers, commanded by Patrick Ogilvy, constable of the Scottish army in France (B.N., fonds français, MS 7858, vol. 50 v). Bishop John of Kirk-Michael, who returned from Blois with the Scottish army of reinforcements, was at Joan's side on May 8 during the thanksgiving procession that went from church to church in the liberated city.

The Scots remained faithful to Charles VII. The alliance was reinforced by the marriage of the dauphin Louis to Margaret of Scotland, celebrated at Tours in the spring of 1436. But as the *Liber pluscardensis* (ed. Felix J. H. Skene, Edinburgh, 1870-1880, vol. 2, p. 288) documents, the little dauphine Margaret died in August 1444, pronouncing words that summarized her life in France: "Fie on life! Speak to me no more of it!" She was buried at Châlons-sur-Marne; her remains were later transferred to Saint-Denis.

What was Joan's importance to the success of the lifting of the siege of Orléans? This is a historically confusing question. Some argue that Joan was peripheral as a military commander, but those arguments are countered by others that recognize the essential need of troops to have faith in their mission and their leader. Although she was untutored in military matters, Joan is considered by many to have been a natural genius at military tactics; her genius is equally reflected in the faith of French troops who believed that she was doing the will of God. She was thought capable of bringing France a huge victory at Orléans, bringing her dauphin to his coronation, and bringing them all to salvation. For a review of this issue, see Kelly DeVries, "A Woman as Leader of Men: Joan of Arc's Military Career," in *Fresh Verdicts on Joan of Arc*.

9. THE TAX EXEMPTION FOR THE INHABITANTS OF DOMRÉMY AND GREUX

On July 31, 1429, Joan of Arc supposedly asked King Charles VII to exempt the inhabitants of her native parish, Domrémy and Greux, from any taxes. An official act granting this favor has not survived, but according to the unreliable Charles du Lys, advocate general at the Cour des Aides under Louis XIII and a self-proclaimed descendant of Joan's brother Jean, people in those Lorraine villages had to struggle to preserve their privilege (in records maintained in Archives Nationales, section domaniale H, 15352). He claimed, moreover, that on February 6, 1459: "In the register of the Cour des Comptes, these two villages were drawn from obscurity under this notation: 'because of the Maid,' and on the registers of the taxes for Domrémy and Greux, one reads: 'nothing due; the Maid.'"

Although the Chamber of Accounts burned down in 1737, a disaster that destroyed most of the financial records, a copy of the missing original act (*Traité sommaire du nom des armes ... de la Pucelle* [Paris, 1633]) dated 1769 is preserved in the Archives Nationales, which can be summarized as follows:

> Charles, by the grace of God king of France, to the bailiff of Chaumont and his successors dealing with taxes. In favor of and at the request of our well-beloved Joan the Maid, and for the great, high, notable, and profitable services that she has done and does every day toward the recovery of our lordship, we have granted to the inhabitants of Greux and Domrémy, of which the aforesaid Joan is a native, that they shall be hereafter free and exempt from any taxes levied or to be levied in the aforesaid district. For so does it please us and we wish it to be done, putting aside whatever ordinances, restrictions, or prohibitions and instructions may be thereto contrary. Given at Chinon (the king was actually at Château-Thierry), on the last day of July in the year of grace, one thousand four hundred twenty-nine and of our reign the seventh, by the king in his council. Bude

On November 8, 1769, a note signed by the royal notary Vivenot was added after the copy of this act. He reported that the people of Domrémy had protested that although their neighbors of Greux had always been exempt, they themselves had enjoyed the exemption for no more than two centuries. The intendant general of Lorraine subsequently explained that the village of Domrémy had come under the domination of the dukes of Lorraine in their capacity as dukes of Bar and thus had been removed from the province of Champagne. In 1771, the inhabitants of Domrémy were referred to some edicts of 1614 and 1634:

> The descendants of the brothers of the Maid of Orléans who at present live nobly will enjoy for the future the privileges of nobility [that is, of not being taxed] and also their posterity from male to male who live nobly as well as those who have obtained our letters patent and the decisions of sovereign courts to that effect; but those who have not lived and who do not at present live nobly will not enjoy any such privilege in the future. The daughters and women also descending from the brothers of the Maid of Orléans will no longer ennoble their husbands in the future.

Article VII of the Edict of 1634 stipulates that:

> The descendants of the brothers of the Maid of Orléans who have been added to . . . the nobility and who at present live nobly will enjoy the privileges of nobility, as will their posterity from male to male living nobly. But those who have not lived and who at present do not live nobly will not in the future enjoy any such privilege; as also the daughters and women descending from the brothers of the Maid of Orléans will no longer ennoble their husbands in the future.

A review of these two claims in 1771 decided that the privilege of Charles VII had been revoked by the edicts of 1614 and 1634. Two years after the accession of Louis XVI, a second decision was made on February 18, 1776:

> The demand of the inhabitants of Domrémy was previously refused in 1771, the edicts of 1614 and 1634 having terminated the privileges accorded to the family of the Maid, and it was not thought that the inhabitants of the village in which she was born should be treated with any more favor. It is for the same reasons, my lord, that the council very recently refused to accept the request for confirmation of the privilege that the inhabitants of Greux had reinstituted upon the accession of His Majesty to the throne. Thus, the inhabitants of Domrémy will no longer envy the difference between themselves and their neighbors; that envy only intensified

their vain pretension without giving them any solid advantage.

The people of Domrémy were demanding the confirmation of their privilege, at the same time as the inhabitants of Greux. The intendant of Champagne, Bouillé d'Orfeuill, responded to these requests at Paris on September 15, 1775, by summarizing these same texts once more. The privileges had been confirmed on the accessions of Louis XI, of Charles VIII, and of Francis I, and thereafter by the letters patent of Henry II (April 9, 1551), Francis II (October 15, 1559), Henry III (January 15, 1584), Henry IV (March 24, 1596), Louis XIII (June 1610), Louis XIV (March 1656), and Louis XV (August 19, 1723). The edicts of 1614 and 1634, he observed, had absolutely nothing to do with these privileges and in any case did not concern the inhabitants of Greux, for Charles IX had ceded Domrémy to Charles III, duke of Lorraine, in 1571. Afterward, that village belonged to Lorraine. In 1767, Bouillé d'Orfeuill added, it had returned to French domination and was part of the Generality of Lorraine. He requested that the inhabitants of Greux be given confirmation of their privilege, but his request was refused. After the Revolution of 1789, the question was moot.

10. JOAN'S CAPTURE AT COMPIÈGNE

Was Joan of Arc betrayed at Compiègne on May 23, 1430? Or to put the question differently: Did Guillaume de Flavy, the captain of Compiègne, raise the drawbridge intentionally so that she could not find refuge within the city? Was the city of Compiègne really in danger at that point? Did Flavy absolutely have to close that gate behind Joan? According to Alexandre Sorel's 1889 treatise, *La prise de Jeanne d'Arc devant Compiègne et l'histoire des sièges de la même ville* [The Capture of Joan of Arc Before Compiègne and a History of the Sieges of That City], Guillaume de Flavy was a traitor. But in 1934 J.-B. Mestre concluded that *Guillaume de Flavy n'a pas trahi Jeanne d'Arc* [Guillaume de Flavy Did Not Betray Joan of Arc], in his book of that title. What is the truth?

In 1430 prospects for Compiègne were grim indeed; the inhabitants had suffered eight attacks between 1415 and 1430. The town had been taken by the Armagnacs, then by the Burgundians, then by the English. The people of Compiègne decided after long deliberation to "serve the king well and loyally." It is easy to understand the attachment that Joan felt for them during her captivity and her desire to repay their fidelity to King Charles.

When they learned about the victories at Orléans and Patay, and then of the march toward Reims, the inhabitants of Compiègne drove out the English garrison and sent the keys to their city to Charles VII and the Maid. They replaced Jean Dacier, the abbot of Saint-Corneille and a committed Burgundian, with Philippe de Gamaches, the abbot of Saint-Faron at Meaux. The inhabitants even expelled a leading citizen, Boudon de La Fontaine, who was accused of collaborating with the Burgundians.

By May 1430 the Burgundians had decided to resume combat jointly with the English. The boy king, Henry VI, debarked at Calais on April 23 with a fleet of forty-seven vessels transporting more than 2,000 men. He was accompanied by the cardinal of Winchester, the duke of Norfolk, and by Huntington, Warwick, Stafford, and Arundel. Bishop Pierre Cauchon had gone before him as an envoy to the city of Calais. At the same time, hostilities had broken out between the English and the Burgundians. Charles VII was, in short, well advised when he wrote to inform the duke of Savoy of the separate peace he wished to offer his cousin, Philip of Burgundy. Disappointed by Philip's reluctance, he proposed a new meeting at Auxerre on June 1. He quickly realized that the English had come seeking further combat because they had yet to return the dukes of Orléans and Bourbon and the count of Eu, as they had agreed. As a consequence, Compiègne and Creil were not handed over to John of Luxembourg.

While the English army occupied itself with the siege of Pont-à-Choisy, Joan entered Compiègne on May 13, and the town councillors welcomed her with every honor. She had nearly 2,000 men under her command and proposed, as was her usual strategy, to surprise the English. She attacked on the fifteenth at first light and initially enjoyed the element of surprise; however, her men were forced to retreat and return to Compiègne. Joan then planned to launch a new operation to separate the two enemy armies by cutting the Ourscamp-Sempigny-Noyon line of communications. She went to Soissons with that intent, but the captain of the city, Guichard Bournel, would not authorize her troops to enter the town, so they had to bivouac in the surrounding fields. Bournel had entered negotiations sometime beforehand with John of Luxembourg and had won the bishop of Soissons, Regnault de Fontaine, to his side. After Joan's arrival, he delivered Soissons to John of Luxembourg for a payment of 4,000 gold saluts.

Since Joan was unable to cross the Aisne without access to the stone bridge of Soissons, she had to return to Compiègne. She was furious at having been tricked by Bournel and having, therefore, to return to Crépy-en-Valois. Meanwhile, Philip the Good had built a temporary bridge across the Oise, and his army set up camp facing Compiègne on the north bank. In the two-volume *La mission de Jeanne d'Arc*, Colonel Ferdinand de Liocourt tells us that this was the way the siege commenced. Alerted to this development, Joan marched her troops through the forest on the evening of May 22, and the following morning she was before Compiègne. She was captured while attempting a sortie in the direction of Margny. A look at the map on page 280 will help clarify her situation.

Joan left Compiègne on May 23 to undertake a skirmish with the English, but found herself facing an army much larger than she had expected. She therefore ordered a retreat and sought refuge inside the ramparts. We know that some of the gates were closed at the time, but which ones? It seems not to have been the main gate that Joan found closed behind her but rather the bridge gate or, more precisely, the gate of the forward rampart—that is, the gate of the palisade and counterscarp protecting the bridge. With these gates closed, Guillaume de Flavy could hardly have believed the city's safety to be in real danger at that moment.

Compiègne was well protected with artillery positioned along the wall; the great tower was solidly fortified, as was the Gate of Notre-Dame; and the bridge across the Oise, 450 feet long, was commanded by an outwork, which was also well defended. Behind that outwork was a rampart, with ditches full of water, the palisade of the counterscarp. Behind that last fortification, Joan was unable to find refuge. The rampart blocking access to the bridge was constructed of planks, earth, and straw and constituted an efficient protection because musket balls and other projectiles either ricocheted off it or penetrated it harmlessly.

Three fifteenth-century accounts lead readers to conclude that Guillaume de Flavy committed treason: the *Chronicle of Flanders* (vol. 19, 1882, p. 62) records that "many said and affirmed that because of the envy of the captains of France and the favor that some of the king's council had for Philip of Burgundy and for my lord John of Luxembourg, they found a way to make the aforesaid Maid die by fire." The *Diarium* or *Chronicle of Heinrich Token* (*Un nouveau témoignage contemporain de Jeanne d'Arc*, Bibliothèque de l'École des Chartes, 1928, pp. 455–

456) says: "By the treason of the captains who found it difficult to accept that a young girl should lead them and that the glory won by them should be attributed to her, she was finally sold to the English by the Bastard of Lorraine [*sic*], who caused her to be made a prisoner by treason." The advocate Rapioux, in a full session of Parlement (preserved in Archives nationales, X2 A24, Registre du Parlement, and cited by Ayroles, *La vraie Jeanne d'Arc*, vol. 4, p. 93) made the accusation: "It is not to be believed that he [Flavy] refused the offer of 30,000 écus if he would close the gates to Joan the Maid, by which act she was taken; it is said that to close the aforesaid gates, he had many ingots of gold." Rapioux, who by virtue of his office was immune from official reprisal, was alluding to sums allegedly offered by the duke of Burgundy to convince Guillaume de Flavy to surrender Compiègne.

Mestre's central argument against the culpability of Guillame de Flavy is that the captain of Compiègne was a man "who protected" his city against the Burgundians. Mestre sees in the imperative of the city's defense a point in Flavy's favor. But Guillaume de Flavy had in fact no commitment other than his personal interest, which was to build up a petty domain around Compiègne. Joan was definitely an obstacle to that ambition. Furthermore, Jean Chartier—in the *Chronique de Charles VII* (ed. A. Vallet de Viriville, 3 vols; Paris, 1858), also cited in Quicherat (vol. 4, p. 52, from BN ms. 8350)— attributed the heroic defense of Compiègne against the Anglo-Burgundians to another commander, Philippe de Garmaches. Careful study of the defense of Compiègne shows that there was no danger to the city even if the first gate of the palisade remained open so that Joan of Arc might have gained refuge. In the worst of cases, even if that gate had been taken, the city's defenses would have remained secure. The argument that Joan was betrayed is therefore at least plausible.

11. THE ABJURATION CEDULA

During the morning sessions of Joan's trial, Guillaume Manchon was one of three notaries who took notes; then, in the afternoons, at Cauchon's residence, he drew up a daily transcript. The notes were taken in French and later translated into Latin, with five authentic copies. Orléans has a copy of the French minutes (translated into English by W. S. Scott).

In the Latin version of the minutes translated after Joan's death, there is a long abjuration formula in both French and Latin, in which Joan confesses to having sinned gravely by pretending to have seen apparitions and received revelations from God. She admits also that she "made superstitious divinations and thereby blasphemed God and His saints, infringing the divine law, Holy Scripture, and canon law by wearing dissolute garments contrary to feminine decency, . . . by wearing armor. . . ." This cedula occupies some forty lines of text.

Witnesses at the nullification trial swore under oath that this cedula was inserted into the trial transcript and was not the one read to Joan. Several witnesses, including Jean Massieu, who read the cedula to Joan, declared that she had signed a text only six or seven lines long. One witness, Pierre Miget, said that it was about as long as a Pater Noster. A longer cedula, however, was disseminated to the pope, the emperor, and Christendom at large. We can imagine Pierre Cauchon's chagrin therefore when, five days after Joan had signed a cedula, several judges proposed that it be read to her again to make clear to her why she was being accused of relapsing. To the French minutes at Orléans is attached a cedula beginning with the word "Jeanne," in which she submits to the church and disavows her voices. She later said that she had signed it because she was afraid of the fire, that she had not understood it well. It is thus highly probable that Cauchon ordered the inclusion in the transcript of a text that was not read to Joan. For a summary of the thorny issues involved in assessing the abjuration cedula, see Pierre Doncoeur and Yvonne Lauhers, eds., *La Minute française des interrogatoires de Jeanne la Pucelle.*

12. JOAN IMPOSTERS

What are the arguments of the survivalists, who assert that Joan escaped burning at the stake? We know that a woman named Claude des Armoises impersonated Joan and that she fooled some people for some time. In 1436 for example, the people of Orléans, who had heard reports of this woman, sent a messenger, the herald Coeur-de-Lys, to Arlon. He left Orléans on July 31 and returned on September 2. In the meantime, Petit-Jean, Joan's brother, was in Orléans on August 5 and said that he was conveying news from his sister to the king. He was offered a meal, after which he left to find the king at Loches. He returned to Orléans on August 21, complaining that the officers of the king had not given him the 100 francs they had promised to pay him on the king's order, but only 20 francs. The people of

Orléans offered him an additional sum of 12 francs. Orléans also received another envoy, the herald Fleur-de-Lys, who was at Orléans on August 9 and again on the twenty-fifth and was allegedly sent by "Joan." The *Chronicle* of the Dean of Saint-Thibault-de-Metz reported the extraordinary adventure of that "Joan" who now called herself "Claude":

> In the year 1436, Sir Philippin Marcoult was the chief alderman of Metz; in the same year, on the 20th day of May, Joan the Maid, who had been in France, came to the Barn of the Elms near Saint-Privas; she was brought there to speak to some of the lords of Metz, and she called herself Claude, and the very same day there came to see her her two brothers; one was a knight called Messire Pierre and the other Petit-Jean, a squire. And they believed that she had been burned; but when they saw her they recognized her and she also recognized them. [Subsequently] Claude . . . met Sir Pierre Louve, a counselor of the duke of Burgundy, who gave her a horse. . . . Her manly warrior's equipment was completed by a lord of Boulay and a certain Nicole Gronart, who gave her a sword.

The chronicler records that this "Joan" spoke in parables, that she left Metz for Arlon along with "the lady of Luxembourg," and that she resided at Metz, where she had married the knight Robert des Armoises.

Some authors identify this "lady of Luxembourg" as the one who had been with Joan during her captivity at Beaurevoir, but she was in fact Elizabeth, daughter of the John of Luxembourg who was duke of Görlitz. She was thus the niece-in-law of the duke of Burgundy—not to be confused with Joan of Luxembourg, who died a spinster in 1430. It also should be noted that the *Chronicle of the Dean of Saint-Thibault-de-Metz* was rewritten at a later date, and its own author gives a second version of this event: "In this year there came a young girl who said she was the Maid of France and played her role so well that many were duped by her, and especially the greatest nobles."

This false Joan with the adventurous life reappeared at Trier to offer her advice about the two contenders for the archiepiscopal throne. At the instigation of the count of Württemberg, she also visited Cologne. These details were remarked upon by the Inquisitor Johann Nider, prior of the Dominicans of Nuremberg and later

of Basel, doctor of the University of Vienna, and author of a famous inquisitorial manual, *Formicarius*. In that work Nider told how two of his colleagues were claiming the archiepiscopal see of Trier. The false Maid "boasted that she could and would set one party upon the throne, even as Maid Joan . . . had done shortly before with Charles, king of France, by confirming him in his kingdom. Indeed, this woman claimed to be this same Joan, raised up by God."

But this "Joan" was to have serious difficulties with the Inquisitor of Cologne, Heinrich Kalt Eysen, who summoned her to appear before him. Johann Nider reports that she had dazzled everyone there by performing such tricks as breaking a glass or tearing a napkin in two and making them whole again. The count of Württemberg, her protector, removed her quickly from Cologne when the Inquisitor failed to find her tricks impressive. Nider reported the rumor that the false Maid had been living as a priest's concubine. We know for certain, from an act published by Dom Calmet, *Histoire de Lorraine* (vol. 3), that she married Robert des Armoises, lord of Tichemont, around November 7, 1436. Little is known of this person whose family, originally from Champagne, were vassals of Lorraine. Robert des Armoises lived in Metz and Luxembourg because he had taken refuge there from René of Anjou, the duke of Bar. After her marriage, Claude began to call herself "Joan." After two years (in which the records are silent), she appears at Orléans on July 18, 1439, when a banquet and reception were given in her honor. On August 1, she was granted a sum of money for "the good she had done for the city during the siege." She then disappeared while a dinner was being prepared in her honor. Had the arrival of the king, announced that very day, encouraged her to flee? In any case, she hastened to locate Gilles de Laval, lord of Rais, who engaged her to make war with him. This is, of course, the same Gilles de Rais (II, 34) who, one year later, in 1440, was arrested, condemned, and both hanged and burned.

Madame des Armoises went to Paris, according to the *Journal of a Bourgeois of Paris*. Certain people began to believe that she was the Maid, but she confessed her imposture before the University of Paris. Although we do not know whether she had been unmasked by the university, by the king, or by the Parlement, after 1440 one hears no more of Claude-Joan des Armoises.

The question remains: How could at least one of Joan's brothers, Petit-Jean, have acknowledged this woman and followed her from May 20 to the beginning of September 1436? We can suspect that Petit-Jean tried to derive some advantage from this adventuress by demanding subsidies in her name from the king.

Joan's brother, Pierre, had followed her throughout her career. He had been taken prisoner with her before Compiègne and, having long remained a prisoner of the English, ruined himself paying his ransom. Only the *Chronicle of the Dean of Saint-Thibault-de-Metz* suggests that Pierre later acknowledged the false Joan. Pierre would later reside at Orléans, whose duke gave him the Ile-aux-Boeufs opposite Chécy, upriver from the city, to recompense him for his imprisonment and for having been forced to sell his wife's inheritance to pay his ransom. Pierre du Lys (as he later called himself) resided in the castle of Bagueneaux. In 1450, he received further financial assistance from the duke of Orléans and in 1452 built a house at Orléans on the rue des Africains. In 1454, he received an annual pension of 61 livres, which was paid regularly. At his death, his son Jean continued to receive some benefits. Pierre and his mother attended the opening of the nullification trial in 1455.

Petit-Jean, failing to gain subsidies from the king, returned to his own country, to Domrémy or to Ceffonds. He married his niece, daughter of his elder brother Jacquemin d'Arc, who lived in Vouthon. In 1452 Jean du Lys, as he had come to call himself, was named bailiff of the Vermandois and captain of Chartres, an important post. He was replaced in 1457, but as compensation he received the captaincy of Vaucouleurs, closer to Domrémy, a post he held for more than ten years. When the captaincy was then given to Jean, the Bastard of Calane, son of the duke of Lorraine, Jean du Lys was well beyond his sixtieth year. He retired on a pension of 25 livres. Petit-Jean was not merely a poor dupe. Although for three months the accomplice of Claude des Armoises, he seems thereafter to have supported the cause of his sister's rehabilitation and assembled proofs of her innocence at Paris and Rouen.

Other adventurers also posed as Joan of Arc. From a letter of pardon from King René (Archives nationales, p. 734, côte 10, vol. 199, published by Lecoy de La Marche), dated February 1457 and granted to a certain Jeanne de Sermaize, we know that this impostor was married to an Angevin named Jean Douillet and that she had been detained in the prison of Saumur for more than three months for representing herself as Joan the Maid.

13. TRIAL TRANSCRIPTS: THE "BOOK OF POITIERS" AND THE DATE OF THE LATIN EDITION OF THE CONDEMNATION TRIAL TRANSCRIPT

In an elegant and tightly argued article in the 1996 *Fresh Verdicts on Joan of Arc,* Charles T. Wood contends that the loss of the transcript of Joan's investigation by pro-Valois clergy at Poitiers between March 11 and 24, 1429 can hardly be accidental. The conclusions of that board of judges were widely disseminated that spring, and in her trial at Rouen, Joan herself frequently appealed to the entire transcript, which she called "the book [more precisely translatable as the "register"] of Poitiers." As Wood points out, it would have been unthinkable in fifteenth-century juridical practice to conduct such an investigation without such a document, normally preserved with some care. Wood surmises that Charles VII or someone close to him—very likely Regnault de Chartres, the archbishop of Reims, a diplomat never sympathetic to Joan—may have been the culprit. He had presided over the Poitiers investigation, and presumably would have kept the transcript among his records.

Wood suggests two moments when suppressing that transcript might have seemed prudent to Charles's advisers. First of all, the disheartening ten months from Joan's failure to take Paris to her capture at Compiègne, when God's favor seemed to have deserted her. Secondly, the fairly extended period of preparation for the nullification trial of the 1450s. The basic fact the Poitiers register may have revealed, according to Wood's speculations, was Joan's initial sense that God had sent her to France to raise the siege of Orléans; only after that miraculous feat, Wood argues, does the existing record show the coronation at Reims as a second "sign" of her mission. Several witnesses at the nullification trial did indeed assert that she arrived at Chinon with the promise to aid her dauphin by achieving both of those miracles, but Wood sees those assertions as either fraudulent or the product of creative hindsight. In the 1450s Charles VII wanted, above all, to have the legitimacy of his royal title confirmed; hence, any downplaying of the Reims coronation would have been most unwelcome.

Perhaps most tellingly, Wood suggests that the limited content and evasive character of the Poitiers transcript, which Joan had only slowly (and sadly) come to understand, explains several of her more enigmatic responses to her judges at Rouen. Why, for instance, did she not jump at the chance to have her trial remanded to Poitiers, an offer made late in the trial? Was it only that she saw through the insincerity of such a ploy on Cauchon's part? Or had she come to realize that the transcript of that investigation would reveal a mission initially more limited than she wanted to assert by the spring of 1431, as well as limited enthusiasm for her cause on the part of those clergymen? So both Joan and Charles may have come in time to consider that register more embarrassing than supportive, and someone in Charles's entourage took care of the problem.

Régine Pernoud's reaction to Wood's argument is respectful but cautious. Hesitant to declare dubious all those voices asserting that Joan came to Chinon with a double mission (Reims as well as Orléans) in her mind, Pernoud pointed out that the transcript is precisely the evidence we lack. Consequently, it seemed to her finally unconvincing to reconstruct that evidence in a way that contradicts sworn evidence we do have. Not a surprising response from a graduate of the École des Chartes. But she had great esteem for Wood's expertise as a close and subtle reader of texts and for his skill in the exercise of historical logic. So, as Wood himself remarks about a disagreement with Jean Fraikin, it is perhaps wisest to leave decision on this matter to the reader.

Entirely opposite has been the history of the transcript of Cauchon's trial, for the perfection and preservation of which he seems to have been obsessively concerned. The transcript of Joan's condemnation trial has come to us in three authenticated manuscripts. The first of them (MS 119), the manuscript Jules Quicherat, Pierre Champion, and Yvonne Lanhers use for their translations, is preserved in the library of the Assemblée Nationale: it is MS Latin 5965.

During the trial itself three notaries—Guillaume Manchon, Guillaume Colles who was known as Boisguillaume, and Nicholas Taquel—recorded the interrogators' questions and Joan's responses and then compared their texts to produce the French minutes. From that text the Latin translation was made by Thomas de Courcelles and Guillaume Manchon; this first register has not come down to us, but five copies were made of it.

Carrying on the research of Vallet de Viriville, "Notes pour servir l'histoire du papier" in *La Gazette des Beaux Arts* (Paris, 1859), Jean Fraikin ("La date de la rédaction latine du procès de Jeanne d'Arc," *Bulletin de l'Association des Amis du Centre Jeanne d'Arc,* no. 8, 1985) has concluded that the Latin translation was made after Joan's death on May 30, 1431, but before August 8, 1432. Since the end of the nineteenth century,

following the conclusions of Denifle and Châtelain, editors of the *Cartulary* of the University of Paris, historians have thought that the Latin edition was composed no earlier than 1435. However, the three authentic copies of the condemnation trial that have survived carry the seal of Pierre Cauchon as bishop and count of Beauvais. Seals always accompany the person who bears the title. Cauchon was named bishop of Lisieux in a papal bull of January 29, 1432, and he took possession of the diocese on the August 8, 1432. At Beauvais Jean Juvénal des Ursins succeeded Cauchon. Cauchon therefore would not have been able to seal a text drawn up in 1435 with his seal as bishop of Beauvais, because by then he had not presided over that diocese for three years. Furthermore, Thomas de Courcelles, editor of the Latin text, left for Rome around the middle of October 1431, and did not return to Paris until 1435. He was unlikely to have undertaken the editing of that text at that time since by then he had become a partisan of Charles VII.

The nullification trial record provides very few indications leading to secure conclusions on this point. The three persons who do speak of it—Simon Chapiteau, Guillaume Manchon, and Nicolas Taquel—are disappointingly vague about the date of the Latin translation. They all say the translation was made "a long time after Joan's death (*longo tempore, longe post mortem permanum temporis*). Manchon used the word *longe* very loosely: he wrote *longe antequam* on one occasion to denote a period of three days, and also used it to describe the duration of interrogations, which took thirty-five days. Therefore, we cannot claim precision for his testimony.

Three reliable documents give us solid information on the sums received by Cauchon for his service to King Henry VI. For Joan's trial, the first is dated January 31, 1431; it is a receipt of 73 livres tournois for the period from May until October of 1430. The second is a letter of the King authorizing his treasurer and governor of finances for Normandy, John Stanlawe, to see to it that Pierre Baule, the receiver general of Normandy, pay 770 livres tournois to the Councillor "Pierre, bishop of Lisieux, formerly bishop of Beauvais . . . for the trial for heresy of the deceased Joan, formerly called the Maid." This letter is dated July 29, 1437, but refers to the receipts of 1431 and 1432. A third document authorizing payment, drawn up at Rouen on August 14, 1437 has to do with 7,070 livres tournois paid by the king of England to "our aforesaid lord" for a period stretching from May 1430 to November 1431. During the time dedicated to negotiations arranging Joan's purchase (May 1 to September 30,

1430), Cauchon received 775 livres; in a second period during which he was busy with the preparation and the unfolding of the trial, from September 30, 1430 to June 30, 1431, he received 1,407 livres and 10 sous as well as a bonus. Finally, for production of the documents of the trial—that is, from July 1 to November 30, 1431—he received another 770 livres. The financial difficulties of the kingdom of England explain these delays; Cauchon's final payment would not arrive until 1437.

For six months, therefore, Pierre Cauchon and Thomas de Courcelles dedicated themselves to the Latin edition of the trial documents. It can be reasonably concluded, then, that November 30, 1431, was the final date on which they spent their time on the affairs of the king of England.

14. JOAN OF ARC IN THEATER AND OPERA

Joan of Arc has enjoyed a flourishing theatrical career. She bestrode the stage for the first time at Orléans in 1435 in *Le Mystère du siège d'Orléans*. Its present form is 20,529 verses long and may in large part be the work of Jacques Millet, revised around the time of the nullification trial from an earlier text. Staged at various times at Orléans, this mystery play includes more than a hundred speaking characters and numerous walk-on figures. Joan of Arc, God, the Virgin, and St. Michael all have significant roles, along with Sts. Euverte and Aignan, patrons of the city.

Not until the end of the sixteenth century did another play on Joan appear: *Histoire tragique de la Pucelle d'Orléans* [The Tragic History of the Maid of Orléans], from the pen of the Jesuit priest Fronton du Duc. Composed in honor of the wife of Henry III, Queen Louise de Vaudémont, who had come to Lorraine to take the water of Plombières as a remedy for her sterility, the play was performed on September 7, 1580, in the presence of Duke Charles III (the Great) of Lorraine. One of that prince's secretaries, Jean Barnet, published the tragedy in 1584 without citing the author's name; it was reprinted in 1859 at Pont-à-Mousson in Lorraine.

In England the Maid figures in Shakespeare's *Henry VI, Part I*, written between 1592 and 1594. Shakespeare presented Joan as a sorceress, cursed by her own father and fittingly condemned to the fire by the English. Only these two plays appeared in the sixteenth century and just three more in the seventeenth, but all five were performed frequently on both sides of the Channel.

La tragédie de Jeanne d'Arcques by Vivrey des Graviers was staged at Rouen in 1600, then in Paris at the Theater of the Marais in 1603 and at the Hôtel de Bourgogne in 1611. The text was republished at Rouen and at Troyes at least eight times. A verse tragedy in five acts, Vivrey des Graviers's work is deeply defective in historical accuracy. Full of long monologues that push the taste for mythology to its limits, it even claims that its heroine was born in the village of Epernay. During the same period, in *Les Intermèdes du pastoral* [Pastoral Interludes] and in *Les amantes* [Women in Love] of Nicholas Chrétien, Joan of Arc appears beside Clovis (who died in 511 as first king of the Franks) and Godfrey of Bouillon (epic hero of the First Crusade, who died in 1100).

In 1629 the Luxembourg dramatist Nicolas Vernulz added to his collection of tragedies a piece inspired by the Maid's story, *Joanna Darcia vulgo puella aurelianensis* [Joan of Arc, in Common Speech, the Maid of Orléans], written in Latin verse the style of which today seems merely pompous. Then, in 1642, the Theater of the Marais staged *Une pucelle d'Orléans*, a tragedy by La Ménardière, the doctor of Monsieur, Louis XIII's brother, and later member of the Académie Française. This play was in fact a rewriting in Alexandrine verse of another play by the Abbé d'Aubignac, *La pucelle d'Orléans*. La Ménardière followed the rule of the three classical unities: All the action occurs on the day of Joan's death. The love Joan feels for Warwick makes Warwick's wife a pitiless rival. The countess strives, with the complicity of the bishop of Beauvais ("Canchon," as the author spells it), to hasten the prisoner's death while Warwick prepares an escape, but Joan refuses. With Joan dead, divine anger strikes the countess who loses her reason. "Canchon" dies onstage declaiming:

> Ah! I am struck by an invisible shaft
> Which gives my heart a painful wound;
> I cannot resist this final assault
> And I die . . .

Although this third play of the seventeenth century received little critical acclaim, it generated a minor literary controversy. Mademoiselle de Scudéry, the author of *L'astrée* [The Woman of Destiny], defended the honor of the Maid against the criticism of André Rivet, a Calvinist pastor who had taken refuge in The Netherlands at Leiden. Scudéry organized what might be described as a literary tournament in honor of the holy warrior.

In the Enlightenment, theatre was more interested in the memory of Joan of Arc, consecrating to it eight dramatic works. Some, influenced by the two epics of Jean Chapelain and Voltaire, were hostile. Chapelain's ponderous epic poem in twelve books, *La pucelle, ou la France délivrée* [The Maid, or France Liberated], of 1656 was called by no less an authority than Quicherat "as disastrous for the memory of Joan as a second condemnation trial," by which Quicherat meant that the heavy, overly didactic verse of this admirer of medieval literature and values tended to antagonize rather than attract public interest in Joan. Too bad, since Chapelain hoped that *La Pucelle* would be the French *Aeneid*. In the eighteenth century Voltaire's *La Pucelle d'Orléans* both stimulated the creativity of numerous playwrights and provoked a reaction. Voltaire's poem is a robustly satirical mock epic in twenty-one cantos, completed in 1730 and circulated widely among the French intelligentsia in manuscript. It was privately printed without Voltaire's permission in 1740; the first of several author-approved editions appeared in 1762. During much of the three decades before the book's wide dissemination in 1762, these scurrilous caricatures of Joan, Dunois (who finally takes her virginity after the victory at Orléans), La Trimouille (Voltaire's spelling), Talbot, Agnès Sorel (who is clearly at least ten years older than her actual age of seven in 1429), and the clergy in general were celebrated with gusto in many salon readings—a quasi-theatrical genre as old as Roman antiquity. At least as unlikely to be accused of feminism as of historical scrupulosity, Voltaire lets loose barrage after barrage against contemporary and recent figures as well as every type of churchman, medieval and modern. The sexual affair of Agnes and Charles VII and the travails of the beautiful Dorothée, a victim of the most bigoted—that is, Italian—variant of the Inquisition are at least as important to the plot as Joan's vaguely historical exploits. The extended action ceases as the final English attempt to storm Orléans fails. Poor Joan is a coarse, even doltish peasant who loves to kill Englishmen, rides a winged ass, and frequently appears nude.

The reaction protective of Joan's reputation was perhaps best stated by Henri Bernardin de Saint-Pierre, the colonial adventurer and then polymathetic man of letters whose masterpiece is *Paul et Virginie* (1787), the romantic, nature-exalting novel that has remained a perennial favorite of the French reading public. Disgusted by Voltaire's gross caricature, Saint-Pierre wrote: "A study of nature: the death of Joan of Arc would yield yet greater insight if a man of genius would dare to confront the ridicule which we have showered on this respectable and unfortunate girl, to whom Greece would have raised altars."

Joan of Arc also became the heroine of a sympathetic but wildly unhistorical pantomime at the theatre of Rognard de Pleinchène, entitled *Programme du fameux siège* [A Tableau of the Famous Siege]: Joan challenges an English general to single combat; wounded by an arrow in the arm, she returns a little later healed and in the ensuing mêlée achieves victory. Pantomime performances were composed and performed at Orléans as well as Paris. A melodrama by Plancher-Valcourt was staged there in 1786. In 1790 Roussin wrote a tragicomic play accepted for performance at the Comédie Française, but there is no record of its actually being staged. (In any event, its author died on the guillotine.) Perhaps the best instance of this generic current is *Jeanne d'Arc ou la Pucelle d'Orléans,* a drama in three acts performed in counterrevolutionary Paris on June 24, 1795.

Across the Channel, Robert Southey rose to the Maid's defense, rendering striking homage to her in his long poem *Joan of Arc* published in 1796 (when he was twenty-two). In the previous year a pantomime entitled *Jeanne d'Arc* had been performed at Covent Garden. In the first version of that pantomime, the Maid was plunged into hell by the devil, but the indignant cries of the spectators obliged the actors to substitute for the devil some angels who raised the heroine to bring her to heaven, all of this to music.

At the turn of the century in 1801, the great German poet and dramatist Johan Christoph Friedrich Schiller composed a *romantische Tragoedie* consecrated to the Maid, *Die Jungfrau von Orléans*. Schiller himself explained, in a poem published the same year, that he was responding to Voltaire: "O virgin, . . . mockery has dragged you in the slime . . . but be without fear. There are still fine souls on fire with that which is great. . . ." Schiller was no more concerned than Voltaire had been with historical precision, however: He makes Joan fall in love with an English soldier and approve of the love of Agnès Sorel for the king. (We should recall once more that Agnès was seven years old when Joan met the dauphin in 1429.) In Schiller's play Joan is a virgin who receives directly from an almighty warrior God the power of arms and an enchanted helmet on condition that she stay faithful to her mission; the helmet of course loses its power once she falls in love. There is no subsequent trial, no stake; Joan, taken prisoner, frees herself miraculously from her chains and returns to die triumphantly before Charles VII and the entire court, which covers her with flags.

At least thirty-four plays based on the story of Joan of Arc were composed between the beginning of the nineteenth century and 1870, the year of France's humiliating defeat by Prussia, and forty-eight from 1870 to 1900. Many nineteenth-century playwrights were heavily indebted to Schiller. A little-known author named Avril produced a plagiarized drama, *Le Triomphe des lis—Jeanne d'Arc ou la Pucelle d'Orléans,* published at Paris in October of 1814. The development is quite original, with Joan carried about on a cloud after the coronation at Reims to a great surge of choral music.

La mort de Jeanne d'Arc, a sympathetic tragedy the prolific playwright Dumolard dedicated to the citizens of Orléans, was presented on the eighteenth Floréal of the year XIII (May 8, 1805) in that city. In this play, Talbot and the duke of Burgundy propose that Joan marry an Englishman and move to England, but despite their efforts Joan is handed over to the secular arm by Isabeau of Bavaria. An edifying play by S. N. Cartier, *Jeanne d'Arc,* was dedicated to Marie-Louise of Austria, Napoleon's second wife. A sympathetic pantomime, *Le crébillon du melodrama* [A Melodramatic Parody (After the Manner of Crébillon)], was presented in 1813 at the Cirque Olympique in Paris and would be restaged many times thereafter, often at the Théâtre de la Gaité.

Jeanne d'Arc à Rouen, a drama composed by Charles-Joseph Laeillard d'Avrigny, was presented for the first time at the Comédie Française in Paris by the actors of Louis XVIII, the restored Bourbon king, on May 4, 1819. The action unfolds at Rouen, and Bedford offers Joan, in vain, the solution of leaving for England; Dunois wishes to wage combat for her. The duchess of Bedford and Talbot strive to save Joan, but she is burned by mistake. The role of Joan in this supportive drama was first played, to wide acclaim, by Mademoiselle Duchesnois.

On the lyric stage, the drama of Jules Barbier, set to music by Gounod in 1873, was so popular that it sold out at the Théâtre de la Gaîté for three months. Jacques Offenbach, director of the theater, under pressure to present his *Orphée aux Enfers* [Orpheus in Hell], had to close it down despite the steady crowd. (Ironically, the Orpheus revival failed financially.) An opera by Mermet was presented at the Opéra in 1876, but without any success. Barbier's musical drama was restaged several years later in 1890, by the Théâtre de la Porte-Saint-Martin with Sarah Bernhardt in the role of Joan of Arc. The enthusiastic spectators saw in this "moral" drama a work that responded fully to their patriotic aspi-

rations. It appeared several times later and was last performed there in 1906.

Serious dramas on Joan followed one another in rapid succession, and the satirists responded to practically every one. Soumet's tragedy of 1819 inspired *La tulipe à Jeanne d'Arc* [A Tulip for Jeanne d'Arc], a parodic potpourri in five acts by Ricard. On June 11, 1819 the Théâtre du Vaudeville performed *Le Procès de Jeanne d'Arc ou le jury littéraire* [The Trial of Joan of Arc, or The Literary Jury], a work by Dupin d'Artois, and *Carmouche,* which was a riposte to Avrigny's drama, was staged on the May 4 of the same year at the Théâtre Français. Pantomimes of the same type flourished throughout the nineteenth century.

The general public of the nineteenth- and twentieth-century French theater became and remained sympathetic to Joan's memory. From the mid-nineteenth century onward, French theatrical performances began to benefit from scholarly research on the Maid. Revival of the medieval *Mystère du siège d'Orléans* was one of the first consequences of this trend. Émile Eude wrote a *Nouveau mystère du siège d'Orléans,* performed there at the Festival of Joan of Arc (see III, 16). In 1895 the pastor of Mesnil-en-Xaintois, a village in Lorraine, staged for his parishioners a mystery play in the medieval style that enjoyed immediate success with people taking the cure at Contrexéville and Vittel. In 1904 Maurice Pottecher, creator of the Théâtre du Peuple of Bussang, produced a *Passion de Jeanne d'Arc.* In 1909 the parish priest of the Church of Saint-Joseph in Nancy (the capital of Lorraine) staged a *Vie de Jeanne d'Arc,* which he presented as a parallel to the Passion of Christ.

At the time of Joan's beatification (1909) and subsequent canonization hearings, interest in the heroine of Domrémy naturally increased. No fewer than seventeen plays about her were composed in 1909 alone. Between the two world wars, after Joan's canonization in 1920, at least twenty-nine plays were written about her, and nineteen appeared between 1945 and 1986. Some of them, more or less hagiographic and written by clerics, were designed for performance in schools for Catholic youth or in adult devotional groups. Side by side with that clerical tendency flourished a secular, nationalist attitude that saw Joan of Arc as a patriot and only a patriot. For Joseph Fabre, author of *La délivrance d'Orléans, Mystère en trois actes,* presented just before World War I at Orléans at the Théâtre Municipal in 1913, the virtue to celebrate was her patriotism.

In discussing the theater devoted to Joan's memory, Charles Péguy of Orléans, who had heard stories of the Maid throughout his childhood, must be mentioned. In 1894 when Péguy, twenty-one, had already broken with Catholicism, he undertook a study of Joan in which he paid close attention to the documents collected by Quicherat. In 1895 he made a trip to Domrémy; upon his return to Orléans, where he had withdrawn to his mother's house, he began writing his three-part drama. He completed the first part, *Domrémy*, in June 1896; by June 1897, he had finished the entire triptych, which appeared that same year under the pseudonym of Marcel and Pierre Baudouin. Its publication was a complete failure, and its first staging did not occur until June 1924, as a benefit for the war wounded and for writers who had served in the military; it was performed at the Comédie Française with Paulette Pax in the title role. Not once during the dozen years that followed that first publication of 1897 do any of Péguy's surviving writings mention Joan's name; at the end of that period, however, he began his return to Christianity. He took part in the parade at Orléans on the May 8, 1909, as a lieutenant in the French army. That was the moment at which he returned to this work and gave it a new title, *Le mystère de Jeanne d'Arc*, which would become *Le mystère de la vocation de Jeanne d'Arc* and finally *Le mystère de la charité de Jeanne d'Arc*. He revised the first part of *Domrémy* with embellishments to his text of 1897. This mystery play was first performed by the Comédie d'Orléans in a production by Olivier Katian in November 1965.

Twentieth-century foreign playwrights also took up the subject of Joan of Arc. The most influential of them, George Bernard Shaw, a nonconforming Irish Protestant, made of his *Saint Joan* a heroine struggling against both church and state, relying instead on her sense of national mission and her personal judgment. The play was performed at New York in 1923 and then recast in Paris by the Pitoëffs in 1925. Shaw's *Saint Joan* was adapted for the screen, to wonderful effect, by Otto Preminger. Holly Hill has recently produced a set of twenty-six interesting interviews, incorporating the full performance history of Shaw's play, in her monograph: *Playing Joan, Actresses on the Challenge of Shaw's* Saint Joan (New York: Theatre Communications Group, 1987), which unfolds the complexities of portraying Joan, from the actress's perspective. Shaw's *Saint Joan* brought in its wake the creation of other Joans who have become ever more dedicated to expressing their authors' personal predilections. *Jeanne avec nous* of Vermorel underlined in 1942 the "existentialist" character

of Joan's mission: its production was forbidden by the Occupation authorities.

Jacques Audiberti (*La Pucelle*, 1950) and Thierry Maulnier (*Jeanne et les juges* [Joan and the Judges], 1949) each voiced distinctively post-World War II sentiments in their presentations of Joan. Maulnier, a rightist in politics, saw Joan as a heroine in the eternal struggle of the individual against the tyranny imposed by societal norms. Jean Anouilh's *L'alouette* [The Lark] is perhaps the most important of post-War dramas about her. It was first produced in 1953; Joan's character is not unlike that of the heroine of Anouilh's *Antigone*. In recent years Péguy's play and *La fenêtre* [The Window] of Andrée Obey have enjoyed great success both in Paris and elsewhere in France. The puppet theater of Père Brandicourt at Nancy has been showing its *Chronique de sainte Jeanne d'Arc* ever since 1955.

Serious musicians of the nineteenth and twentieth centuries have also found inspiration in Joan of Arc. A musical variant of her dramatic tradition has enjoyed great success since 1945. *Jeanne au bûcher* [Joan at the Stake], a dramatic oratorio with text by Paul Claudel and music by Arthur Honegger, composed in response to a request by Ida Rubinstein, has been performed worldwide. It was first staged at Basel in 1938, then at Orléans and Paris, and frequently in America. In 1995 it was performed at the Berkshire Festival. Claudel's intention was to celebrate at once Joan's humility, peasant simplicity, and lofty spirituality. Honegger complements with freshness and serenity the naive authenticity of Claudel's language.

Honegger and Jolivet had quite a number of predecessors: More than four hundred plays, cantatas, symphonies, and other musical works were tallied by Émile Huet in 1894 in his *Jeanne d'Arc et la musique*. A major opera on that list is Gounod's *Jeanne d'Arc* of 1873, adapted from Barbier's play. Verdi had already exalted France's liberation in *Giovanna d'Arco* in 1845. In 1879, Tchaïkovsky dedicated his first opera to Joan, *La Pucelle d'Orléans*, some selections from which were performed during the Orléans Festival in 1979 by Vera Kousmitchova.

15. TOWARD AN ICONOGRAPHY OF JOAN OF ARC

"O Joan, without a grave and without a portrait!" André Malraux once exclaimed. Sympathetic though his sentiment may have been, Malraux's facts were wrong. There have in fact been many "portraits" of Joan of Arc, the first one drawn on May 10, 1429—two days after the liberation of Orléans—by Clément de Fauquembergue. He was a notary appointed by the Parlement of Paris to keep a daily register of that high court's cases, of relevant decrees emanating from high authority, and of major events of the moment. The resulting document resembled an official journal of that branch of government. Fauquembergue's appointment to that post must have been acceptable to Bedford even if not formally approved by the regent. This effigy was not known or appreciated until our time, when recourse to authentic documents has become decisive in the formation of historical images.

On that Tuesday the tenth, the news circulating in Paris was not good for Plantagenet partisans: On the previous Sunday, the dauphin's troops had taken the "*bastides* which William Glasdal and the other captains and men at arms" had occupied on the bridge of Orléans. Fauquembergue added that "the enemies had in their company a Maid who had only a banner with her." In a burst of creative curiosity not normally recommended for notaries, Fauquembergue embellished his report by sketching in the margin the silhouette of this unforeseen Maid; he gave her a robe and long hair, not knowing that Joan had a taste for functional clothing. But he retained two details that everyone was mentioning: the sword that she would not use to kill and the standard.

Others would later attempt portraits of the heroine. First was the Scotsman who painted her at Reims. (The notary who recorded that artistic effort misunderstood and wrote "Ras," which led the first editors of the trial to conclude that this painting was done in Arras.) During the coronation Joan, who appreciated fine clothes, must have been superbly dressed, since Archbishop Regnault of Chartres was displeased—Joan had become prideful "because of the rich garments which she had taken it upon herself to wear." This critical opinion helps us assess her; she did not present herself as a virago who "should have been a boy." When she was on horseback, she wore "leggings well fitted and firmly tied," but for her king's anointing, sumptuous garments. When she was taken prisoner, the archer who succeeded in throwing her "flat on the ground" pulled her "by her doublet of cloth-of-gold." The taste for fine clothes had not abandoned her.

None of these garments has survived, however; nor has the Reims portrait. The disconcerting speed of Joan's destiny—one year of public action, one year of prison, then the fire that consumed all, with any charred remains thrown into the Seine—largely explains this disappearance.

The oldest dated miniature portrait of Joan was made twenty years after her death; it is an illustration in *Le champion des dames*, the work by Martin Lefranc. In that miniature we see that Joan had already been swept into legend: She appears at the side of Judith at the tent of Holofernes; she has long hair beneath a hat with a very broad brim, and beneath her armor a long robe. She is depicted in the same manner for the *Chronique de Charles VII* of Jean Chartier, which dates from the end of the fifteenth century, when she is represented in the council of the king, along with those who freed the kingdom at different moments of the Hundred Years War—Dunois, Richemont, and the brothers Bureau. She is also depicted with a long robe and long hair in the MS français 4811 of the Bibliothèque Nationale, which is an abridgment of that chronicle. The Maid had also been depicted some fifty years after her death, in 1484, in the *Vigiles du roi Charles VII*, a chronicle illustrated by some 400 miniatures.

A miniature that could be contemporary to Joan shows her in a guise perhaps edifying but hardly historically accurate. This portrait has in fact been separated from the text that it was suppose to illustrate, and the manuscript from which it was removed has not been identified. This is the miniature known as "Joan at the Standard" that the Archives Nationales au Musée de l'histoire de France holds today. In it, Joan carries her armor well, holding in her hand the standard and the sword. Her clear gaze recalls the letter of the youthful Guy de Laval to his mother, reporting with admiration how he had seen the Maid "in full armor, except for her head, a little ax in her hand. . . ." Her feat "seemed something divine, as did seeing and hearing her."

Another depiction of Joan of Arc from her own century and her own homeland may just have been revealed in a fresco in the hermitage of Notre-Dame de Bermont. That chapel seemed about to collapse in ruins until a recent rescue operation underwritten by individual philanthropy undertook its preservation. In the course of restoring the seventeenth-century frescoes, two earlier figures of young women were revealed. One is a peasant girl at prayer, dressed in a red dress. The other has blonde hair and is dressed in male attire; she wears hose and a jacket descending to mid-thigh, belted at the waist. Analysis of these frescoes is under way at this writing (August 1998), but Marie-Véronique Clin reports that there is good reason to assign them to the late fifteenth century. It is worth remembering that

Joan loved to visit Notre-Dame de Bermont to pray. On Saturdays she often went there with her sister Catherine, carrying a candle to the statue of the Virgin—a habit likely to have been preserved in local memory. Several sources mention the red dress she wore around Domrémy and Vaucouleurs, again a memorable detail. So these figures may be among the earliest and, in some sense, the most reliable representations of Joan of Arc.

The iconography of Joan of Arc soon began to accompany literary history and the history of the theater. Since there were no accurate drawings made of her during her lifetime and since none of her portraits survives, artists have been able to give free rein to their imagination in three major traditions: Joan the shepherdess to whom the saints appear; Joan the female soldier carrying armor, the sword, and the standard; and finally, Joan the saint at the stake in Rouen. Thereafter, most images of Joan have centered principally around these three paradigms: the visionary, the warrior, or the martyr. Within these three traditions, Joan conforms to the canons of feminine beauty of the age. She has the opulent flesh of Rubens in a portrait of her that he liked so much that it was kept in his room until his death, and later the slim silhouette of the 1920s' flapper. Until quite recently images of Joan were not expected to defy cultural norms: Even though she wore men's clothes and usually armor, the armor was always covered by a robe; since until the twentieth century a woman was expected to have long hair, Joan of Arc's coiffure conformed.

The earliest surviving painted portrait in the proper sense of the term is the "Portrait of the Échevins" (town councilmen of Orléans) ordered by that group for installation in the city hall in 1557; it was later moved to the Hôtel Groslot. In it Joan is represented as a good bourgeoise. Any rich merchant's wife could have posed for this painting, wearing that robe with slashed sleeves; only the sword and the label with her name permit us to identify her as Joan of Arc. The plume—a symbol of martial victory—underlines the ambiguity between the woman and the warrior: A plume was then part of masculine costume. But the fashion was set; it is as a woman wearing a plume that Joan is depicted until the nineteenth century.

The "Portrait of the Échevins" became her official portrait; it was copied in 1606 by the engraver Léonard Gaultier to illustrate the work of Léon Tripault, *Histoire et le discours au vray du siège qui fut mis devant la ville d'Orléans* [True History and Recollections of Orléans under Siege]. It was reproduced also in *Heroïnae nobi-lissimae Joannae Darc* [On the Most Noble Heroine Joan of Arc], in which Jean Hordal celebrated his claim to collateral descent from the Maid. One or the other of these two engravings would be imitated throughout the seventeenth and eighteenth centuries. Richelieu ordered from Philippe de Champaigne a portrait of Joan of Arc in that tradition for his Gallery of Illustrious Men. That painting has disappeared, but the engraving that Claude Vignon did from it to illustrate the *Portraits des hommes illustres* [Portraits of Famous Men] of Vulson de La Colombière has survived: Joan here resembles a heavy peasant woman disguised as a soldier, wearing above a long dress a breastplate that shapes her bosom; the sword that she seems to drag behind her does nothing to correct the unflattering effect of this portrait. In the eighteenth century Joan of Arc was depicted on a whole series of Aubusson tapestries: The cartoons were based on Vignon's illustrations for Chapelain's mythic epic in twelve parts, *La Pucelle ou la France délivrée* [The Maid, or France Liberated] (1656).

In the second half of the eighteenth century, we find a number of engraved portraits such as that by Noël Lemire in 1774 as well as numerous depictions in etchings. During the Revolution, the traditional plume became a Phrygian cap. Then under Napoleon Joan became the happy symbol of the force and the durability of the Empire. During that period the sculptor Edmé-Etienne-François Gois, at Orléans, cast her in a robe with the features of a melodramatic heroine.

With the Restoration of the Bourbon monarchy in 1815, Joan's popularity grew. Just as the "Portrait of the Échevins" had been the model for previous centuries, Joan's iconography from the Restoration onward was shaped by the statue of the princess Marie d'Orléans. Instead of the manly virago one saw now the humble servant of God: "Joan of Arc, her head bowed in modesty and sweetness, sure of her sword, sure of her faith, who although armored is no less an expression of pity," as Pierre Marot concluded in his article "De la réhabilitation à la glorification de Jeanne d'Arc."

Under the July Monarchy (1830–1848), many painters and sculptors chose the theme of Joan of Arc for the works that they presented at the great Paris Salons. Practically every year's Salon had its version of Joan: "Joan Hearing Her Voices," "Joan the Martyr," "Joan the Expression of Sanctity," "Joan in Torment," "Joan in Combat," "Joan at the Stake," and so on. Numerous illustrated books featuring Joan appeared, among them those of Alexandre Guillemin and of the Baron de Barante on the dukes of Burgundy

(1824), which enjoyed a considerable success. Barante's liberal interpretation of the Burgundian dynasty won him membership in the French Academy. After the defeat of 1870 Joan of Arc came to incarnate the spirit of revenge against Germany; postal cards and patriotic posters appealed to her warlike aspect in the hope of restoring France. During the two world wars, official propaganda appealed to her image as well: She was either the angel of comfort to the dying soldier or the general who led her troops to victory.

Sculptures of Joan appeared within a century of her death. A monument erected in 1502 on the bridge at Orléans showed Joan and Charles VII kneeling at either side of the crucified Christ. During the Napoleonic First Empire Gois produced a histrionic bronze statue of her, as has been mentioned. Then with the Bourbon Restoration and the July Monarchy of the Orléans dynasty came the normative statue of the Princess Marie d'Orléans. In 1855 under the second Empire of Napoleon III (1849–1870), the massive bronze equestrian statue of Joan by Royaltier—with bas-reliefs on the pedestal by Vital Dubray—was erected in the Place du Martroi at Orléans. In that heroic statue Joan's long hair spills out from beneath her helmet. In the first decades of the Third Republic (1870–1940), public sculptures of Joan became common. In 1875, Emmanuel Frémiet's equestrian statue was installed in Paris in the Place des Pyramides just beyond the Louvre (a copy inspires the New Orleans riverfront); in 1882, Frederic Leroux's was dedicated at Compiègne; in 1891 Domrémy ordered one from Marius Mercié.

After Joan's beatification (1909) and canonization (1920), statues appeared everywhere; every city, every village, every church wanted its own Joan of Arc: Some wanted the saint, others the patriot. Even commercial advertising began to make use of her. Joan's picture appeared on boxes of cheese, packets of green beans, on chickens and coffee sacks.

The Maid still attracts artists in our own day. Since she is no longer the banner bearer of one group or another, since she has no more cause to defend, she appears simpler and more human. [Translator's note: This was written before LePen's National Front reappropriated her in its propaganda.] Albert Decaris in his engravings shows us a Joan of Arc who is young, spare, introspective. Rouault shows us a plausible warrior despite the aureole of divine grace surrounding her, and Bernard Buffet depicts a woman who is also a war commander at the head of her troops. Between the two world wars, Maxime Real del

Sarte conveyed a Joan who suffered, the martyr at the stake. George Mathieu in his "La Libération d'Orléans" gave her no face but suggested in a halo of victory the force and the hope that she knew how to awaken in the troops.

In the summer of 1979 an exhibition entitled *Jeanne d'Arc: Images d'une légende* was held at the Bibliothèque Muncipale in Rouen. It contained some 500 images and other articles relating to Joan and her "legend," ranging in date from 1458 to 1979. The catalogue for this exhibition was produced by the Musée des Beaux-Arts, and features detailed information on all the images displayed. This publication proves indispensable to anyone who studies the kaleidoscope of images spiraling out through the centuries and engulfing Joan of Arc, the Maid of Orléans.

16. JOAN OF ARC IN FOLKLORE: THE ORLÉANS FESTIVALS

On May 8, 1429 at the moment that the English were raising the siege and withdrawing from Orléans, the inhabitants of the city organized solemn processions to thank God and the patron saints of the city, Sts. Aignan and Euverte. This spontaneous thanksgiving celebration became a procession that continues today, every May 8. With some exceptions during periods of warfare, Orléans has thus celebrated Joan for more than five and a half centuries. The ritual developed little by little, and the account books of the city detailed the subject carefully. Amplified and modified over the course of years, the ceremony's major elements have remained essentially unchanged.

In the fifteenth and sixteenth centuries, the bells began ringing on the evening of May 7 and heralds passed through the city announcing the procession. Platforms were set up on the main crossroads and at battle sites of the siege. A particularly splendid festival occurred in 1435 when the *Mystère du siège d'Orléans* was first performed. That pageant drama evoked historical events with startling accuracy, and one of Joan's most improbable companions, Gilles de Rais, was among its financial backers as well as a performer.

The city government paid for these ceremonies. The members of the procession were the civil and religious authorities, including the twelve procurators of the city each holding in his hand a candle of new wax weighing three pounds, decorated with the city's coat of arms. Then came the canons of the cathedral, the clergy of the region, the chantry priests, the choirboys of Sainte-Croix, of Saint-Aignan, of Saint-Pierre-

Enpont. The sergeants of the duke of Orléans supervised the orderliness of the procession so as to prevent laymen from mixing with the clergy. When Joan of Arc had been rehabilitated, Cardinal d'Estouteville granted an indulgence of one year and ten days to anyone taking part in this celebration. The city government of Orléans also assumed responsibility for paying the preacher who was to deliver a sermon on that day and the bellringers; it provided for adequate offerings at mass and paid for dressing the choir boys and the banner-bearer in new clothes.

That evening a large banquet brought together the preacher and the town councilmen. A young boy carried a reconstruction of the banner of Joan of Arc. At the end of the fifteenth century, another banner borne by privileged citizens appeared. These festivals were interrupted during the Wars of Religion (1562–1589) but the processions began soon thereafter, "strong, devout, and solemn," as the city account books describe them. The ceremony remained essentially unchanged across the centuries; the most significant alteration was that the banquet at the city hall was suppressed occasionally because of "the misery of the time."

In the eighteenth century two new characters appeared in the procession: In 1725 arrived a young boy called le Puceau (the virginal boy) wearing a vestment of the period of King Henry III with the red and gold colors of the city and on his head a hat of scarlet enriched by two white plumes. Chosen by the mayor and the city councilmen, a boy would play that role until the Revolution. In 1786 the Puceau was joined by la Rosière—a girl who had won the prize rose of her village for her outstanding virtue. That role was an invention of the duke and duchess of Orléans who also wished to celebrate the festival of May 8 by "the marriage of a young woman who was both poor and virtuous, born within the ramparts of the city walls;" she was granted a dowry of 1,200 livres provided by their highnesses.

In 1771 the Pont Royal was built, passing over the site of the Tourelles, and a bronze monument to Joan was dedicated on the rue Royale. That monument was melted down in 1792 and recast as a cannon named "Jeanne d'Arc." (In the twentieth century, several naval vessels bore that name.)

After the 1792 celebration of the festival (including the Puceau and the Rosière), Joan's rescue of the city was ignored for eleven years. Napoleon's Consulate revived the festival in 1803. In 1802, the mayor of Orléans, Grignon-Désormeaux, requested that a monument in honor of Joan of Arc be restored. A commission exam-ined the project, which was awarded to Gois. The Consular government approved the recommendation and forwarded it to Bonaparte, who reestablished the festival with a burst of his favorite declamatory rhetoric:

> The illustrious Joan of Arc has proved that it is no miracle that the French genius can be productive in circumstances in which the national independence is threatened. Unified, the French nation has never been conquered, but our neighbors, more calculating and more clever than we, abusing the freedom and the loyalty of our character, have constantly striven to sow among us that dissension from which were born the calamities of that epoch and of all the disasters which our history recalls—Paris, the 16th Pluviôse, the year XI. (Document preserved at the Centre Jeanne-d'Arc)

In addition, the bishop of Orléans requested the restoration of religious ceremonies, which the First Consul approved wholeheartedly.

In 1817 the mayor, the count of Rocheplatte, wished to reestablish the ceremony in all its ancient splendor. On that occasion a new Puceau was chosen, and a cross was erected on the rue Croix-de-la-Pucelle on the site of the rampart of the Tourelles. During the reign of Louis-Philippe (1830–1848), these festivals underwent a curious transformation: May 8 became a national feast day and thus required an essentially secular ceremony. The bust of Joan of Arc surrounded by the National Guard and by the civil and military authorities was carried in triumph past the sites that bore witness to her glory. In 1848, the feast resumed its traditional form. Joan's banner was handed by the mayor to the bishop of Orléans on May 7, 1855; that same year Monseigneur Dupanloup, the bishop, delivered a panegyric sermon insisting on the Maid's beatification. In that year the statue by Royaltier was set up on the place du Martroi. In 1869, Dupanloup announced publicly his intention to introduce the cause of Joan's canonization in the Roman Curia.

In 1920 the religious festival and the national festival of Joan of Arc, joining in a common fervor church and state, were finally combined. But the people of Orléans had anticipated this joint statement of collective gratitude several centuries before, giving homage almost without fail across the span of time to the woman who freed them. The festival has been revised in that spirit since the beginning of the twentieth century. It is only since 1912 that a young woman has been assigned the task and privilege of incarnating Joan of Arc.

17. BEATIFICATION AND CANONIZATION

Félix Dupanloup, bishop of Orléans from 1849 to 1878, laid the groundwork for the beatification of Joan of Arc. The son of a poor peasant woman from the Alpine frontier of France, a moderate liberal in politics who was elected to the French National Assembly and then the Senate, a pioneer in the education of women and a romantically rhetorical preacher elected to the French Academy, Dupanloup called a meeting of all the bishops through whose dioceses Joan had passed when alive. Arguing that whatever else she may have been or had come to represent, Joan was at base a genuine saint, he persuaded his episcopal colleagues in 1869 to send a petition to Pope Pius IX (hardly his greatest admirer in Rome). In 1874 Dupanloup established a diocesan court to hold a preliminary inquest. Two years later, its conclusions were submitted to the Congregation of Rites, along with a biography.

After Dupanloup's death in 1878, this project was taken up by his successor, Monseigneur Couillié. Meanwhile, at Rome, the cardinals of the Congregation of Rites decided to submit Joan's cause to the pope for his signature. On January 27, 1894, Leo XIII signed the brief. During that year Monseigneur Touchet succeeded Couillié and took upon himself the expense of the next stages of the project. He went to Rome himself in 1896 and in the following year was asked formally to undertake a study of the heroic character of Joan's virtues—that is, her sanctity. The results were brought to Rome in person by Touchet, the bishop of Orléans in 1898.

During 1902 and 1903 Rome studied the Orléans tribunal's conclusions concerning the virtues of Joan of Arc. This study led, on January 6, 1904, to the proclamation by Pope Pius X that her virtues were indeed heroic. The formal beatification took place at the basilica of St. Peter in Rome on April 18, 1909.

Touchet pushed forward, requesting that the cause of her canonization be opened. He worked unceasingly on the dossier, which was presented at Rome on April 17, 1914. Matters proceeded slowly, and the death of Pope Pius X aggravated other pressures to which the tribunal was subject. But on September 3, 1914, Pope Benedict XV agreed to a canonization trial. Finally, on July 6, 1919, he approved its conclusions. On May 16, 1920, the ceremony took place at St. Peter's. For a surprising view of the whole canonization process in Rome, see H. A. Kelly's "Joan of Arc's Last Trial: the Attack of the Devil's Advocates" in *Fresh Verdicts on Joan of Arc*.

18. SELECT FILMOGRAPHY

1898   Georges Hatot, *Jeanne d'Arc*. (French). A fragment is preserved at the Centre Jeanne d'Arc in Orléans.

1900   Georges Méliès, *Jeanne d'Arc*. Star Films (French). A historical reconstruction in twelve scenes. Joan played by Louise d'Aley.

1908   Albert Capellani, *Jeanne d'Arc*. Pathé (French). Joan played by Léontine Massart.

1909   Mario Caserini, *Vie de Jeanne d'Arc*. Cinés (Italian). Joan played by Maria Gasperini. Based on Schiller's *Die Jungfrau von Orléans*.

1913   Nino Oxilia, *Giovanna d'Arco*. Pasquali (Italian). Joan played by Maria Jacobini.

1917   Cecil B. de Mille, *Joan the Woman*, Paramount (USA). Based on Schiller's *Die Jungfrau von Orléans*. Joan played by Geraldine Farrar (Photo CJA, n 2).

1928   Carl Dreyer, *La Passion de Jeanne d'Arc*. Société générale de Films (French). Historical advisor: Pierre Champion. Joan played by Renée (a.k.a. Maria) Falconetti.

1928   Marc de Gastyne, *La Merveilleuse vie de Jeanne d'Arc*. Auliert-Natan (French). Joan played by Simone Genevoix.

1935   Gustav Ucicky, *Das Mädchen Johanna*. UFA (Germany). Joan played by Angela Salloker.

1948   Victor Fleming, *Joan of Arc*. Production RKO (USA). Religious advisor: R. P. Doncoeur. Based on *Joan of Lorraine* by Maxwell Anderson. Joan played by Ingrid Bergman.

1952   Carl Dreyer, *La Passion de Jeanne d'Arc*. The 1928 Gaumont silent film equipped with a sound track by Lo Duca. Music: Bach, Vivaldi, Albinoni.

1954   Roberto Rossellini, *Giovanna d'Arco al Rogo*. A Franco-London-Film and PCA (Franco-Italian) co-production. Based on the text of Paul Claudel and on the oratorio by Paul Claudel and Arthur Honegger. Joan played by Ingrid Bergman.

1954   Jean Delannoy, *Destinées (Jeanne)*. This film is one of three sketches of a long film entitled *Destinées* and consecrated to *La Femme et la guerre*. Joan played by

Michèle Morgan. A Franco-London-Film and Continental Produzione Coproduction.

1956   Robert Enrico, *Jehanne*. A SINPRI-Guy Perol Production (French). A short film relating the life of Joan of Arc from miniatures of a manuscript of the fifteenth-century. Text read by Alain Cuny. Music reconstructed by a fifteenth century specialist, Madeleine Bourlat.

1957   Otto Preminger, *Saint Joan*. Wherel Productions (USA). Script by Graham Greene adapting the play of Bernard Shaw. French subtitles by Jean Anouilh. Joan played by Jean Seberg.

1961   Claude Antoine, *Jeanne au vitrail*. Films Claude Antoine (French). This short film relates the life of Joan of Arc according to the stained glass windows depicting the principal moments of her life: Domrémy, Vaucouleurs, Chinon, Orléans, Reims, Rouen.

1962   Robert Bresson, *Le Procès de Jeanne d'Arc*. Agnès Delahaie (French). A film based on the minutes of the condemnation and nullification trials. Joan played by Florence Canez.

1962   Francis Lacassin, *Histoire de Jeanne*. Lux-CCF (French). A short film based on the documents and engravings of the fifteenth century in the Bibliothèque Nationale and Bibliothèque Municipale of Lyon.

1970   Gleb Panfilov, *Nachalo—Le Début*. Studio-Len Film (USSR). Black and white. A satiric comedy; Joan played by Inna Tchourikova.

1983   Gina Newson, *Joan of Arc*. British Film Institute. Black and white. Commentator, Marina Warner.

1993   Jacques Rivette, *Jeanne la Pucelle*. (French). Joan played by Sandrine Bonnaire.

For a complete bibliography through 1988, including films now lost or unavailable for viewing, see Robin Blaetz, *Strategies of Containment: Joan of Arc in Film*, a dissertation in the Department of Cinema Studies for the Ph.D., New York University (New York City, 1989). A selective but fully annotated filmography concludes Nadia Margolis's broad treatment of *Joan of Arc in History, Literature, and Film* (New York: Garland, 1990). More recently, Kevin Harty has examined Joan's cinematic interpretations in his essay: "Jeanne au Cinéma," in *Fresh Verdicts on Joan of Arc* (New York: Garland, 1996).

THE LETTERS
OF JOAN OF ARC

THREE LETTERS TO WHICH JOAN OF ARC affixed her signature have survived to our day, and they are moving documents. The first was addressed to the inhabitants of Riom on November 9, 1429; the second, dated March 16, 1430, went to the people of Reims; and Joan's handsomest and best-composed signature appears at the end of the letter of March 28, 1430, to the people of Reims.

It can reasonably be concluded that the Maid learned not only to sign her name but to read as well during her two years of activity and imprisonment, since in the course of her trial at Rouen she asked that a certain number of documents be sent her so that she could read them in their entirety at leisure in her cell. (This interpretation is contested by some scholars.)

We also have, in the original, six further letters Joan dictated and copies of others, such as her letter to the inhabitants of Tournai or the famous "Letter to the English," which was cited during her trial. Several references to other letters of hers appear in additional sources, so it is quite clear that far more than three letters once existed. We know, in fact, that Joan of Arc made use of a code, as she said during the trial that condemned her: When she wished her orders to be ignored or disobeyed, she signaled that intention by a cross within a circle. She was thus used to exchanging letters with other captains or with the royal chancery.

In this appendix, we refer only to documentary evidence. Each letter of Joan's is accompanied by a translation into modern English (either in this appendix or in part I), as are several of the original allusions to her letters. We indicate how each letter or reference to one has survived, and where possible we include the date and place of composition. Every available text and some further bibliographical references follow.

1. REFERENCE TO A LETTER OF JOAN TO HER PARENTS

Sent from Sainte-Catherine-de-Fierbois or from Chinon at the end of February 1429. In Quicherat I, p. 129. Tisset I, p. 123; II, p. 113.

> Asked if she thought she was doing well to leave home without her parents' permission, since one should honor one's father and mother, she answered that she had obeyed her parents well in everything but this departure; but then she wrote them about it and they pardoned her.
>
> (Condemnation Trial, session of Monday, March 12, 1431)

2. REFERENCE TO A LETTER FROM JOAN TO CHARLES VII, ANNOUNCING THAT SHE WAS COMING TO HIS AID

Sent from Sainte-Catherine-de-Fierbois at the end of February or beginning of March 1429. In Quicherat I, pp. 77, 222, 248. Tisset I, p.76; II, pp. 75, 191, 228.

> She said that she sent letters to her king in which it was stated that she was sending them to know if she were to enter the city where her aforesaid king was and if she had done well to travel 150 leagues to come to him, to his aid, and that she knew many good things for him to hear. And it seemed to her that in those same letters it was stated that she would recognize her aforesaid king among all the others.
>
> (Condemnation Trial, session of Tuesday, February 27, 1431)

3. REFERENCE TO A LETTER OF JOAN TO THE CLERGY OF SAINTE-CATHERINE-DE-FIERBOIS

Sent from Chinon around March 6, 1429. Known to Jean Chartier. Ed. Vallet de Viriville, p. 70. *Le Journal du siège,* ed. Charpentier, p. 49. *Chronique de la Pucelle,* ed. Vallet de Viriville, ch. 42, p. 277. Quicherat I, p. 76. Tisset I, p. 77; II, pp. 75-76.

She said again [that] while she was at Tours or Chinon, she sent to find in the church of Sainte-Catherine-de-Fierbois a sword behind the altar; and shortly thereafter they found it all rusted. And she wrote to the men of the church of that place.

(Condemnation Trial, session of Tuesday, February 27, 1431)

4. THE "LETTER TO THE ENGLISH"

Dictated around March 22, 1429 at Poitiers, sent from Blois between April 24 and 27, 1429, unsigned. Quicherat I, p. 240; II, p. 24, 27, 74, 107, 126; III, pp. 139, 215, 306; V, pp. 95. Tisset I, p. 82; II, pp. 82-83; the text in I, pp. 120-122; II, pp. 185-86. The text is cited by: article 22 of d'Estivet, Tisset II, p. 185; *Chroniques de Flandre et d'Angleterre; la Geste des Nobles Français,* ed. Vallet de Viriville, p. 280; *Chronique de la Pucelle,* ed. Vallet de Viriville, p. 281; the *Registre delphinal* of Mathieu Thomassin; *Journal du siège d'Orléans,* ed. Charpentier, pp. 62-63; *the Chronicle of Windecken,* ed. G. Lefèvre-Pontalis, pp. 52, 55-63.

+IHESUS MARIA+

Roy d'Angleterre, et vous, duc de Bedford, qui vous dictes regent le royaume de France; vous, Guillaume de la Poule, conte de Sulford; Jehan, sire de Talebot; et vous, Thomas, sire d'Escales, qui vous dictes lieutenans dudit duc de Bedford, faictes raison au Roy du ciel; rendez a la pucelle, qui est cy envoiee de par Dieu, le Roy du ciel, les clefs de toutes les bonnes villes que vous avez prises et violees en France. Elle est toute preste de faire paix, se vous lui voulez faire raison, par ainsi que France vous mectrés jus et paierez ce que vous l'avez tenu. Et entre vous, archiers, compaignons de guerre, gentilz et autres qui estes devant la ville d'Orleans, alez vous ent en vostre païs, de par Dieu; et se ainsi ne le faictes, actendez les nouvelles de la Pucelle qui vous ira voir briefment, a vos bien grans dommaiges. Roy d'Angleterre, se ainsi ne le faictes, je sui chief de guerre, et en quelque lieu que je actaindray voz gens en France, je les en feray aler, vueillent ou non vueillent. Et si ne veullent obeir, je les feray tous occire; je sui cy envoiee de par Dieu, le Roy du ciel, corps pour corps, pour vous bouter hors de toute France. Et si veullent obeir, je les prandray a mercy. Et n'aiez point en vostre oppinion, quar vous ne tendrez point le royaume de France [de] Dieu, le Roy du ciel, fils saincte Marie; ains le tendra le roy Charles, vray heritier; car Dieu, le Roy du ciel, le veult, et lui est revelé par la Pucelle; lequel entrera a Paris a bonne compagnie. Se ne voulez croire les nouvelles de par Dieu et la Pucelle, en quelque lieu que vous trouverons, nous ferrons dedens et y ferons ung si grant hahay que encore il a mil ans que en France ne fu si grant, se vous ne faictes raison. Et croyez fermement que le Roy du ciel envoiera plus de force a la Pucelle que vous ne lui sariez mener de tous assaulx, a elle et a ses bonnes gens d'armes; at aux horions verra on qui ara meilleur droit de Dieu du ciel. Vous, duc de Bedford, la Pucelle vous prie et vous requiert que vous ne vous faictes mie destruire. Si vous lui faictes raison, encore pourrez venir en sa compaignie, l'ou que les Franchois feront le plus bel fait que oncques fu fait pour la chrestienté. Et faictes response se vous voulez faire paix en la cité d'Orleans; et se ainsi ne le faictes, de vos bien grans dommages vous souviengne briefment. Escript ce [mardi] sepmaine saincte.

(Modern English translation appears in I-5, pp. 33-34.)

5. REFERENCE TO AN ULTIMATUM TO THE ENGLISH:

Sent on May 5, 1429 from Orléans. Cited by Jean Pasquerel during the Nullification Trial, May 4, 1456. In Quicherat III, p. 107. Duparc I, p. 393.

(This letter survives only in the Latin trial transcript; it is translated into modern English in I-5, 44, 45.)

6. REFERENCE TO A LETTER TO PHILIP THE GOOD:

Facsimile in the Musée des Arts Décoratifs, Reims, n. June 1, 1429. Known by this reference:

Et à trois semaines que je vous envoye escript et envoie bonnes lectres par ung herault que feussiez au sacre qui aujourd'hui dimenche XVIIeme jour de ce present mois de juillet ce fait en la cite de Rains dont je nay eu point reponse ne nouy oncques puis nouvelles dudit herault.

[Three weeks ago I sent you by a herald a friendly letter asking you to be at the anointing performed today, Sunday the seventeenth day of the present month of July, in the city of Reims; but I have had no reply to it, and I have heard nothing further of that herald.]

7. LETTER TO
THE INHABITANTS OF TOURNAI

Sent on June 25, 1429. Delivered at Tournai July 6, 1429. Contained in the city registers. Published by F. Hennebert: *Une lettre de Jeanne d'Arc aux Tournaisiens 1429,* in Archives historiques et littéraires du Nord de la France et du Midi de la Belgique, Nouvelle série I, 1837. Quicherat V, pp. 125-126. The letter was copied and transmitted to the "36 Banners," or thirty-six sections of the city. It is preceded by these notices:

> Et pource que nous savons vous estre tousiours desirans de oyr et savoir bonnes nouvelles de lestat et prospérité du roy nostre sire nous avons fait copier les lectres que la Pucelle qui de present est devers le roy nostre sire nous a envoies qui contiennent de la fourme qui s'ensuit. . . .

> [And since we know that you are always eager to hear good news about the estate and prosperity of our lord the King, we have had copies made of the letters which the Maid, who at present is with our lord the King, sent us. They contain the following. . . .]

In the same register is found this further reference:

> A Thery de Maubray qui le VIème jour de julet raporta nouvelles de Roy nostre sire et de ses victoires et recouvrement de son roiaume, avoecq lettres de la Pucelle et du confesseur d'icelle, pour ce, par don 60 s.

> [To Thierry de Maubray who on the sixth day of July brought news of our lord the King and of his victories and the recovery of his kingdom, along with letters of the Maid and of her confessor, a gift of 60 sous.]

> Jhesus Maria
>
> Gentilz loiaux Franchois de la ville de Tournay, la Pucelle vous fait savoir des nouvelles de par decha que en VIII jours elle a cachie les Angloix hors de toutez les places quilz tenoient sur le revire de Loire par assaut et autrement ou il en eu mains mors et prins et lez a desconfis en bataille, et croies que le conte de Suffort, La Poulle son frere, le sire de Tallebort, le sire de Scallez et messire Jehan Falstof et plusieurs chevaliers et capitainez ont este prins, et le frere du conte de Suffort et Glasias mors. Maintenes vous bien, loiaux Franchois, je vous en pry.
>
> Et vous pry et vous requier que vous soies tous prestz de venir au sacre du gentil roy Charles a Rains ou nous serons briefment; et venes audevant de nous quant vous saures que nous aprocherons. A Dieu vous commans, Dieu soit garde

de vous et vous doinst grace que vous puissies maintenir la bonne querelle du royaume de France. Escript a Gien le XXVe jour de juing.

Aux loiaux Franchois de la ville de Tournay

[Jhesus Maria,

Gracious loyal Frenchmen of the city of Tournai, the Maid sends you the news that from here in eight days, whether by assault or otherwise, she has chased the English out of every place they held on the river Loire. Many of them are dead or taken prisoners and they are discomfited in battle. And may you well believe that the Earl of Suffolk, La Pole his brother, the Lord Talbot, the lord of Scales and my lord John Fastolf and many knights and captains have been taken, and that the brother of the Earl of Suffolk and Glasdale are dead. Hold yourselves fast, loyal Frenchmen, I pray you.

And I pray and demand that you be ready to come to the anointing of the gracious King Charles at Reims, where we shall soon be; come before us when you hear that we are approaching. I commend you to God; may God keep watch over you and give you grace to be able to sustain the good cause of the kingdom of France. Written at Gien the twenty-fifth day of June.]

8. LETTER TO THE BURGESSES OF THE CITY OF TROYES

Written at Saint Phal, July 4, 1429. The original has disappeared. Preserved in the register of Jean Rogier (1637): *Recueil fait par moi Jean Rogier l'aisnel des Chartes, tiltres, arretz et anciens mémoires quy se trouvent en la maison et Hostel de ville comme aussy en la chambre de l'Eschevinage de la ville de Reims.* A copy of this collection has been preserved as B.N. ms. fr. 8334. Quicherat IV, pp. 284-288.

Jésus Maria

Très-chers et bons amys, s'il ne tient à vous, seigneurs, bourgeois et habitants de la ville de Troyes, Jehanne la Pucelle vous mande et faict savoir de par le roy du ciel son droitturier et souverain Seigneur, duquel elle est chacun jour en son service royal, que vous fassies vraye obeissance et recognoissance au gentil roy de France, quy sera bien bref à Reims et à Paris, quy que vienne contre, et en ses bonnes villes du sainct royaume à l'ayde du roy Jésus. Loyaulx François, venes au-devant du roy Charles et qu'il n'y ait poinct de faulte et ne vous doubtes de vos corps ne de vos biens, sy ainsy les faictes; et, sy ainsy ne le faictes, je vous promectz et certifie sur vos vies que nous entrerons, à l'ayde de Dieu, en toultes les villes quy doibvent estre du sainct royaume, et y ferons bonne paix fermes, quy que vyenne contre. A Dieu vous commant; Dieu soit garde de vous, s'il luy plaist. Responce brief. Devant la cité de Troyes; escrit à SaintFale, le mardy quatrième juillet.

[Jhesus Maria

Very good and dear friends—lords, townsmen, and residents of the city of Troyes— Joan the Maid commands and informs you on behalf of the King of Heaven our rightful and sovereign Lord, in whose royal service she serves daily, that you should truly obey and recognize the gracious king of France, who will soon be at the city of Reims and at Paris, come who may against him. And with the aid of King Jesus he will be in all the good cities of this holy kingdom. Loyal Frenchmen, come before King Charles. Do not fail to do so; have no hesitation about your lives and property if you. And if do not do so, I promise and assure you for your lives' sake that with God's aid we shall enter all the cities that should belong to the holy Kingdom; and we will establish a firm peace there, whoever comes against us. I commend you to God, may God protect you, if it please Him. Reply soon. Written before the city of Troyes at Saint-Phal, Tuesday the fourth of July.]

9. LETTER OF JOAN TO PHILIP THE GOOD, DUKE OF BURGUNDY

Dictated July 17, 1429 at Reims, unsigned. Original preserved in the Archives du Nord at Lille, B. 300/23612 a. Quicherat V, pp. 126-127. Tisset I, pp. 215-216; II, p. 180, cites it from d'Estivet's brief: "To this item Joan answers that, as to the Duke of Burgundy, she demanded by letters and through his ambassadors that there be peace between the duke and the king."

Jhesus Maria

Hault et redoubté prince, duc de Bourgoingne, Jehanne la Pucelle vous requiert de par le Roy du ciel, mon droicturier et souverain seigneur, que le roy de France et vous, faciez bonne paix ferme, qui dure longuement, pardonnez l'un à l'autre de bon cuer, entièrement, ainsi que doivent faire loyaulx christians; et s'il vous plaist à guerroier, si alez sur les Sarazins. Prince de Bourgoingne je vous prie, supplie et requiers, tant humblement que requerir vous puis que ne guerroiez plus au saint Royaume de France, et faictez retraire incontinent et briefment vos gens qui sont en aucunes places et forteresses du dit saint Royaume; et de la part du gentil Roy de France, il est prest de faire paix à vous, sauve son honneur, s'il ne tient en vous, et vous faiz à savoir de par le Roy du ciel, mon droicturier et souverain seigneur, pour vostre bien et pour vostre honneur et sur voz vie, que vous n'y gaignerez point bataille à l'encontre des loyaulx François, et que tous ceulx qui guerroient ou dit saint Royaume de France, guerroient contre le roy Jhesus, Roy du ciel et de tout le monde, mon droicturier et souverain seigneur. Et vous prie et requiers à jointes mains, que ne faictes nulle bataille ne ne guerroiez contre nous, vous, voz gens ou subgiez; et croiez seurement que, quelque nombre de gens que vous amenez contre nous, qu'iz n'y gaigneront mie, et sera grant pitié de la grant bataille et du sang qui y sera respendu de ceux qui y vendront contre nous. Et à trois sepmaines que je vous avoye escript et envoié bonnes lettres par ung hérault, que feussiez au sacre du roy qui, aujourd'hui dimanche XVIIe jour de ce présent mois de juillet, ce fait en la cité de Reims: dont je n'ay eu point de response, ne n'ouy oncques puis nouvelles dudit hérault. A Dieu vous commens et soit garde de vous, s'il lui plaist; et prie Dieu qu'il y mecte bonne pais. Escript audit lieu de Reims, ledit XVIIe jour de juillet.

(Modern English translation in I, 4, pp. 67-68.)

10. LETTER TO
THE INHABITANTS OF REIMS

Sent from Provins, August 5, 1429. Unsigned. Original kept at Reims in the Archives Municipales. Quicherat V, pp. 139-40. Reproduced in facsimile in *Les Lettres de Jeanne d'Arc, et la pretendue abjuration de Saint-Ouen,* ed. Count Conrad de Maleissye-Melun (Paris, 1911).

Mes chiers et bons amis les bons et loiaulx Franczois de la cite de Rains, Jehanne la Pucelle vous fait assavoir de ses nouvelles et vous prie et vous requiert que vous ne faictes nulle doubte en la bonne querelle que elle mayne pour le sang roial; et je vous promeit et certiffi que je ne vous abandonneray point tant que je vivroy; et est vroy que le Roy a fait trêves au duc de Bourgoigne quinze jours durant par ainsi qu'il li doit rendre la cité de Paris paisiblement au chieff de quinze jours. Pourtant ne vois donner nulle mervoille si je ne y entre si brieffvement; combien que des trêves qui ainsi sont faîctes je ne suy point conteinte, et ne scey si je les tendroy; maiz si je les tiens ce sera seulement pour garder lonneur du Roy, combien aussi que ilz ne cabuseront point le sang roial, car je tendroy et maintendroy esemble l'armée du roy pour estre toute prestre au chieff desdis quinze jours si ilz ne font la paix. Pour ce, mes tres chiers et parfaiz amis, je vous prie que vous ne vous en donner malaise tant comme je vivroy, maiz vous requiers que vous faictes bon guet et gardés la bonne cite du roy et me faictes savoir se il y a nulz triteurs qui vous veullent grever et au plus brieff que je pourray je les en osteray et me faictes savoir de voz nouvelles.

A Dieu vous commans qui soit garde de vous. Escript ce vendredi V jour daoust empres Provins, un logeiz sur champs ou chemin de Paris.

[My dear and good friends the good and loyal Frenchmen of the city of Reims, Joan the Maid sends you her news, and begs and requires you to have no doubt about the good fight she is waging for the blood royal. I promise and certify that I shall never abandon you as long as I shall live. And it is true that the king has made a truce with the duke of Burgundy for a period of fifteen days, by which the duke will surrender the city of Paris to him peacefully at the end of those fifteen days. Nevertheless you should not wonder at seeing me not enter that city so swiftly. No matter how many truces are made, I am never content and do not know if I will keep them. But if I do, it will be only to preserve the King's honor. No matter how much they mock the blood royal, I shall hold the King's army and keep it together lest, at the end of those fifteen days, they do not make peace. On that account, my very dear and perfect friends, I beg you not to grieve yourselves about this as long as I shall live, but I do require that you keep good watch and guard the king's good city. Let me know if there are any traitors who would do you grief. Briefly, I shall do all I can to combat them; let me know your news.

I commend you to God; may He protect you. Written on Friday, the fifth day of August, near Provins, from lodgings in the fields, on the road to Paris.]

11. LETTER OF
JOAN TO THE COUNT OF ARMAGNAC

August 22, 1429, from Compiègne. Unsigned. Reproduced in the Condemnation Trial. Quicherat I, p. 246. Tisset I, pp. 81, 225-226; II, pp. 188-190.

Jhesus Maria

Conte d'Armignac, mon trés chier et bon ami, Jehanne la Pucelle vous fait savoir que vostre message est venu pardevers moy, lequel m'a dit que l'aviés envoié pardeça pour savoir de moy auquel des trois papes, que mandez par mémoire, vous devriés croire. De laquelle chose ne vous puis bonnement faire savoir au vray pour le présent, jusques à ce que je soye à Paris ou ailleurs, à requoy; car je suis pour le présent trop empeschiée au fait de la guerre; mes quant vous sarez que je seray à Paris, envoiez ung message pardevers moy, et je vous feray savoir tout au vray auquel vous devrez croire, et que en aray sceu par le conseil de mon droiturier et souverain Seigneur, le Roy de tout le monde, et que en aurez à faire, à tout mon pouvoir. A Dieu vous commans; Dieu soit garde de vous. Escript à Compiengne, le XXIIe jour d'aoust.

[Jhesus Maria

Count of Armagnac, my very dear and good friend, Joan the Maid wants you to know that your message has reached me, the one which you sent me to let you know which of the three popes whom you mentioned you should believe. On that matter I cannot tell you truly what to think at present, nor until I shall be in Paris or somewhere else later, for at present I am too occupied with the reality of war. But when you know that I am in Paris, send me a message, and I will let you know the full truth about which of them you should believe, as well as what you should do. I will have learned that from the counsel of my rightful and sovereign Lord, the King of the whole world. I will do all that is within my power. I commend you to God; may God take care of you. Written at Compiègne, the twenty-second day of August.]

12. REFERENCE TO
A LETTER SENT BY JOAN AND BY THE
CONSTABLE D'ALBRET TO THE INHABITANTS
OF CLERMONT

November 7, 1429. Quicherat V, p. 146. Taken from the *Livre des mémoires et diligence de la ville de Clermont ou papier du chien,* fol. 47 v.

Memoyre soit que la pucelle Jehanne, message de Dieu, ei monseigneur de Lebret, envoyèrent à la ville de Clermont le VIIe jour de novembre l'an mil quatre cens et vint et neuf, unes lettres faysant mencion que la ville leur voulsist ayder de poudre de canon et de traict et d'artillerie pour le sciege de La Charité.

[Let it be remembered that Joan the Maid, God's messenger, and Monseigneur d'Albret sent to the city of Clermont on the eighth day of November in the year 1429, a letter urging that the city aid them willingly with cannon powder transport, and artillery for the siege of La Charité.]

13. LETTER TO
THE CLERGY, THE BOURGEOIS, AND ALL THE
INHABITANTS OF THE CITY OF RIOM

Sent from Moulins, November 9, 1429. The original, on paper, is kept at Riom in the Archives Communales de Riom AA.33. (Jules Quicherat saw the seal and a black hair caught in the wax, which today have disappeared.) Signed, with

Joan's first known signature. Facsimile in Maleissye-Melun, *Les Lettres de Jeanne d'Arc*. Quicherat V, p. 147-48.

> Chers et bon amis, vous savez bien comment la ville de Saint Pere le Moustier a esté prinse d'assault, et à laide de Dieu ay entencion de faire vuider les autres places qui sont contraires au Roy; mais pour ce que grant despense de pouldres, trait et autres habillemens de guerre a este faicte devant la dicte ville et moy en sommes pourveuz pour aler mectre le siege devant La Charité, où nous alons prestement. Je vous prie, sur tant que vous aymez le bien et honneur du Roy, et aussi de tous les autres de par deçà, que vueillez incontinant envoyer et aider pour le dit siege de pouldres, salepestre, souffre, trait, arbelestres fortes et d'autres habillemens de guerre; et en ce faictes tant que par faulte desdites pouldres et autres habillemens de guerre la chose ne soit longue et que on ne vous puisse dire en ce estre négligens ou refusans. Chiers et bons amis, nostre Sire soit garde de vous. Escript a Molins le neufiesme jour de novembre.
>
> Jehanne

> [Dear and good friends, you know well how the city of Saint-Pierre-le Moûtier was taken by assault; with God's help I intend to empty the other places which are hostile to the king. But because major expenses in powder, transport and other necessities of war had to be made in besieging that city, and because I and my men are making preparations to go lay siege to La Charité, where we will go soon, I pray you and everyone else nearby, inasmuch as you love the well-being and honor of the King, send aid to us in that effort as soon as you can: powder, saltpeter, sulfur, transport, strong arbalests and other necessities of war. Do it both so that the affair won't last long for lack of powder and other war supplies, and so that people won't be able to say that you were negligent or uncooperative. Dear and good friends, may our Lord protect you. Written at Moulins on the ninth day of November.
>
> Jehanne]

(See chapter 5, p. 81.)

14. REFERENCE TO A LETTER OF JOAN TO CHARLES VII ABOUT CATHERINE DE LA ROCHELLE

Sent from Montfaucon in Berry November 20(?), 1429. Quicherat I, p. 107. Tisset I, p. 104; II, p. 200. "And she wrote to the king that she would tell him what he should do about it": Condemnation Trial session of March 3, 1431, and article 56 of Jean d'Estivet's brief: Tisset II, p. 223.

(See chapter 5, pp. 79-80.)

15. LETTER TO THE MEN OF THE CHURCH, BOURGEOIS, AND OTHER INHABITANTS OF THE CITY OF REIMS:

Written at Sully March 16, 1430. Signed with her second known signature. Original preserved; facsimile in *Lettres de Jeanne d'Arc*, de Maleissye-Melun. Quicherat, in V, p. 160, gives a transcription of the letter that had been copied by Nogier in the eighteenth century; a certain number of errors have crept into this copy.

> Très chiers et bien aimes et bien désiries a veoir, Jehenne la Pucelle ey receu vous lettres faisent mancion que vous vous doptiés davoir le sièscge. Vulliés savoir que vous nares point, si je les puis rencontryer bien bref, et si ainsi fut que je ne les recontrasse ne eux venissent devant vous, si fermes vous pourtes car je serey bien brief vers vous, et ci eux y sont je leur ferey chousier leurs esperons si a aste que ne savent par ho les prandre, et lever cil y et se brief que ce cera bien tost. Autre chouse ne vous escri pour le present, mès que soyez toutiours bons et loyals. Je pri à Dieu que vous ait en sa guarde. Escrit a Sully le XVIe jour de Mars. Je vous mandesse anquores auqunes nouvelles de quoy vous series bien joyeux mes je doubte que les lettres ne feussent prises en chemin et que l'on ne vît les dites nouvelles.
>
> Jehanne

Excerpted in modern English in chapter 5, p. 83; the last two sentences are included here and translated as follows:

> [Written at Sully on the sixteenth day of March. I would send you some news at which you would be very joyful; but I fear that those letters might be intercepted, and the wrong people see that news.
>
> Jehanne.]

16. LETTER TO THE HUSSITES

Written at Sully-sur-Loire March 23, 1430. Signed by Pasquerel. Original in Latin, preserved in German translation in the Vienna *Reichsregister* D. f. 236 r. 237. Quicherat V, p. 156, knew only the German translation. Johann Nider mentions this letter. Quicherat IV, p. 503. This letter was not dictated by Joan; it is the work of Pasquerel, her confessor.

Jesus-Maria (in the margin: Puella de Anglia [the Maid from England: *sic!*])

For some time now, rumor and public information have reported to me, Joan the Maid, that from true Christians you have become heretics and that, like the Saracens, you have destroyed true religion and worship; embracing a shameful and criminal superstition and wishing to protect and propagate it, there is no shameful deed or belief you do not dare. You ruin the sacraments of the Church, you rend the articles of Faith, you destroy churches, you smash and burn the statues which have been erected as memorable monuments, you massacre Christians simply because they have kept the true Faith.

What is this frenzy? What rage or madness drives you? This Faith, which Almighty God, which the Son, which the Holy Spirit have revealed, established, given sway and glorified a thousandfold through miracles is the faith which you persecute, which you wish to overturn and obliterate. You are blind, not because you lack eyes or foresight. Do you think that you will not be punished for this? Or do you not realize that God will block your criminal efforts? Do you think He will allow you to remain in darkness and error? The more you give yourselves over to criminal sacrilege, the more He will ready great punishment and torment for you.

As for myself, I tell you frankly that if I were not kept busy with these English wars I would have come to see you a long time ago. But if I do not hear that you have corrected yourselves, I may well leave these English and set off against you, so that, by the sword if I cannot otherwise, I may remove your madness and foul superstition, taking away either your heresy or your lives. But if you choose instead to return to the Catholic faith and to the original source of light, send me your ambassadors and I shall tell them what you must do. If you do not wish to do so and persist in resisting the spur, recall how much criminal harm you have done and wait for me, who will deal with you comparably with the aid of divine and human force.

> Given at Sully, the 23d of March,
> to the heretics of Bohemia.
> (signed) Pasquerel

17. LETTER TO THE PEOPLE OF REIMS

Lettre à mes très chiers et bons amis, gens d'Église, échevins, bourgeois et habitants et manants de la bonne ville de Reyns

[Letter to my very dear and good friends, the men of the Church, judges, bourgeois, and residents and dwellers in the good city of Reims]

Sent from Sully on March 28, 1430. Original preserved by the family de Maleissye-Melun. Joan's third and best written signature. Facsimile in the Count de Maleissye-Melun's *Les Lettres de Jeanne d'Arc,* 1911. Quicherat V, p. 161.

Très chiers et bons amis, plese vous savoir que je ay rechu vous lectres, lesquelles font mencion comment on ha raporte au roy que dedens la bonne cite de Rains il avoit mult de mauvais. Si veulez sovoir que c'est bien vray que on luy a raporté voirement quil y en voit beaucop qui estoient dune aliance et qui devoient trair la ville et mettre les Bourguignons dedens. Et depuis le roy a bien seu le contraire pour ce que vous luy en avez envoie la certaineté dont il est très content de vous. Et croiez que vous estes bien en sa grasce et se vous aviez à besongnier, il vous secouroit quant au regard du siege. Et congnoist bien que vous avez moult à souffrir pour la durté que vous font ces traitrez bourguignons adversaires; si vous en delivrera au plesir Dieu bien bref, c'est a savoir le plus tost que fere se pourra, si vous prie, requier, tres chiers aimiz, que vous guardes bien la dite bonne cite pour le roy et que vou faciez tres bon guet, vous orrez bien tost de mes bonnez nouvellez plus à plain. Austre chose quant à présent ne vous rescri fors que toute Bretaigne est fransaise et doibt le duc envoier au roy III mille combatans paiez pour iy moys. A Dieu vous commant qui soit guarde de vous. Escript a sully le XXVIIIe de mars.

Jehanne.

[Very dear and good friends, may it please you to know that I have received your letters which mention the report to the king that in the good city of Reims there are many wicked people. If you want to know the real truth, this report said to him that there are many who are part of a plot to betray the city and install the Burgundians. And since the king has learned that from you, it will not happen, and he is very pleased with you. Believe that you are high in his grace and that if you have to fight he will assist you in the event of any siege. He knows well that you have suffered much because of the hardships these treasonous Burgundians have imposed on you. So surrender yourselves to the will of God; rest assured that relief will be sent as soon as possible. I pray and require you, very dear friends, to guard your good city well for the king; keep good watch; you will soon get good news more directly from me. Another thing: for the present I will not write you any more than the fact that all of Brittany has come over to the French, and the duke should be sending the king four thousand soldiers who are already paid for four months' service. I commend you to God, that he may protect you. Written at Sully on the twenty-eighth of March.

Jehanne.]

(See chapter 5, p. 83)

These texts are not exhaustive. References exist to other letters of Joan of which we have no trace. Joan of Arc certainly dictated more than seventeen letters. The following reference can be found in the archives of the city of Compiègne, for the year 1428-1429:

> A Tassart du Tielt, pour avoir allé en la ville de Compiegne et ailleurs devers le roy nostre Sir, pour savoir et enquerre des nouvelles, dont il raporta lettres de la pucelle qui estoit devers le Roy; auquel voyage il vaqua XV jours finans le XVIe jour dudit mois d'Aou est CV s.

> [To Tassart du Tielt, 105 sous for having gone into the city of Compiègne and elsewhere to the lord the King, to seek out and discover news, from which trip he brought back letters of the Maid who was in the King's company; on which trip he spent fifteen days ending with the sixteenth day of the month of August.]

A little further on, there is this notice:

> Au même pour avoir allé à St Denis et autres villes devers le Roy nostre Sir pour enquerre et savoir de ses nouvelles, dont il raporta lettres dudit seigneur et aussi de la pucelle; auquel voyage il vacqua XVIII jours finans le XIVe jour de septembre ensuivant CV s IX d.

> [To the same, 105 sous and 9 deniers for having gone to Saint-Denis and other cities to our lord the King to seek out and discover news, from which trip he brought back letters of the aforesaid lord and also from the Maid; on which trip he spent eighteen days ending with the fourteenth day of September.]

Then, in the archives of the Department of the Aube at Troyes, under September 22, 1429:

> Registre des assemblées faictes des congié, licence et auctorité de M. le bailli de Troie ou son lieutenant, par MM. les gens du clergé, bourgois et habitans de la ville de Troies, depuis le mercredi XXIe jour du mois de semptembre l'an 1429.

> [Register of the assembly held with the permission and under the authority of Monseigneur the bailiff of Troyes or his lieutenant, consisting of Messieurs the clergy, the bourgeois and residents of the city of Troyes, from Wednesday the twenty-first day of the month of September in the year 1429.]

Under October 11, 1429, we find:

Le dimenche, IIe jour du mois d'octobre l'an mil CCCCXXIX furent assemblez en la Sale royal à Troies, par l'ordonnance et commandement de Mgr. le bailli de Troies, les personnes qui s'ensuyvent, c'est assavoir, etc. . . . et aultres plusieurs, en grant nombre advenuz, pour oïr la lecture de certaines lectres envoyeez par le roy à MM. le clergié, bourgois et habitans; . . .

Furent en la dicte assemblée publiées certaines lectres de Jehanne la Pucelle, escriptes à Gien, XXIIe jourt dudict mois, par lesquelles elle se recommande à MM., leur fait sçavoir de ses nouvelles, et qu'elle a esté bléciée devant Paris. [Published by Quicherat in V, p. 145.]

[On Sunday, the second day of the month of October in the year 1429 there were assembled in the Royal Hall at Troyes, acting upon the decree and command of Monseigneur the bailiff of Troyes, the following persons. . . . and many others, who had arrived in great number to hear the reading of certain letters sent by the king to Messieurs the clergy, bourgeois, and residents. . . .

Certain letters of Joan the Maid were made public in that assembly. They were written at Gien on the twenty-second day of that month; in them she commended herself to those Messieurs and transmitted her news, including that she had been wounded at Paris.]

In the *Register of Deliberations* of the city of Tours under the dates January 19-February 7, 1430 (preserved in the Archives of the Mairie of Tours) can be found, under the rubric "Gifts and Presents," the following references:

Le XIXe jour de janvier, l'an mil IIIIe XXIX, au tablier de la dite ville, présent Guion Farineau, juge de Touraine, es sont assemblez etc. Pour délibérer sur unes lettres closes envoyées par Jehanne la Pucelle au quatre esleus de la ville et sire Jehan Dupuy, faisans mencion que on baille à Heuves Polnoir, paintre, la somme de C. escus pour vestir sa fille, et que on la lui garde.

[On the nineteenth day of January in the year 1429, in the court of the aforesaid city, in the presence of Guion Farineau, judge of Tourraine, were assembled the following persons, . . . to deliberate some sealed letters sent by Joan the Maid to the four elected councilmen of the city and Sir Jehan Dupuy: these letters contained the recommendation to pay Heuves Polnoir the painter the sum of 100 livres to buy his daughter [wedding] clothes, and to take her under (the city's) protection].

And also:

Le VIIe jour de fevrier, l'an mil IIIIe XXIX, au lieu de la Massequiere, presens Jehan Godeau, lieutenant etc., et Guion Farineau, juge de Touraine, se sont

assemblez les esleus, etc, Par les quelx a este delibere que a la fille de Heuves
Poulnoir, paintre, qui de nouvel est mariée, pour lonneur de Jehanne la Pucelle,
venue en ce royaume devers le roy pour le fait de sa guerre, disant à lui avoir este
envoyee de par le roy du ciel contre les anglois ennemis de ce royaume, la quelle
a rescript a la ville que pour le mariage de ladite fille, icelle ville lui paie la somme
de C. escuz;—que, de ce, riens ne lui sera paie ne baille pour ce que les deniers de
la ville convient emploier es reparacions dé ladite ville et non ailleurs;—mais pour
lamour et honneur de ladite Pucelle, iceulx gens deglise, bourgeois et habitans
feront honneur a ladite fille a sa benediction qui sera juedi prouchain; et dicelle
feront priee ou nom de ladite ville; et pour faire ladite priere aux hommes notables
dicelle ville, est ordonne Michau Hardoin, notaire de ladite ville, et a icelle fille
sera donne du pain et du vin le jour de sadite benediction; c'est assavoir; le pain,
d'un sextier de froment, et quatre jalayes de vin.

A Colas de Montbazon, pour lui et Heuves Polnoir, paintre, baillé par
mandement desd. esleus, donné le XIXe jour de fevrier l'an MCCCCXXIX cy
rendu avec quittance sur ce, la somme de IIII liv. X sous tournois, qui deue leur
estoit, c'est assavoir, aud. Colas XL sous tourn., pour IIII jalayes de vin blanc
et claret donné de par lad. ville le IXe jour de ce moys, à Héloite, dud. Heuves
fille, qui, cellui jour, fut espousée, et aud. Heuves L sous tourn. pour estre
convertiz en pain pour les noces d'icelle fille, pour l'onneur de Jehanne la
Pucelle qui avoit recommandée lad. fille à lad. ville par ses lettres clouses, cy
rendues; pour ce IIII livres X sous tourn.

[On the seventeenth day of February in the year 1429, in the presence of Jehan
Goudeau, lieutenant, and of Guion Farineau, judge of Tourraine, were assembled the councilmen. They deliberated the question of the daughter of Heuves
Poulnoir, painter, who was to be married. Out of respect for Joan the Maid, who
came into this kingdom into the king's presence to wage war, saying to him that
she had been sent by the king of heaven against the English enemies of this
kingdom, and who had written the city a letter concerning the marriage of
Heuves' daughter and said that the city should pay her the sum of 100 écus—
of which amount nothing will be paid or contracted because the revenues of the
city should be used for repairing the damage done to the city—nevertheless,
from love of the Maid and for her honor, the men of the church, the bourgeois
and residents will render honors to Heuves' daughter at her nuptial benediction
next Thursday. and prayers will be said for her in the city's name: Michau
Hardoin, the city notary, will deliver the prayer before the notable men of the
city. To that young woman bread and wine will be given on the day of her
nuptials: to wit, the bread made from a sextier of grain, and four jalayes of wine.

To Colas of Montbazon, for himself and for Heuves Polnoir the painter, 4
livres and 10 sous tournois are awarded by command of the aforesaid

councilmen; paid the nineteenth day of February of the year 1429 with a receipt; that is, 40 sous to Colas, for four jalayes of white wine given by the city on the ninth day of this month, to Héloite, Heuves' daughter, who was married on that day. Fifty sous tournois to purchase bread for his daughter's wedding, in honor of Joan the Maid who commended that daughter to the city in sealed letters delivered here: that is, 4 livres and 10 sous tournois].

In the margin:

Par mandement et quittance cy rendu avec les lettres de la Pucelle.

[By order and with the receipt attached here along with the Maid's letter.]

CHRONOLOGY AND ITINERARY

1412?

January 6 ?: Domrémy: Joan's birth.

Cf. Letter of Perceval de Boulainvilliers to the duke of Milan (June 29, 1429). But no one else, neither Joan's mother nor the witnesses at the rehabilitation trial, mentions the feast of the Epiphany. In the course of the trial of condemnation, Joan "answered that she was nineteen or thereabout."

Sometime during that January?:

Joan's baptism in the church of Domrémy, by Jean Nivet, the parish priest. Numerous witnesses attested to it, including some godfathers and godmothers, as well as Joan herself (condemnation trial in Tisset II, p. 40).

1424 ?

Domrémy, in Jacques d'Arc's garden.

"She was thirteen years old; she heard a voice coming from God to help her control herself. And the first time she felt a great fear. And that voice came about midday, in the summer, in her father's garden"(Tisset II, p. 46).

1425

Domrémy.

> Henri d'Orly steals cattle belonging to the inhabitants of the village. The lady of Domrémy, Jeanne de Joinville, makes him return them.

1428

May: Burey-le-Petit.

> Joan stays with Durand Laxart (Quicherat II, p. 443).

May 13: Vaucouleurs.

> First meeting with Robert de Baudricourt, around Ascension Thursday.

July: Neufchâteau.

> The inhabitants of Domrémy leave their village for fear of armed bands of soldiers. Joan and her family are housed with a woman named La Rousse for a fortnight.

?: Toul.

> Joan is denounced before the authorities for breaking a promise of marriage, which she denies.

1429

January: Burey-le-Petit.

> Second stay with Durand Laxart.

Vaucouleurs.

> Second meeting with Robert de Baudricourt.

February?: Nancy.

> Meeting with Duke Charles of Lorraine.
>
> Return to Vaucouleurs by way of Saint-Nicolas-du-Port.

Vaucouleurs.

> With the Le Royer couple.

Saturday, February 12, 1429: "Day of the Herrings."

> Joan announces it during her third meeting with Robert de Baudricourt. Exorcism by the parish priest of Vaucouleurs, Fournier. Her escort is gotten ready.

Tuesday, February 22: Departure from Vaucouleurs.

> Late afternoon. The distance to Saint-Urbain is covered at night. Joan is accompanied by Jean of Metz and his servant, Jean de Honnecourt;

Bertrand de Poulengy and his servant, Julien; Colet de Vienne, the royal courier; and Richard the archer.

"Eleven days to reach the king" (rehabilitation trial, Deposition of Bertrand de Poulengy). This date seems more likely for the departure than for their arrival at Chinon. (For the itinerary and the dates of the journey, see the *doctorat d'état* thesis of Maurice Vachon, University of Reims, October 1985.)

Wednesday, February 23: Saint-Urbain—Clairvaux.

Thursday, February 24: Clairvaux—Pothières.

Friday, February 25: Pothières—Auxerre.

Saturday, February 26: Auxerre—Mezilles.

> In Auxerre, Joan attends mass in the "great church" (Tisset II, p. 52).

Sunday, February 27: Mezilles—Viglain.

Monday, February 28: Viglain—La Ferté.

Tuesday, March 1: La Ferté—Saint-Aignan.

Wednesday, March 2: Saint-Aignan—Sainte-Catherine-de-Fierbois.

Thursday, March 3: Sainte-Catherine-de-Fierbois—L'Ile-Bouchard.

> From Sainte-Catherine, Joan has a letter written to the king, asking him to receive her (Tisset II, p. 52).

Friday, March 4: L'Ile-Bouchard—Chinon.

> Joan arrives at Chinon about midday. She takes up lodging in a hostelry.

Saturday, March 5: Chinon.

Sunday, March 6: Chinon.

> In late afternoon, Joan is received by the king.

Monday, March 7: Chinon.

> First meeting with John of Alençon.

Tuesday, March 8: Chinon.

Thursday, March 10: Chinon.

> Interrogation session.

Friday, March 11: Poitiers.

> The interrogations held at the residence of Master Jean Rabateau, where Joan is lodged.

Tuesday, March 22: Poitiers.

> Joan sends an ultimatum to the king of England (the "Letter to the English").

Thursday, March 24: Departure for Chinon.

Saturday, April 2:

> A horseman is sent to find the sword of Sainte-Catherine-de-Fierbois.

Tuesday, April 5: Joan leaves Chinon for Tours.

> Her armor, her standard, and her pennon are produced.

Thursday, April 21: Departure from Tours for Blois.

There Joan joins the royal army and the convoy of food for Orléans. The banner for the priests to carry is produced.

?: departure for Orléans.

Friday, April 29:

Joan reaches Chécy and enters Orléans in the evening by the Burgundy Gate; she takes up lodging with the treasurer of the duke, Jacques Boucher.

Saturday, April 30: Orléans.

Joan "went to the rampart of Belle-Croix" on the bridge and speaks with "Glacidas" (*Journal du siège d'Orléans*).

Sunday, May 1: Orléans.

Dunois leaves Orléans to find the rest of the royal army at Blois. (He will be away until May 4.) Joan rides about in the city.

Monday, May 2: Orléans.

Joan, on horseback, reconnoiters the English *bastides*.

Tuesday, May 3: Orléans.

Feast of the Finding of the Holy Cross. A procession in the city.

Wednesday, May 4: Orléans.

Joan confronts Dunois. The Saint-Loup *bastide* is taken.

Thursday, May 5: Orléans.

Ascension Day: no combat. Joan sends the English an ultimatum.

Friday, May 6: Orléans.

Bastide of the Augustinians taken.

Saturday, May 7: Orléans.

Bastide of the Tourelles taken.

Sunday, May 8: Orléans.

The English raise the siege. Thanksgiving procession throughout the city.

Monday, May 9: Joan leaves Orléans.

Friday, May 13: Tours.

Meeting between Joan and the king.

Between 13 and 24 May: Joan goes to Saint-Florent-lès-Saumur.

She meets John of Alençon, his wife, and his mother.

Sunday, May 22: The king is at Loches.

Tuesday, May 24: Joan leaves Loches.

Sunday, May 29: Selles-en-Berry.

Monday, June 6: Selles-en-Berry. Departure for Romorantin.

Joan meets Guy de Laval at Selles-en-Berry.

Tuesday, June 7: Romorantin.

Thursday, June 9: Orléans.

The army is regrouped.

Friday, June 10: Sandillon.

Saturday, June 11: Attack on Jargeau.

Sunday, June 12: Jargeau.

> Jargeau taken.

Monday, June 13: Return to Orléans.

Tuesday, June 14: Joan leaves the city.

Wednesday, June 15: Attack on Meung-sur-Loire.

Thursday, June 16: Attack on Beaugency.

Saturday, June 18: Battle of Patay.

> "The gentle king will have today the greatest victory he has ever had. And my counsel has told me that they will all be ours" (deposition of John of Alençon at the rehabilitation trial).

Sunday, June 19: Joan and the captains reenter Orléans.

Wednesday, June 22: Châteauneuf-sur-Loire.

> Meeting of the king's council.

Thursday, June 23: The king returns to Gien.

Friday, June 24: The army leaves for Gien.

> Joan tells the duke of Alençon, "Have trumpets sounded and mount horse; it is time to go before the gentle Dauphin Charles and put him on the road to his coronation at Reims" (Perceval de Cagny).

Saturday, June 25: Gien.

> Joan dictates letters to the inhabitants of Tournai and the duke of Burgundy to invite them to the anointing.

Sunday, June 26: Gien.

THE CORONATION ROUTE

Monday, June 27: Joan leaves Gien.

Wednesday, June 29: The royal army sets off toward Auxerre.

Monday, July 4: Briennon—Saint-Florentin—Saint-Phal.

> From Saint-Phal, Joan writes to the inhabitants of Troyes.

Tuesday, July 5: The army before Troyes.

Saturday, July 9: Troyes.

> The city of Troyes agrees to receive the king.

Sunday, July 10: Troyes.

> The king and Joan enter the city.

Tuesday, July 12: Troyes—Arcy-sur-Aube.

Wednesday, July 13: Arcy-sur-Aube—Lettrée.

Thursday, July 14: Lettrée—Châlons-sur-Marne.

> Joan encounters her fellow villagers from Domrémy.

Friday, July 15: Châlons-sur-Marne—Sept-Saulx.

Saturday, July 16: Sept-Saulx—Reims.

Sunday, July 17, 1429:

> Anointing of Charles VII in the cathedral of Reims.

Thursday, July 21: Departure from Reims for Corbeny.

> Charles VII touches for scrofula.

Saturday, July 23: Soissons

Wednesday, July 27: Château-Thierry

Sunday, July 31:

> Letter of Charles VII granting immunity from taxation to the inhabitants of Domrémy and Greux.

Monday, August 1: Montmirail.

Saturday, August 6: Provins.

> Letter of Joan to the inhabitants of Reims.

Sunday, August 7: Coulommiers.

Wednesday, August 10: La Ferté-Milon.

Thursday, August 11: Crépy-en-Valois.

Friday, August 12: Lagny.

Saturday, August 13: Dammartin.

Monday, August 15: Montépilloy.

> Heavy skirmishing with the English, who withdraw toward Paris.

Wednesday, August 17–Saturday, August 28: Compiègne (the royal residence).

Monday, August 23: Joan leaves Compiègne.

Thursday, August 26: Saint-Denis.

Monday, September 7: Saint-Denis.

> The king arrives in the town.

Tuesday, September 8: Attack on Paris, at the Saint-Honoré Gate.

Wednesday, September 9: Return to Saint-Denis.

Thursday, September 10:

> The order is given to abandon the attack on Paris.

Saturday, September 12: The army returns to the Loire.

> Monday, September 14–Monday, September 21: Provins—Courtenay—Châteaurenard—Montargis.

Monday, September 21: Gien.

> Dissolution of the army.

Late September: Preparation for the La Charité campaign.

October: Departure for Saint-Pierre-le-Moûtier.

Wednesday, November 4: Fall of Saint-Pierre-le-Moûtier.

Late November: The army marches toward La Charité.

> They follow the Allier and then the Loire (whether on the right or the left bank has not been settled). The army crosses the Loire between Nevers and Décize. It ascends the valley of the Nièvre and then cuts sharply

westward toward La Charité, which isolates Perrinet Gressart from whatever help he could expect from Varzy.

Tuesday, November 24:

At the request of Charles d'Albret, the inhabitants of Bourges send 1,300 gold écus to the royal troops. The siege begins shortly before this date and lasts a month.

Saturday, December 25: Joan returns to Jargeau.

1430

January: Meung-sur-Yèvre?—Bourges.

Wednesday, January 19: Orléans.

February: Sully-sur-Loire?

March: Sully-sur-Loire.

Wednesday, March 29: Lagny.

Monday, April 24: Melun.

Joan waits for the reinforcements requested from Charles VII.

Tuesday, April 25–May 6: Crépy-en-Valois.

Saturday, May 6: Compiègne.

Thursday–Friday, May 11–12: Soissons.

Guichard Bournel refuses authorization to pass through the city.

Monday–Tuesday, May 15–16: Compiègne.

Wednesday–Friday, May 17–18: Crépy-en-Valois.

May 19–21:

Joan waits for reinforcements.

Monday, May 22: Return to Compiègne.

Tuesday, May 23: Capture of Joan of Arc before Compiègne.

Philip the Good comes from Coudun to Margny to see Joan.

Wednesday, May 24: Clairoix?

May 27 and 28: Beaulieu-lès-Fontaines.

Monday, July 10: Departure from Beaulieu.

July 11–early November: Beaurevoir.

Asked whether she spent a long time in the tower of Beaurevoir, Joan answered: "Four months or thereabout."

Thursday, November 9: Arras.

November 21–December 9: Le Crotoy.

Wednesday, December 20: Crossing of the estuary of the Somme between Le Crotoy and Saint-Valéry.

Saturday, December 23: Joan arrives at Rouen.

1431

Tuesday, January 9: Rouen.

First day of the trial. Inquest undertaken at Domrémy and Vaucouleurs.

Saturday, January 13:

The assessors read the information so far gathered on the Maid.

Tuesday, February 13:

Oath swearing by the officers of the court appointed by the bishop of Beauvais.

Monday, February 19:

Summons sent to the vice-inquisitor.

Tuesday, February 20:

The vice-inquisitor questions whether he has competence in the matter. A new letter from the bishop of Beauvais.

Wednesday, February 21:

First public session. Joan is presented to the court.

Thursday, February 22:

Trial sessions.

Saturday, February 24:

Trial sessions.

Tuesday, February 27:

Trial sessions.

Thursday, March 1:

Trial sessions.

Saturday, March 3:

Trial sessions.

Sunday–Friday, March 4–9:

Meeting, before which Joan does not appear, in the residence of the bishop of Beauvais.

Saturday, March 10:

Trial session in prison.

Monday, March 12:

Second session in prison.

Tuesday, March 13:

The vice-inquisitor takes part in the trial for the first time.

Wednesday, March 14:

Sessions in prison.

Thursday, March 15:

Sessions in prison.

Saturday, March 17:

Sessions in prison.

Sunday–Thursday, March 18–22:

>Meetings in the residence of the bishop of Beauvais.

Saturday, March 24:

>The transcript of questions and answers read to Joan.

Monday, March 26:

>Regular ("ordinary") trial sessions begin.

Tuesday, March 27:

>The seventy articles are read to Joan.

Wednesday, March 28:

>The seventy articles are read to Joan.

Saturday, March 31:

>The seventy articles are read to Joan.

Monday–Thursday, April 2–5:

>Deliberation of the assessors and drafting of the twelve articles.

Monday, April 16:

>Joan falls ill after eating a carp sent her by the bishop of Beauvais.

Wednesday, April 18:

>Charitable exhortation delivered to Joan in her cell.

Wednesday, May 2:

>Public admonition.

Wednesday, May 9:

>Joan threatened with torture in the great tower of the castle.

Sunday, May 13:

>Formal dinner party hosted by Richard Beauchamp, earl of Warwick, to which are invited the bishop of Beauvais, the bishop of Noyon, Louis of Luxembourg, Earl Humphrey of Stafford, and others. Late in the evening, they go see Joan in her prison cell.

Saturday, May 15:

>Deliberation of the masters of the University of Paris and of the masters and doctors present in the palace of the archbishop of Rouen.

Wednesday, May 23:

>Explanation of the charges and admonition to Joan by Pierre Maurice, canon of Rouen, in the castle of Bouvreuil.

Thursday, May 24:

>Public sermon in the cemetery of Saint-Ouen followed by Joan's "abjuration." She is led back to the English prison, where she dresses in women's clothes.

Monday, May 28:

>In prison, Joan resumes men's clothes; the charge that she is a relapsed heretic is opened.

Tuesday, May 29:

Deliberation of the doctors and other assessors.
Wednesday, May 30:
> Joan is burned alive in the Old Marketplace at Rouen.

1449

Charles VII requests that Pope Nicholas V authorize a new trial for Joan.

1455

Pope Calixtus III authorizes a new trial.
November 17: Paris.
> Guillaume d'Estouteville, papal legate to France (and cousin of Charles VII), opens the first session of the new trial.

December 12: The trial moves to Rouen.

1456

January 28: Inquest begins at Domrémy.
February 12–March 16: Inquest at Orléans.

July 7: Rouen.
> The trial adjourns, declaring the nullity of the 1431 trial, on the basis of procedural flaws.

France around 1430

FLANDRE

CALAIS

ARTOIS

Tournai

La Manche

Escaut

Meuse

Somme

Rouen

Oise

Aisne

Compiègne

Reims

Seine

Marne

Mt. St. Michel

Paris

Vaucouleurs

Seine

Orléans

Yonne

Vilaine

Gien

La Charité

DUCHÉ
DE
BOURGOGNE

Luxeuil

Cte DE
BOURGOGNE

Loire

Cher

Chinon

Bourges

St. Pierre-le-Moutier

Creuse

Riom

Clermont

Charente

Vienne

AUVERGNE

Loire

Isère

Océan Atlantique

Dordogne

Allier

Rhône

Lot

GUYENNE

Tarn

ARMAGNAC

Adour

Garonne

Aude

Hérault

Durance

SOULE

Mer Méditerranée

English territory

Burgundian territory

Valois (Armagnac) territory

Armagnac-held cities

N

0   400
kilometers

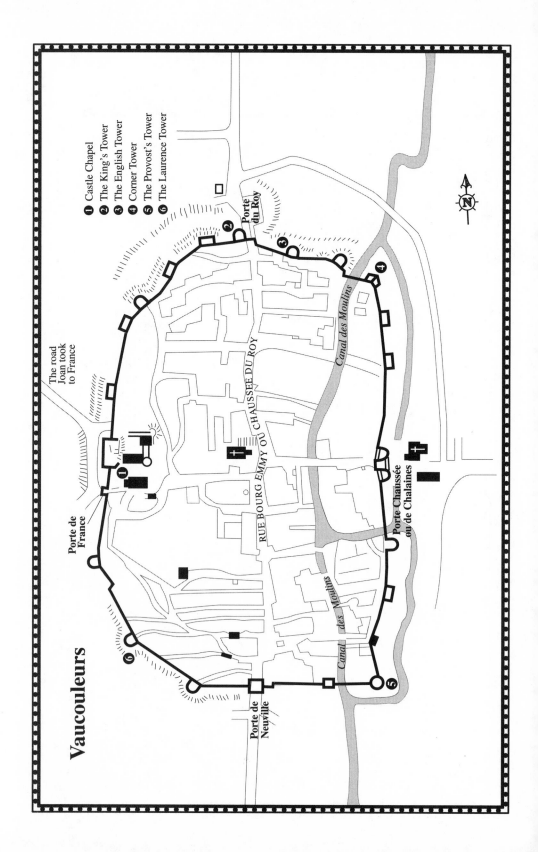

Vaucouleurs

1 Castle Chapel
2 The King's Tower
3 The English Tower
4 Corner Tower
5 The Provost's Tower
6 The Laurence Tower

Porte du Roy

The road Joan took to France

Porte de France

Canal des Moulins

RUE BOURG EMMY OU CHAUSSEE DU ROY

Porte Chaussée ou de Chalaines

Canal des Moulins

Porte de Neuville

N

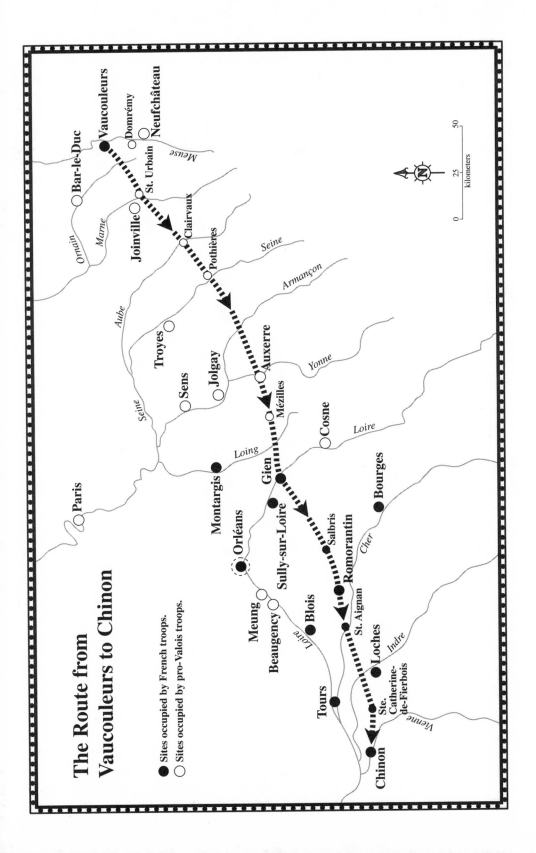

The Route from
Vaucouleurs to Chinon

● Sites occupied by French troops.
○ Sites occupied by pro-Valois troops.

Vaucouleurs
Bar-le-Duc
Domrémy
Neufchâteau
St. Urbain
Meuse
Joinville
Clairvaux
Pothières
Seine
Marne
Ornain
Armançon
Aube
Troyes
Jolgay
Sens
Auxerre
Mézilles
Yonne
Seine
Cosne
Loire
Loing
Montargis
Gien
Paris
Orléans
Sully-sur-Loire
Salbris
Bourges
Meung
Beaugency
Romorantin
Blois
Cher
Loire
St. Aignan
Indre
Tours
Loches
Ste.
Catherine-
de-Fierbois
Vienne
Chinon

N
0 25 50
kilometers

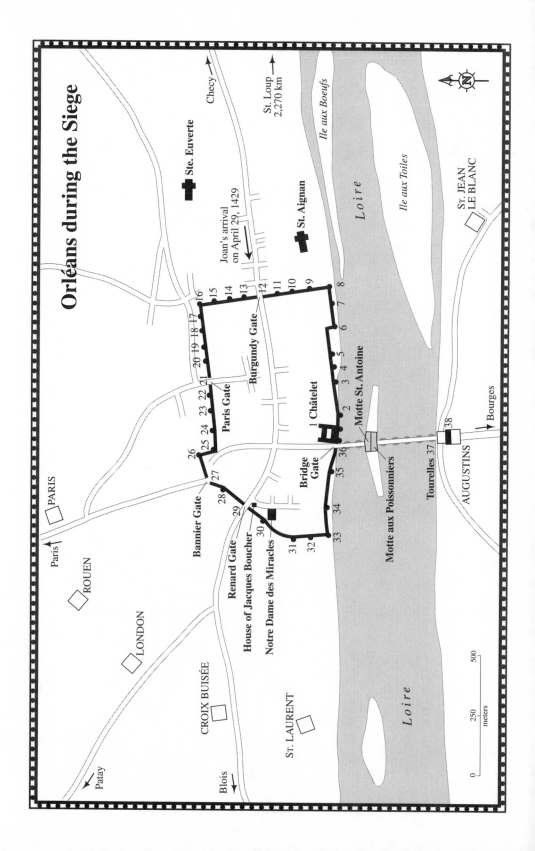

Orléans during the Siege

1. The Châtelet

2. Tower of Master Pierre Le Queux

3. Tower of the Meffroy jetty

4. Chesneau postern-gate
   (with portcullis)

5. Aubert or Wicket Tower
   (its gate walled up)

6. unnamed tower with eight square
   turrets

7. August Tower and Tanner's Gate
   (walled up)

8. New Tower

9. White Tower

10. Avalon Tower

11. Saint-Flou Tower

12. Burgundy or Saint Aignan Gate

13. Saint-Stephen's Tower

14. Tower of Champ-Egron

15. Auvillain Tower (or Tower of
    Messire Baudes)

16. Tower of the Falconry or of My
    Lord the Bishop

17. Tower of the Bishop's Plea

18. tower of unknown name

19. Tower of the Holy Cross

20. Saltworks Tower (or Tower of the
    Hôtel-Dieu Granaries)

21. Paris Gate

22. Jehan Thibault's Tower

23. Tower of Saint-Mesmin's Allod
    (freeholding)

24. Tower of Saint Samson's
    Orchards

25. Saint Samson's Tower

26. Helmet Tower

27. Bernier or Bannier Gate

28. Michaut-Quanteau Tower

29. Renard (Fox) Gate and Joan of
    Arc House

30. Saint Paul Tower
    (with a projecting screen-wall)

31. André Tower

32. tower of unknown name

33. Tower of la Barre-Flambert
    (or Frambert Tower or Tower of
    the Basin)

34. Our Lady's Tower

35. Horse-trough Tower and Gate
    (walled up)

36. Portcullis Gate and (adjacent)
    Bridge Gate

37. Fortress of the Tourelles

38. Tourelles rampart

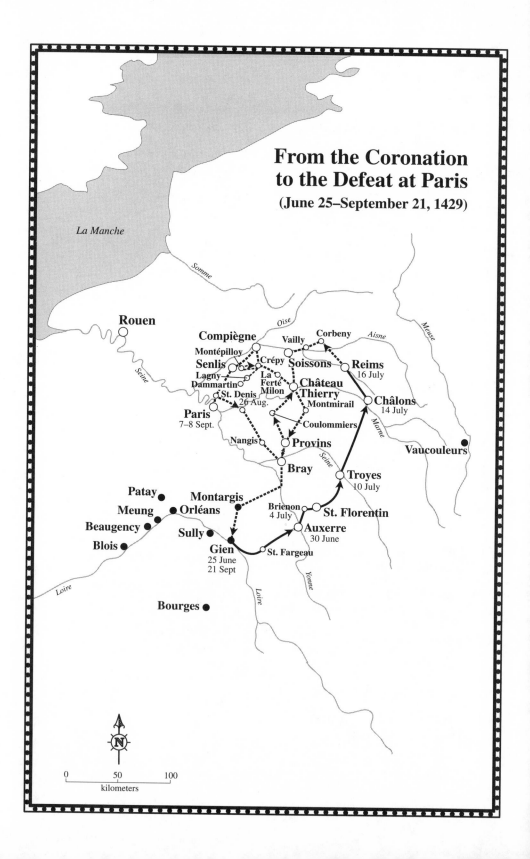

From the Coronation to the Defeat at Paris
(June 25–September 21, 1429)

La Manche

Rouen

Compiègne

Montépilloy

Senlis

Lagny

Dammartin

St. Denis
26 Aug.

Paris
7–8 Sept.

Nangis

Bray

Crépy

Vailly

Corbeny

Soissons

La
Ferté
Milon

Château
Thierry

Montmirail

Coulommiers

Provins

Reims
16 July

Châlons
14 July

Vaucouleurs

Troyes
10 July

Brienon
4 July

St. Florentin

Montargis

Patay

Meung

Orléans

Beaugency

Sully

Blois

Gien
25 June
21 Sept

St. Fargeau

Auxerre
30 June

Bourges

Somme

Oise

Aisne

Meuse

Seine

Marne

Seine

Loire

Loire

Yonne

N

| 0 | 50 | 100 |
kilometers

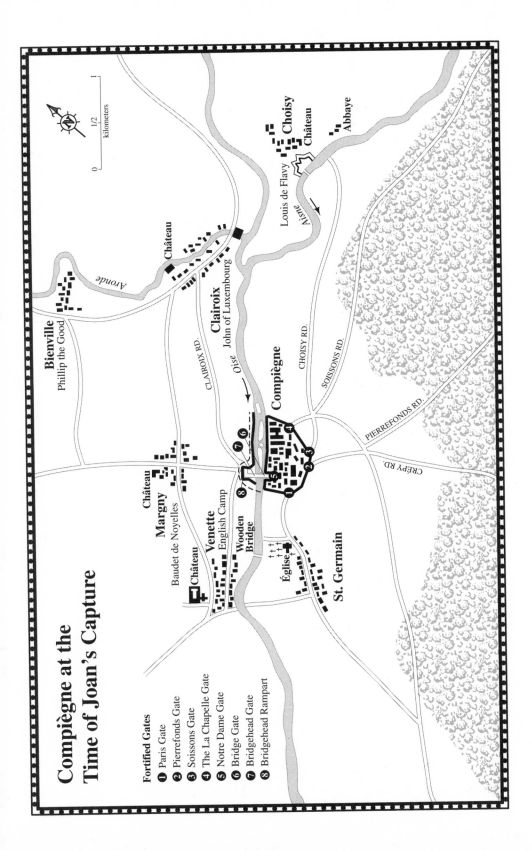

Compiègne at the
Time of Joan's Capture

Fortified Gates

① Paris Gate
② Pierrefonds Gate
③ Soissons Gate
④ The La Chapelle Gate
⑤ Notre Dame Gate
⑥ Bridge Gate
⑦ Bridgehead Gate
⑧ Bridgehead Rampart

Bienville
Phillip the Good

Aronde

Château

Château

Margny
Baudet de Noyelles

Venette
English Camp

Château

Wooden Bridge

Église

St. Germain

Clairoix
John of Luxembourg

Oise

Compiègne

CLAIROIX RD.

CHOISY RD.

SOISSONS RD.

PIERREFONDS RD.

CRÉPY RD.

Choisy
Château

Louis de Flavy

Aisne

Abbaye

0   1/2
kilometers

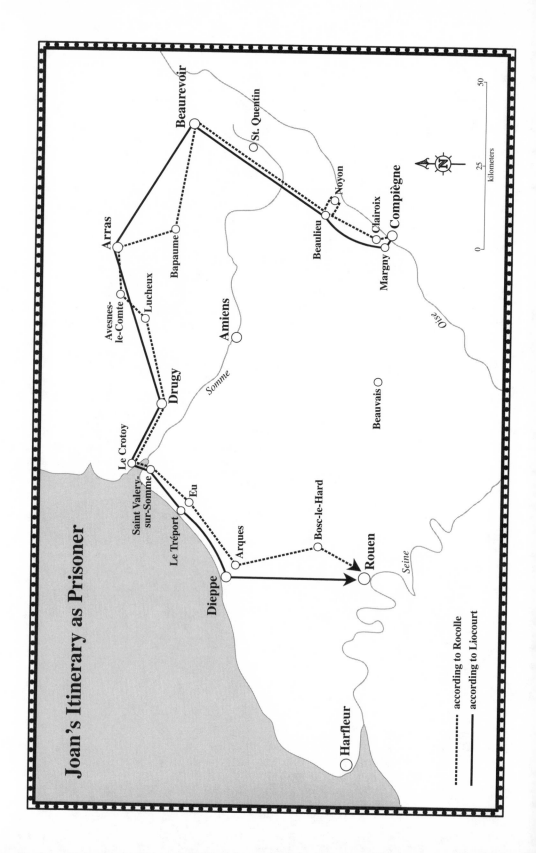

Joan's Itinerary as Prisoner

Harfleur

Dieppe

Le Tréport

Saint Valery-sur-Somme

Eu

Arques

Bosc-le-Hard

Rouen

Seine

Le Crotoy

Drugy

Avesnes-le-Comte

Lucheux

Bapaume

Arras

Beaurevoir

St. Quentin

Amiens

Somme

Beauvais

Beaulieu

Noyon

Clairoix

Margny

Compiègne

Oise

N

0   25   50
kilometers

- - - - - according to Rocolle
———— according to Liocourt

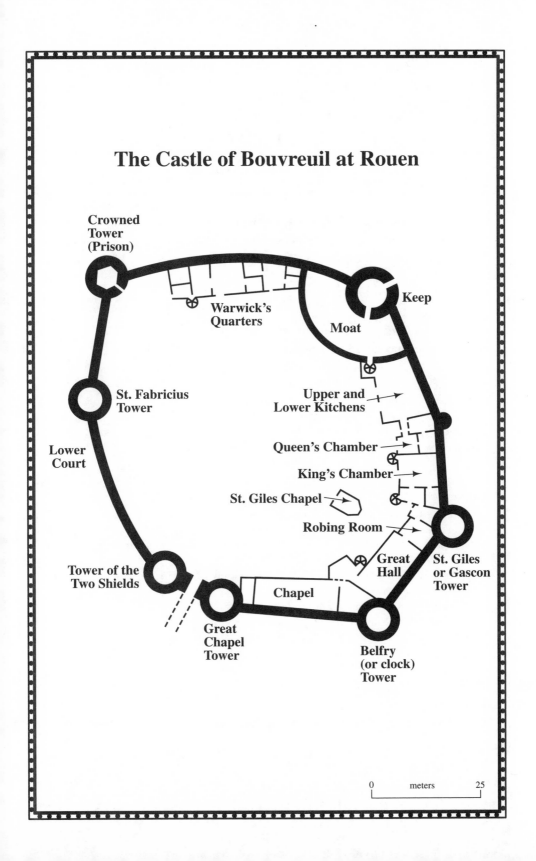

The Castle of Bouvreuil at Rouen

Crowned
Tower
(Prison)

Warwick's
Quarters

Keep

Moat

St. Fabricius
Tower

Upper and
Lower Kitchens

Lower
Court

Queen's Chamber

King's Chamber

St. Giles Chapel

Robing Room

Tower of the
Two Shields

Great
Hall

St. Giles
or Gascon
Tower

Chapel

Great
Chapel
Tower

Belfry
(or clock)
Tower

0 meters 25

TOPICAL BIBLIOGRAPHY

For any problems arising from the condemnation trial, such as Joan's voices or her leap from the tower of Beaurevoir, see volume 3 of the *Procès de condamnation de Jeanne d'Arc* by Tisset and Lanhers, especially Pierre Tisset's introduction.

For a detailed study of the rehabilitation trial, see:
Volume 3 of Doncœur and Lanhers.

On the possibility of Joan's being a royal bastard, see:
Brown, Mary Milbank, *The Secret History of Jeanne d'Arc, Princess, Maid of Orléans.*
Caze, Pierre, *La vérité sur Jeanne d'Arc, ou éclaircissements sur son origine.* 2 vols.
Schneider, Eugène, *Jeanne d'Arc et ses lys: La légende et l'histoire.*

For the many theories about Joan's possible survival see:
Comminges, Élie de, "Quelques lettres inédites sur le *Problème historique* de Daniel Polluche et sur la *Jeanne d'Arc* de Lenglet Dufresnoy." In *Jeanne d'Arc: Une époque, un rayonnement. Colloque d'histoire médiévale, Orléans, Octobre 1979.*
Lang, Andrew, "The False Jeanne d'Arc." In Andrew Lang, *The Valet's Tragedy and Other Studies.*
Lefèvre-Pontalis, Germain, *La Fausse Jeanne d'Arc.*
Lenglet-Dufresnoy, Nicolas, *Remarques sur la Pucelle d'Orléans.*
Polluche, Daniel, *Problème historique sur la Pucelle d'Orléans.*

On the question of Joan's literacy, the "secret" at Chinon, and the so-called Celtic theory, see (respectively):
Millot, Stanislas. *Le langage de Jeanne d'Arc: Deux récentes découvertes* (Algiers: Jules Carbonel, 1931).
Thomas, Antoine, "Le 'Signe Royal' et le secret de Jeanne d'Arc," *Revue Historique,* 278-282.
André, Francis, *Les dessous de l'histoire. La vérité sur Jeanne d'Arc. Ses ennemis, ses auxiliaires, sa mission.*

On the psychological and medical issues surrounding Joan and the question of her voices see:

Clin, Marie-Veronique, "Joan of Arc and Her Doctors." in *Fresh Verdicts on Joan of Arc.*

Lang, Andrew, "The Voices of Jeanne d'Arc." In Andrew Lang, *The Valet's Tragedy and Other Studies.*

Madden, Richard Robert. "Jeanne d'Arc." In *Phantasmata, or Illusions and Fanaticisms of Protean Forms Productive of Great Evils.*

Pinzino, Jane Marie, "Speaking of Angels: A Fifteenth-Century Bishop in Defense of Joan of Arc's Mystical Voices." in *Fresh Verdicts on Joan of Arc.*

Russell, Josiah C, "Muhammad, Joan of Arc, Hitler: Leaders Influenced Possibly by Extrasensory Perception." *TAIUS: Texas A & I University Studies.*

Sullivan, Karen, "'I do not name to you the voice of St. Michael': The Identification of Joan of Arc's Voices." in *Fresh Verdicts on Joan of Arc.*

For the issue of Joan's involvement in witchcraft, see:

Cohn, Norman, *Europe's Inner Demons.*

Murray, Margaret A., *The Witch-Cult in Western Europe.* See especially appendix 4, on Joan of Arc and Gilles de Rais.

Russell, Jeffrey Burton, *Witchcraft in the Middle Ages.*

For on-line discussion of Joan of Arc, see:

The International Joan of Arc Society: http://dc.smu.edu/ijas

BIBLIOGRAPHY

I. MANUSCRIPTS OF THE CONDEMNATION AND REHABILITATION TRIALS

London. British Library. Stowe 84.
Orléans. Bibliothèque Municipale 518 (anc. 411).
Paris. Bibliothèque de l'Assemblée Nationale 1119.
Paris. Bibliothèque Nationale MS lat. 5965.
Paris. Bibliothèque Nationale MS lat. 5966.
Paris. Bibliothèque Nationale MS lat. 5970.
Paris. Bibliothèque Nationale MS lat. 8838.
Paris. Bibliothèque Nationale MS lat. 17013 (anc. Notre-Dame 138).

II. THE TRIAL TRANSCRIPTS

The trial of condemnation and the trial of nullification (or rehabilitation) were edited and published for the first time in their entirety by Jules Quicherat between 1841 and 1849. His edition of the condemnation trial was reedited for the Société de l'Histoire de France by Pierre Tisset and Yvonne Lanhers in three volumes published between 1960 and 1971. The rehabilitation trial was reedited by Pierre Duparc (3 vols., 1977–1989). Since his edition, it is customary to refer to the second inquest as the nullification trial.

Champion, Pierre. *Le Procès de condamnation.* 2 vols. Bibliothèque du XVe siècle 22 & 23. (Paris: Edouard Champion, 1920–1921).

Doncœur, Rev. Paul and Yvonne Lanhers, eds. *Documents et recherches relatifs à Jeanne la Pucelle.* 5 vols. (Melun: d'Argences, 1952–1961; except vol. 5).

———. *Documents et recherches* Vol. 1: *La minute française de l'Interrogatoire de Jeanne la Pucelle, d'après le réquisitoire de Jean d'Estivet et les manuscrits d'Urfé et d'Orléans* (1952). A complete and reliable edition of the manuscripts cited, including that of Orléans, which was long considered useless but which has since been proven essential as the closest representation of Joan's own words.

———.*Documents et recherches* Vol. 2: *Instrument public des sentences portées les 24 et 30 mai 1431 par Pierre Cauchon et Jean Le Maître contre Jeanne la Pucelle* (1954). An edition of the Latin text produced by the judge and vice-inquisitor with translation and full apparatus.

———.*Documents et recherches* Vol. 3: *La réhabilitation de Jeanne la Pucelle. L'Enquête ordonnée par Charles VII en 1450 et le codicille de Guillaume Bouillé*

(1956). Edition with translation and critical apparatus of Charles VII's preliminary investigation toward rehabilitation.

———.*Documents et recherches* Vol. 4: *L'enquête du cardinal d'Estouteville en 1452* (1958). The text of the inquest of Cardinal d'Estouteville in 1452 edited, translated, and annotated.

———.*Documents et recherches* Vol. 5: *La rédaction épiscopale du procès de 1455–1456* (Paris: Desclée de Brouwer, 1961). An edition of the "episcopal redaction" of the trial which led to Joan's rehabilitation.

Duparc, Pierre, ed. *Procès en nullité de la condamnation de Jeanne d'Arc*. 5 vols. CNRS and Société de l'Histoire de France (Paris: Klincksieck, 1977–89). The definitive, complete edition of the documents relating to the rehabilitation trial. It is in this work that Duparc coins the phrase "nullification process" (*procès en nullité*).

Oursel, Raymond, ed. *Le procès de condamnation de Jeanne d'Arc*. Preface by Michel Riquet (Paris: Club du meilleur livre, 1953). A modern French abridgement of Quicherat and Champion meant for the public at large.

———. *Le procès de réhabilitation de Jeanne d' Arc* (Paris Denoël, 1954). Same as the last work, but for the rehabilitation trial.

———. *Le procès de condamnation et le procès de réhabilitation de Jeanne d'Arc* (Paris: Éditions Denoël, 1959). The more easily obtained edition of both of the preceding works.

Quicherat, Jules-Étienne-Joseph, ed. *Procès de condamnation et de réhabilitation de Jeanne d'Arc dite la Pucelle. Publiés pour la première fois d'après les manuscrits de la Bibliothèque Nationale, suivis de tous les documents historiques qu'on a pu réunir et accompagnées de notes et d'éclaircissements*. 5 vols. Société de l'Histoire de France (Paris: Jules Renouard, 1841–1849; reprinted, New York: Johnson, 1965). The classic, exhaustive edition.

Tisset, Pierre and Yvonne Lanhers, eds. and trans. *Procès de condamnation de Jeanne d'Arc*. 3 vols. Société de l'Histoire de France (Paris: Klincksieck, 1960–1971). An update and revision of Quicherat's condemnation segment—a continuation of the work begun by Pierre Champion.

EXCERPTS FROM THE TRIALS

Barrett, W.P., ed. and trans. *The Trial of Jeanne D'Arc, Translated into English from the Original Latin and French Documents*. With biographical essays by Pierre Champion translated by Coley Taylor and Ruth H. Kerr. (New York: Gotham House, Inc., 1932).

Pernoud, R. *Jeanne d'Arc, par elle-même et ses témoins* (Paris: Seuil, 1962; reprinted: Livre de Vie, 1975). Published in English as *Joan of Arc by Herself and Her Witnesses*. Edward Hyams, trans. (London: MacDonald, 1964; New York: Stein & Day, 1966; 1969).

———. *Vie et mort de Jeanne d'Arc: Les témoignages du procès de réhabilitation, 1450–1456* (Paris: Hachette, 1953). Published in English as *The Retrial of Joan of Arc: The Evidence at the Trial for Her Rehabilitation*, Régine Pernoud, ed. and J. M. Cohen, trans. with preface by Katherine Anne Porter (New York: Methuen, 1955).

III. CONTEMPORARY SOURCES

Actes de la chancellerie d'Henri VI concernant la Normandie sous la domination anglaise (1422–1435). Paul Casimir Noël Marie Joseph Le Cacheux, ed. 2 vols. (Rouen: A. Lestringant, 1907–1908).

d'Auvergne, Martial. *"Vigiles du roi Charles VII."* In *Poésies*, Martial d' Auvergne, 2 vols. (Paris: Urbain Coustelier, 1724).

Basin, Thomas. *Histoire de Charles VII*. Ch. Samaran, ed. and trans. 2 vols. (Paris: "Les Belles Lettres," 1933 and 1944; revised, 1964).

———. *Histoire de Louis XI*. Ch. Samaran & M.-C. Gavand, eds. and trans. 2 vols. (Paris: "Les Belles Lettres," 1963, 1966).

Bochon, J. Alexandre. *Choix de chroniques et mémoires sur l'histoire de France avec notes et notices*. Panthéon littéraire, vol. 34 (Paris: A. Desrez, 1838; Delagrave, [n.d.]; Orléans: Herluison, 1875).

Bouvier, Jacques or Gilles le [The Berry Herald]. *Chroniques du roi Charles VII*. Henri Courteault and Léonce Celier with Marie-Henriette Jullien de Pommerol, eds. Société de l'Histoire de France, (Paris: Klincksieck, 1979).

[Bueil, Jean de, Count de Sancerre]. *Le Jouvencel par Jean de Bueil, suivi du commentaire de Guillaume Tringant*. Camille Favre and Léon Lecestre, eds. 2 vols. (Paris: Renouard, H. Laurens, successeur, 1887–1889).

Cagny, Perceval de. *Chronique des ducs d'Alençon*. Henri Moranvillé, ed. Société de l'Histoire de France (Paris: Klincksieck, 1902; 1982).

Chartier, Alain. *Epistola de puella*. In *Œuvres latines*. Pascale Bourgain-Hemeryck, ed. Sources d'Histoire Médiévale/IRHT (Paris: CNRS, 1977).

Chartier, Jean. *Chronique de Charles VII*. Auguste Vallet de Viriville, ed. 3 vols. (Paris: P. Jannet, 1858).

———. "La chronique latine de Jean Chartier (1422–1450)." Charles Samaran, ed. *Annuaire-Bulletin de la Société de l'Histoire de France* (1926): 183-273.

Chastellain, Georges. *Chronique des ducs de Bourgogne*. Kervyn de Lettenhove, ed. In Lettenhove's edition of the *Œuvres* of Chastellain. 5 vols. (Brussels: Académie Royale de Belgique, 1863–1866).

[The Monk of Saint-Rémy/Michael Pintoin (1349?-1421)]. *Chronicorum Karoli Sexti/ Chronique du religieux de Saint-Denys, contenant le règne de Charles VI de 1380 à 1422/Chronique de Charles VI*. Louis-François Bellaguet, ed. and trans. Introduction to 1994 edition by Bernard Guenée. (6 vols.: Paris: Impr. de Crapelet, 1839-1852; 6 vols. in 3: Paris: Editions du Comité des travaux historiques et scientifiques, 1994).

Chronique de la Pucelle ou chronique de Cousinot, suivie de la chronique Normand de P. Cochon, relatives aux règnes de Charles VI et de Charles VII, restituées à leurs auteurs et publiées pour la première fois intégralement à partir de l'an 1403, d'après les manuscrits, avec notices, notes, et développements. Auguste Vallet de Viriville, ed. Bibliothèque gauloise (Paris: Adolphe Delahaye, 1859; reprinted, Garnier, 1888).

Chronique du Mont-Saint-Michel (1343–1468). Siméon Luce, ed. Société des Anciens Textes Français. 2 vols. (Paris: Firmin Didot, 1879–1883).

[Mâcon, Jean de]. *Chronique du siège d'Orléans et de l'établissement de la fête du 8 mai 1429*. Boucher de Molandon, ed. In *Mémoires de la Société historique de l'Orléanais* 18 (1884): 241-348 (Orléans: Herluison, 1883); also edited by André Salmon in *Bibliothèque de l'École des Chartres* 8 (1847): 500–509. An anonymous chronicle found in the Vatican and in St. Petersburg.

Chronique Martiniane. Edition critique d'une interpolation pour le règne de Charles VII restituée à Jean Le Clerc. Pierre Champion, ed. Bibliothèque du XVe siècle (Paris: Honoré Champion, 1907).

Chroniques de France/Chronique de Saint-Denis, depuis les Troiens jusqu'à la mort de Charles VII en 1461. J. Viard, ed. Société de l'Histoire de France. 3 vols. (Paris: Renouard, 1920–1953).

Cochon, Pierre. *Chronique normande.* Ch. de Robillard de Beaurepaire, ed. (Rouen: Le Brument, 1870).

Gerson, Jean [le Charlier de]. *De mirabili victoria.* In *Opera.* Ellies Dupin, ed. vol. 4 (Antwerp/The Hague, 1706).

———. *De quadam puella.* In "Jean Gerson's Theological Treatise and Other Memoirs in Defence of Joan of Arc." (Modern English translation only.) *Revue de l'Université d'Ottawa* 41 (1971): 58-80. Not in Gerson's *Œuvres Complètes.* P. Glorieux, ed. 10 vols. (Paris: Desclée, 1960–1973), the modern edition of his works. There are no other editions after Dupin until Quicherat and Monnayeur, although there were several editions prior to Dupin in the fifteenth, sixteenth, and seventeenth centuries.

———. *Traité de Jean Gerson sur la Pucelle.* Dom. J.-B. Monnayeur, ed. (Paris: Champion, 1910). A full-length study and Modern French translation of *De quadam puella.*

Girau[l]t, Guillaume. "Note de Guillaume Giraut sur la levée du siège d'Orléans." Boucher de Molandon, ed. *Mémoires de la Société Archéologique de l'Orléanais* 4 (1858).

Gruel, Guillaume [the Younger]. *Chronique d'Arthur de Richemont.* Achille Levavasseur, ed. Société de l'Histoire de France (Paris: Renouard, 1890).

Fauquembergue, Clément de [Fauquemberque]. *Journal de Clément de Fauquembergue.* Alexandre Tuetey and Henri Lacaille, eds. Société de l'Histoire de France 3 vols. (Paris: Renouard, 1903–1915).

Journal d'un Bourgeois de Paris, 1405–1449. Alexandre Tuetey, ed. Société de l'Histoire de France (Paris: Renouard, 1881).

Journal d'un Bourgeois de Paris, sous Charles VI et Charles VII. André Mary, ed. (Paris: Jonquières, 1929). [In modern French].

Journal du siège d'Orléans [et du Voyage de Reims] 1428–29, augmenté de plusieurs documents, notamment des Comptes de ville. P. Charpentier and Ch. Cuissard, eds. (Orléans: Cuissard, 1896).

Le Fèvre de Saint-Rémy, Jean. *Chronique.* F. Morand, ed. Société de l'Histoire de France. 2 vols. (Paris: Renouard, 1876–1881).

Monstrelet, Enguerran[d] de. *Chronique: 1400–1444.* L. Douët d'Arcq, ed. Société de l'Histoire de France. 6 vols. (Paris: Renouard, 1857–1862).

Le Mistére du siège d'Orléans, publié pour la première fois, d'après le manuscrit unique conservé à la Bibliothèque du Vatican. François Guessard and Eugène de Certain, eds. Documents inédits sur l'histoire de France (Paris: Imprimerie impériale, 1862).

Morisini, Antonio. *Chronique: Extraits relatifs à l'histoire de France.* Léon Dorez, ed. and trans. With introduction and notes by Germain Lefèvre-Pontalis. Société de l'Histoire de France (Paris: Renouard, 1898–1902).

Nangis, Guillaume de [Continuator of]. *Chronique parisienne anonyme de 1316 à 1339, précédée d'additions à la Chronique française dite de Guillaume de Nangis.* A. Hellot, ed. Mémoires de la Société de l'Histoire de Paris et de l'Ile-de-France 2 (1884): 1-207 (Paris: Renouard, 1884)

Wavrin [du Forestel], Jean de. *Anchiennes chroniques d'engleterre*. Emilie Dupont, ed. Société de l'Histoire de France. 3 vols. (Paris: Renouard, 1858–1863).

———. *Recueil de chroniques et anchiennes istoires de la Grant Bretaigne a present nommee Engleterre*. William Hardy, ed. and trans. Rolls Series 39. 5 vols., 1-2 in English trans. (London: Her Majesty's Stationer's Office, 1891).

von Windecken, Eberhard. *Denkwürdigkeiten zur Geschichte des Zeitalters Kaiser Sigmunds*. In *Les sources allemandes de l'histoire de Jeanne d'Arc*. Germain Lefèvre-Pontalis, ed. and trans. Société de l'Histoire de France (Paris: Renouard, 1903); also edited by P. Beckmann (Berlin, 1893).

IV. USEFUL MODERN SCHOLARSHIP

Allmand, C. *Henry V* (Berkeley: University of California Press, 1992).

———. *The Hundred Years War: England and France at War c. 1300–1450* (Cambridge: Cambridge University Press, 1988).

———. *Lancastrian Normandy, 1415–1450. The History of a Medieval Occupation* (Oxford: Oxford University Press, 1983).

André, Francis. *Les dessous de l'histoire. La verité sur Jeanne d'Arc. Ses ennemis, ses auxiliaires, sa mission* (Paris: Chamuel, 1895).

Bataille, Henri. "Qui était Baudricourt?" *Revue lorraine populaire* 51 (1983): 140-142; 52 (1984): 184-188.

Beauvoir, Simone de. *Deuxième sexe* (Paris: Gallimard, 1949). Published in English as *The Second Sex*. Howard Madison Parshley, trans. (New York: Knopf, 1953 [c. 1952]).

Belisle, Jennifer. "St. Joan of Arc: The Primacy of Conscience," *The Catholic Worker* 62, No. 3 (1995): 1-4.

Bell, Rudolph M. *Holy Anorexia* (Chicago: University of Chicago Press, 1985).

Bossuat, André. *Perrinet Gressart et François de Surienne, agents de l'Angleterre: contribution à l'étude des relations de l'Angleterre et de la Bourgogne avec la France sous le règne de Charles VII* (Paris: E. Droz, 1936).

Boutet de Monvel, M. *Jeanne d'Arc* (Paris: Plon-Nourrit, 1896). Reprinted with introduction by Gerald Gottlieb, New York: Pierpont Morgan Library/Viking, 1980); published in English as *Joan of Arc* (Philadelphia: David McKay, 1918; New York: Century, 1926); many other editions of this work have been published, and are beautifully illustrated.

Brown, Mary Millbank. *The Secret History of Jeanne d'Arc, Princess, Maid of Orléans* (New York: Vantage, 1962).

Bynum, Caroline Walker. *Holy Feast and Holy Fast: The Religious Significance of Food to Medieval Women* (Berkeley: University of California Press, 1987).

Caze, Pierre. *La Vérité sur Jeanne d'Arc, ou éclaircissements sur son origine. 2 vols.* (Paris: Rosa/London: Treuttel & Wurtz, 1819).

Clin, Marie-Veronique. "Joan of Arc and Her Doctors." in *Fresh Verdicts on Joan of Arc*, edited by Bonnie Wheeler and Charles T. Wood (New York: Garland Publishing, 1996).

Clin-Meyer, Marie-Veronique. *Le registre de comptes de Richard Beauchamp, comte de Warwick, 14 mars 1431-1415 mars 1432* (École des Hautes Études en Sciences Sociales, 1981 thesis).

———Cohn, Norman. *Europe's Inner Demons* (New York, Basic Books, 1975).

Commings, Élie de. "Quelques lettres inédites sur le *Problème historique* de Danielle Polluche et sur la *Jeanne d'Arc* de Lenglet-Dufresnoy." In *Jeanne d'Arc: Une époque, un rayonnement. Colloque d'histoire médiéval, Orléans, octobre 1979.* Preface by Régine Pernoud (Paris: CNRS, 1982).

Contamine, Philippe. *La Guerre au Moyen Age* (Paris: Presses Universitaires de France, 1980). Published in English as *War in the Middle Ages*. Michael Jones, trans. (Oxford: Blackwell Press, 1984).

———. *Guerre, état et société: Etudes sur les armées des Rois de France, 1337–1494* (Paris: Presses Universitaires de France, 1972).

———. *De Jeanne d'Arc aux guerres d'Italie* (Orléans: Paradigme, 1994). A collection of Contamine's essays on a wide range of subjects related to Joan.

———. *La vie quotidienne pendant la guerre de Cent Ans en France et en Angleterre* (Paris, 1976).

Crane, Susan. "Clothing and Gender Definition: Joan of Arc," *Journal of Medieval and Early Modern Studies* 28, no. 2 (1996): 297-320.

Davis, Natalie Zemon. *Society and Culture in Early Modern France: Eight Essays* (Stanford, CA: Stanford University Press, 1975).

Delaruelle, Étienne [Canon]. "La spiritualité de Jeanne d'Arc." *Bulletin de littérature ecclésiastique* 1-2 (1964); reprinted, Toulouse, 1964. Widely considered one of the best studies of Joan's spirituality.

DeVries, Kelly. "A Woman Leader of Men: Joan of Arc's Military Career," in *Fresh Verdicts on Joan of Arc,* edited by Bonnie Wheeler and Charles T. Wood (New York: Garland Publishing, 1996), pp. 3-18.

Famiglietti, Richard C., *Royal Intrigue: Crisis at the Court of Charles VI, 1392–1420* (New York: AMS Press, Inc., 1986).

Fraioli, Deborah. "The Literary Image of Joan of Arc: Prior Influences." *Speculum* 56 (1981): 811-830.

Garber, Marjorie B. *Vested Interests: Cross-Dressing and Cultural Anxiety* (New York: Routledge, 1992).

Harmand, Adrien. *Jeanne d'Arc: ses costumes, son armure. Essai de reconstitution* (Paris: Leroux, 1929).

van Herwaarden, Jan, ed. *Joan of Arc: Reality and Myth* (Hilversum & Rotterdam: Uitgeverij Verloren, 1994).

van Herwaarden, Jan. "Joan of Arc: A Gender Myth." In *Joan of Arc: Reality and Myth,* van Herwaarden, ed.

Jackson, Richard A. *Ordines Coronationis Franciae. Texts and Ordines for the Coronation of Frankish and French Kings and Queens in the Middle Ages* (Philadelphia: University of Pennsylvania Press, 1995).

———. *Vive le roi!: A History of the French Coronation from Charles V to Charles X* (Chapel Hill: University of North Carolina Press, 1984).

Jeanne d'Arc: Images d'une légende. Anne Jardin, Conservateur. An exhibition at the Bibliothèque Municipale, Rouen, May 19th-September 16th, 1979, (Paris, Musée des Beaux-Arts, 1979). A brilliant exhibition of images of Joan spanning 500 years.

Jordan, Constance. *Renaissance Feminism: Literary Texts and Political Models* (Ithaca, NY: Cornell University Press, 1990).

Kelly, Henry Ansgar. "Joan of Arc's Last Trial: The Attack of the Devil's Advocates," in *Fresh Verdicts on Joan of Arc,* edited by Bonnie Wheeler and Charles T. Wood (New York: Garland Publishing, 1996), pp. 205-236.

Kelly, Joan. *Women, History and Theory: The Essays of Joan Kelly* (Chicago: University of Chicago Press, 1984).

King, Margaret L. *Women of the Renaissance* (Chicago: University of Chicago Press, 1991).

Krumreich, Gerd. *Jeanne d'Arc in der Geschichte* (Sigmaringen: Thorbecke, 1989).

Lang, Andrew. "The False Jeanne d'Arc." In Andrew Lang, *The Valet's Tragedy and Other Studies* (London: Longmans, Green, 1903).

———. "The Voices of Jeanne d'Arc." In Andrew Lang, *The Valet's Tragedy and Other Studies* (London: Longmans, Green, 1903).

Le Cacheux, Paul Casimir Noël Marie Joseph. *Rouen au temps Jeanne d'Arc et pendant l'occupation anglaise, 1419–1449* (Rouen: A. Lestringant, 1931).

Lefèvre-Pontalis, Germain. *La fausse Jeanne d'Arc* (Paris, 1895).

Lenglet-Dufresnoy, Nicolas. *Remarques sur la Pucelle d'Orléans* (Amsterdam, 1735).

Lewis, P. S. *Later Medieval France: The Polity* (London: St. Martin's Press, 1968).

Lightbody, Charles Wayland. *The Judgements of Joan* (Cambridge, MA: Harvard University Press, 1961).

Liocourt, [Colonel] Ferdinand de. *La mission de Jeanne d'Arc: I. Le plan d'action; II. L'exécution*. 2 vols. (Paris: Nouvelles Editions Latines, 1974, 1976).

Luce, Siméon. *Jeanne d'Arc à Domrémy. Recherches critiques sur les origines de la mission de la Pucelle* (Paris: Champion, 1886).

Madden, Richard Robert. "Jeanne d'Arc." In *Phantasmata, or Illusions and Fanaticisms of Protean Forms Productive of Great Evils*. vol 2 (London: T.C. Newby, 1857).

Maleissye, Conrad [Count] de. *Les lettres de Jeanne d'Arc et la prétendue abjuration de Saint-Ouen*, Preface by Gabriel Hanotaux (Paris: André Marty, 1911).

———. *Les reliques de Jehanne d'Arc. Ses lettres* (Paris: Bloud, 1909).

Margolis, N. *Joan of Arc in History, Literature, and Film. A Select, Annotated Bibliography* (New York: Garland Publishing, Inc., 1990).

———. "Trial by Passion: Philology, Film, and Ideology in the Portrayal of Joan of Arc (1900–1930)." *Journal of Medieval and Early Modern Studies* 27, no. 3 (1997): 445-493.

Marot, P. *Jeanne la bonne Lorraine à Domrémy. La marge de la Haute-Meuse. La mission de Jeanne d'Arc. Souvenir et culte de l'héroïne dans son pays* (Colmar: SAEP, 1980).

McNamara, Jo Ann. "Sexual Equality and the Cult of Virginity in Early Christian Thought." *Feminist Studies* 3 (1976), pp. 145-158.

Merkle, Gertrude. "Martin Le Franc's Commentary on Jean Gerson's Treatise on Joan of Arc." in *Fresh Verdicts on Joan of Arc,* edited by Bonnie Wheeler and Charles T. Wood (New York: Garland Publishing, 1996), pp. 177-188.

Merkle, Gertrude. *Palingenesis of Joan of Arc*. Harvard Ph.D. Thesis, 1988.

Michelet, Jules. *Jeanne d'Arc et autres textes*. Paul Viallaneix, ed. (Paris: Gallimard, 1974).

Millot, Stanislas. *Le langage de Jeanne d'Arc: Deux récentes découvertes* (Algiers: Jules Carbonel, 1931).

Murray, Margaret A. *The Witch-Cult in Western Europe* (Oxford: Clarendon Press, 1921, 1962).

Nora, Pierre, ed. *Les Lieux de Mémoire*. (Paris: Editions Gallimard, 1992). Published in English as *Realms of Memory, Rethinking the French Past*. Arthur Goldhammer, trans. 3 vols. (New York: Columbia University Press, 1996). A compilation of selected English translations from the original.

Pernoud, Régine. *Dans les pas de Jeanne d'Arc* (Paris: Hachette, 1956).

Perroy, Edouard. *La Guerre de Cent Ans*. La suite des temps 13 (Paris: Gallimard, 1945). Published in English as *The Hundred Years War*. W. B. Wells, trans., with introduction by David C. Douglas (London: Eyre & Spottiswoode, 1951; reprinted, New York: Capricorn, 1965).

Plaisse, André. *Robert de Flocques: un chef de guerre du XVe siècle: bailli royal d'Évreux: maréchal héréditaire de Normandie: conseiller et chambellan du roi / Chef de guerre du Xve siècle, Robert de Flocques* (Évreux: Société libre de l'Eure, c. 1984).

Pinzino, Jane Marie. "Speaking of Angels: A Fifteenth-Century Bishop in Defense of Joan of Arc's Mystical Voices." In *Fresh Verdicts on Joan of Arc,* edited by Bonnie Wheeler and Charles T. Wood (New York: Garland Publishing, 1996).

Polluche, Daniel. *Problème historique sur la Pucelle d'Orléans* (Orléans: Couret de Villeneuve, 1749).

Rocolle, Pierre. *Une prisonnière de guerre nommée Jeanne d'Arc* (Paris: S.O.S., 1982) The best overall book-length study of this period of her life.

Rousseau, François. *La Hire* (Mont-de-Marsan: Lacoste, 1969).

Russell, Jeffrey Burton. *Witchcraft in the Middle Ages* (Ithaca, NY: Cornell University Press, 1972)

Russell, Josiah C. "Muhammad, Joan of Arc, Hitler: Leaders Influenced Possibly by Extrasensory Perception." *TAIUS: Texas A & I University Studies* 3, no. 1 (June 1970).

Sackville-West, Victoria. *Saint Joan of Arc* (London: Cobden-Sanderson, 1936; New York: Doubleday, 1936; most recent reedition: Library of Great Lives. Norwalk, CT: Easton, 1990).

Schibanoff, Susan. "True Lies: Transvestism and Idolatry in the Trial of Joan of Arc," in *Fresh Verdicts on Joan of Arc,* edited by Bonnie Wheeler and Charles T. Wood (New York: Garland Publishing, 1996), pp. 31-60.

Schneider, Eugène. *Jeanne d'Arc et ses lys: La légende et l'histoire* (Paris: Grasset, 1952).

Scott, W[alter] S[idney]. *Jeanne d'Arc* (New York: Harper & Row/Barnes & Noble, 1974).

Searle, William. *The Saint and the Skeptics: Joan of Arc in the Work of Mark Twain, Anatole France, and Bernard Shaw* (Detroit, MI: Wayne State University Press, 1976).

Seward, Desmond. *The Hundred Years War: The English in France, 1337–1453* (New York: Atheneum, 1978).

Sullivan, Karen. "'I do not name to you the voice of St. Michael': The Identification of Joan of Arc's Voices." In *Fresh Verdicts on Joan of Arc,* edited by Bonnie Wheeler and Charles T. Wood (New York: Garland Publishing, 1996).

Thomas, Antoine. "Le 'Signe Royal' et le secret de Jeanne d'Arc." *Revue Historique* 102 (1910).

Thompson, Guy Llewelyn. *Paris and Its People Under English Rule. The Anglo-Burgundian Regime 1420–1436* (Oxford: Clarendon Press, 1991).

Twain, Mark [Samuel Langhorn Clemens]. *Personal Recollections of Joan of Arc, by the Sieur Louis de Conte (Her Page and Secretary), Freely Translated Out of the Ancient French into Modern English from the Original Unpublished Manuscript in the National Archives of France by Jean François Alden*. Illustrated by F. V. du Mond (New York: Harper's 1896; reprinted with introduction by John Seelye, Hartford, CT: Stow-Day Foundation, 1980; also in *The Writings of Mark Twain*. Vols. 17-18, New York: Harper's 1922–1925).

———. "Joan of Arc." In *The Writings of Mark Twain.* vol. 22 (New York: Harper's, 1922–1925). 1899. Produced originally as the introduction to T. Douglas

Murray's edition of the trial, Twain withdrew it after an editorial dispute with
Murray.

Vachon, Maurice. *La topographie auxiliaire de l'histoire,* Reims, 1985. This thesis for
the *doctorat ès lettres* is the most recent and best documented study of the stages
of Joan's journeys.

Vale, Malcolm Graham Allan. *Charles VII* (Berkeley: University of California Press,
1974).

———. *English Gascony, 1399–1453: A Study of War, Government, & Politics During
the Later Stages of the Hundred Years War* (Oxford: Oxford University Press,
1970).

———. *War and Chivalry. Warfare and Aristocratic Culture in England, France, and
Burgundy at the End of the Middle Ages* (Athens, GA: University of Georgia
Press, 1981).

Vauchez, André. *Sainthood in the Later Middle Ages.* Jean Birrell, trans. (Cambridge:
Cambridge University Press, 1997).

Vaughan, Richard. *John the Fearless. The Growth of Burgundian Power* (London:
Longmans, 1966).

———. *Philip the Good. The Apogee of the Burgundian State* (Harlow: Longmans,
1970).

———. *Valois Burgundy* (Hamden, CT: Archon Books, 1975).

Warner, Marina. *Joan of Arc. The Image of Female Heroism* (New York: Alfred A. Knopf,
1981).

Weiskoff, Steven. "Readers of the Lost Arc: Secrecy, Specularity, and Speculation in the
Trial of Joan of Arc," in *Fresh Verdicts on Joan of Arc,* edited by Bonnie Wheeler
and Charles T. Wood (New York: Garland Publishing, 1996), pp. 113-132.

Wheeler, Bonnie. "Joan of Arc's Sword in the Stone," in *Fresh Verdicts on Joan of Arc,*
edited by Bonnie Wheeler and Charles T. Wood (New York: Garland Publishing,
1996), pp. xi-xvi.

Wheeler, Bonnie and Charles T. Wood, eds. *Fresh Verdicts on Joan of Arc* (New York:
Garland Publishing, Inc., 1996).

Winwar, Frances. *The Saint & the Devil, Joan of Arc & Gilles de Rais. A Biographical
Study in Good & Evil* (New York: Harper & Brothers, 1948).

Wood, Charles T. *Joan of Arc & Richard III: Sex, Saints, and Government in the Middle
Ages* (New York: Oxford University Press, 1988).

Wood, Charles T. "Joan of Arc's Mission and the Lost Record of Her Interrogation at
Poitiers," in *Fresh Verdicts on Joan of Arc,* edited by Bonnie Wheeler and Charles
T. Wood (New York: Garland Publishing, 1996), pp. 19-20.

Woodward, Kenneth L. *Making Saints: How the Catholic Church Determines Who
Becomes a Saint, Who Doesn't, and Why* (New York: Simon & Schuster, 1990).

INDEX